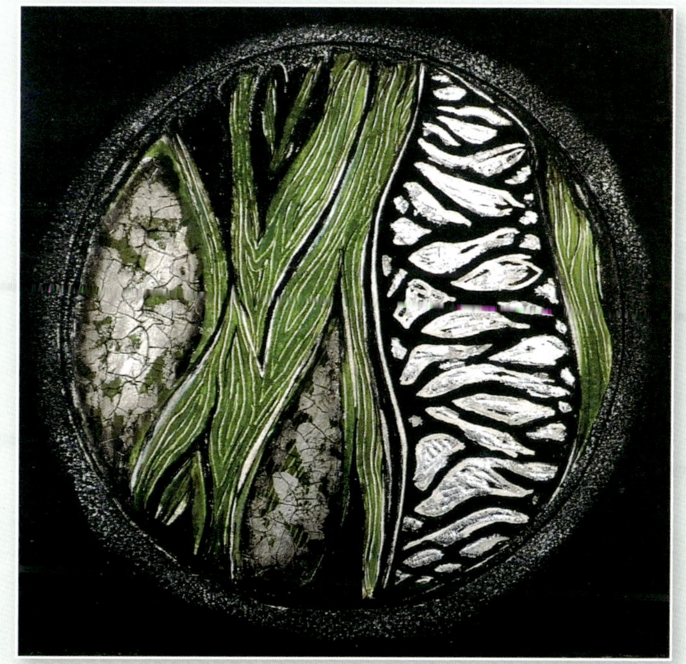

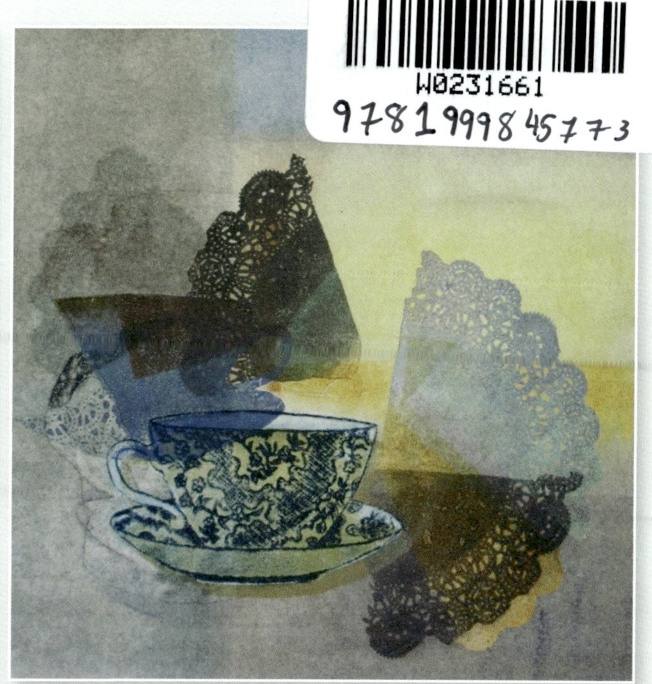

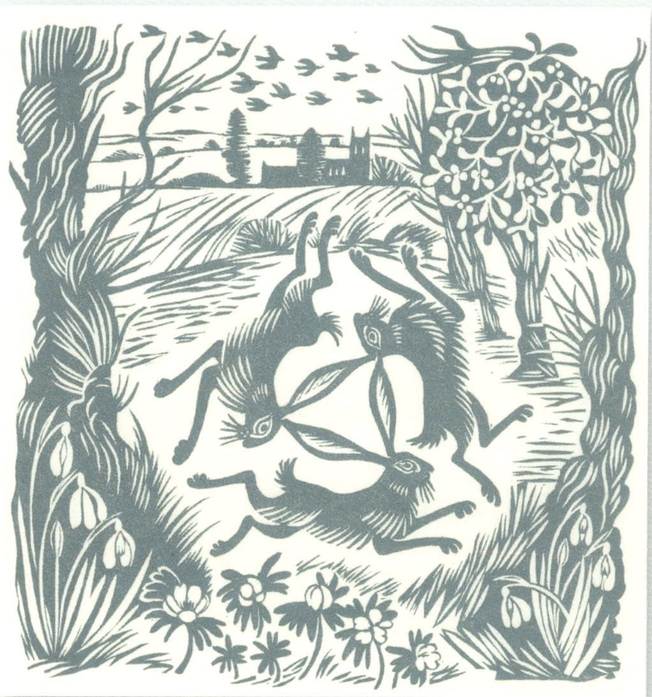

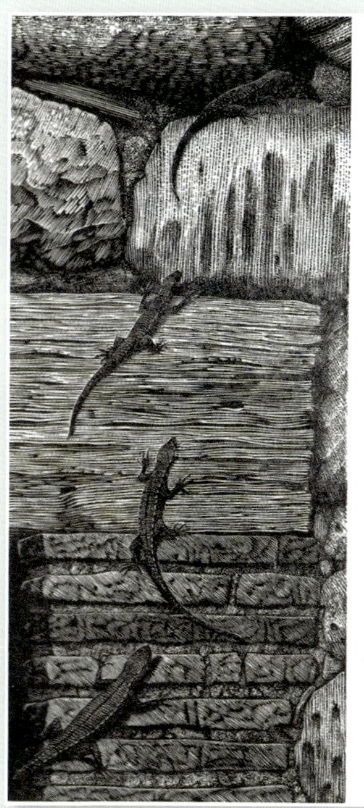

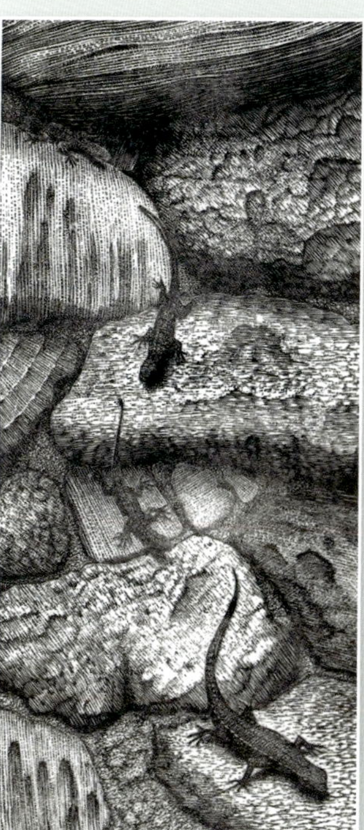

WHEN TWO THOUGHTS COLLIDE

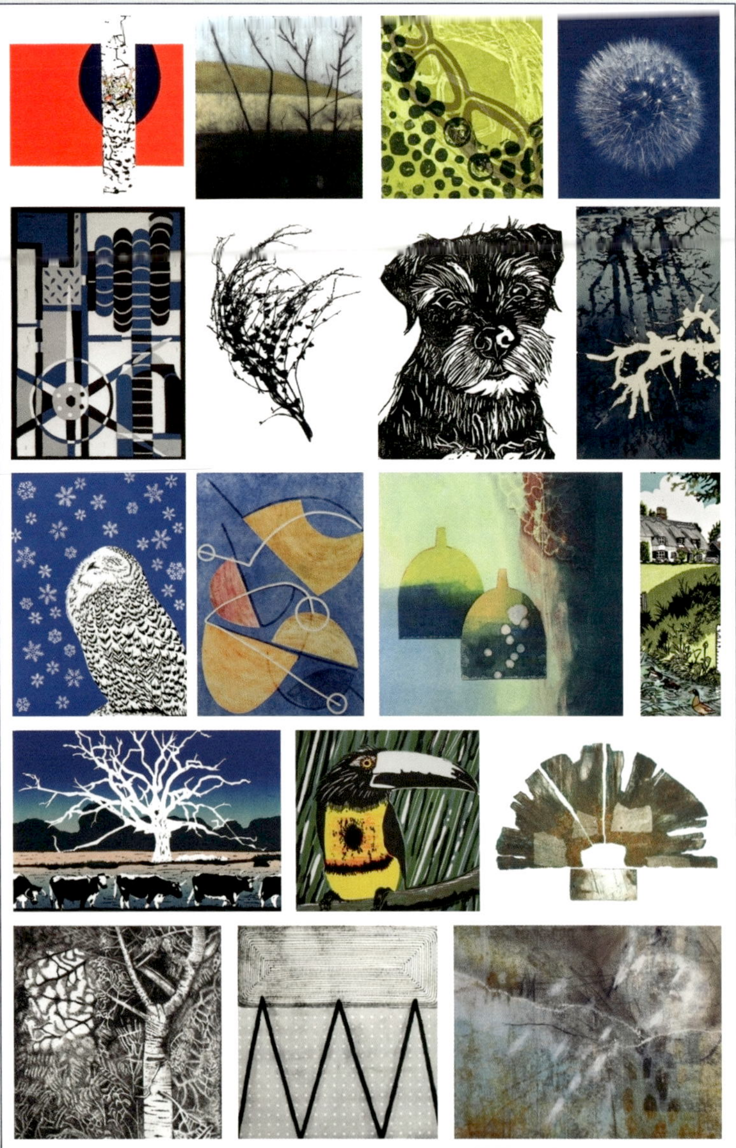

CAMBRIDGE ORIGINAL PRINTMAKERS HAVE ALWAYS been ambitious, aiming to promote the rich diversity of work being made in the area, to make that work available for sale and to give each artist an opportunity to show several pieces together through their Biennale. There is also an understated but very important educational role through the comparison of process, approach and the sheer joy of great craft allied to interesting ideas. Best of all, the Biennale is run by committed volunteers who, rightly, see the work and the business of making and showing the work as important, indeed essential. Coming together to present it all in a professional manner has produced a like-minded community who, through their efforts, have made something that was hidden much more widely understood.

There are qualities in an etched line, a lithographic wash, a cut negative mark or the overlay of transparent printing inks for which there is no equivalent; they are themselves. As with all graphic media, the printed marks have their own vocabulary and do not need to be validated by equivalence. It is always the image that counts, not the medium or its manipulation.

Virtuosity is something else. A deep knowledge of the materials, an instinctive control of the processes and an underlying ability to manage the chaotic nature of the way things behave give the artist a chance to deliver a good performance.

Each element in a print, each plate, stone, block or screen, is a discrete thought. When a second element is added the two thoughts collide, merge and then produce a third, new thought. The complexity of the conversation grows as more layers are added. However this works, the aim must be that, eventually, they all co-exist as a single

Kip Gresham, The Print Studio, Cambridge

(www.theprintstudio.co.uk)

unified statement in which all the voices are identifiable – but it is the totality that catches the eye and the mind.

In light of this, judging submitted work for a mixed exhibition is quite an invidious task. The questions one must ask are. Does the medium match the image? Do the constituent parts come together as a whole? Does the whole piece have a transforming or enlightening aspect that sits outside the issue of craft? Does it have poetry? In short, does it work?

There are no rules for all of this. Everyone sees work differently, and we all carry our predilections and cultural baggage into decisions as to whether we love something or hate it. I chose love, respect for fine drawing, pleasure in a well-resolved thought and, above all, those pieces that work.

The standard of work for each Biennale is remarkably high. Many of the choices are marginal. It is a great feeling to know that work of such a standard is being made in quantity in a small part of the country.

Technology moves on. Printmaking has a long history of appropriating commercial printing materials and processes and, through wild invention, turning them into creative tools. Many mainstream printing methods started life in artists' studios. So it is good to see 3D printing being used to make a relief printing block. The logic is impeccable: an image of an old press (see back cover of this book), captured and 3D printed by digital means only to revert to a handmade print from that press.

The image of the press speaks volumes. The press is inert without a human to make it come alive. In turn, the print from the block is nothing until someone sees it.

Through their Biennale, Cambridge Original Printmakers celebrate creativity, commitment and hope for the future.

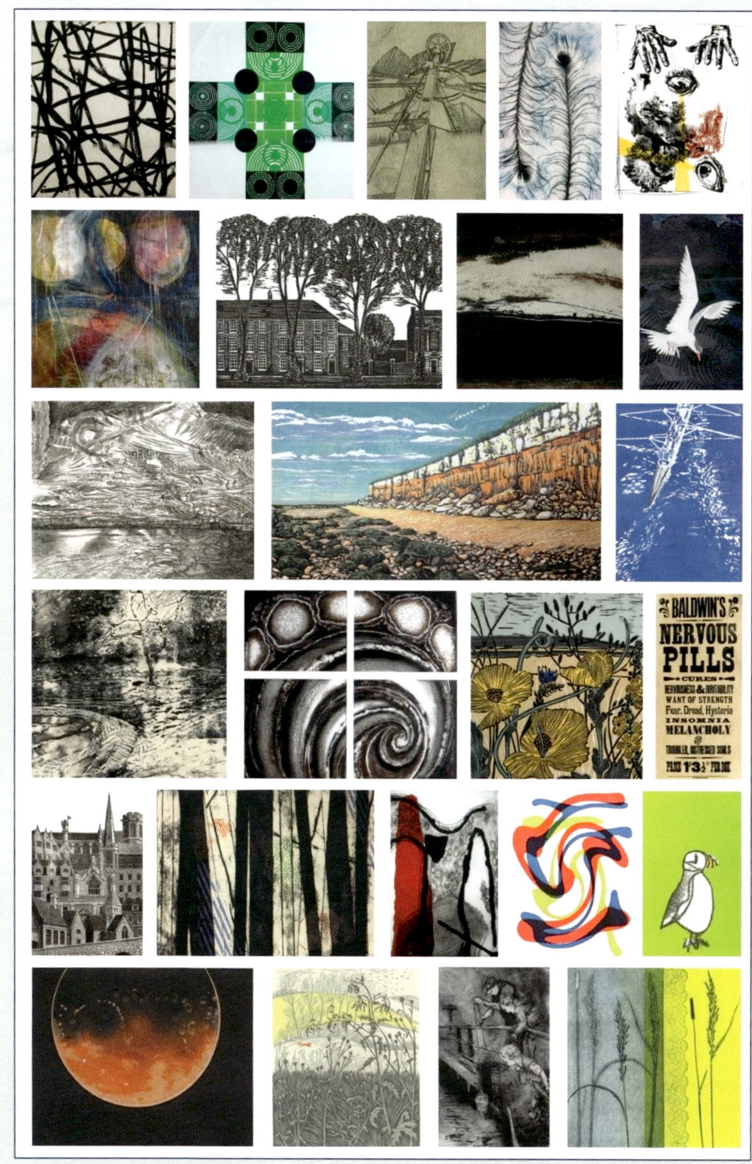

THE ARTISTS

LEADERS IN PRINTMAKING

Background image: John Preston – 'Fen Veteran', plate and print

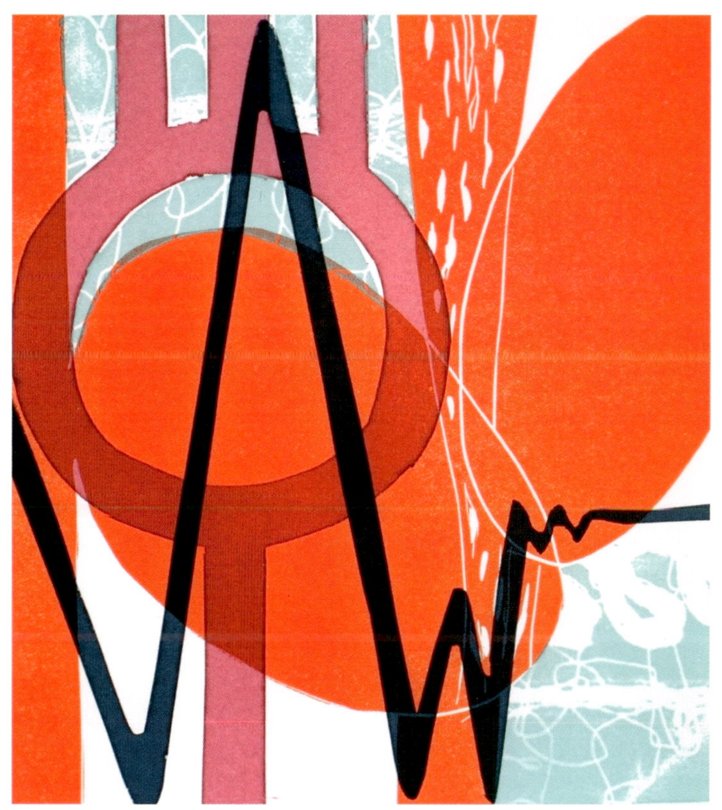

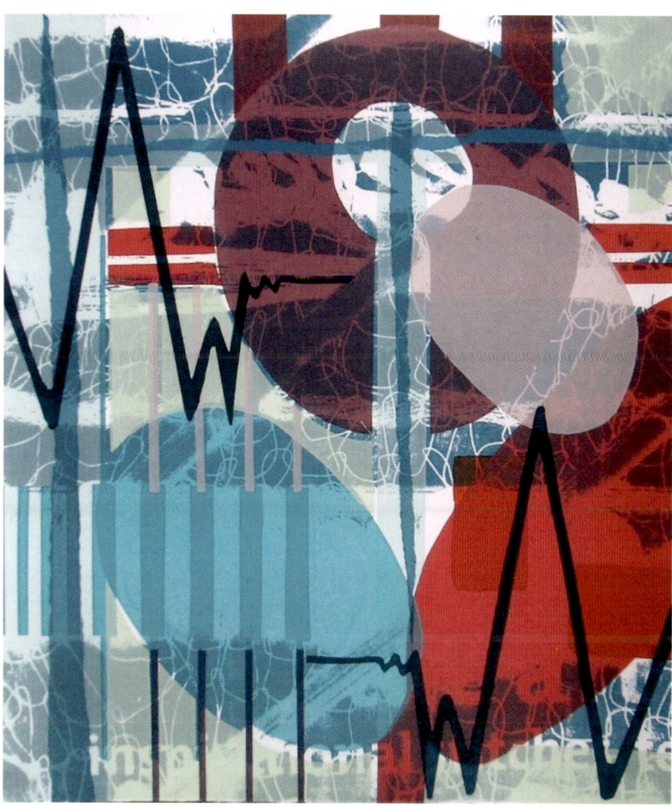

Above, from left: 'Anomaly I' (silkscreen), 20cm x 21cm, edition of 6; 'Anomaly III' (silkscreen and linocut), 20cm x 21cm, edition of 8

TRACEY ASHMAN

Textiles inspire Tracey Ashman's prints. From the age of five, she was taught to sew and knit by her mother, and the legacy of the crafts continues today.

She first incorporated stitching into her printmaking in 2014. Her 'Evocation' series used stitch as a mark-making tool; the texture and form of stitch create marks that mimic those found in nature.

Subsequently, Tracey explored her personal connection to stitch. "Stitch has always been a constant in my life, and I wanted to fuse it with printmaking in imagery that considers stitch as a metaphor for growth and renewal; a healing and mending of both mind and body."

Her 'Anomaly, Series I' examined the experience of open-heart surgery when nine years old. The series imparts her

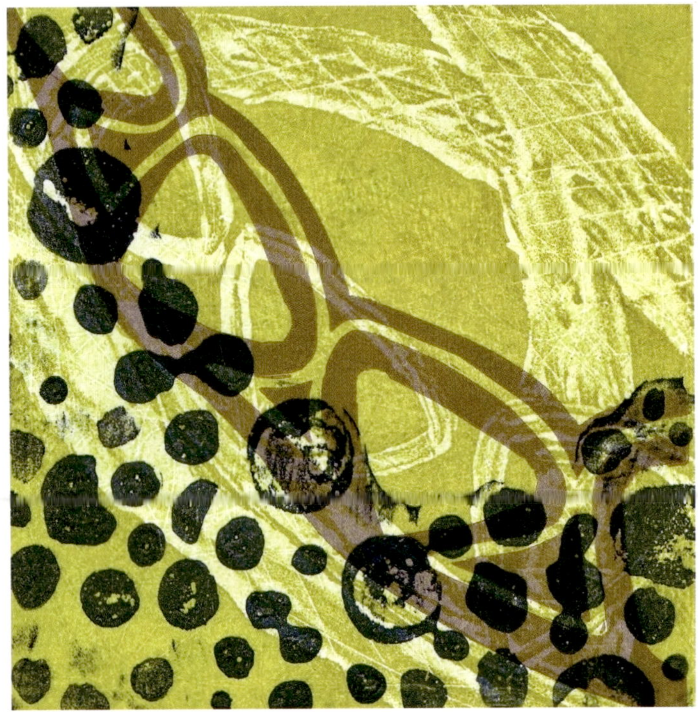

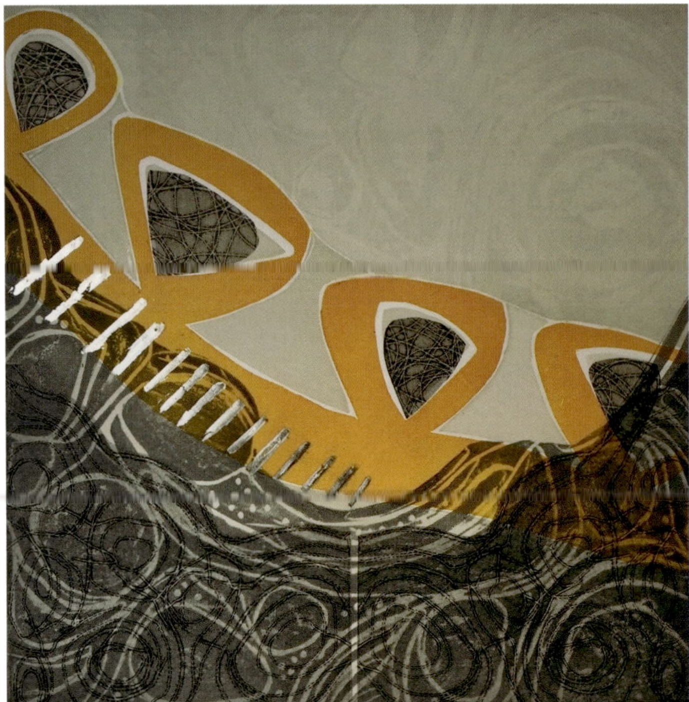

memory of the recuperative powers of knitting with her mother. "Metaphorically, the twofold aspects of physical and emotional healing are evident in human tissue that binds, seals and protects, and the casting of stitches to create a fabric; both actively heal and protect the body and psyche."

Tracey's recent series 'Summons' explores a brain tumour operation in 2016. "The emotional and physical impact is communicated by machine stitch, which underpins imagery to translate my experience."
www.traceyashmanprints.org

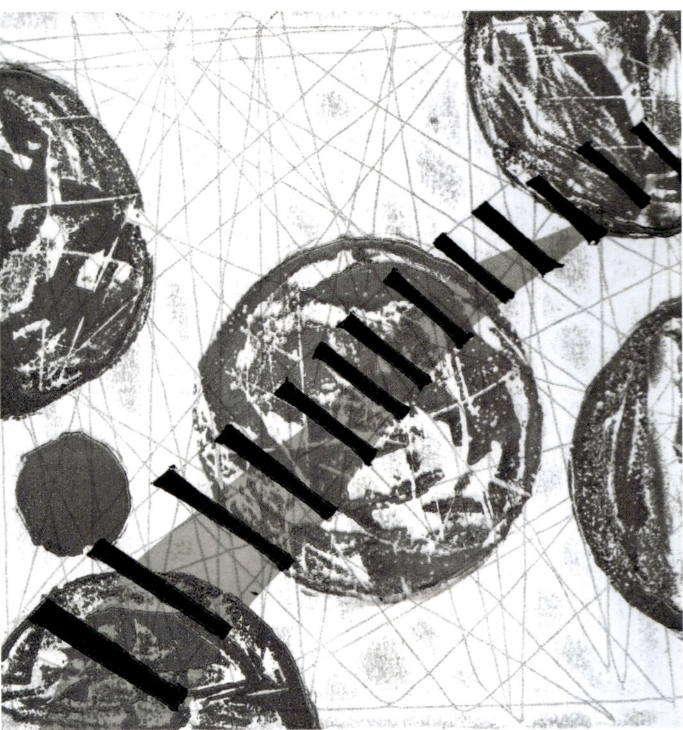

From top left, clockwise: 'Summoning Laso' (etched linocut), 15cm x 15cm, edition of 10; 'Summoning Minerva' (etched linocut and chine-collé), 30cm x 30cm, edition of 10; 'Summoning Athena' (etched linocut), 15cm x 15cm, edition of 10; Facing page: 'Evocation IV (Series I)' (monoprint and chine-collé), 33cm x 38cm, unique

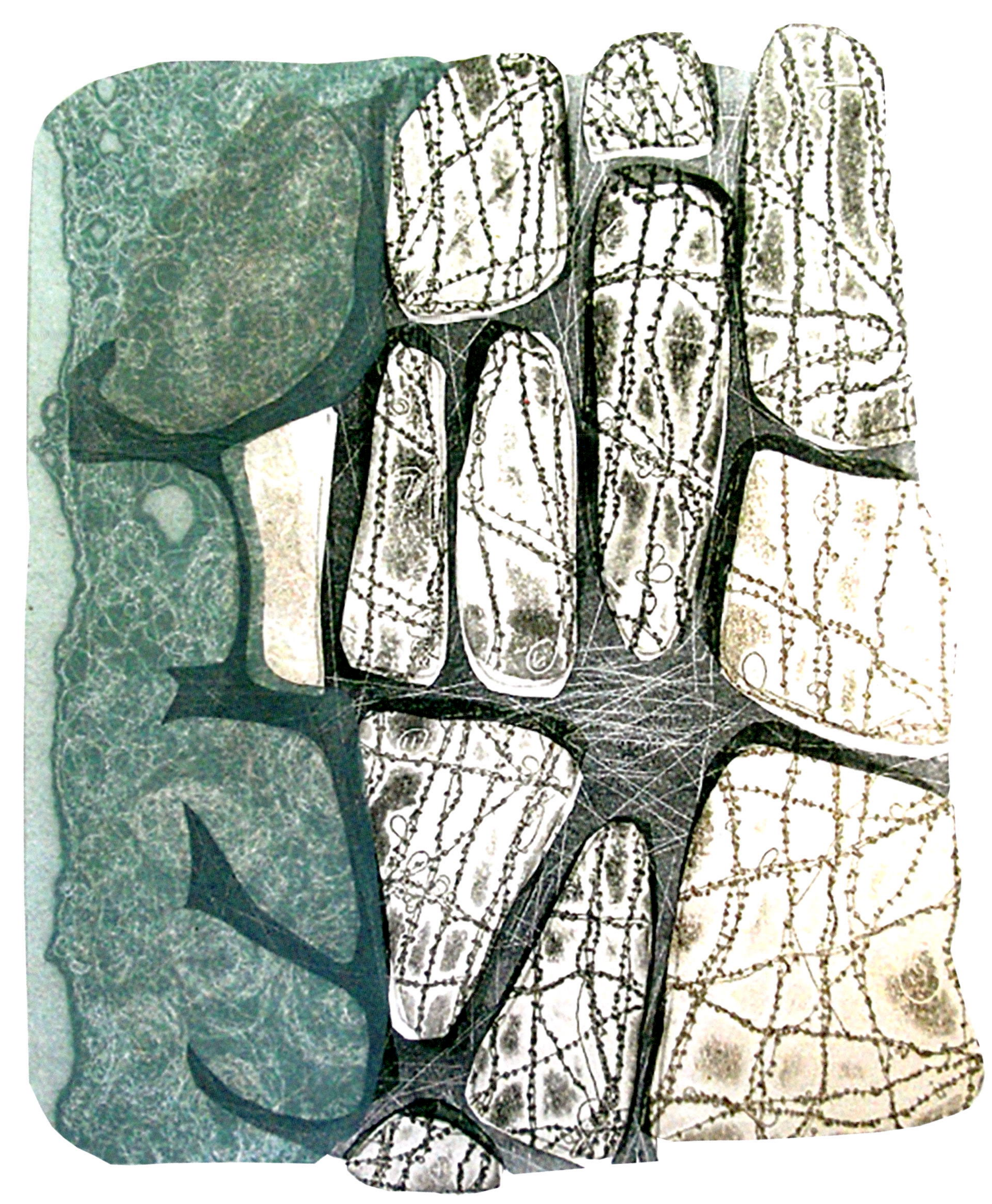

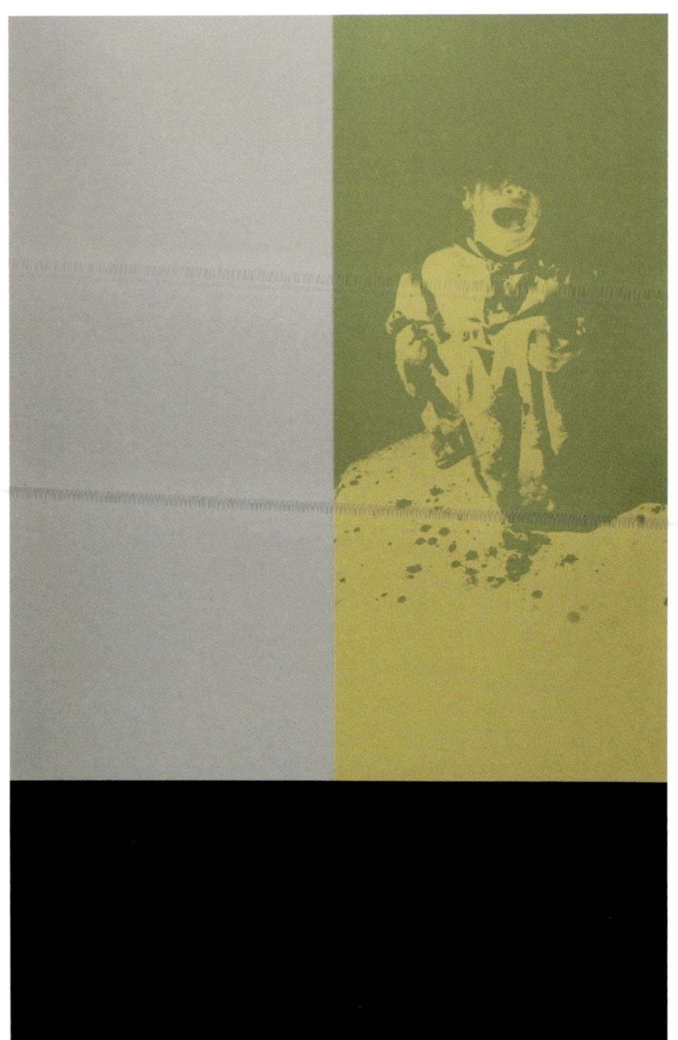

RAMZIEH BAJ

Ramzieh Baj was born in Jordan to Circassian parents from the Caucasus region of Russia. After the scorched earth campaign of 1864, tsarist Russia deported her Circassian ancestors, uprooting almost the entire population from their homeland – those who survived were dispersed all over the world.

"My work, which often explores contemporary and historical issues such as conflict and displacement,

Above left: Untitled (screenprint), 120cm x 80cm, edition of 3; Above right: Untitled (screenprint/graphite), 100cm x 70cm, unique; Opposite: 'Red Gate' (screenprint and watercolour), 56cm x 56cm, edition of 10

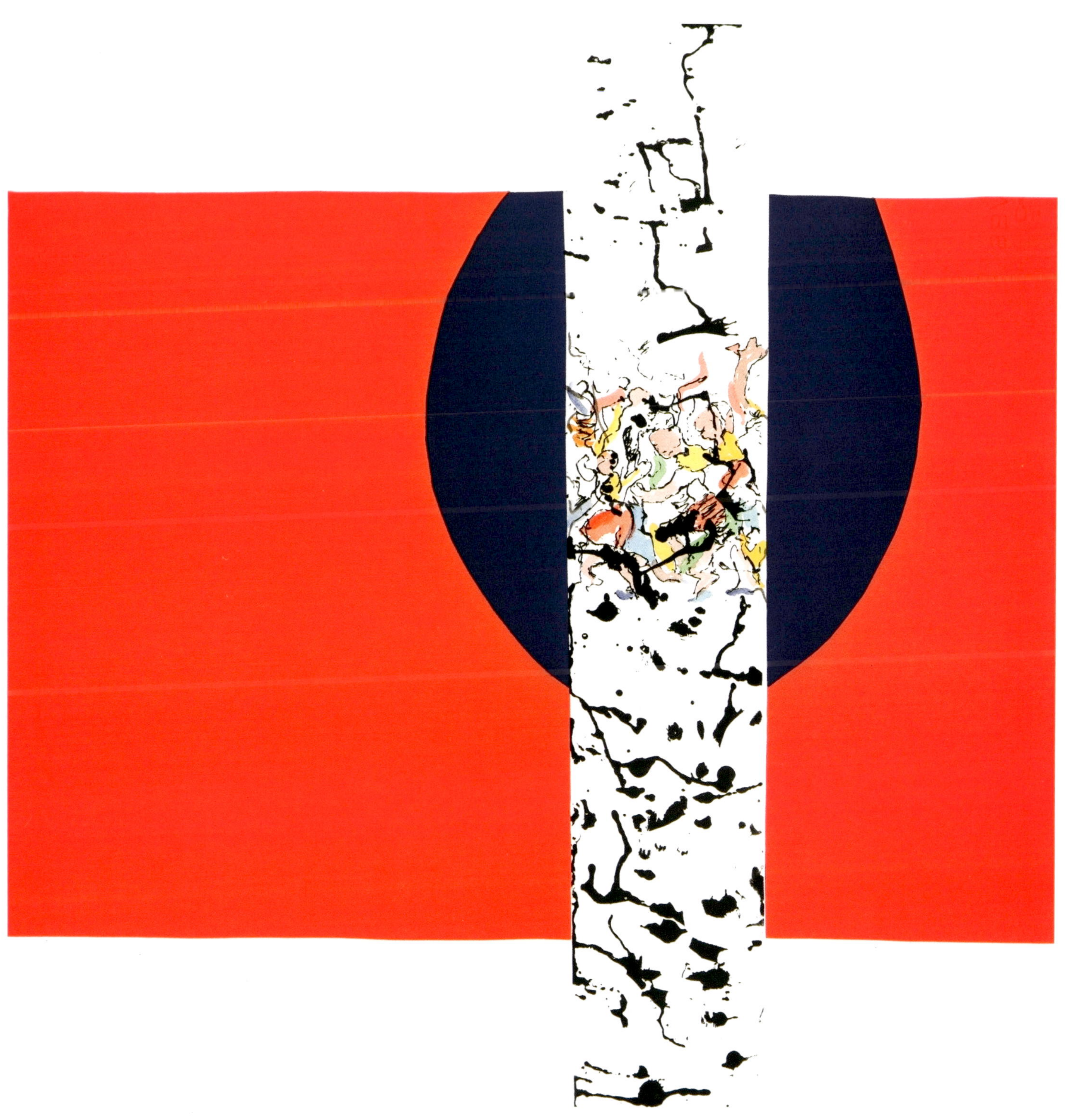

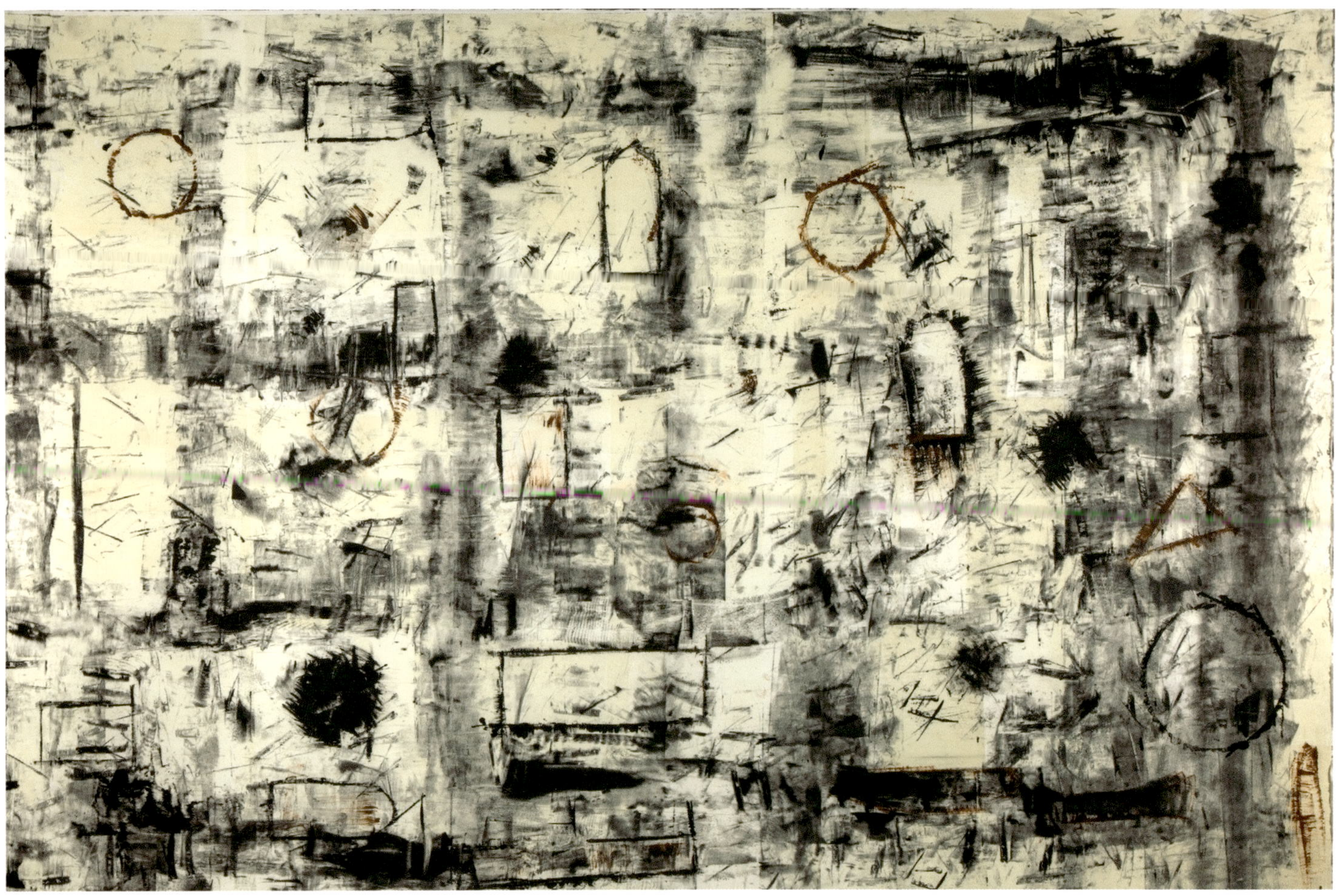

Above: 'Fragments of Evidence I' (monoprint), 80cm x 120cm, unique

consists of monoprints and screenprints with multi-layered constructions of symbolic forms, some of which include photographic images embedded within the layers of reconstituted marks," she explains.

In 2008 Ramzieh was awarded an MA in Fine Art Printmaking from Cambridge School of Art – she had previously studied Fine Art at Brighton College of Art, and at the Academy of Fine Art in Baghdad under Faiq Hassan.

As well as shows in London, Brighton and Cambridge, she has also exhibited internationally in the capitals of Jordan, Egypt, Qatar, Serbia and Botswana. In 2016 she participated in the Cambridge Original Printmakers Biennale where she was awarded the John Purcell Prize.

www.ramziehbaj.com

BERRY BIRDSALL

Berry Birdsall's prints are personal, showing scenes of people and places from her own experiences. Her cityscapes are of New York, London and Cambridge, cities in which she has lived. "I also enjoy portraying the interactions of children with their environment; I want my artwork to catch the atmosphere of a particular moment."

Berry grew up in New York City and studied music at the High School of Music and Art. She then switched to science, moved to England, obtained her PhD from Cambridge University, and became a research scientist at the National Institute for Medical Research in London, where she worked for many years. She took up painting in 2005, and now pursues printmaking and painting full time.

An exhibitor at the 2016 and 2018 Cambridge Original Printmakers Biennales, she also had a print selected for the 2017 exhibition of the Society of Women Artists at the Mall Galleries in London.
www.berrybirdsall.com

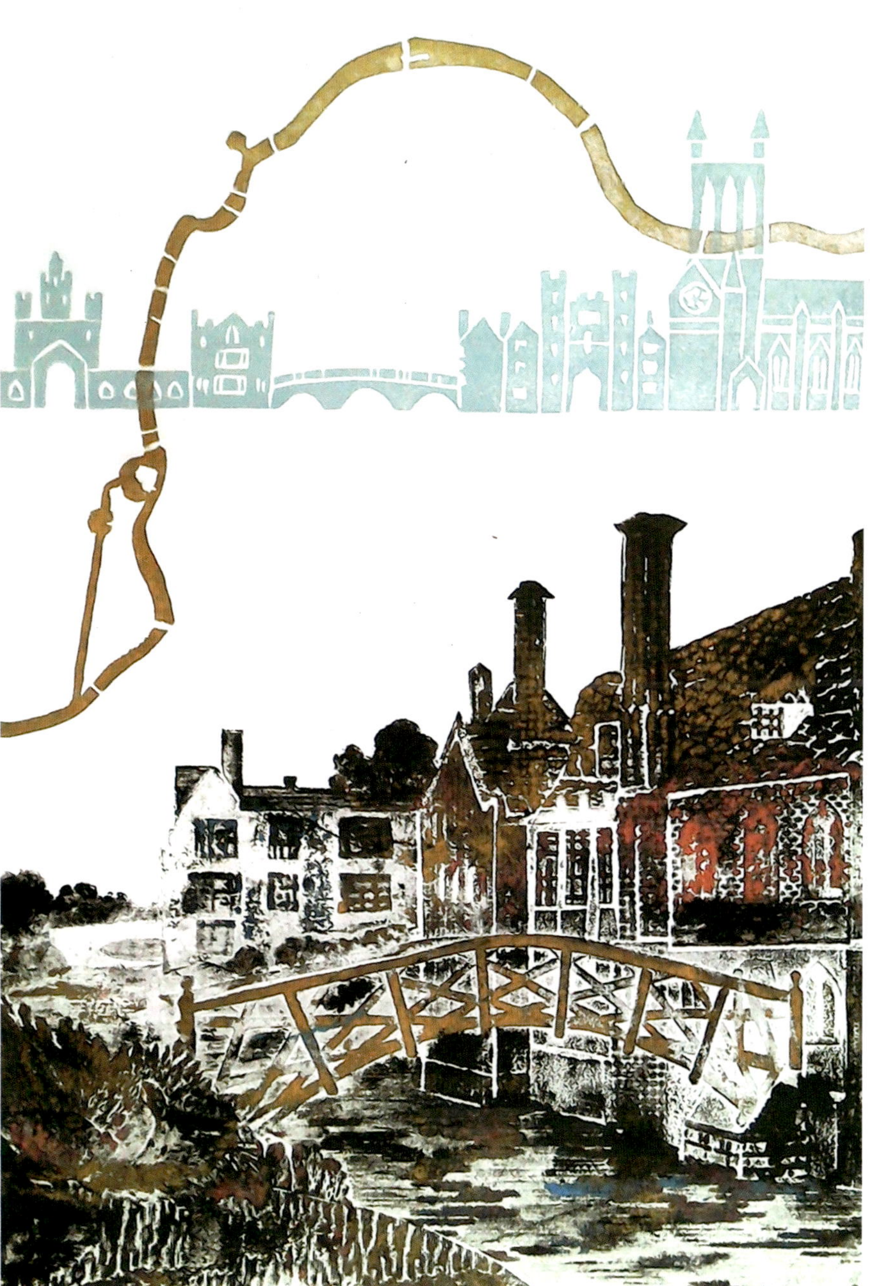

Right: 'River Cam' (collagraph), 33cm x 53cm, edition of 25

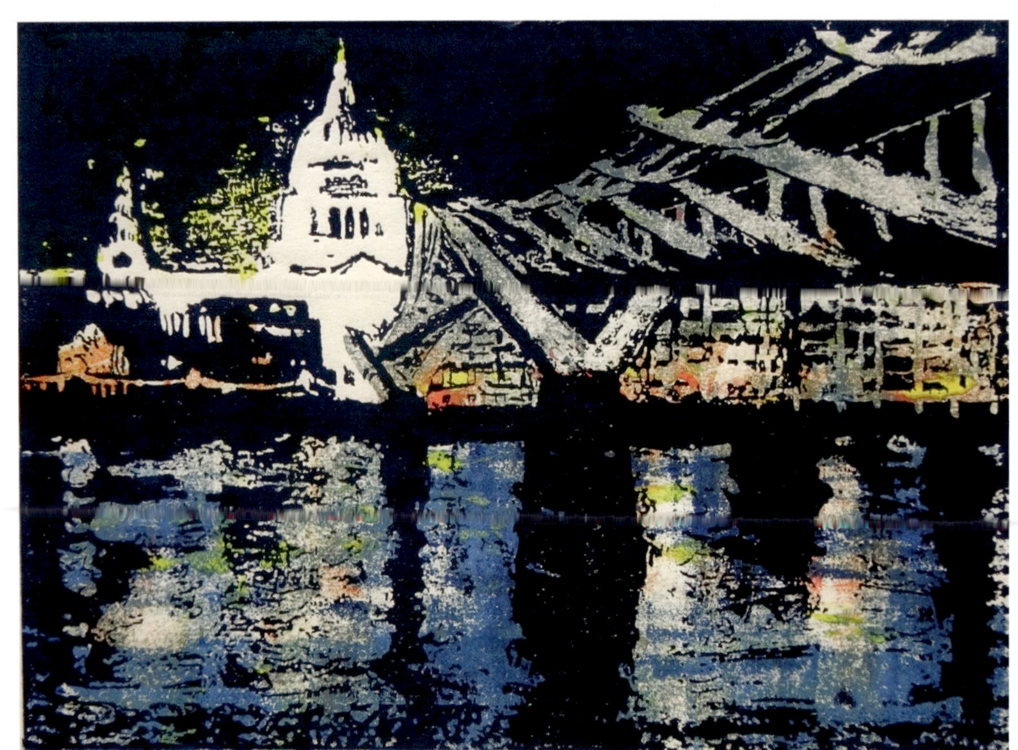

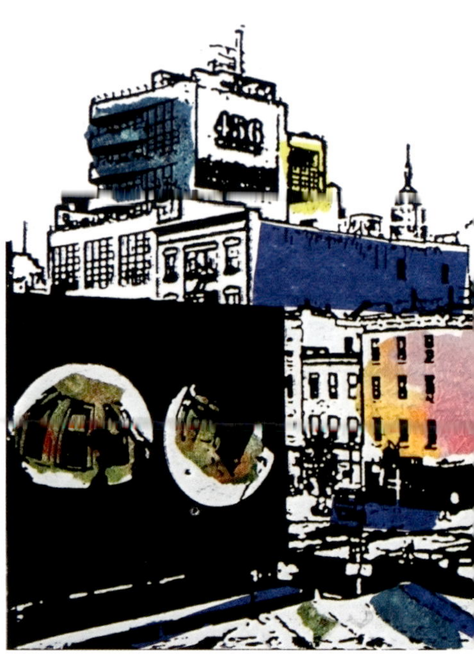

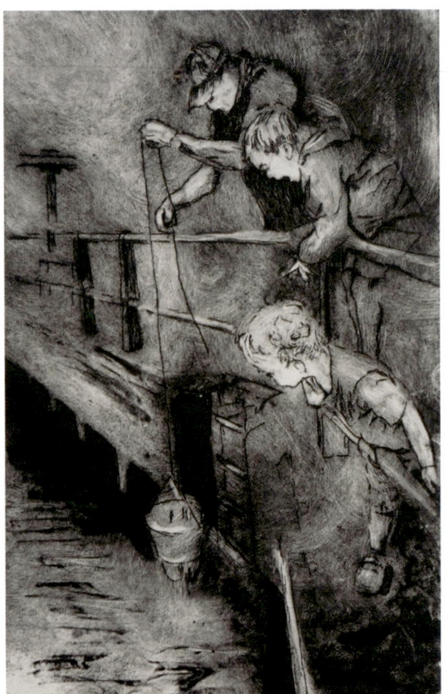

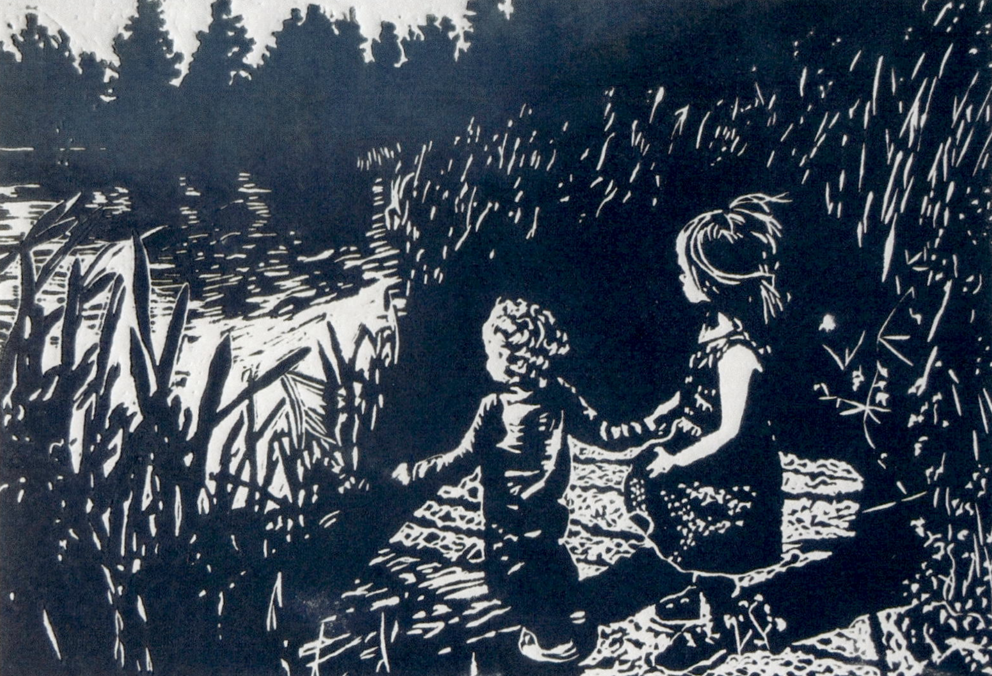

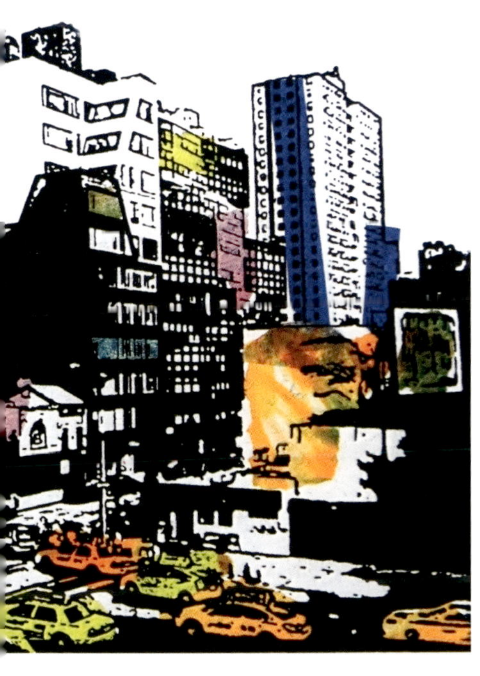

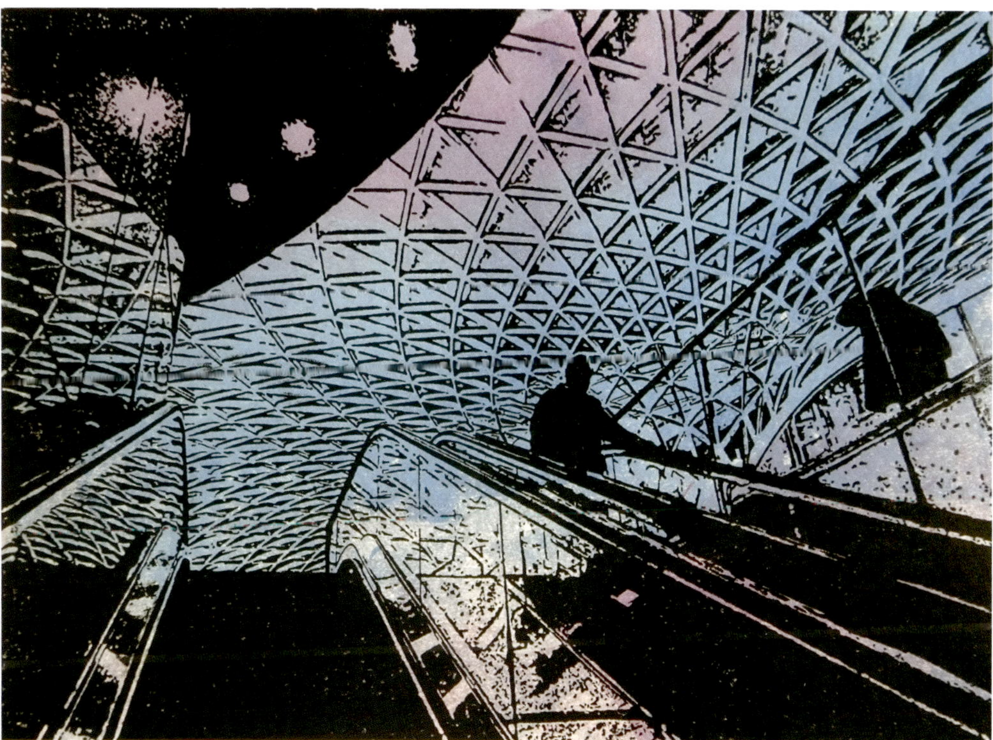

Top row, from far left: 'Millennium Bridge, St Paul's' (Solarplate), 30cm x 21cm, edition of 25; 'New York High Line' (Solarplate and chine-collé), 30cm x 21cm, edition of 25; 'King's Cross' (Solarplate), 30cm x 21cm, edition of 25; Bottom row, from far left: 'Crabbing' (drypoint), 18cm x 28cm, edition of 20; 'Careful!' (linocut), 19cm x 29cm, edition of 40; 'Looking for Kingfishers' (silkscreen), 22cm x 16cm, edition of 25; 'Toe in the Water' (drypoint), 11cm x 21cm, edition of 25 – all Berry Birdsall

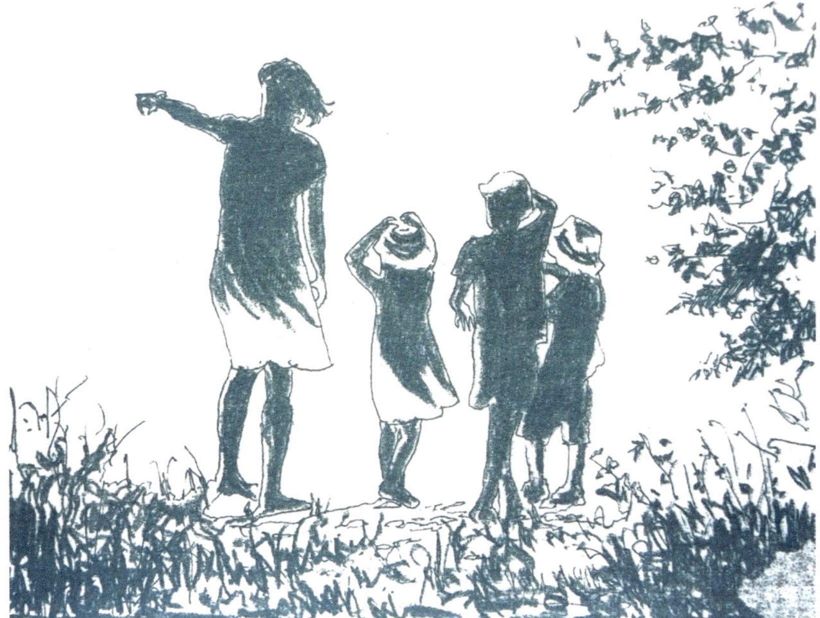

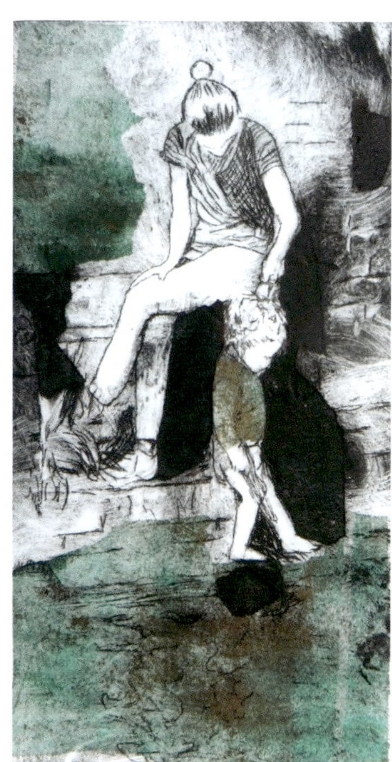

A J BLUSTIN

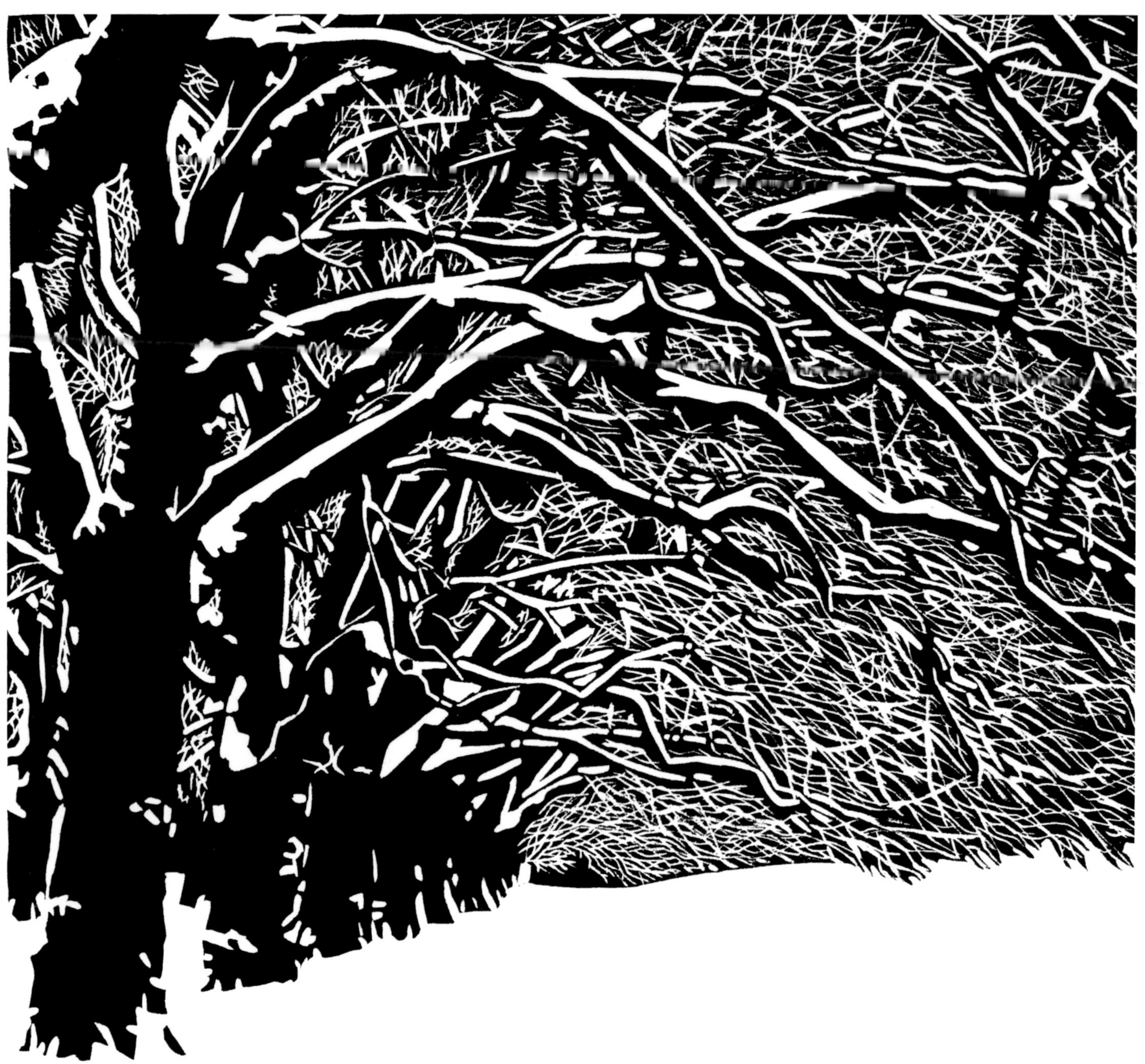

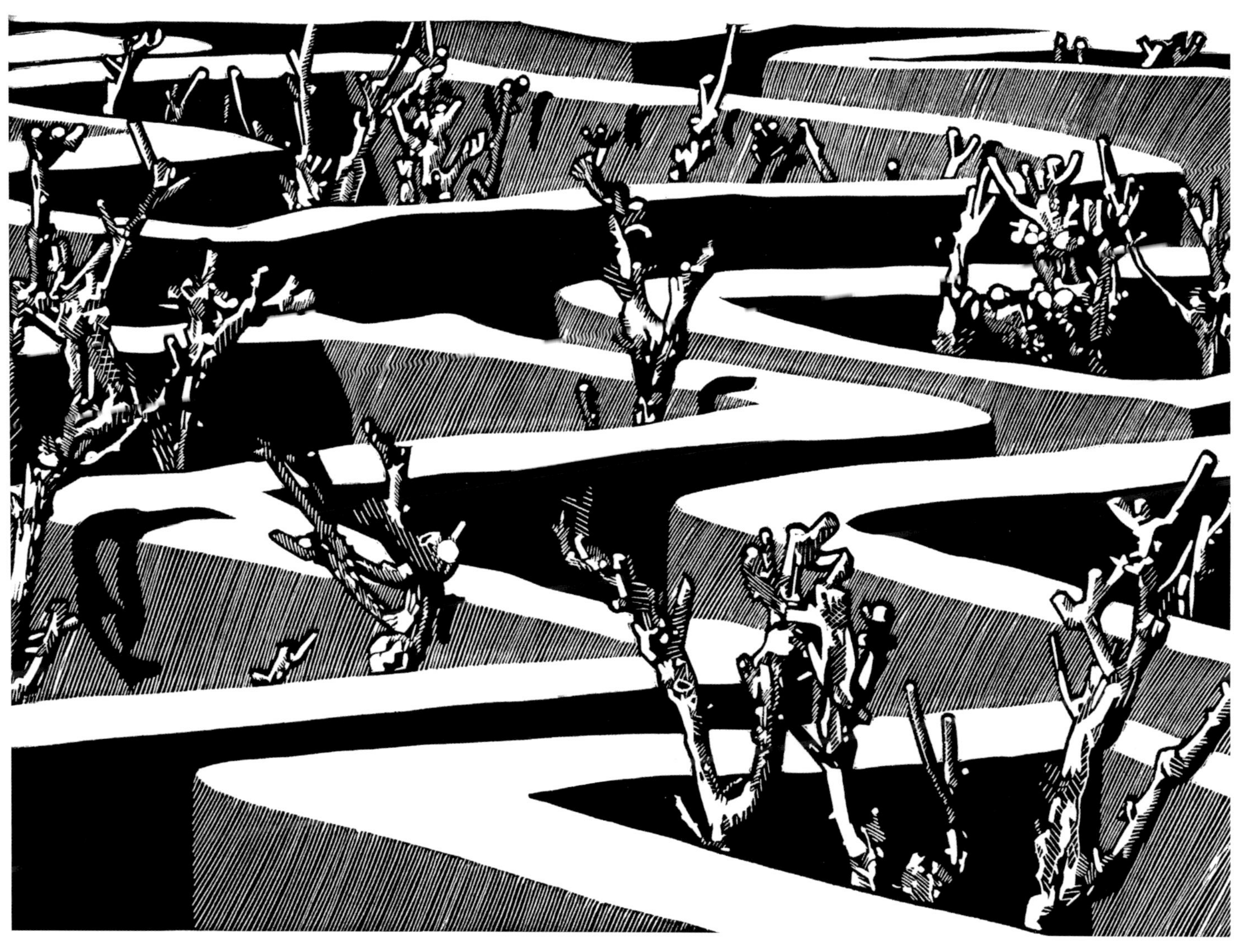

Facing page: 'Hymn of Winter' (linocut), 23.0cm x 23.0cm, edition of 30; Above: 'The Bishop's Topiary, Ely' (linocut), 23.0cm x 32.1cm, edition of 30

Astronomer-turned-artist A J Blustin's work continues to be influenced by the effects of light, "and the search for underlying structure in observed phenomena".

"My printmaking focuses principally on linocuts," he says, "playing with shapes, patterns, flow, connections, light and shade, through imagery of landscape and architecture. Natural forms often stand in for human figures and situations, and certain images have a musical subtext."

Alongside the lino and vinyl prints

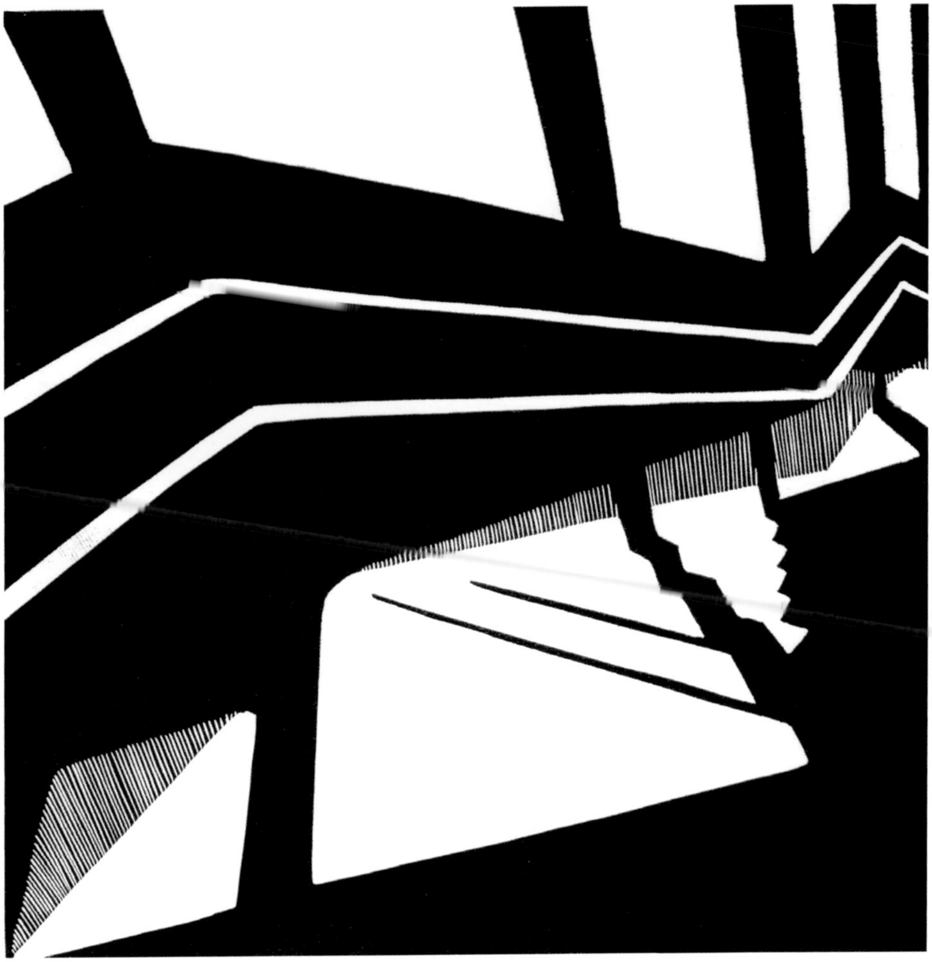

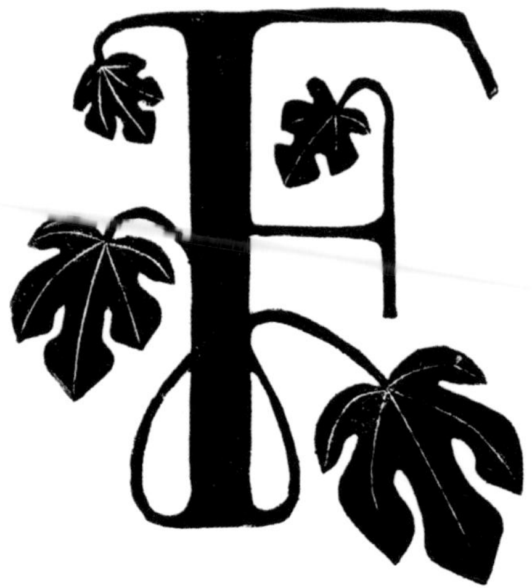

that indulge his penchant for relief carving, the artist also has an interest in illustration and the relationship between text and image.

"This can find expression in drawing-based forms of printmaking such as drypoint, or in the production of small hand-made multiples including my *Word of the Day* illustrated poetry pamphlet," he explains.

"My 'Floccinaucinihilipilification' linocut is a small illustration from *Word of the Day*, a pamphlet of limericks based upon rare vocabulary illustrated by punning linocuts. In this case, 'F' stands for floccinaucinihilipilification (valuing at little or nothing), and also 'fig leaf', the purpose of the ridiculous word for the over-inflated character in the poem:

Floccinaucinihilipilification
Is par for the course for a man of his station;
To sneer with requisite degrees of pomposity
Requires quite exceptional powers of verbosity,
And words of preposterous conglomeration.

"'The Bishop's Topiary, Ely' reveals twisted figures trapped in a nightmare maze (this is not a comment on the Bishop!), while the form of the branches in 'Hymn of Winter' (depicting the avenue of trees across Jesus Green, Cambridge, in the snow) implies the interweaving lines of Renaissance polyphonic choral music. The overall structure of the image is reminiscent of a phase diagram for the solid, liquid and gaseous states of matter – snow being a solid form of water.

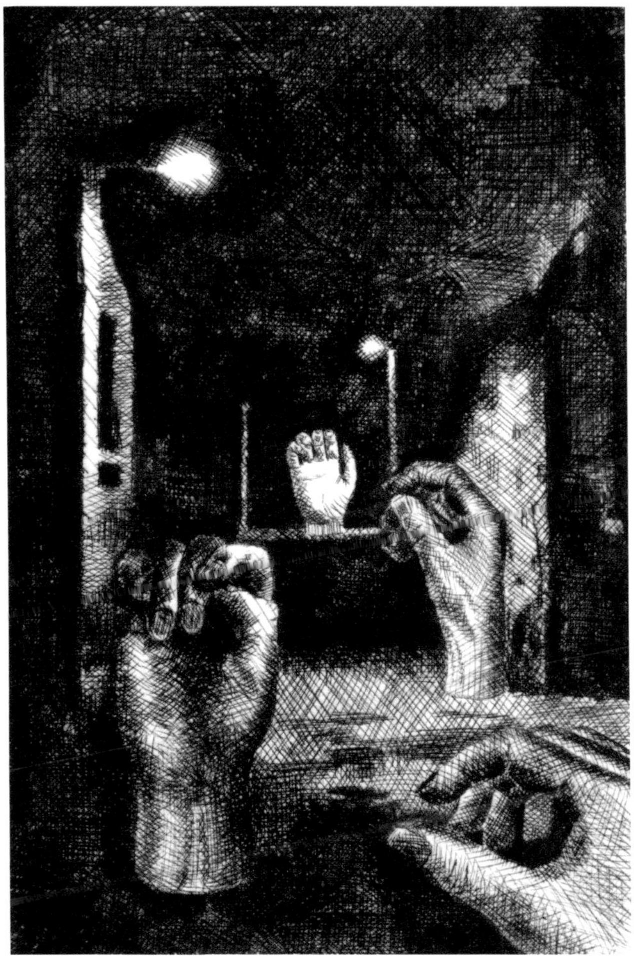

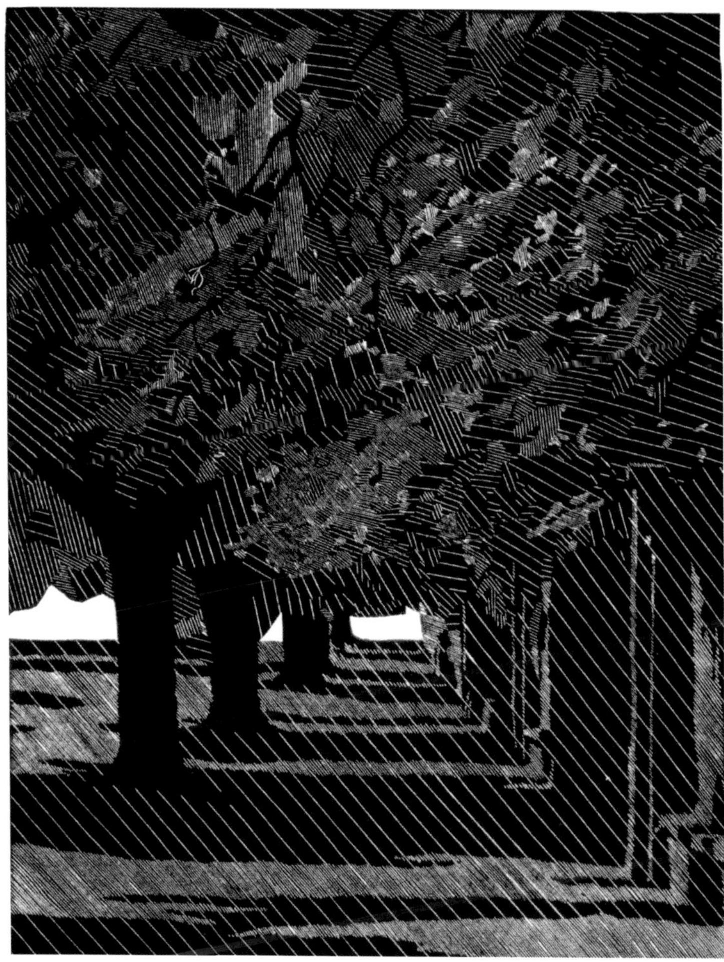

"'Ipswich Station' shows shadows and light in motion on a staircase; 'The Cloister' (the outer boundary of Jesus College, Victoria Avenue, Cambridge) is a study of how sunlight filters through the trees; and 'The Recruiters' reflects strange goings-on in Garret Hostel Lane, a favourite haunt of notorious occultist Aleister Crowley when he was a student at neighbouring Trinity College, Cambridge."

A J Blustin has participated in numerous open exhibitions, including the RA Summer Exhibition, Eastern Open and Cambridge Open Studios. In 2013 he had a solo exhibition at the Mercury Theatre, Colchester; and in 2014 was elected to the Cambridge Drawing Society. *https://tinyurl.com/AJBlustin*

Facing page, from left: 'Ipswich Station' (vinyl cut), 23.0cm x 23.5cm, edition of 30; 'Floccinaucinihilipilification' (linocut), 11.5cm x 10.5cm, not editioned (illustration for photocopied pamphlet); Above, from left: 'The Recruiters' (drypoint), 28.0cm x 18.7cm, unique; 'The Cloister' (linocut), 29.5cm x 22.8cm, edition of 30

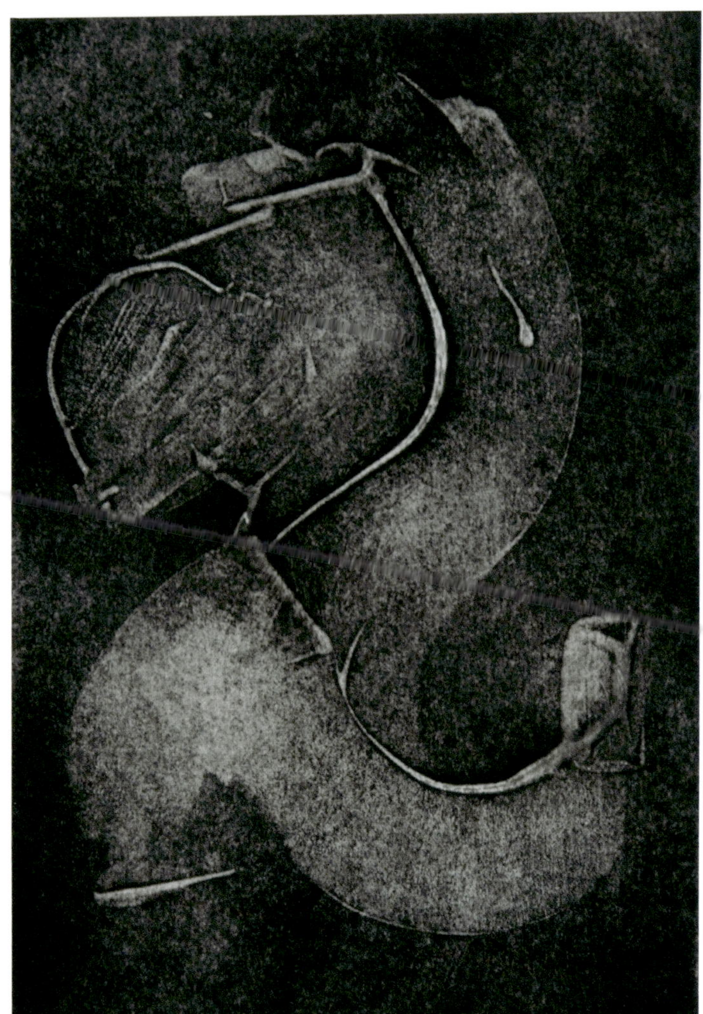

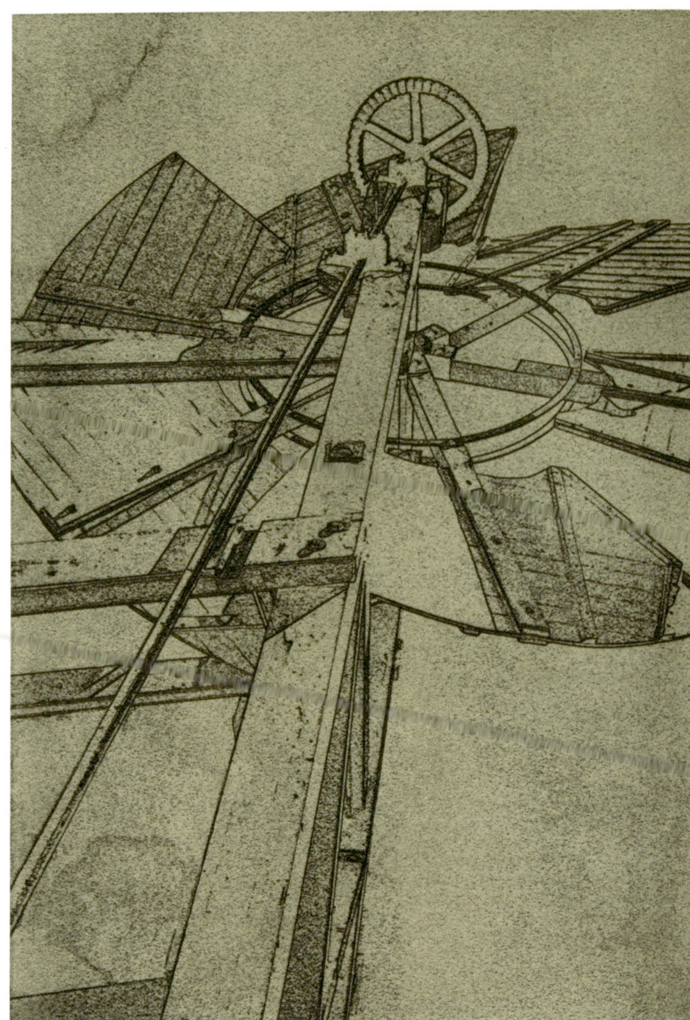

TERRY BRYAN

Graphic artist and printmaker Terry Bryan works from his studio and print workshop in the tranquillity of rural Essex. For more than four decades he worked in the uncompromising world of commercial graphic design. "In 2013 a line was drawn, a journey begun, a passion born, expressed through the framework of printmaking."

From this starting point, his desire to experiment is a process of continual exploration and development. Currently, he is interpreting his graphic and photo imagery, together

Above left: 'Reversed Two' (collagraph), 30cm x 38cm, unique; Above right: 'Slowly Turning' (photo etching), 54cm x 43cm, edition of 5; Facing page, top: 'Basil the Barbarian' (collagraph), 50cm x 45cm, unique; Bottom: 'Across the Fields' (Solarplate etching), 51cm x 33cm, edition of 10

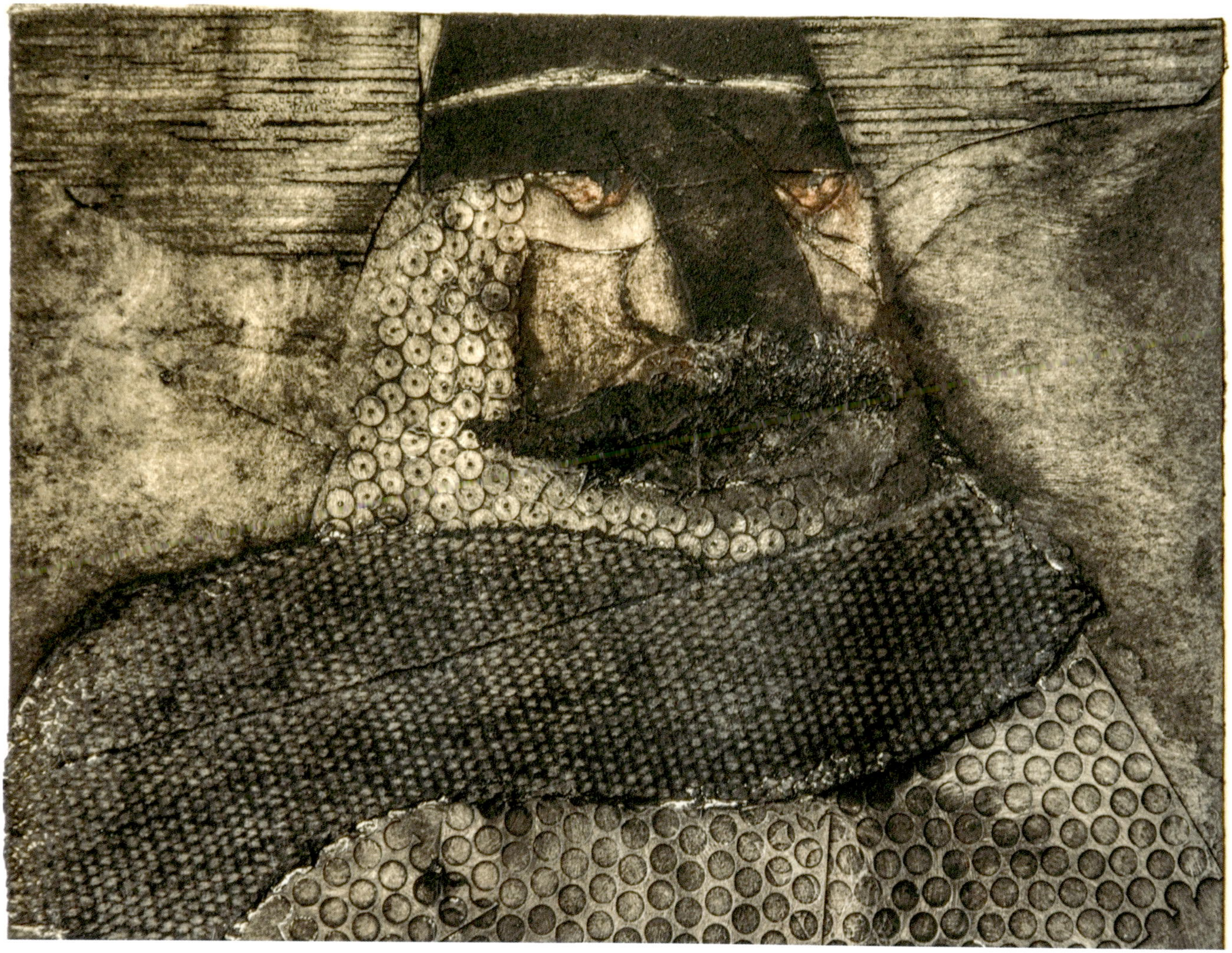

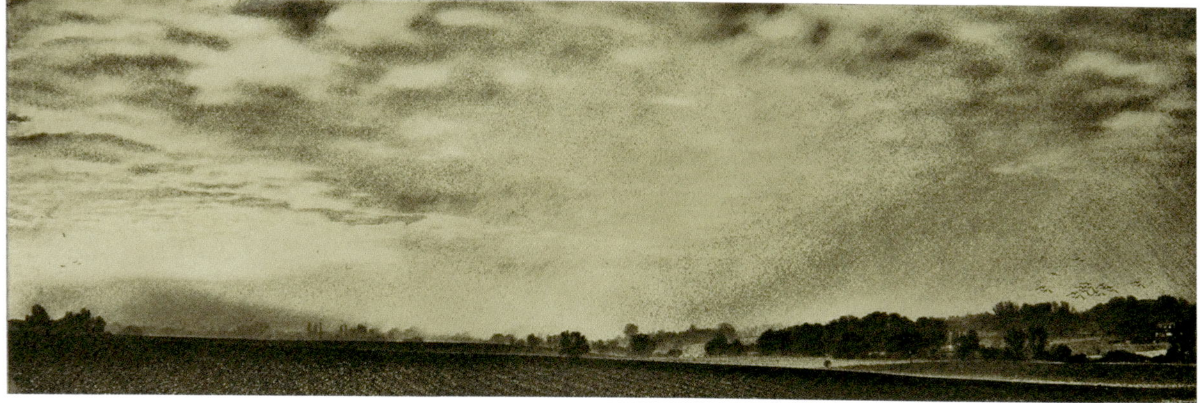

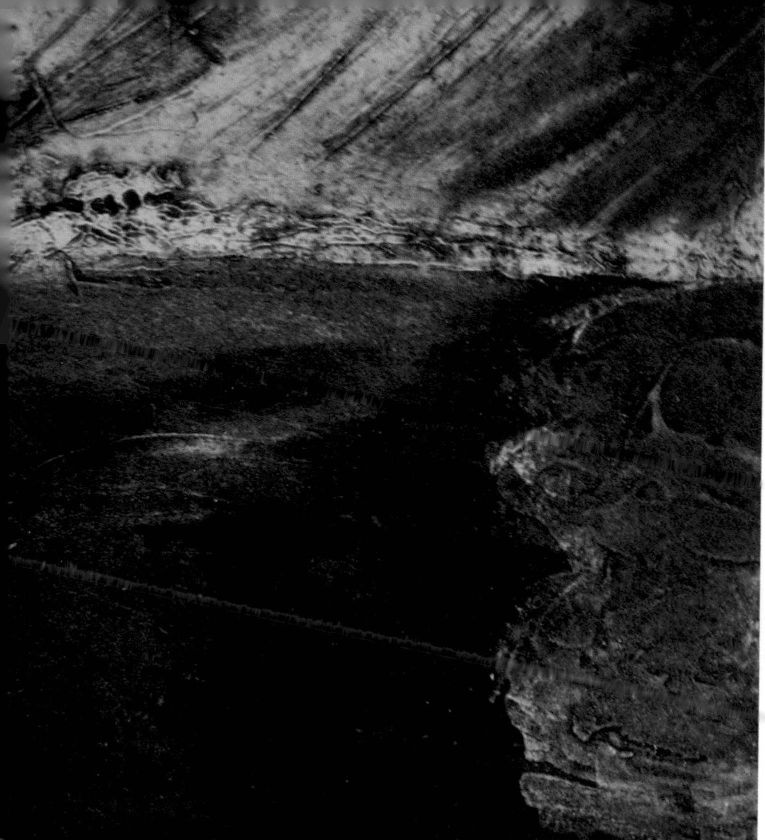

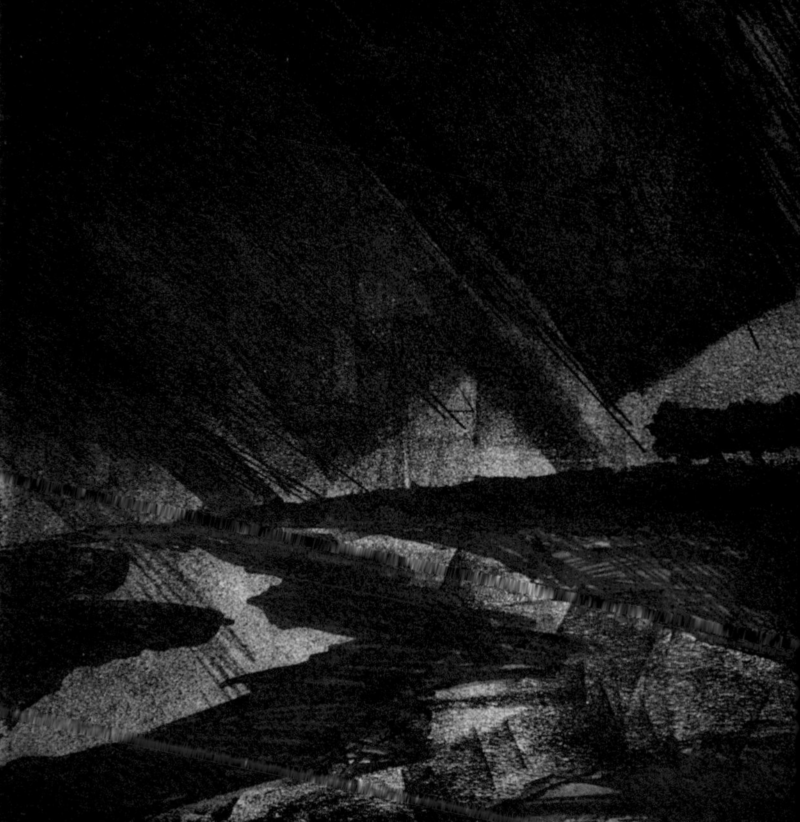

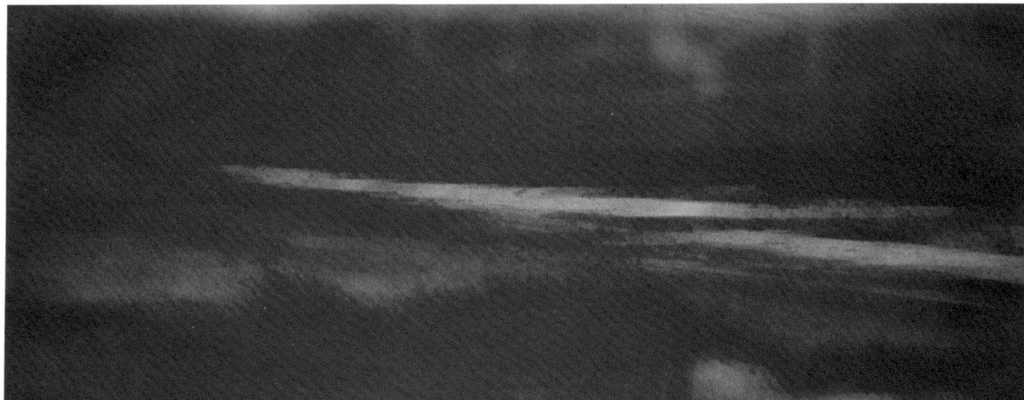

Above left: 'Three Trees Beach' (collagraph), 40cm x 44cm, unique; Above right: 'Dawn Storm' (etching/ aquatint), 50cm x 48cm, unique; Left: 'Moon Surf' (Solarplate etching), 63cm x 38cm, edition of 2

with his visual thoughts, through his sketchbooks, using the media of Solarplate™ etching, photo etching, drypoint, carborundum, collagraph and monoprint to produce contemporary editions encompassing land and seascapes, architecture, calligraphy and his specific interest, "military uniforms and the warrior class through the ages".

Terry was shortlisted for the National Open Art Exhibition in both 2016 and 2017; and selected for the Small Print International, Leicester Print Workshop Exhibition, for its UK tour 2017. He is a member of the Gainsborough's House Print Workshop.

Email: visconuk@yahoo.co.uk

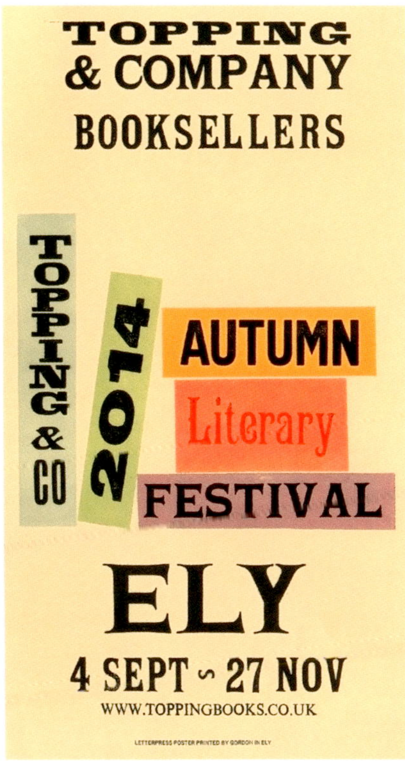

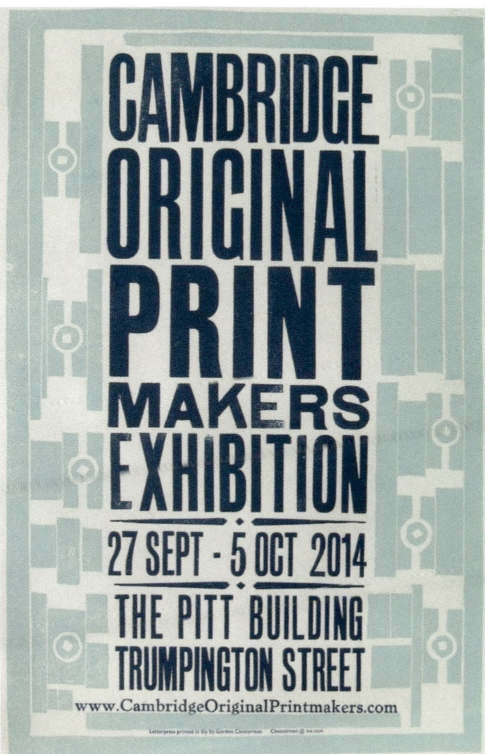

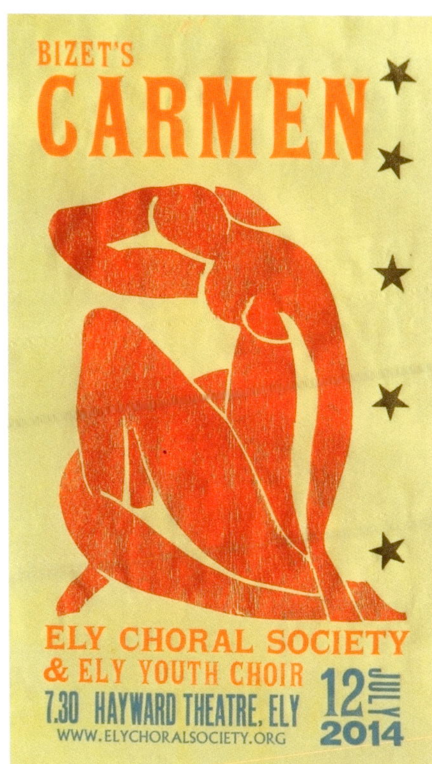

GORDON CHESTERMAN

Ely-based Gordon Chesterman started letterpress printing at the age of 12 and has been printing ever since, pressing on through the technology's extinction in the early 1980s, killed off by computers, to helping in its popular resurgence over the last decade.

After studying at the London College of Printing in the late 1970s, he joined De La Rue, a company designing and printing banknotes for more than 80 countries around the world, where each note was subjected to all three printing processes (letterpress, gravure and litho). Following a varied career that reluctantly took him further away from printing, he continued as a 'hobby' printer, with a good array of type acquired

WEDDED SOULS

I am as a Spirit who has dwelt within his heart of hearts, and I have felt his feelings, and have thought his thoughts, and known the inmost converse of his soul, the tone unheard but in the silence of his blood, when all the pulses, in their multitude image the trembling calm of summer seas.

I have unbarred the golden melodies of his deep soul, as with a master-key, and loosened them and bathed myself therein - even as an Eagle in a thunder-mist clothing his wings with lightning.

Above, from left: 'Topping & Co' (to help the Ely bookshop promote its visiting author events, letterpress printed in six colours, 20" x 12"); 'Cambridge Original Printmakers' (printed "just for fun" to help promote the first Cambridge Original Printmakers' exhibition in 2014, linocut quoins, furniture and reglet as a border, and printed in two colours, 23" x 16"); 'Carmen' (printed for the Ely Choral Society using a hand-cut piece of plywood for Matisse's famous 'cut-out', letterpress printed in three colours, 32" x 18"); 'Wedded Souls' (Shelley's poem, printed in 30pt Times New Roman with initial caps by William Morris, letterpress printed, 18" x 10")

over the years, three presses and a long, growing list of happy recipients of his printed work – including the Fine Press Book Association.

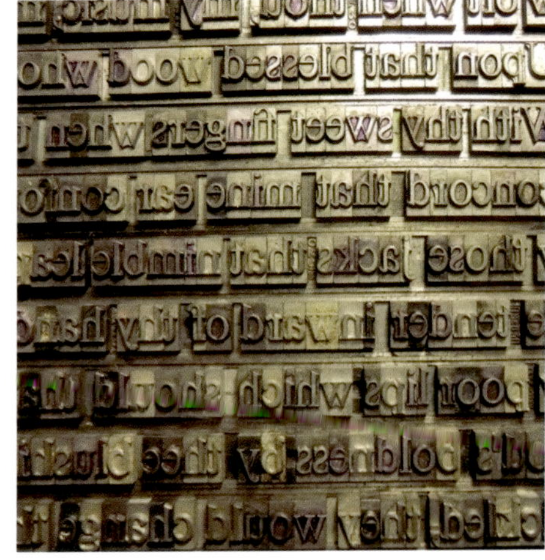

His letterpress work covers three main areas: large posters, small books and printed ephemera. For the posters, he uses wooden type, much of it hand-cut in the 1890s, printed on a very large Stephenson Blake proofing press. Recently, to help 'strengthen' some fonts of wooden type, he has been successfully using the latest 3D printing technology to reproduce perfect replicas of letters, flourishes and fleurons – "computers finally come to the aid of letterpress printers!". In addition to conventional wooden type, Gordon also experiments with type-high plywood, linen and even sandpaper to get the desired tone and texture.

His books are hand-bound with marbled end-papers and gold-blocked covers, usually volumes of poetry, and often given away to friends – "printed solely for creative fun and not for profit". His printed ephemera covers wedding invitations, menus, dinner invitations, business cards, correspondence cards and stationery.

Gordon's work has been displayed in the Bodleian Library, Oxford; the Senate House, University of Cambridge; and Ely Cathedral.

Email: chestermen@me.com

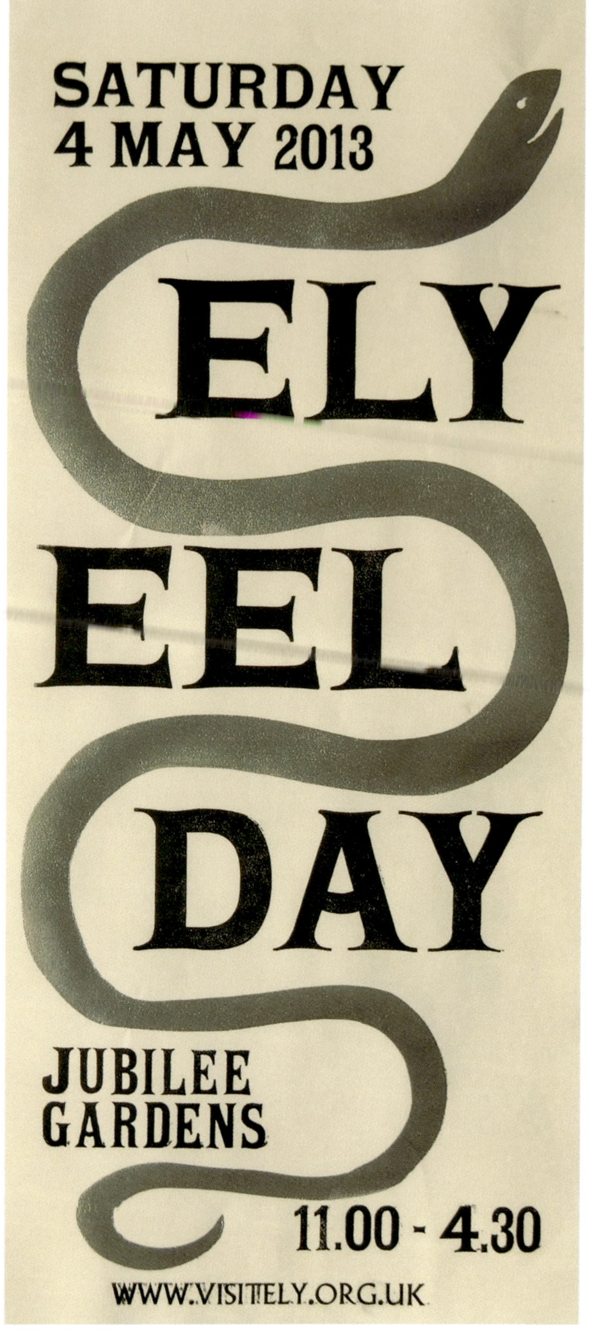

Right: 'Ely Eel Day' (printed "just for fun" to help promote Ely's Eel Day, hand-cut plywood for the eel, using thermography powders on silver ink to create the sheen, 24" x 12"); Facing page, from left: 'Nothing Compares To The Simple Pleasure Of A Bike Ride (John F Kennedy's quote, letterpress printed with a linocut bike, 29" x 13"); 'Being Male...' (Vin Diesel's quote, printed for a friend to give to her son, letterpress printed, 28" x 11"); 'Look Up At The Stars...' (Stephen Hawking's quote, letterpress printed with linocut stars from an illustration by Fiona Whitehouse, www.fionawhitehousepaintings.com, 33" x 12")

NOTHING COMPARES TO THE SIMPLE PLEASURE OF A BIKE RIDE

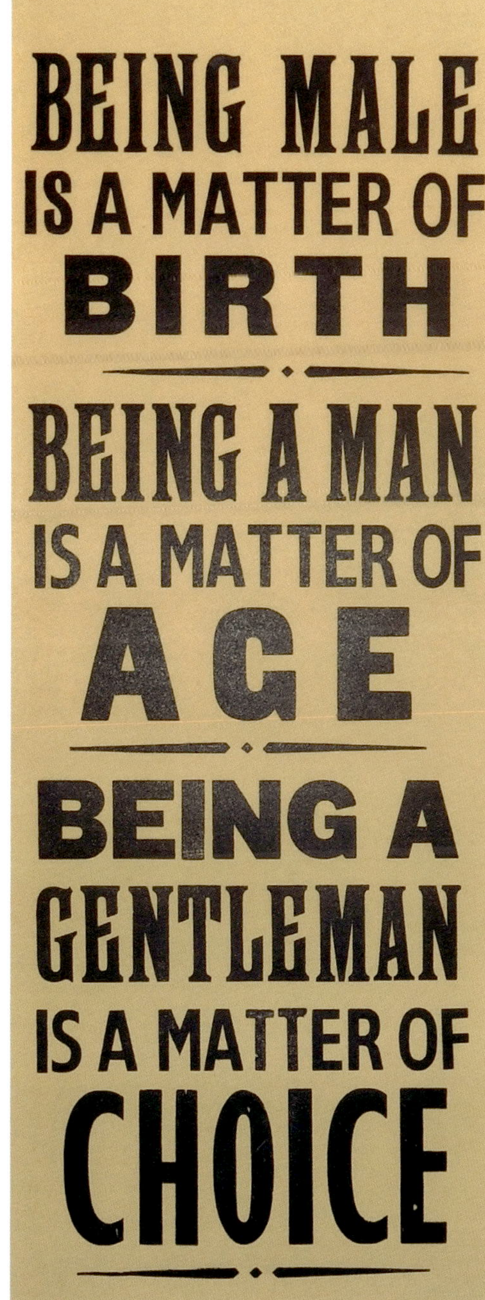

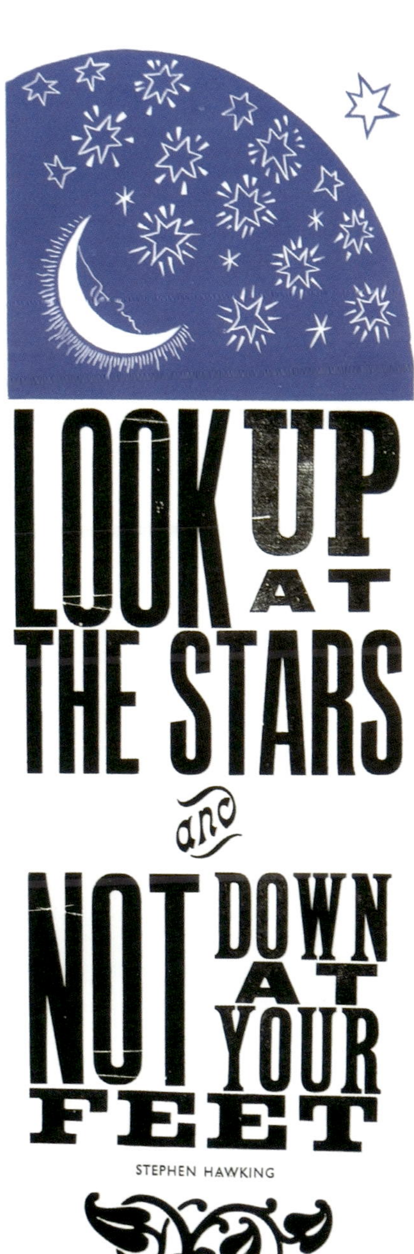

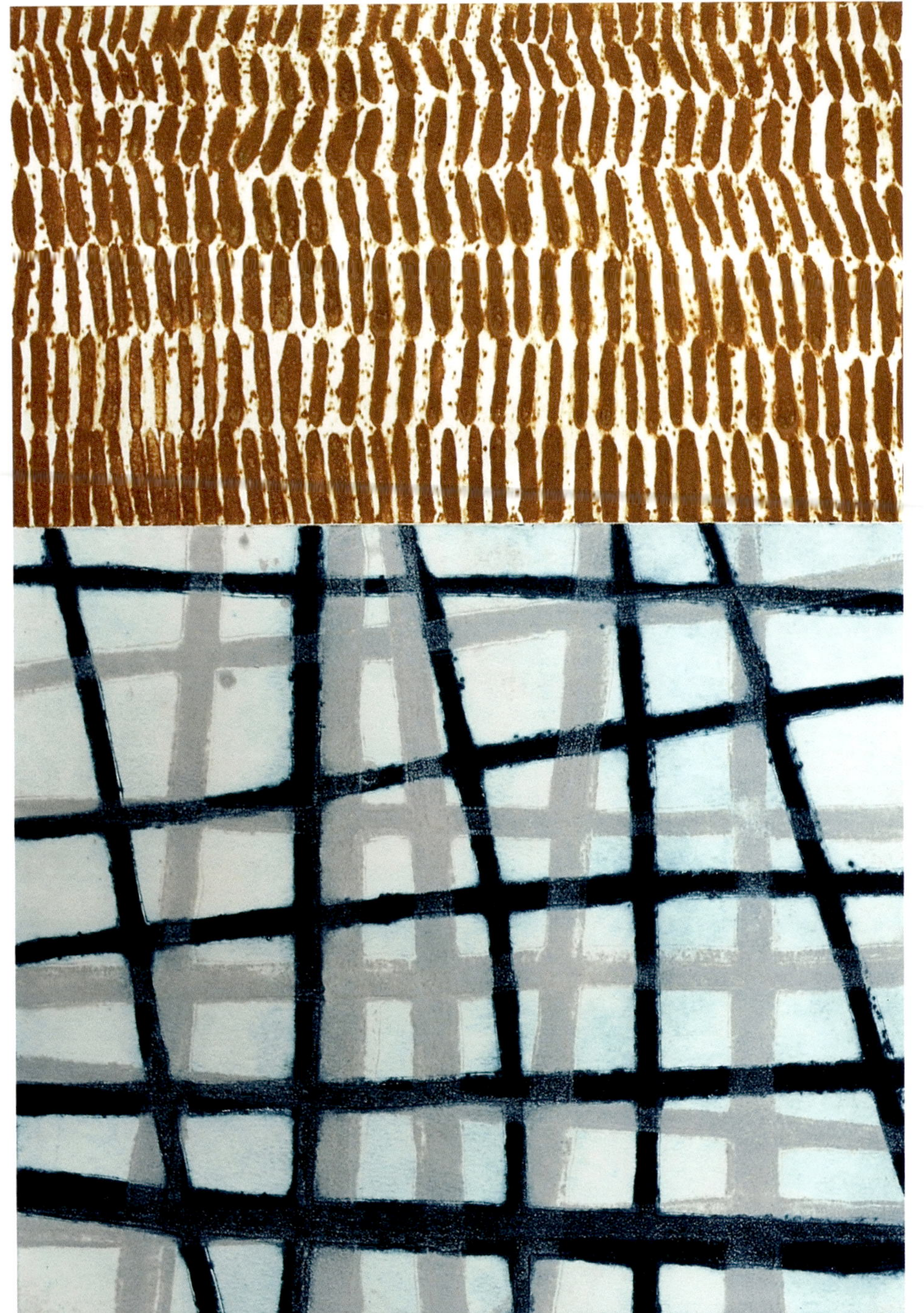

CLARE CROUCHMAN

Cambridgeshire-based printmaker and ceramic artist Clare Crouchman's recent prints are created using both intaglio and relief printing techniques, often layering several plates together. She combines materials that have texture and a richness of surface such as carborundum and collagraph with subtle lines and shapes created with linocut and drypoint etching.

"My fascination for the landscape has deepened over the years into an appreciation of the details," she says. "These fragments suggest that there is an orderly process in the chaos of the natural world.

"I work with abstracted forms, particularly rhythmical and repetitive patterns, which offer reference to this ordered nature. Finding my own order in the chaos of the world is explored through the concepts of systems and mathematical patterns while maintaining a visual language of reduced and economical form."

Clare, who has an MA in Printmaking from Anglia Ruskin University, Cambridge, was awarded the Cambridge Contemporary Art Award for 'Best Print in Show' at the Cambridge Original Printmakers Biennale in 2016. She exhibits regularly in the UK and abroad, and her ceramic wall panels and prints are held in many private and corporate collections worldwide including in the USA and Japan.

www.clarecrouchman.com

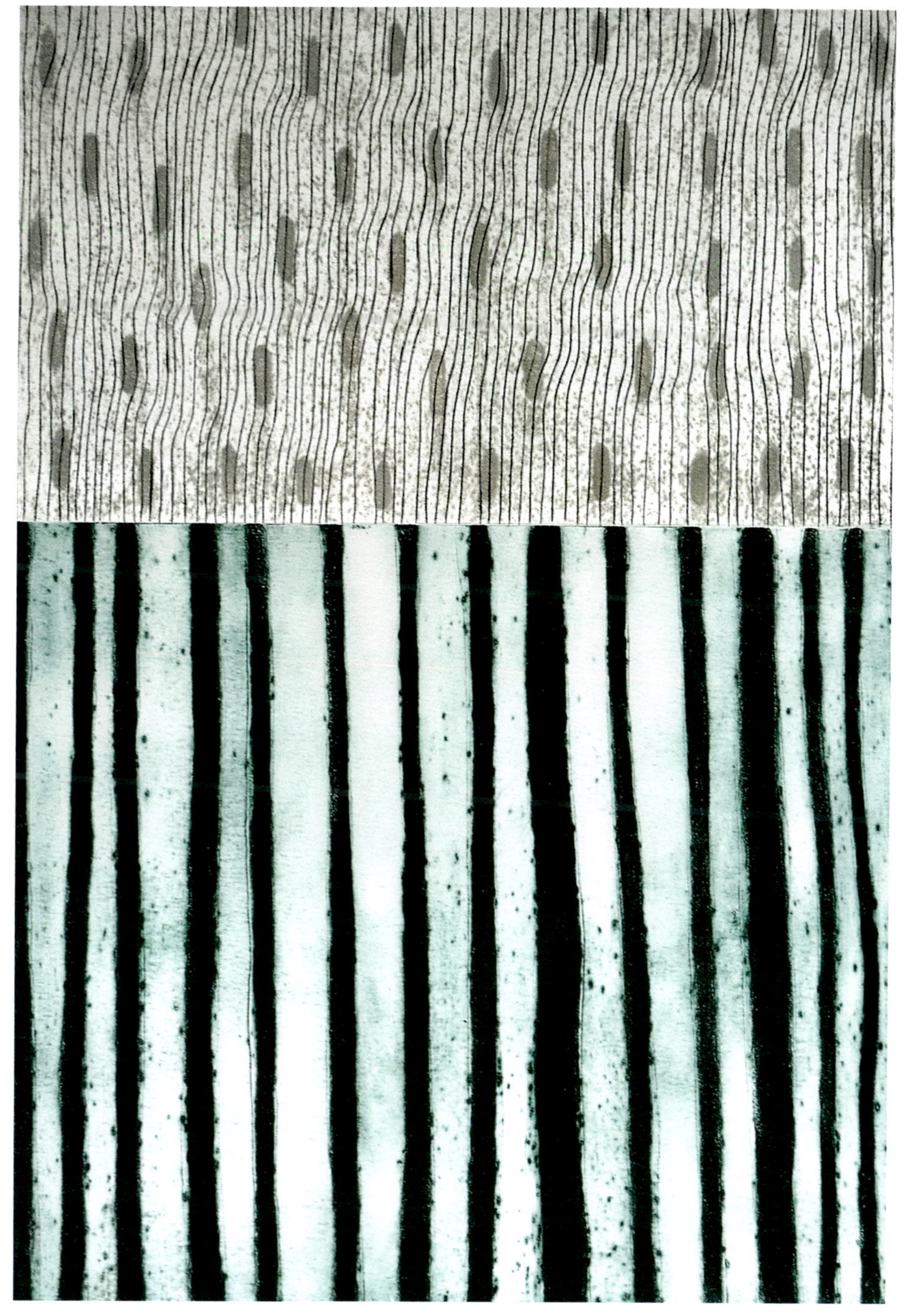

Facing page: 'Quintessence II' (carborundum collagraph), 59cm x 41cm, edition of 15; Right: 'Field' (carborundum collagraph with drypoint etching), 59cm x 41cm, edition of 15

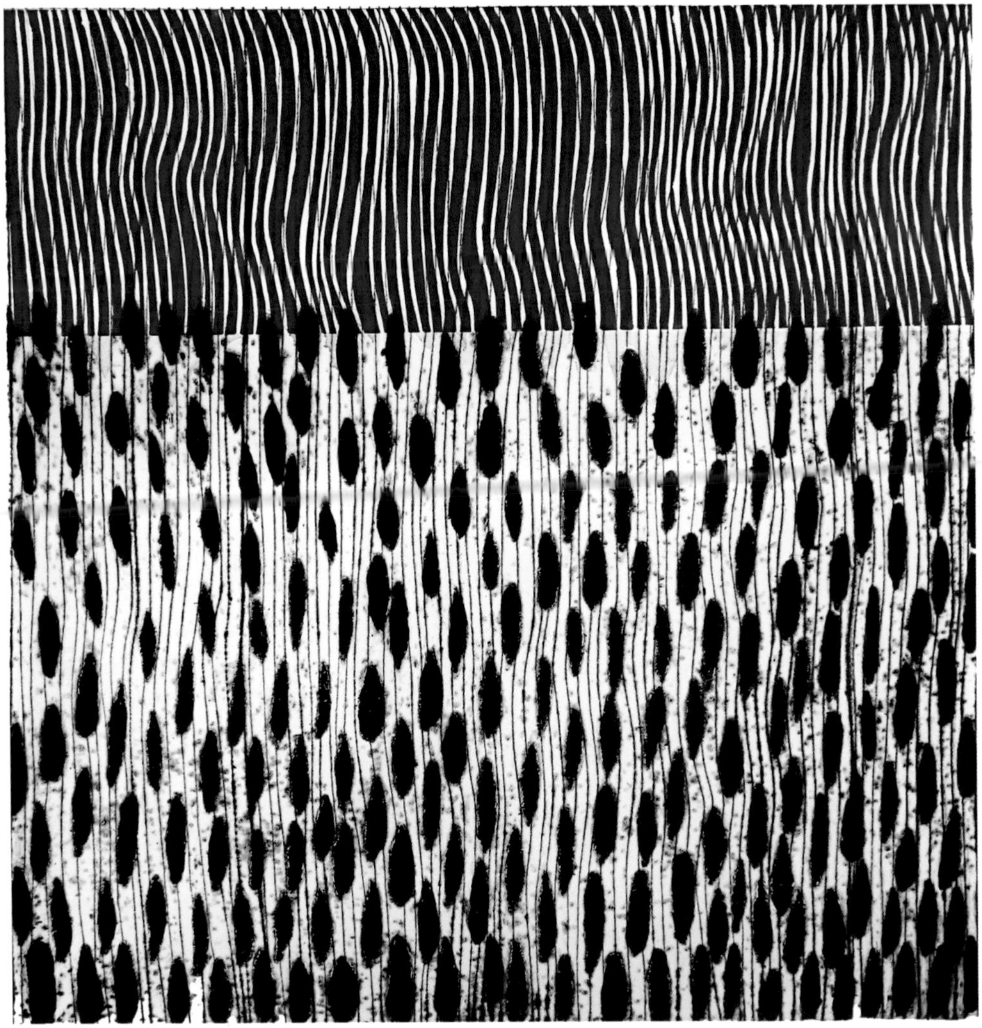

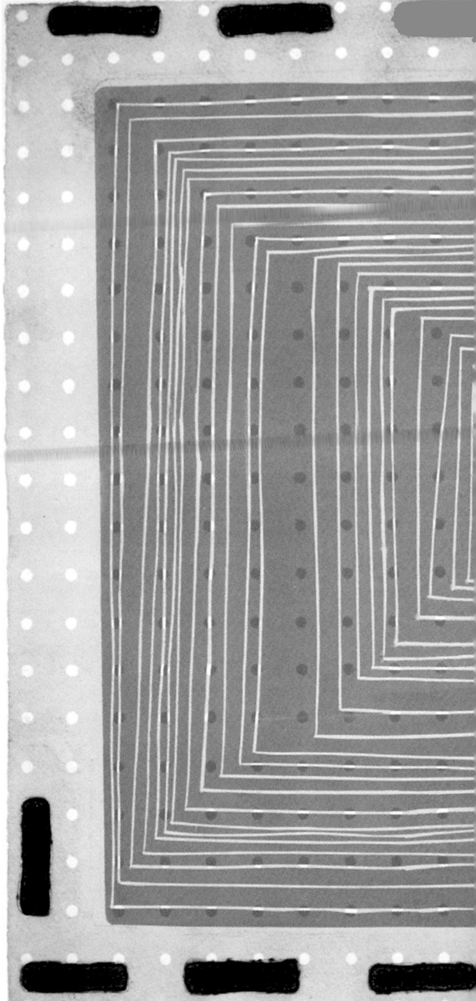

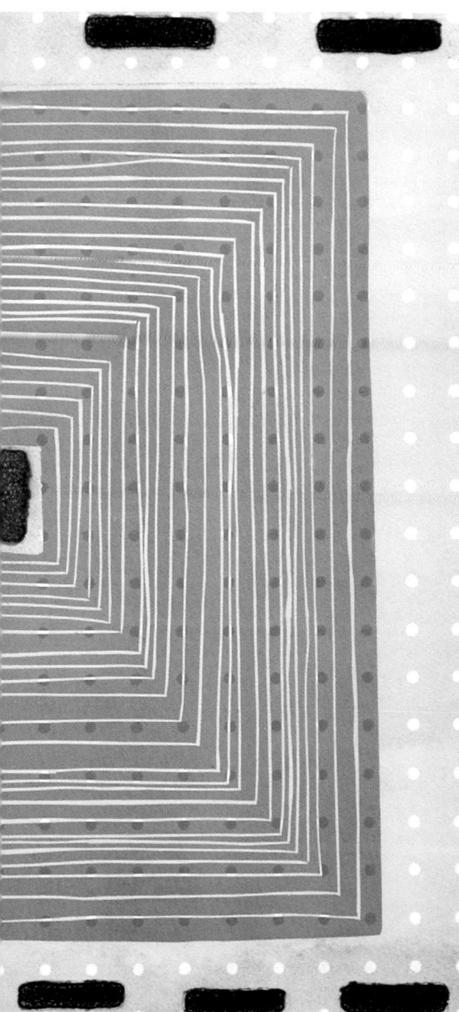

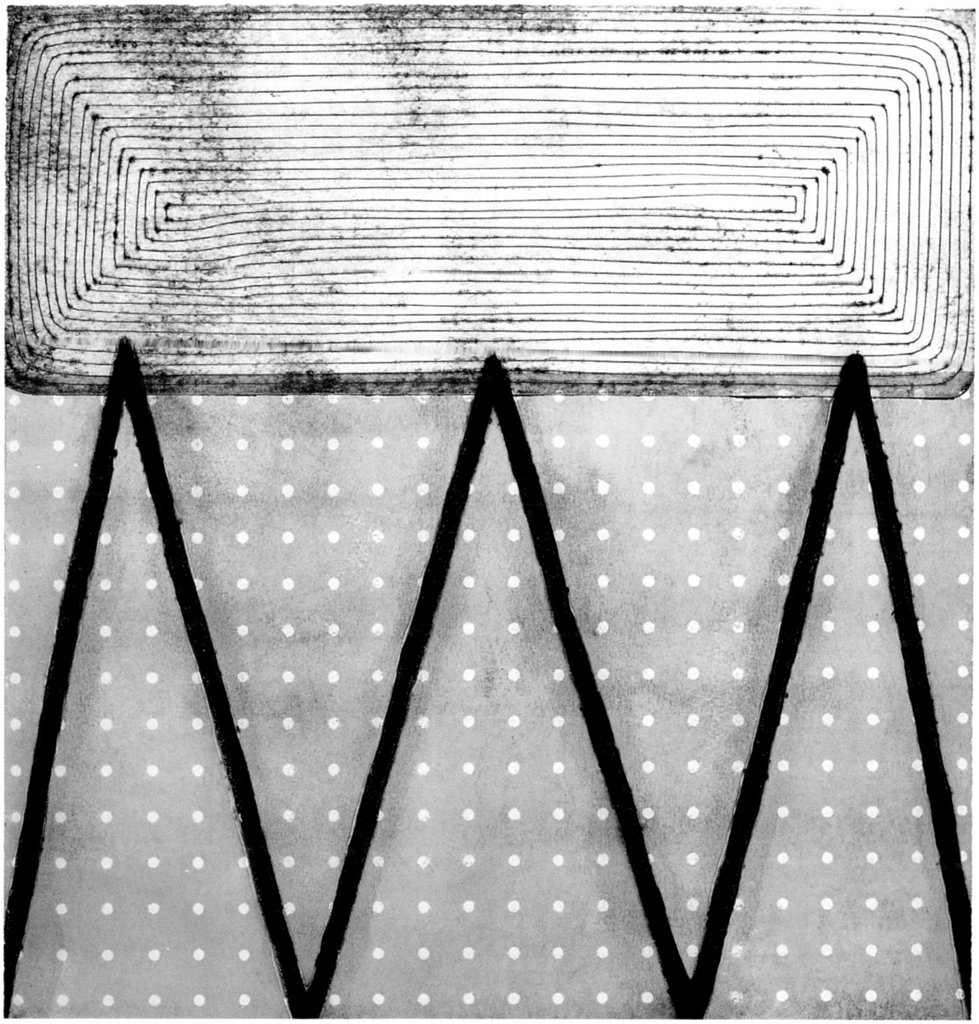

From left: 'Serenity' (carborundum collagraph with linocut); 'Focus' (carborundum collagraph with linocut); 'Troika' (carborundum collagraph with drypoint etching), all 43cm x 43cm, editions of 15 – Clare Crouchman

FELICITY DE VRIES

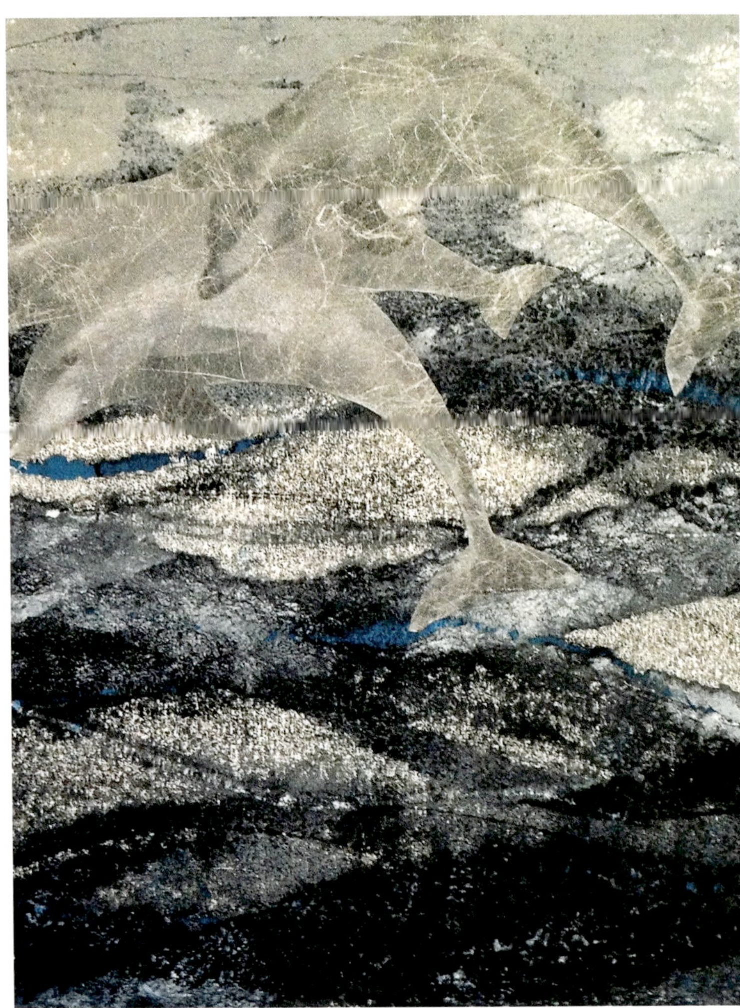

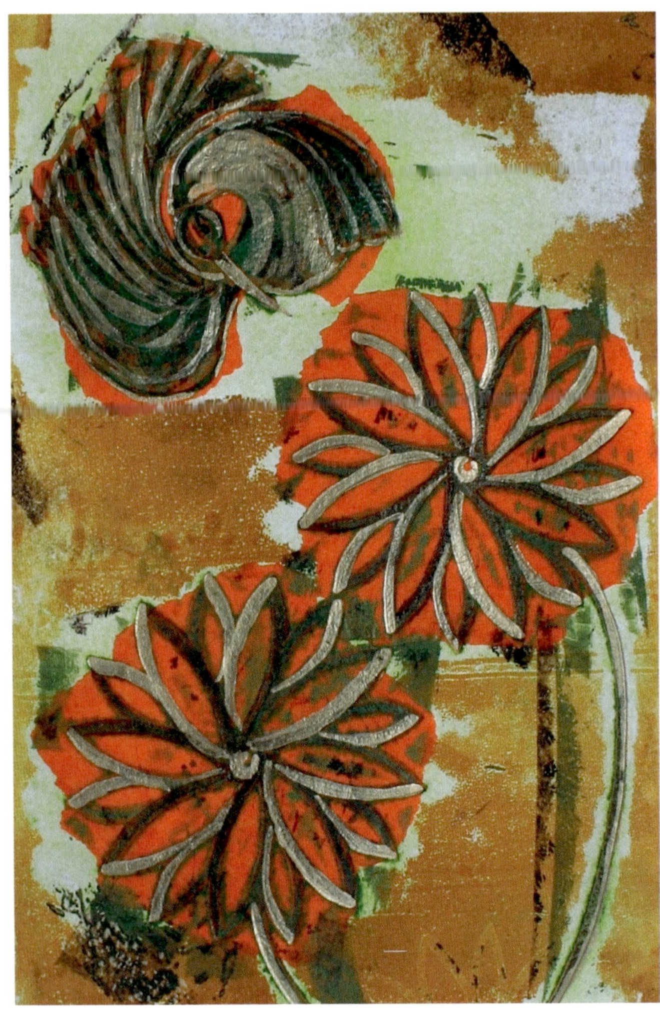

Cambridgeshire-based Felicity de Vries came to printmaking while working as a photographer for Curwen Print Studios, studying under Stanley Jones MBE and Chloe Cheese.

She travels widely – most recently to the Galapagos Islands, Myanmar and India – and brings back the vibrancy, colour and experiences of those trips to explore the natural world, wildlife, people and landscape in her work. She uses photography and sketchbooks to record the shapes and colours that will find their way into her print works.

Felicity works with reduction and multi-block linocut, or linocut in combination with other printmaking techniques such as collagraph and monoprinting with found objects, to produce multi-layered prints that often have monotype backgrounds – making each piece either unique or one of a variable small edition.

www.felicitydevries.com

Above left: 'Seascape with Dolphins' (linocut), 30cm x 30cm, variable edition of 4; Above right: 'Hummingbird' (collagraph), 24cm x 15.5cm, unique; Right: 'Sailing Deep Oceans' (linocut), 30cm x 30cm, edition of 2

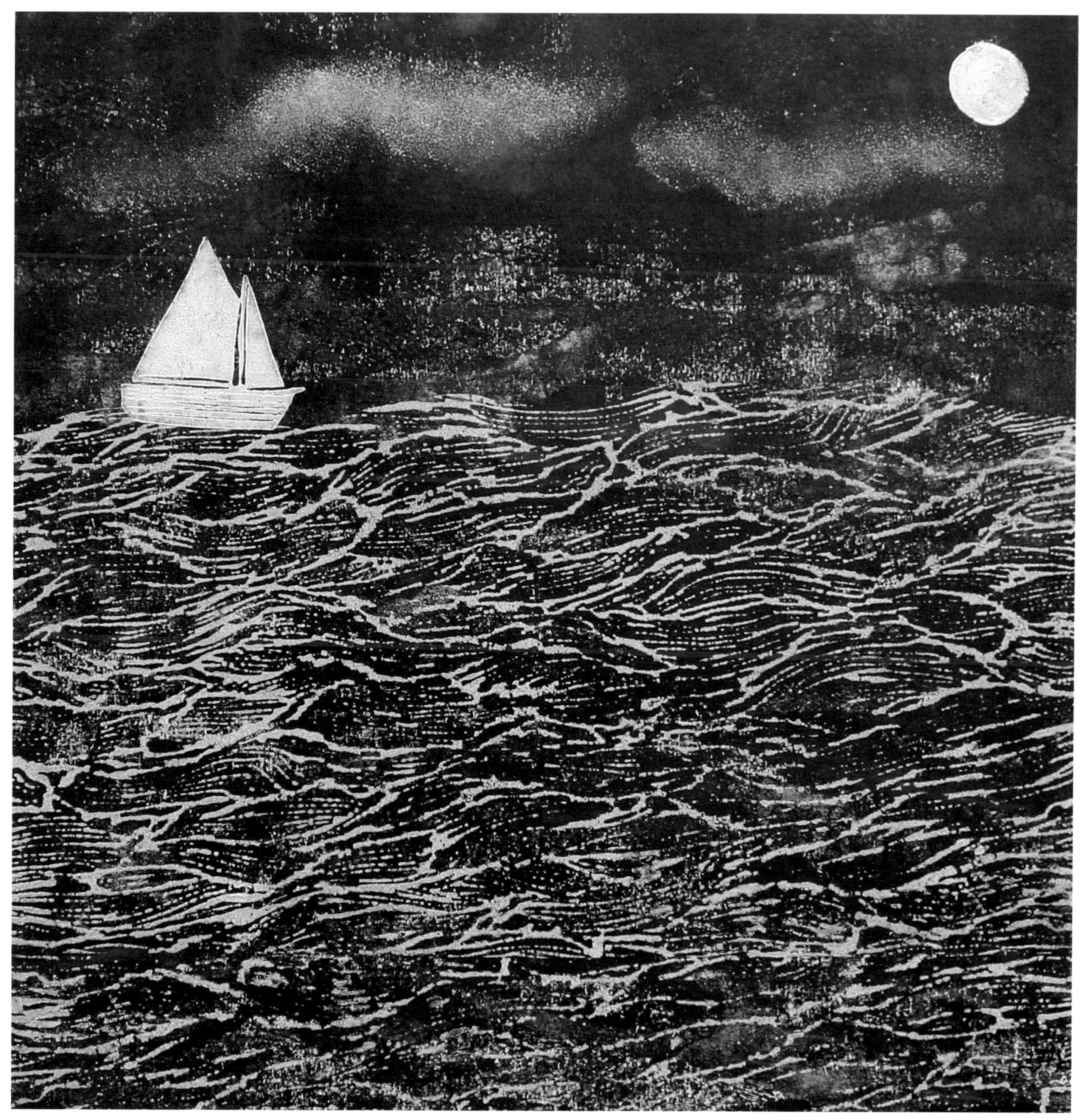

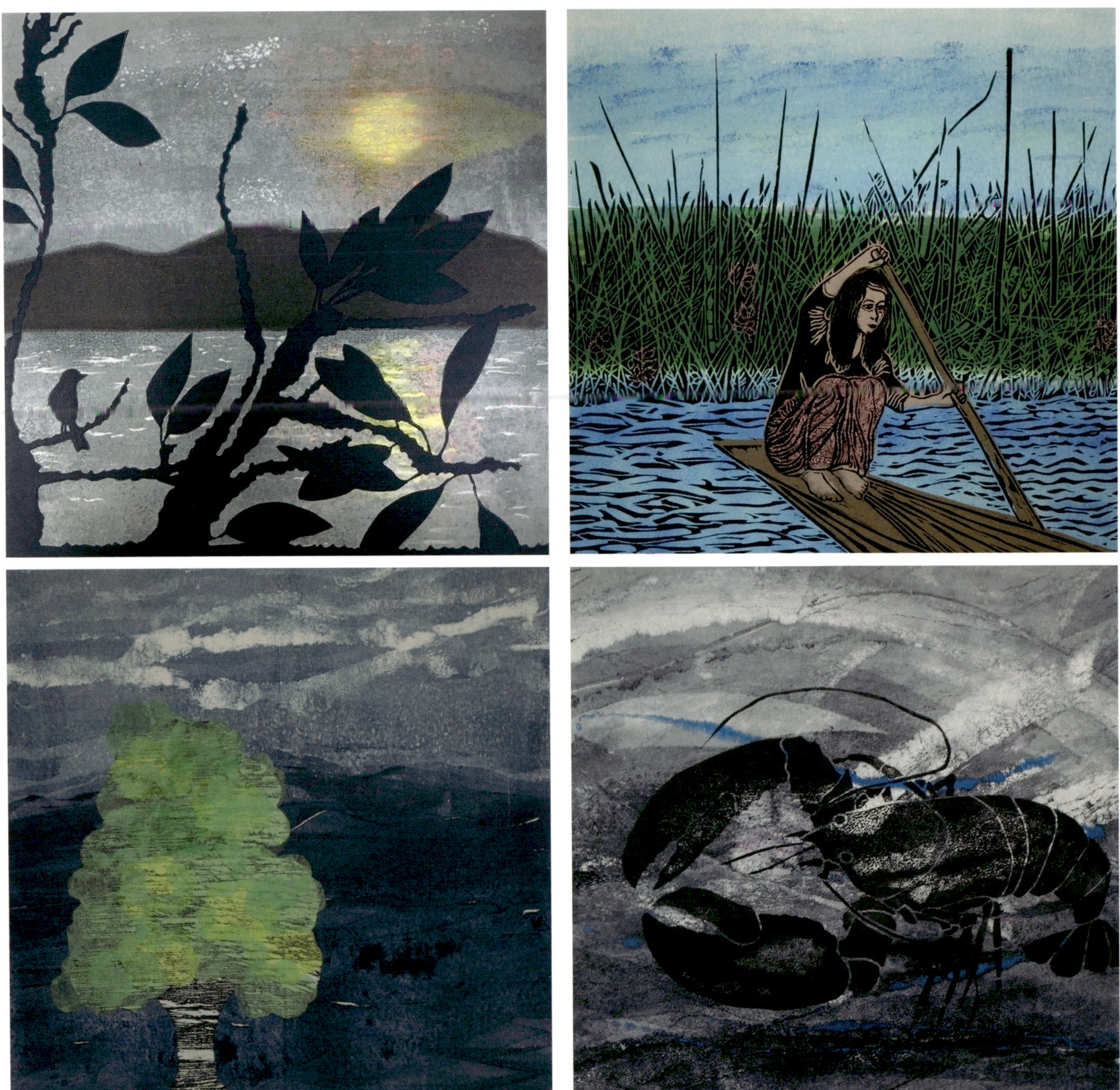

Clockwise from top left: 'The Road to Mandalay' (linocut), 30cm x 30cm, variable edition of 2; 'Inle Lake' (linocut), 30cm x 30cm, edition of 6; 'Lobster' (linocut/monotype), 30cm x 30cm, unique; 'Chestnut Tree' (linocut/woodcut), 30cm x 30cm, unique – all Felicity de Vries

JACKIE DUCKWORTH

At the age of 18, Jackie Duckworth exchanged her artistic ambitions for a career in science, but eventually her first loves returned in force. A chance remark followed by some hard work led to studying Illustration at Cambridge School of Art and becoming a full-time artist.

At art college she fell in love with printmaking. "I have always loved to work with my hands – sewing, knitting, even building a chicken coop! Working in linocut, the physical skill and patience needed to carve out the shapes employs that instinct to make art."

She finds reduction linocuts particularly rewarding. "There is a thrill in both the compositional puzzle and the unforgiving technique." The history of printmaking as illustration also appeals. "Even in a single image, I like to tell a story," she says. Her works encompass myth, legend, history and narratives of all kinds, often expressed through bold images of birds and animals.

In common with all artists, Jackie loves to experiment, using hand colouring, monoprint and collagraph alongside her linocut practice. She also makes illustrations for magazines and other projects, and for artists' books.
www.jackieduckworthart.co.uk

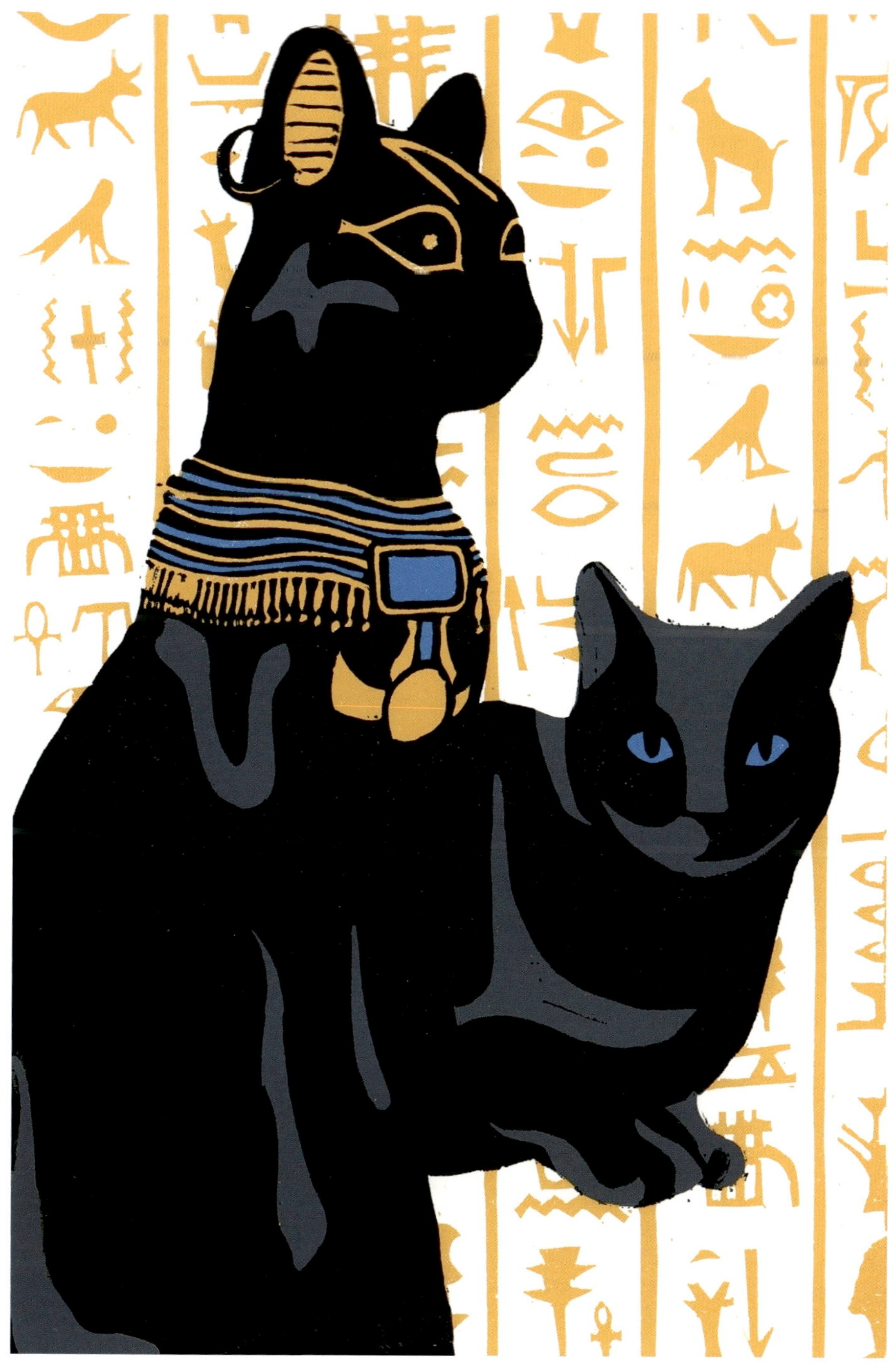

Above: 'Bastet' (reduction linocut), 30cm x 20cm, edition of 13

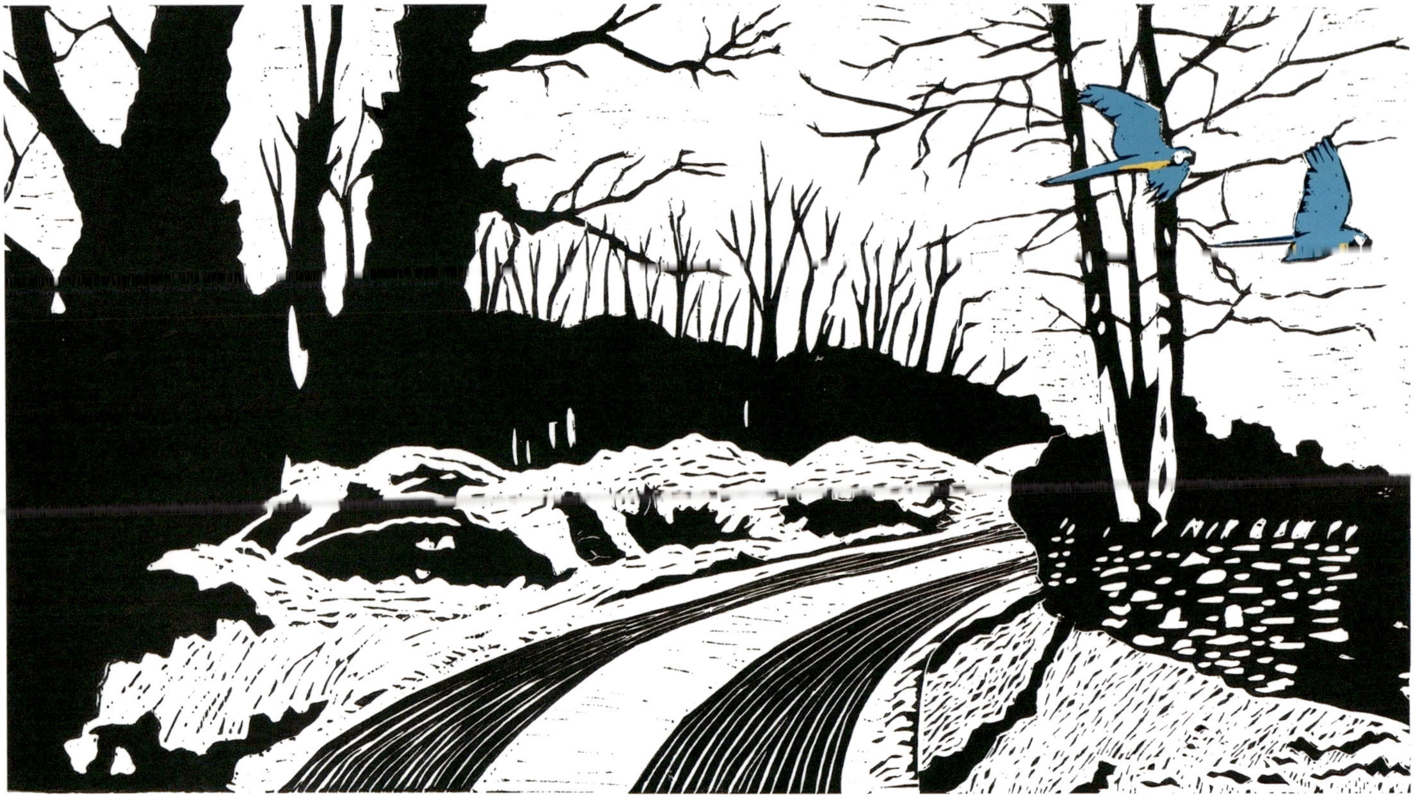

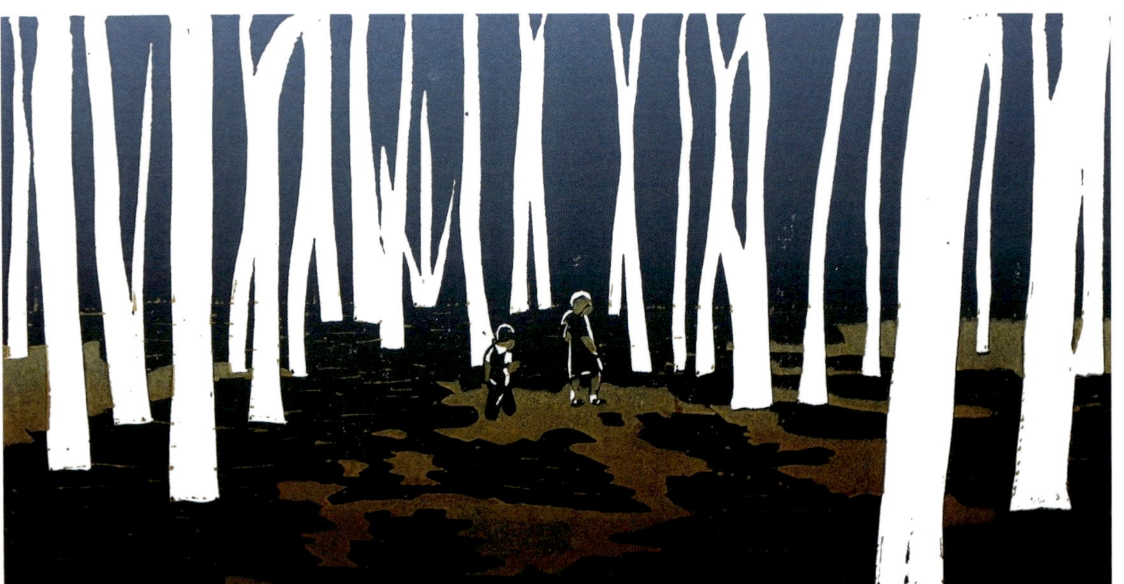

This page, from top: 'As I Drove Home from Kendal' (hand-coloured linocut), 25cm x 42cm, edition of 20; 'Into the Woods' (reduction linocut), 15cm x 30cm, edition of 13; Facing page: 'Castle Corbin' (linocut), 20cm x 20cm, edition of 20 – all Jackie Duckworth

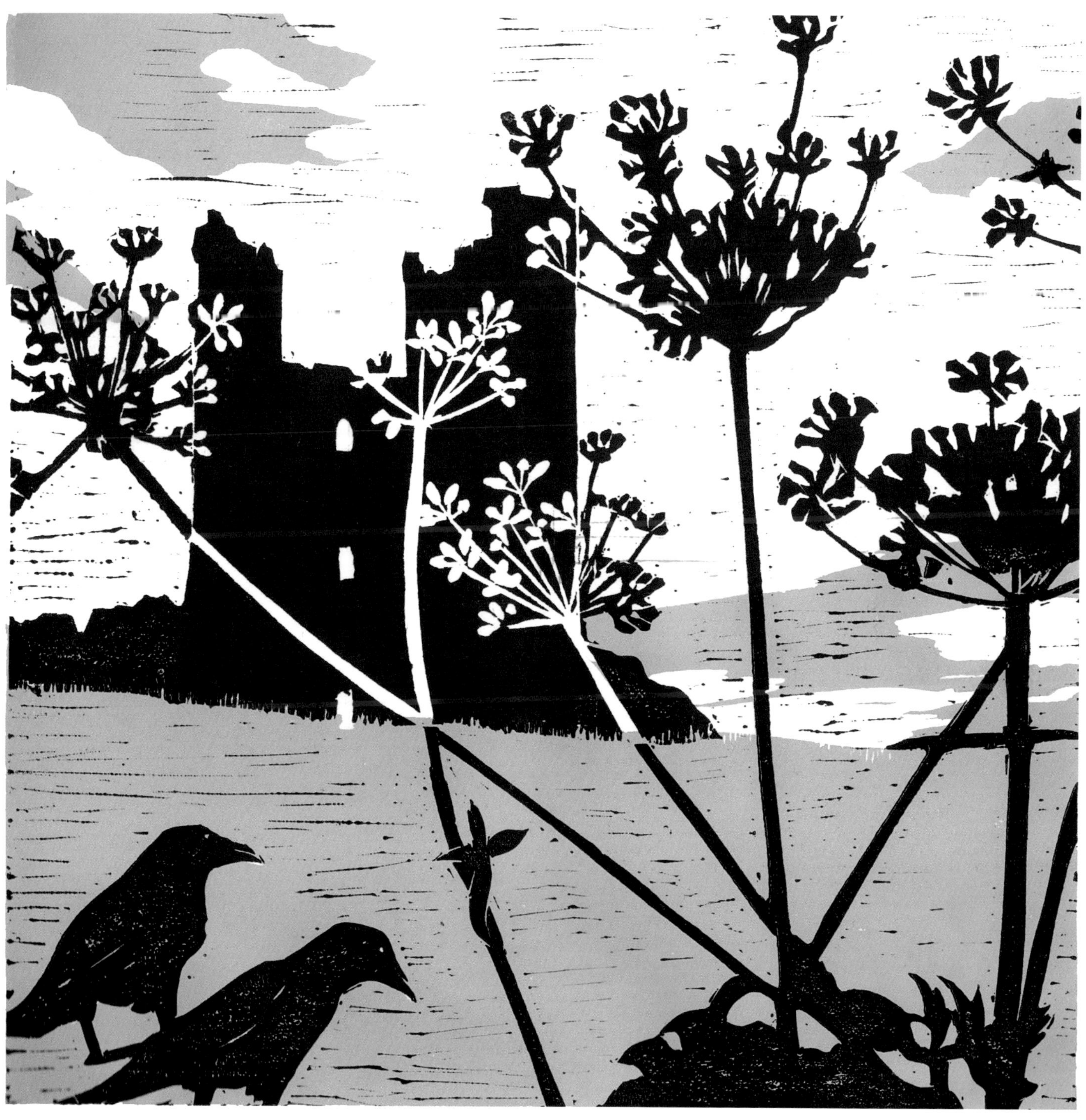

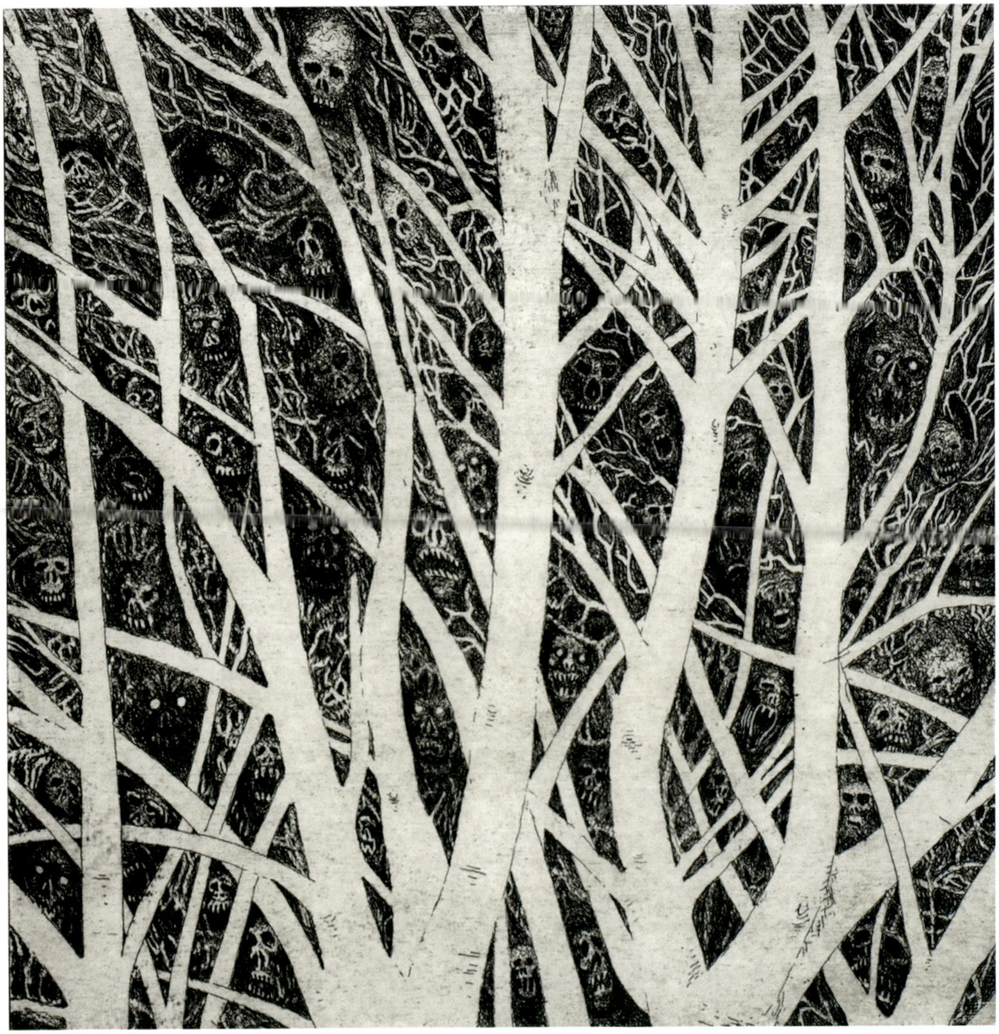

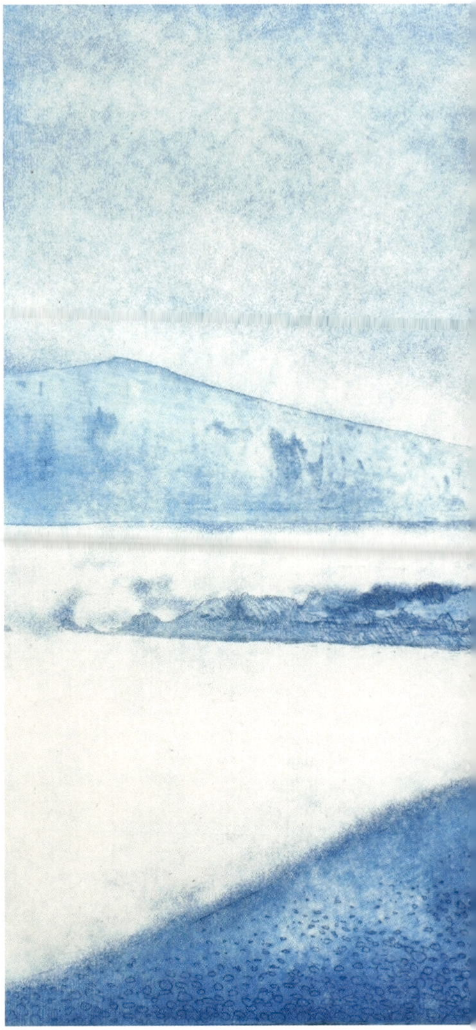

DAVID GRAHAM

David Graham came to printmaking through drawing. He uses pencil and graphite to make sketch studies which are then translated into images through the etching process of mark-making on to zinc plates. The intensity of marks form intimate landscapes: sometimes small scenes; sometimes large, bold physical elements. He makes scenes that are taken out of context, semi-abstracted or augmented by his imagination.

"I like to play with the perception of natural forms. I find wonder in the spaces that surround us, be they garden scenes or small natural urban oasis to large geographical forms. I intend through my work to instil a sense of intimacy with wilderness."

David has found that the process of

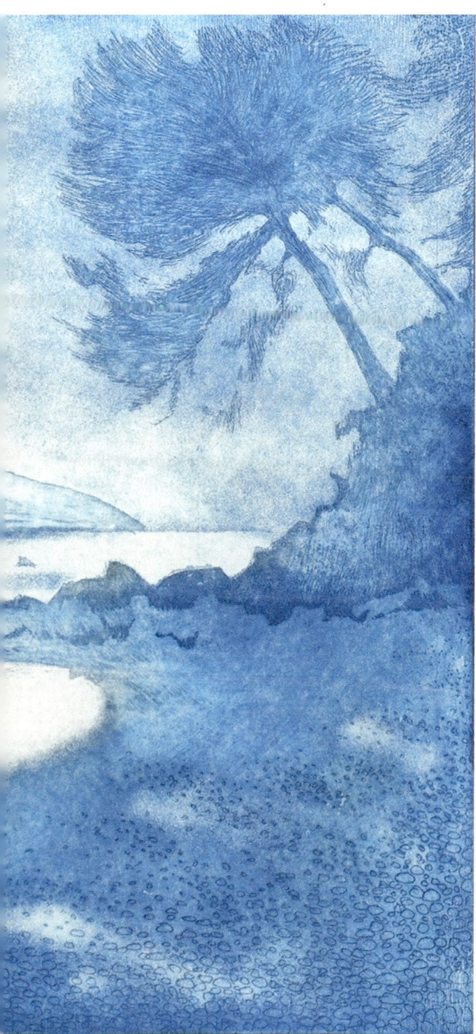

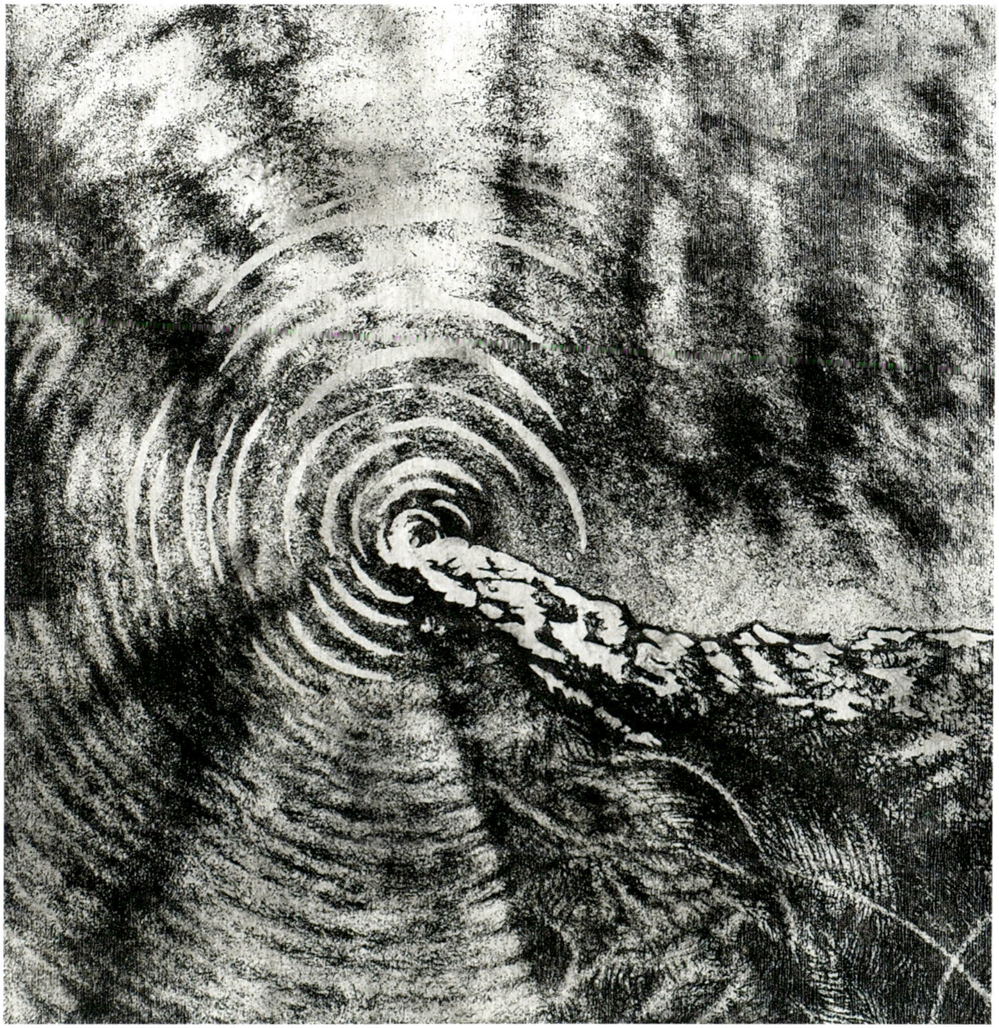

etching and intaglio printmaking achieves a successful unification between idea, mark-making and – finally – print to produce a homogeneous picture. He uses non-toxic printmaking techniques such as copper sulphate etching of zinc plates and water-soluble printing inks that are less damaging to the environment.
www.cargocollective.com/davidg

From left: 'Late One Night' (etching), 20cm x 20cm, edition of 5; 'The Other Place' (etching and aquatint), 20cm x 20cm, edition of 5; 'Water's Edge 2' (etching), 20cm x 20cm, edition of 5

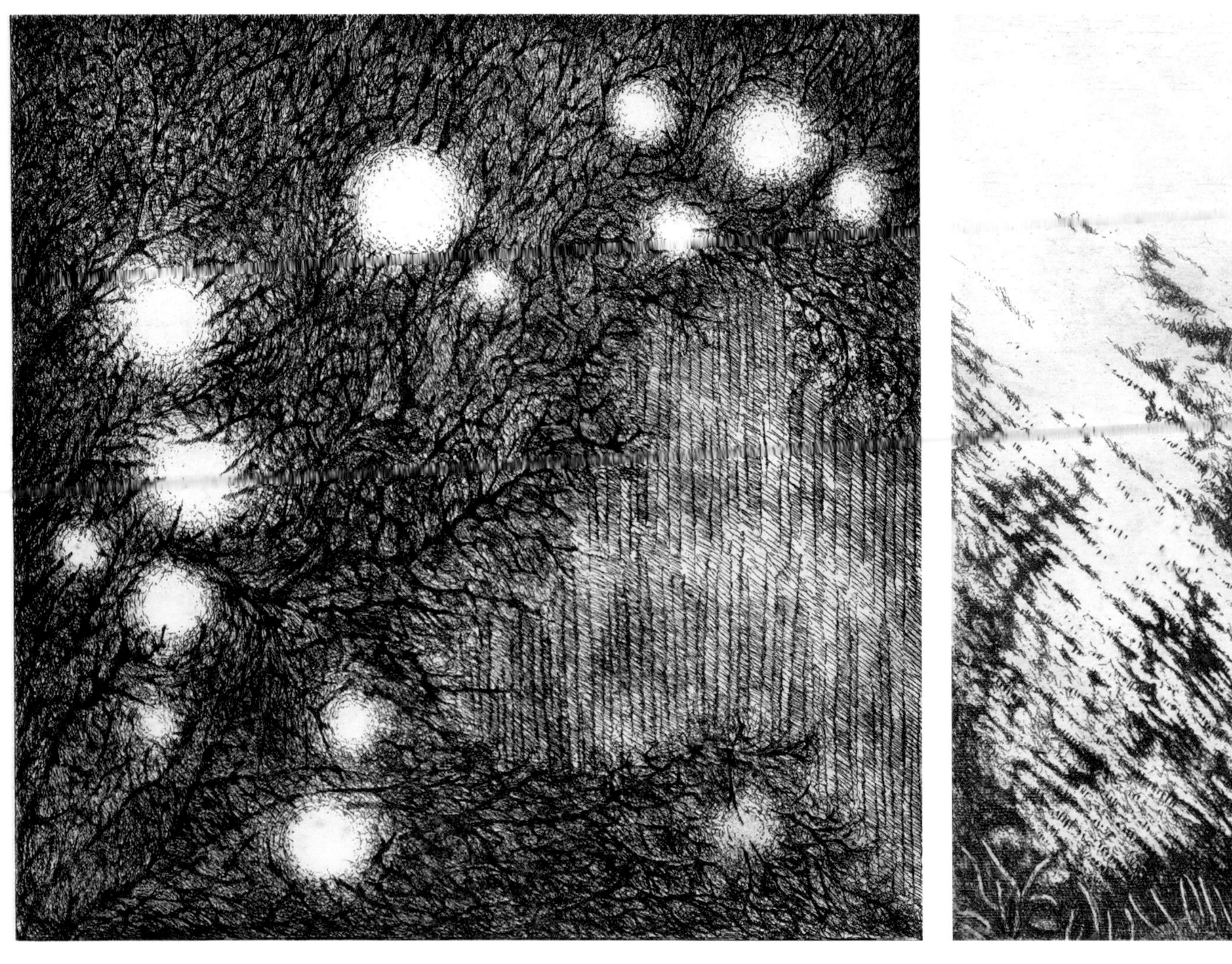

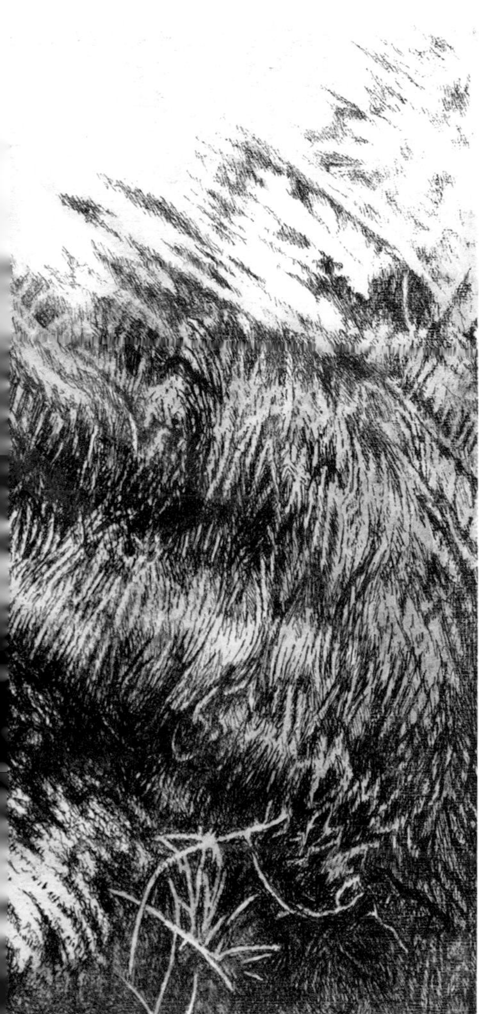

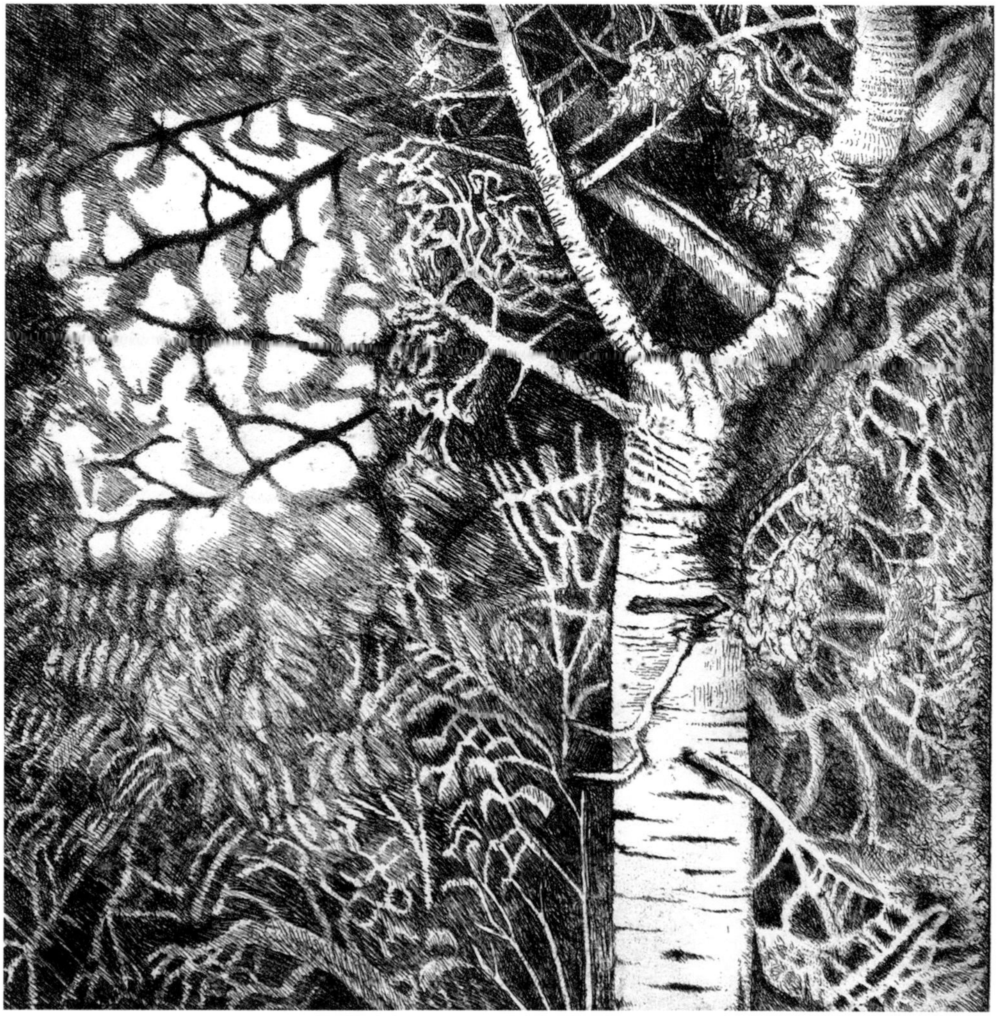

From left: 'Light Amongst the Trees 6', 20cm x 20cm, edition of 5; 'Water's Edge 1' (etching), 20cm x 20cm, edition of 5; 'Light Amongst the Trees 1', 20cm x 20cm, edition of 5 – all David Graham

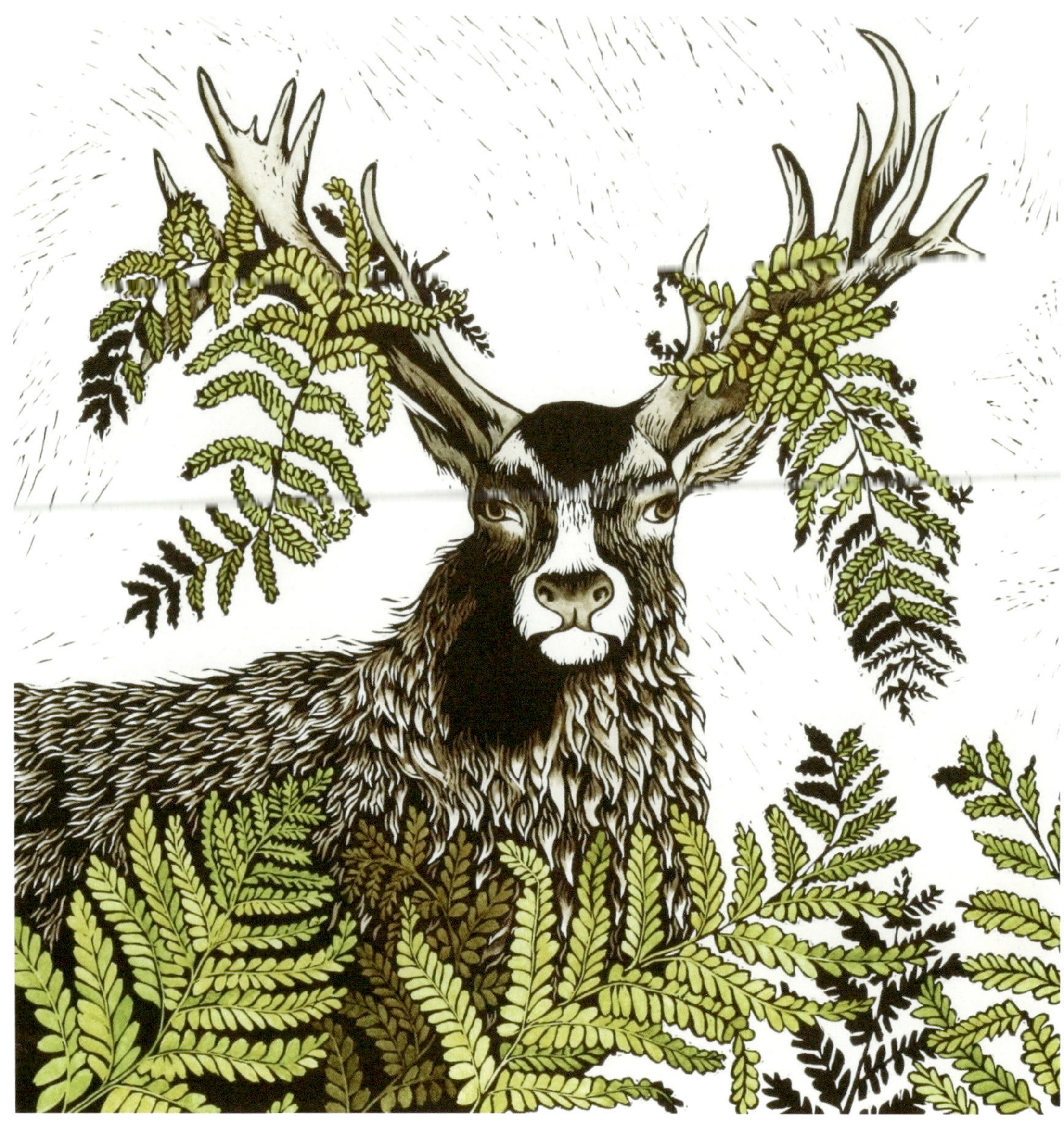

Left: 'Stag Do' (linocut handpainted with watercolour), 30cm x 30cm, edition of 25

KATHARINE GREEN

Katharine Green was fascinated by the natural world from a young age. "Living on the outskirts of Letchworth Garden City, much of the flora and fauna found in my garden and along The Greenway has inspired my work – from my pet cats hiding among flower borders to a passing visit from the neighbourhood fox. Even the famous black squirrels associated with the town can often be seen chasing each other through the trees.

"The surrounding countryside also holds constant new ideas for my work. I am particularly lucky to live near several

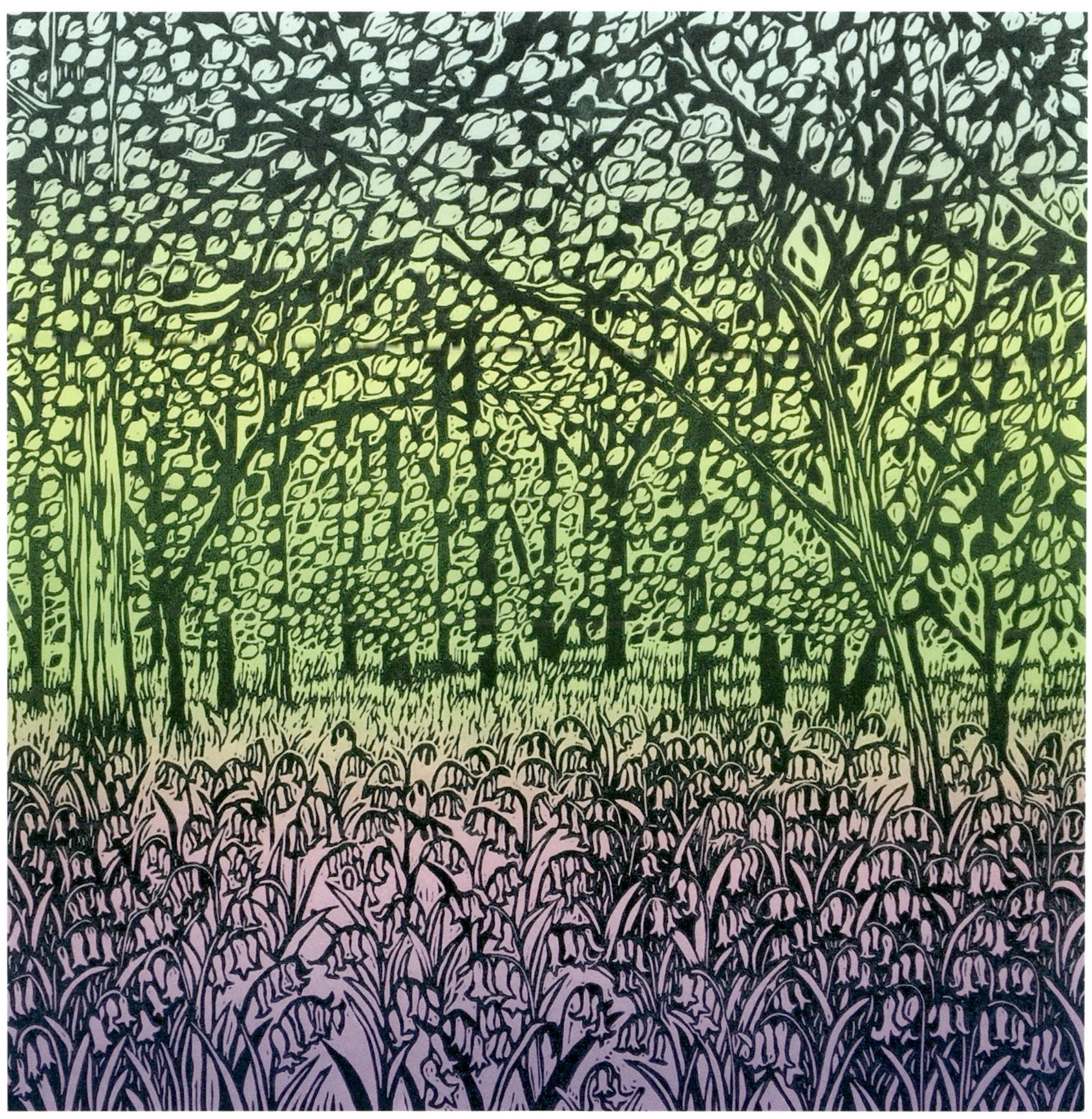

Right: 'The Bluebell Wood' (two-plate coloured linocut), 30cm x 30cm, edition of 10

bluebell woods, and when the land becomes a magical carpet of deep blue I can't resist grabbing my camera and sketchbook and heading to draw this lovely spring show. I have often seen hares looking out among the highly scented flowers."

Katharine's earliest memories of drawing and painting are of spending time in the garden drawing her Dad's prized collection of fuchsias. "I loved their ballerina-shaped flowers."

She went on to study Illustration at the University of Portsmouth, and graduated with a BA Honours degree

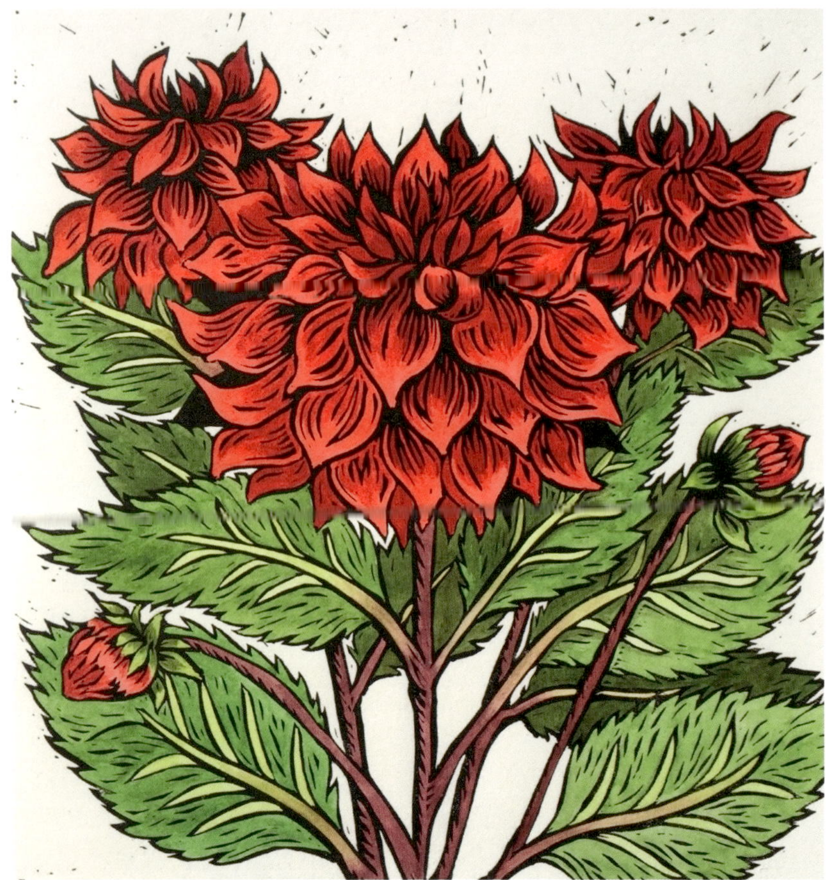

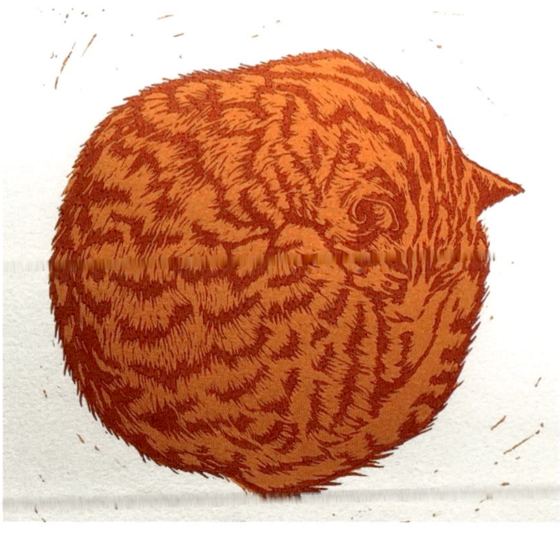

From left, clockwise: 'Dahlia' (linocut handpainted with watercolour), 20cm x 20cm, edition of 20; 'Catnap' (two-plate coloured linocut), 15cm x 15cm, edition of 30; 'Fuchsia' (linocut handpainted with watercolour), 15cm x 20cm, edition of 20

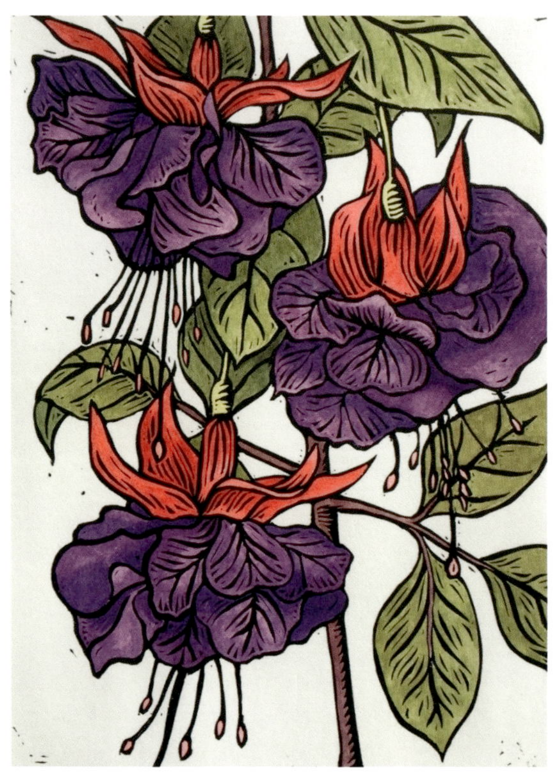

in 1997. Her love of printmaking was reignited in 2013 when she had one of her watercolours, 'Female Sparrow Hawk', exhibited at the Royal Academy's Summer Exhibition. "I was so taken with all the wonderful prints on show that I immediately wanted to revisit the medium I first tried back at school – linocuts.

"Having only a limited budget, I bought some black ink and a few blocks of lino and began to create small prints of the flowers from my garden. Wanting to add colour, I began experimenting by adding watercolour tints to my prints.

"I enjoy mixing both media. I like the gentle nature that watercolour gives, a translucent light in contrast to the boldness of the printing process associated with linocuts. Although I mainly use watercolour in my work, I am increasingly using coloured inks for both the reduction method and multi-block pieces."

Katharine's work has been shown in galleries around the UK, and many of her prints have been reproduced as artist greetings cards by Suffolk publisher Green Pebble. *www.katharinegreen.com*

LIZ HALES

Artist and printmaker Liz Hales works in a number of different media, and is a member of the Cambridge Drawing Society. In 2016 she completed the Certificate Course in Printmaking at the Curwen Print Study Centre. Since then she has been exploring the potential of combining different techniques and materials to produce monoprints in an "ongoing voyage of discovery".

The starting point for all her work is her sketchbook, and she is inspired by observations, drawings and paintings made while travelling in the UK and overseas. Recently she has moved to more abstract forms, exploring the impact of line and colour on the final image.

Email: lah397@gmail.com

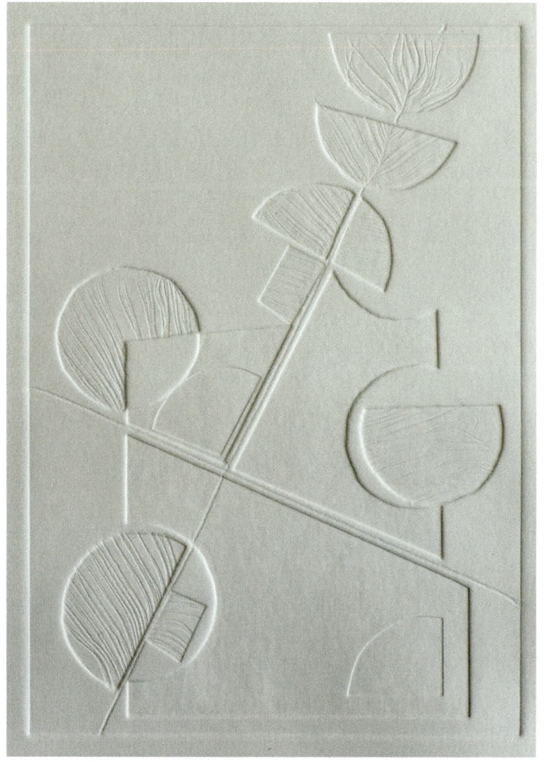

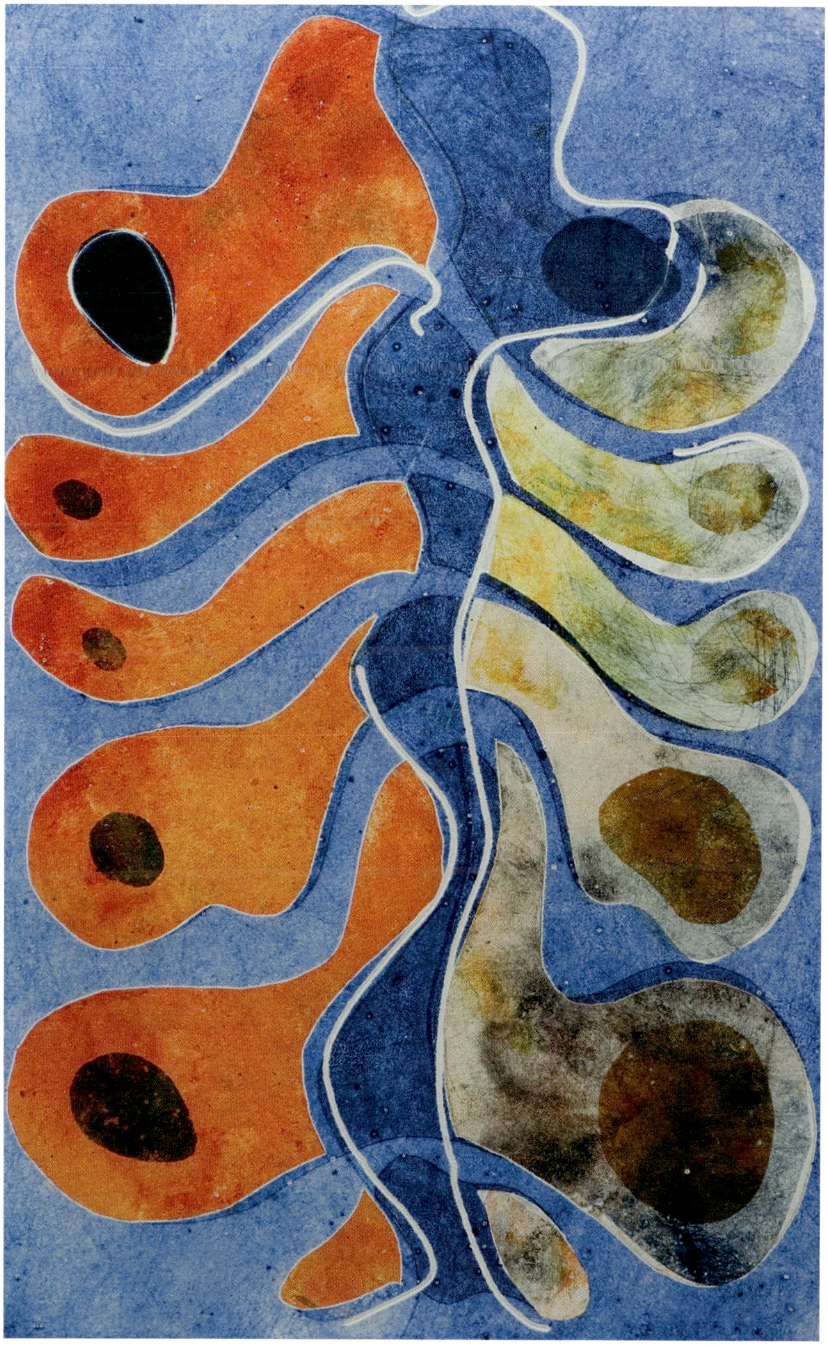

Left: 'Flying Up' (embossed print), 21cm x 29.5cm, edition of 20; Above: 'Bilateral' (monoprint from acetate plates), 25cm x 39.5cm, unique

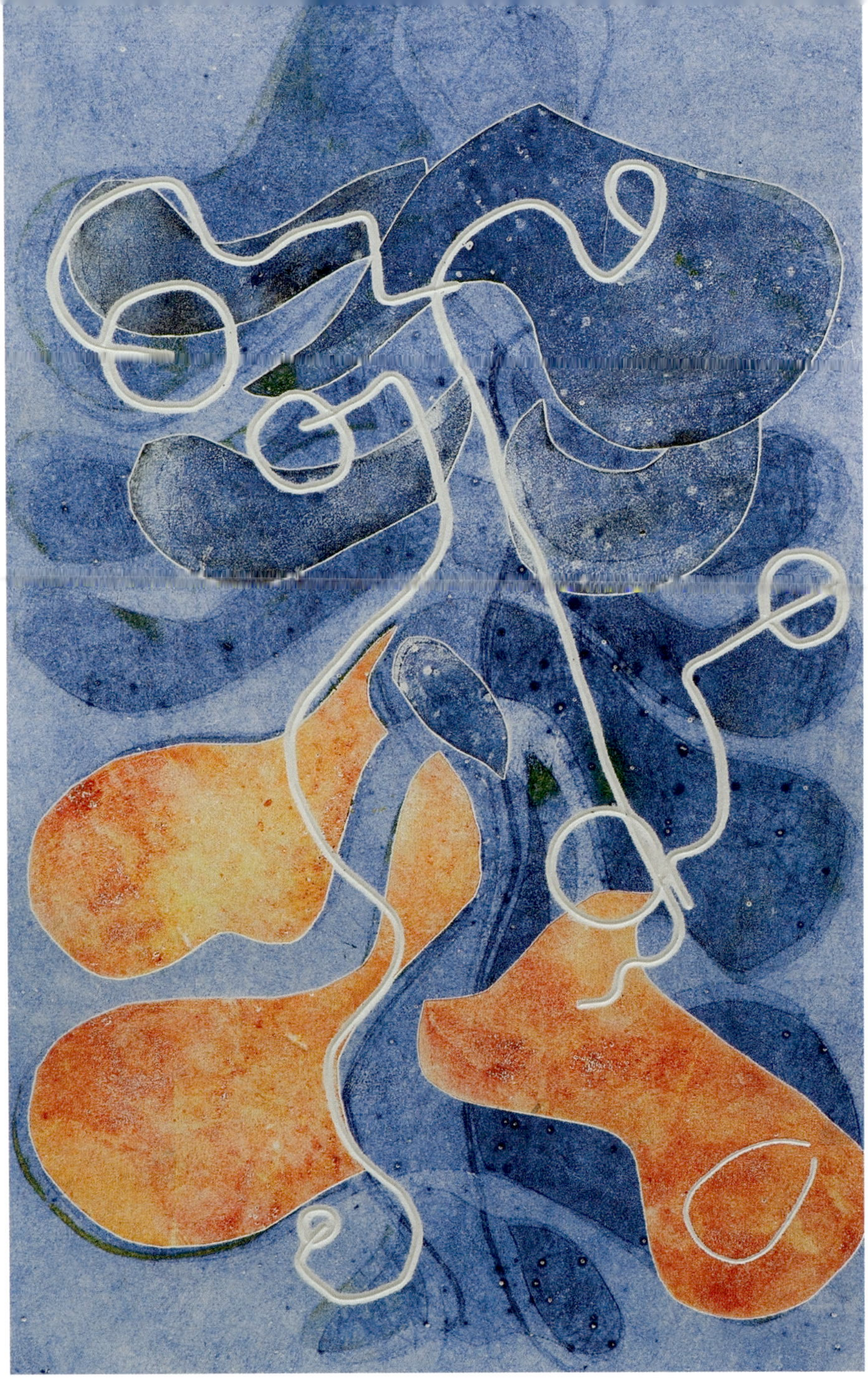

Above: 'Breaking Back' (monoprint from acetate plates), 25cm x 39.5cm, unique;
Above centre: 'Dusk Reflection' (photopolymer plate of ink drawing), 29cm x 21cm, 1 VE

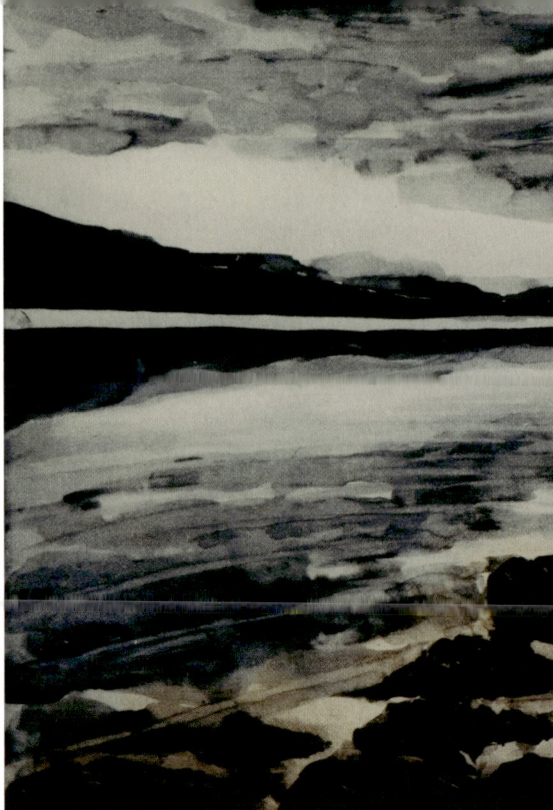

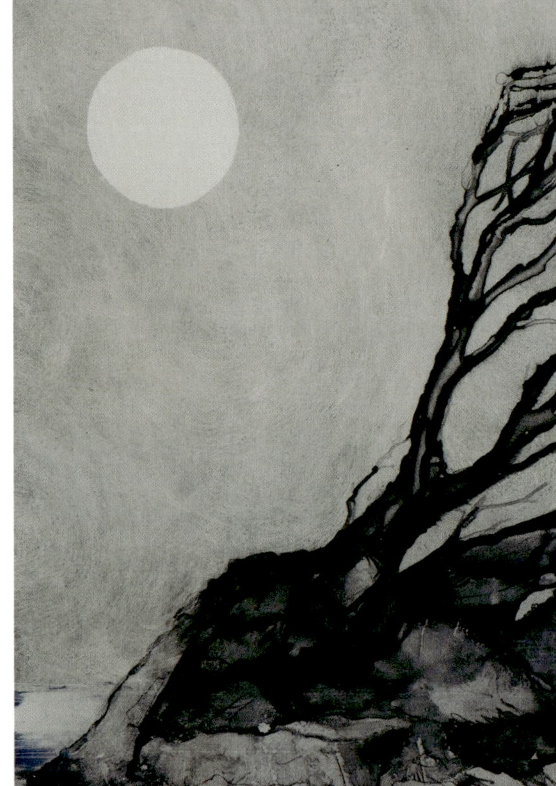

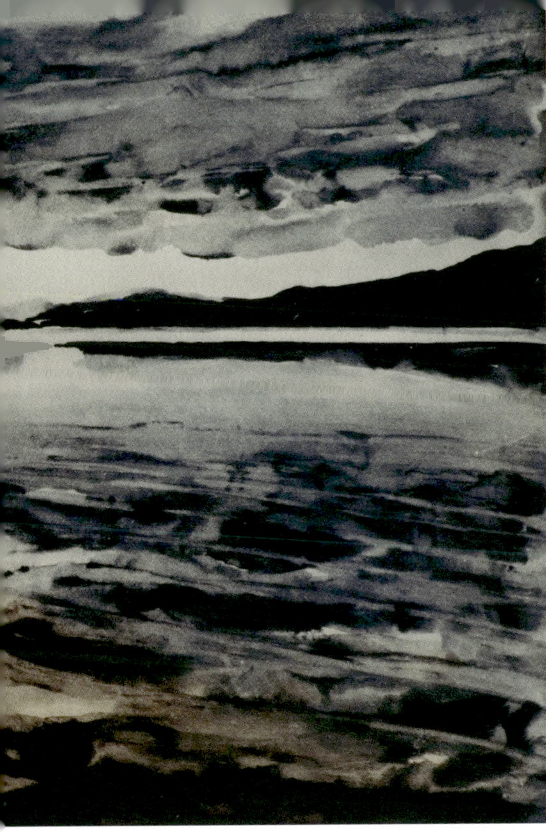

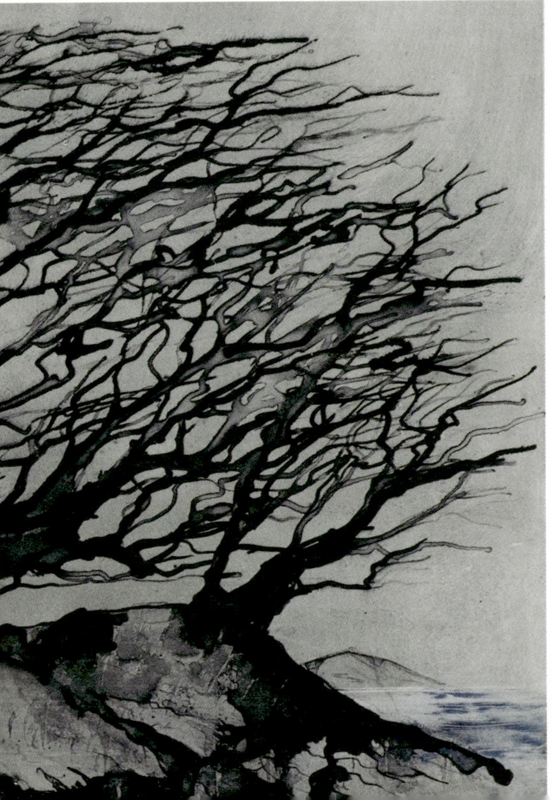

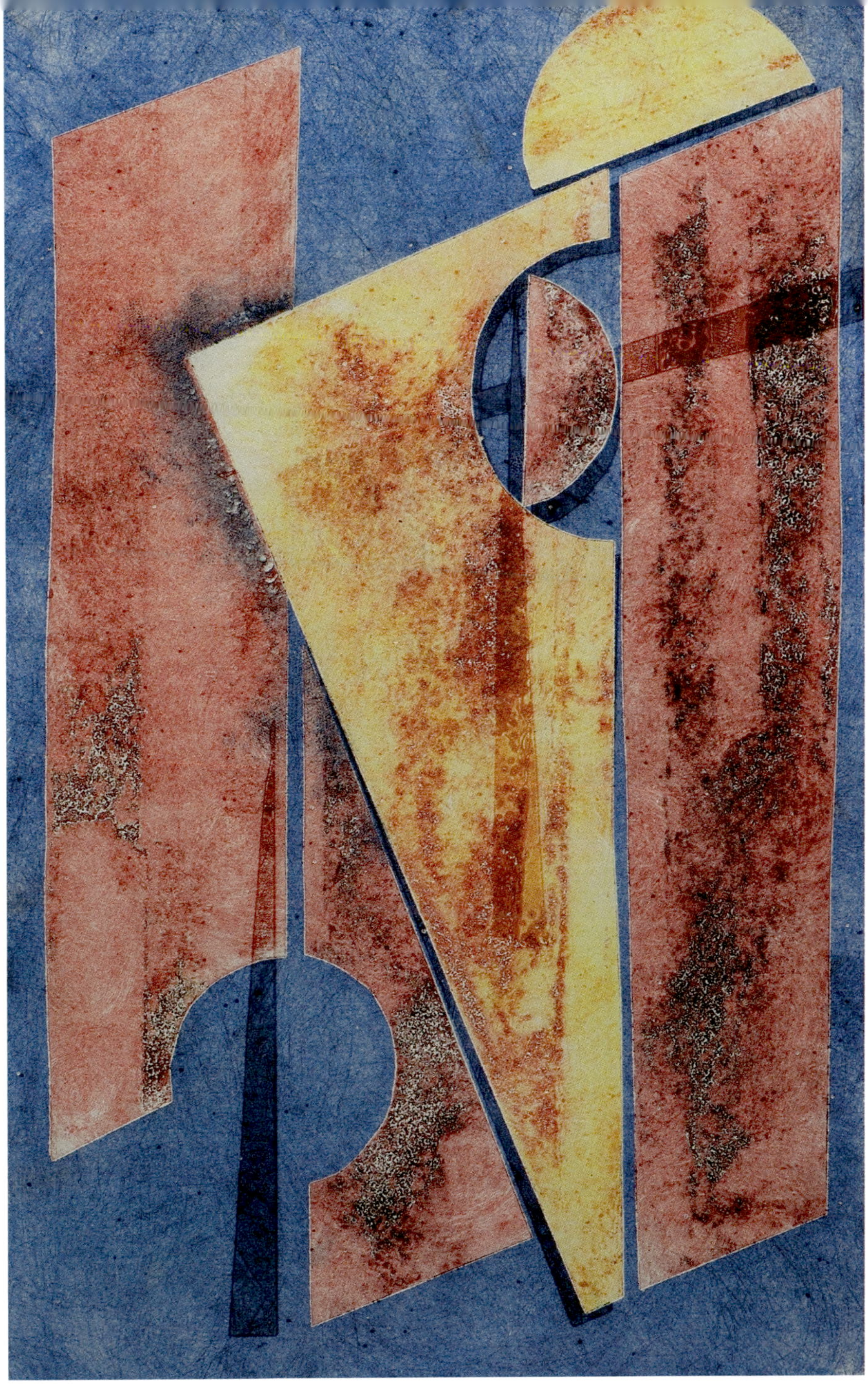

Bottom centre: 'Moon Wind' (photopolymer plate of ink drawing), 29.5cm x 21cm, 1 VE;
Above: 'Statues' (monoprint from acetate plates), 25cm x 39.5cm, unique

CELIA HART

Celia Hart works without a press, producing hand-burnished linocuts and woodcuts on Japanese papers. She enjoys using the negative and positive shapes and the marks of the chisels to create depth and variety in the composition.

After gaining a degree in Visual Communication at Brighton, she worked for publishers as a designer and illustrator. A trip to Japan in 2003 rekindled her enthusiasm for printmaking and the illustrative print. From April 2015 to December 2017 she illustrated Frank Ronan's column for *Gardens Illustrated* magazine, inspired by his words but including visual asides of her own.

"I collect inspiration for my prints of landscapes and wildlife while walking the footpaths and ancient tracks near my home in the south-west corner of Suffolk and the Fens, which I have known since childhood," she says.

Celia works with designers and publishers on varied projects from book jackets to wine labels, combining her block prints with digital artwork.
www.celiahart.co.uk

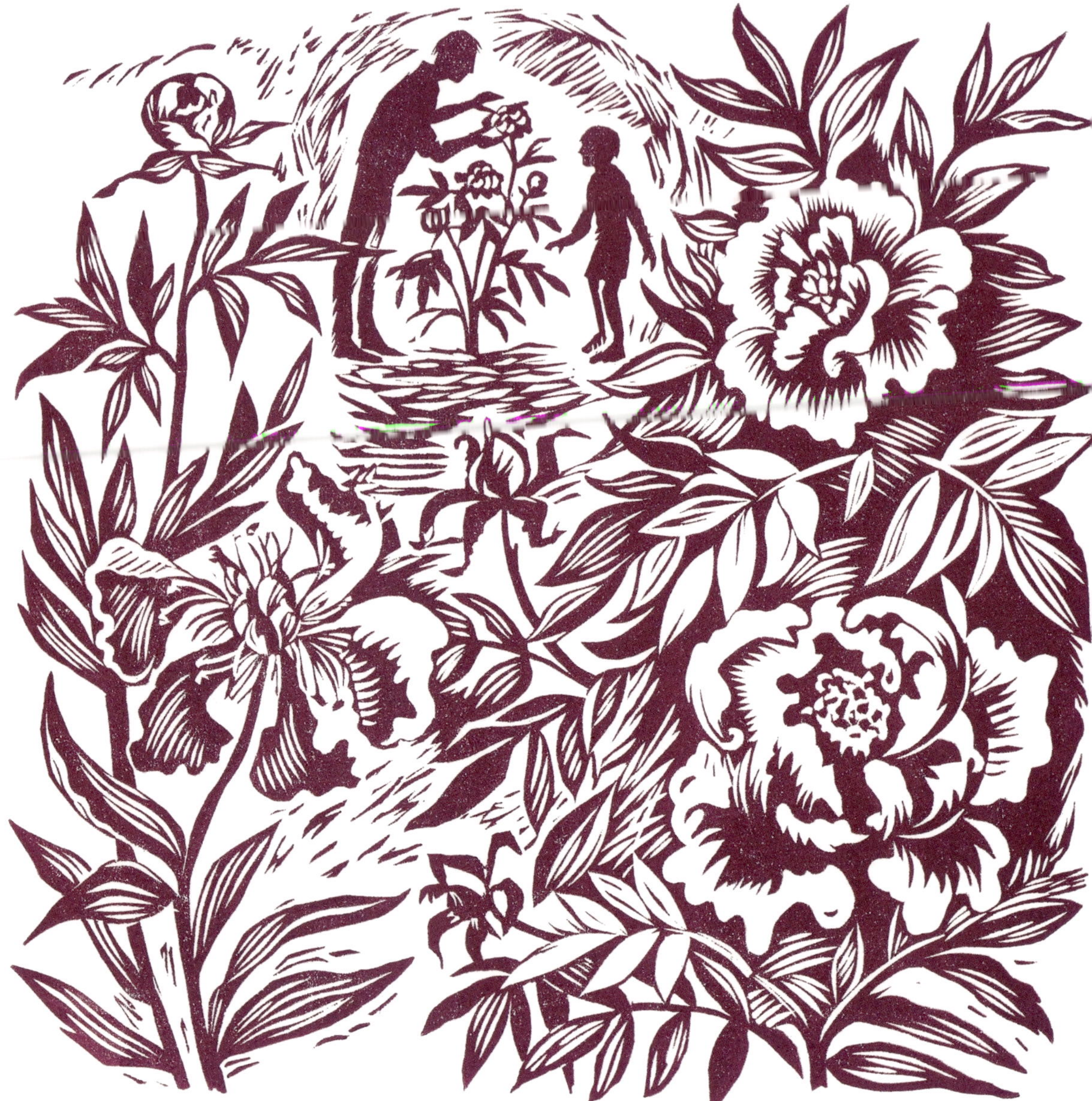

Above: 'Peonies', 19cm x 19cm; Facing page, from top left clockwise: 'Over the Moon', 21cm x 21cm; 'The Orchard', 19cm x 19cm; 'The Goldfinch', 19cm x 19cm; 'Cyclamen and Nerines', 19cm x 19cm, all linocuts and editions of 50

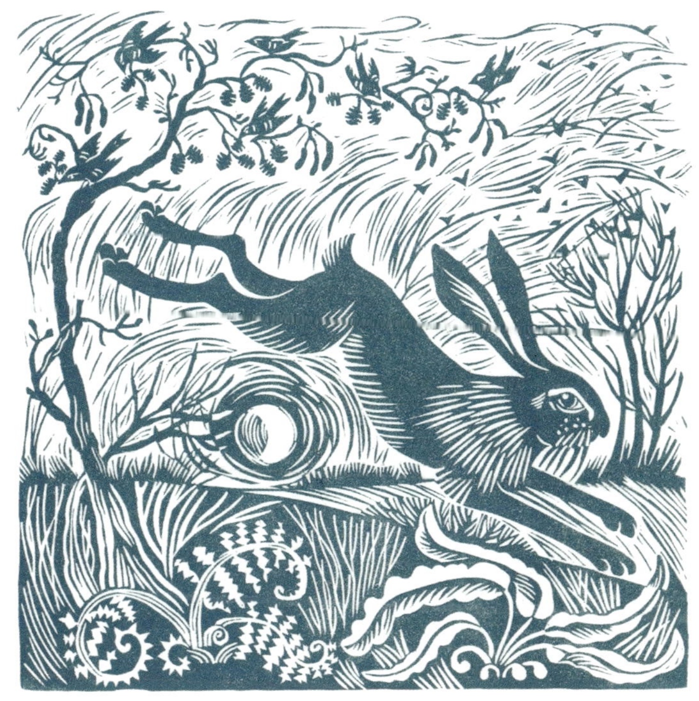
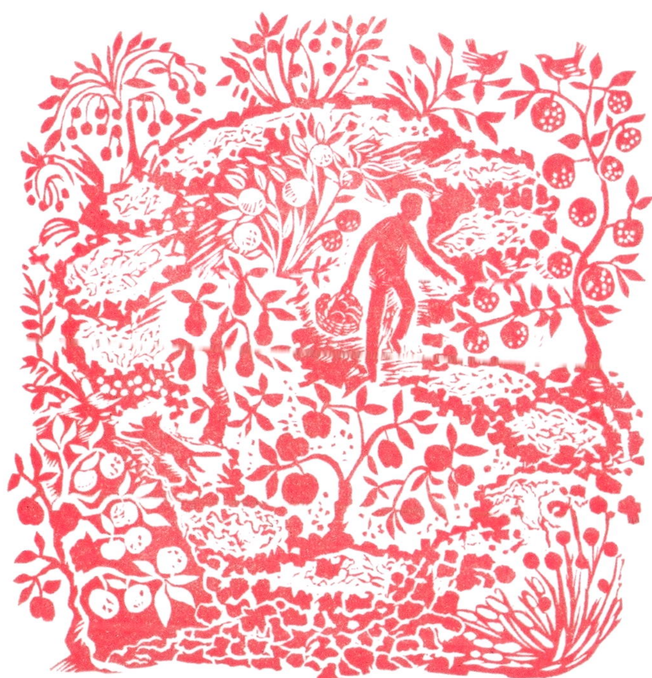
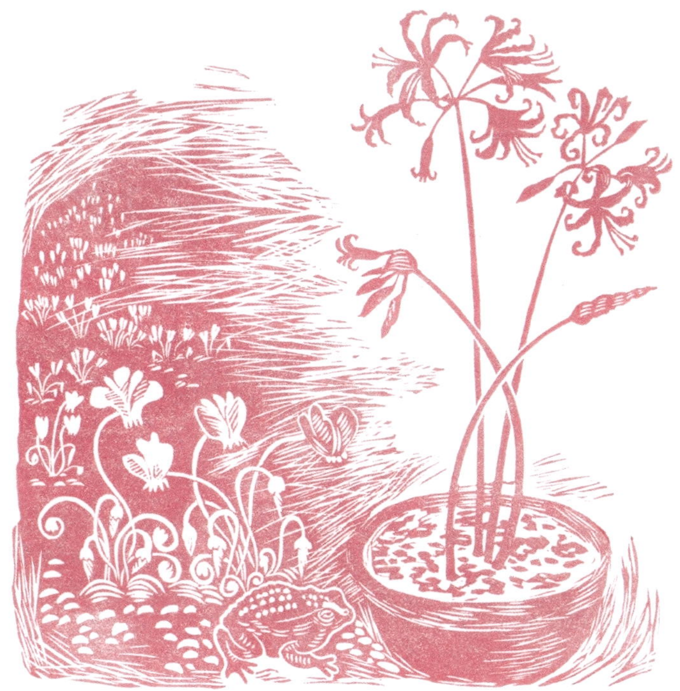
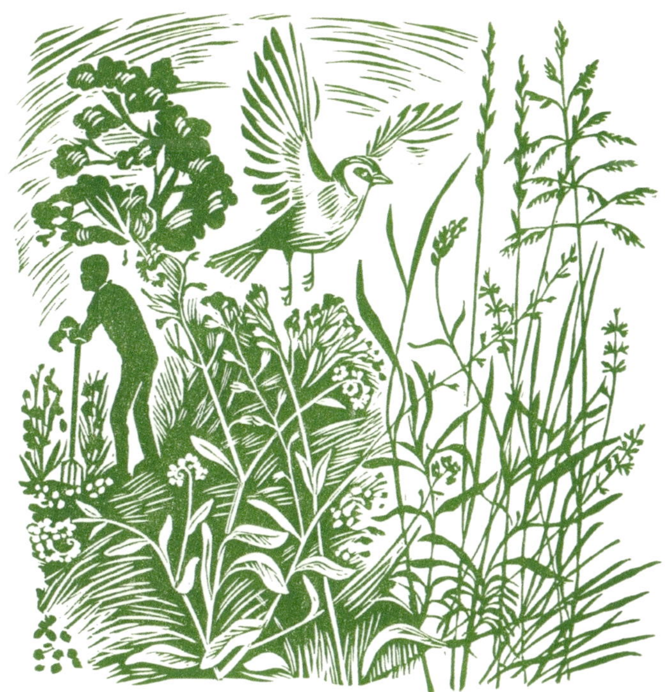

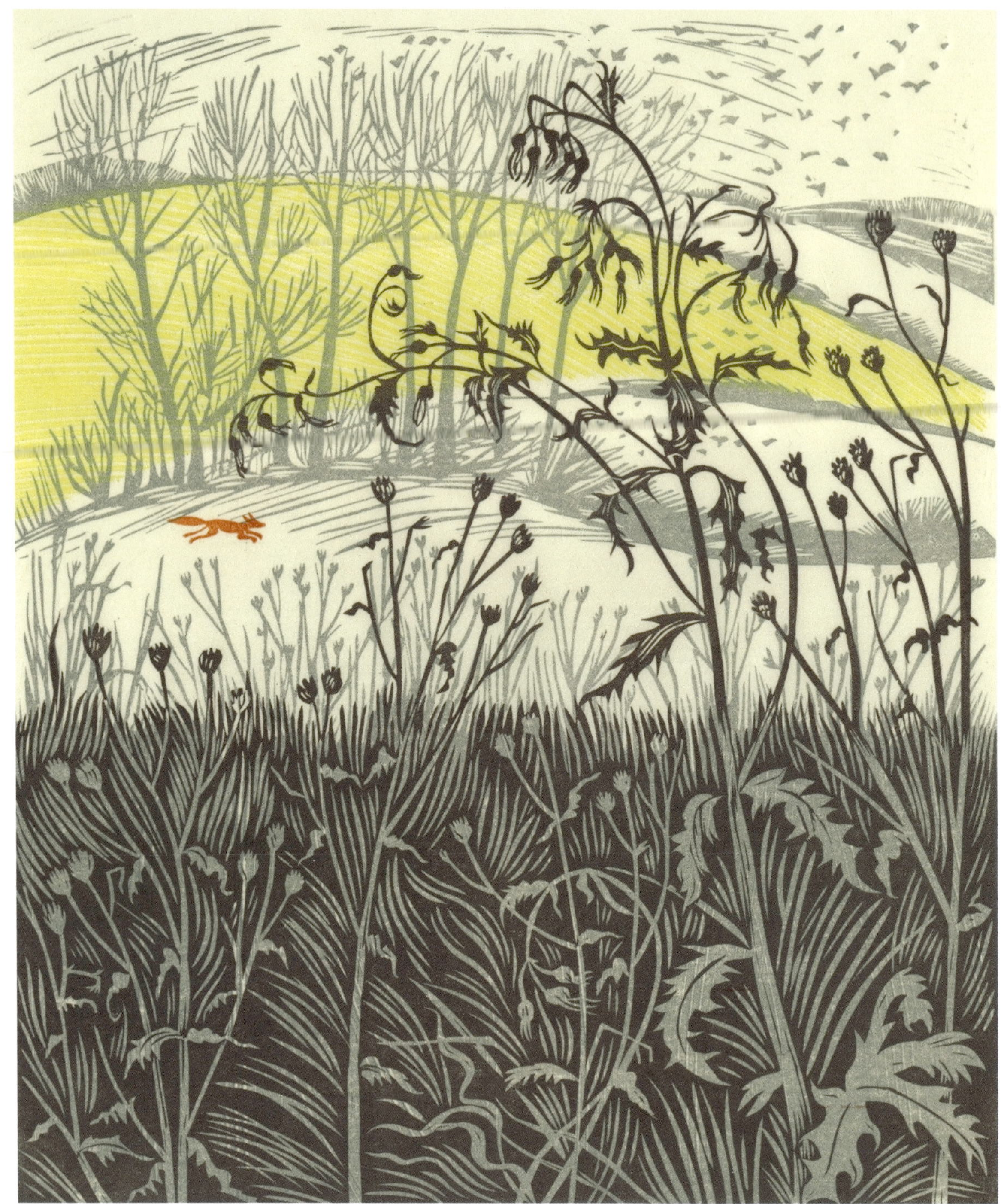

Above: 'The Red Fox' (wood and linocut), 36cm x 30cm, edition of 5 – Celia Hart

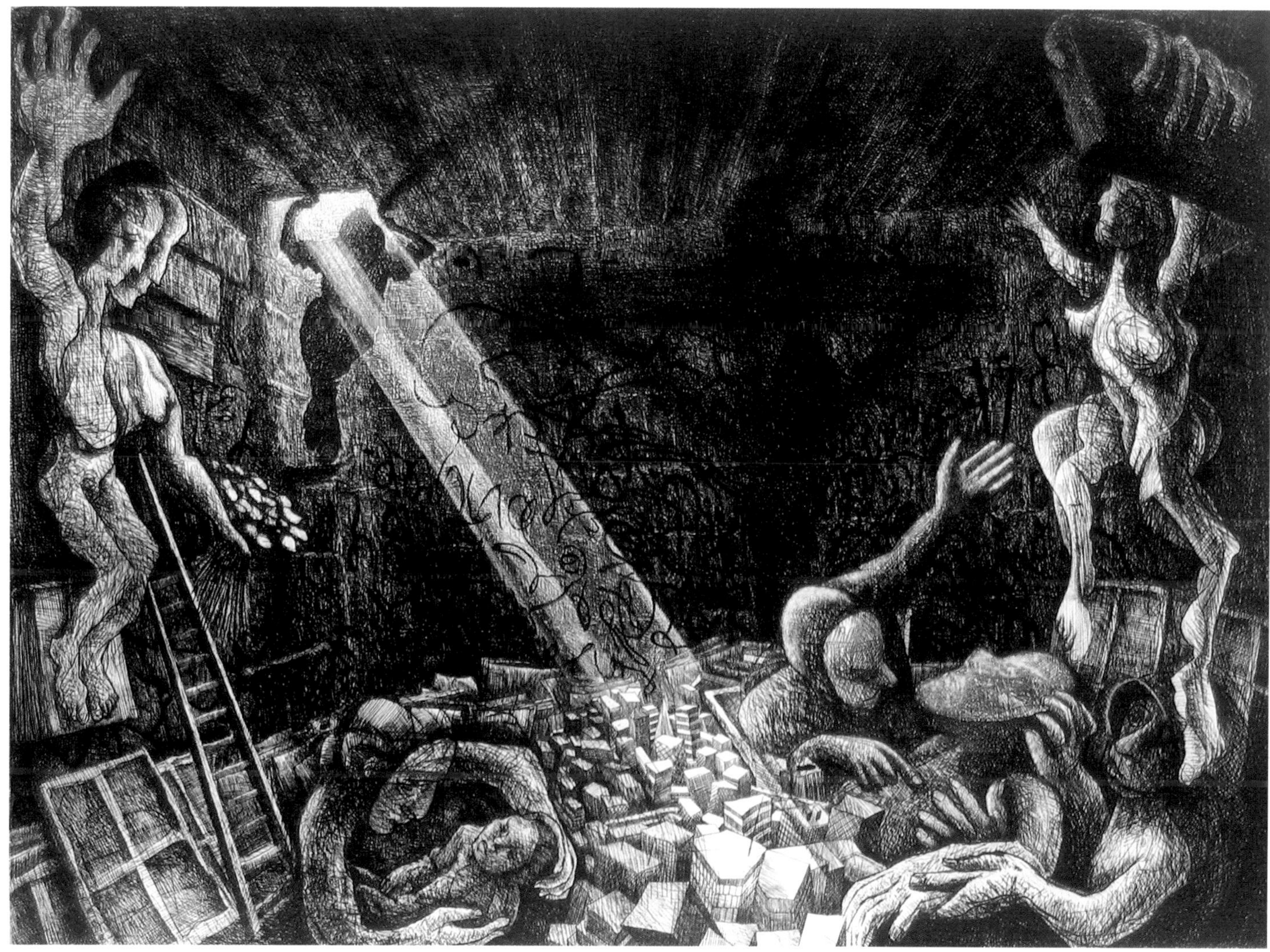

PAUL HAWDON

Cambridge-based painter and printmaker Paul Hawdon's main form of expression is through etching. "I have a great love of drawing, using the simplicity of line and mark, with their infinite abilities, to define and express. The marks can often be unrelated to subject matter or description.

"Each etching is a gradual process of exploration and can take many months and stages to complete. The time taken to make the etching is very important to me. It becomes like a long meditation as we develop a gradual understanding together. I tend to use a needle into a hard ground, although I sometimes use

Above: 'Depart and Forget' (etching), 60cm x 80cm, edition of 40

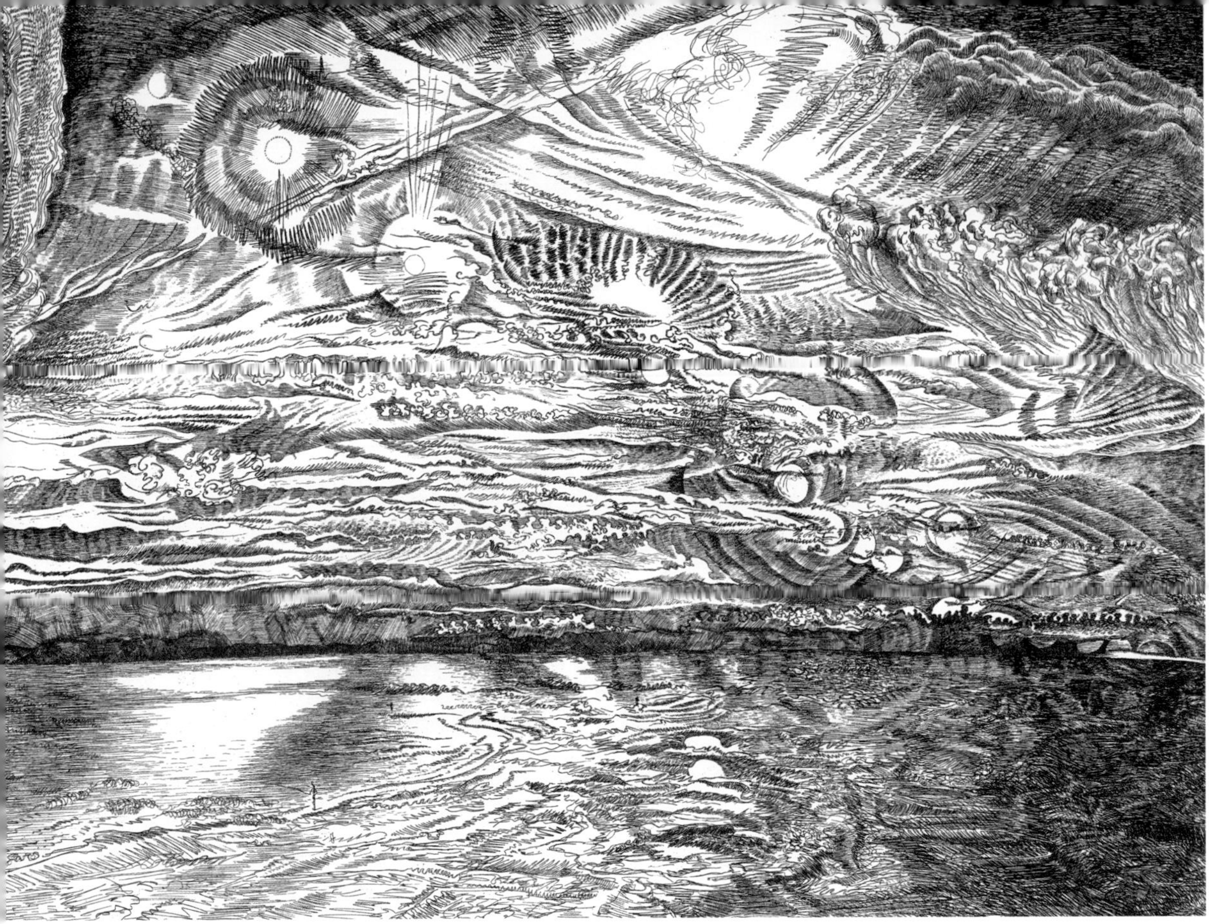

random interventions in order to provoke and surprise myself into making decisions.

"Sometimes my work is based upon drawings that I make in the landscape, but at other times I may draw directly on to the plate to see what appears – and these works can be more symbolic and perhaps difficult to understand. However, I see the works as a conversation with an interested observer, which allows the viewer freedom of interpretation."

Paul prints his own plates, finding that the printing process and inking can be just as interesting as drawing the plates. "My aim is not repetitive technical perfection but some form of expressive content. Sometimes I become so interested in the printing that I produce a varied range of prints from the same plate."

He studied Fine Art at Saint Martins School of Art, with three years' postgraduate study at the Royal Academy Schools. Following this he won an Italian Government Scholarship, which allowed him to study in Italy for a year. Subsequently he was awarded a Prix de Rome in Printmaking, and studied at the British School at Rome for 12 months.

His etchings have been seen in exhibitions at

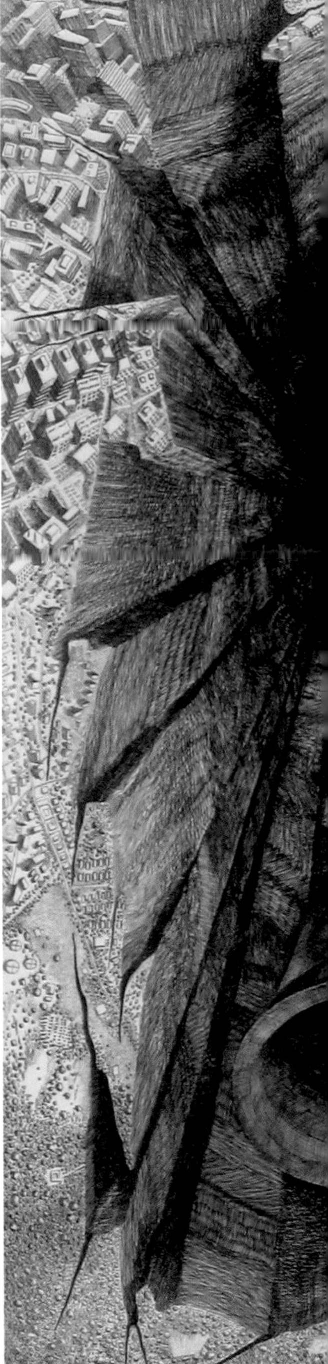

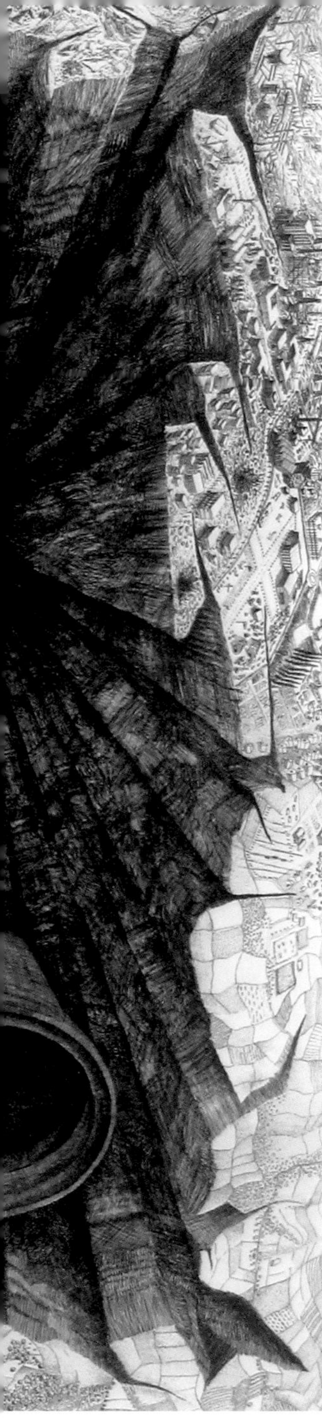

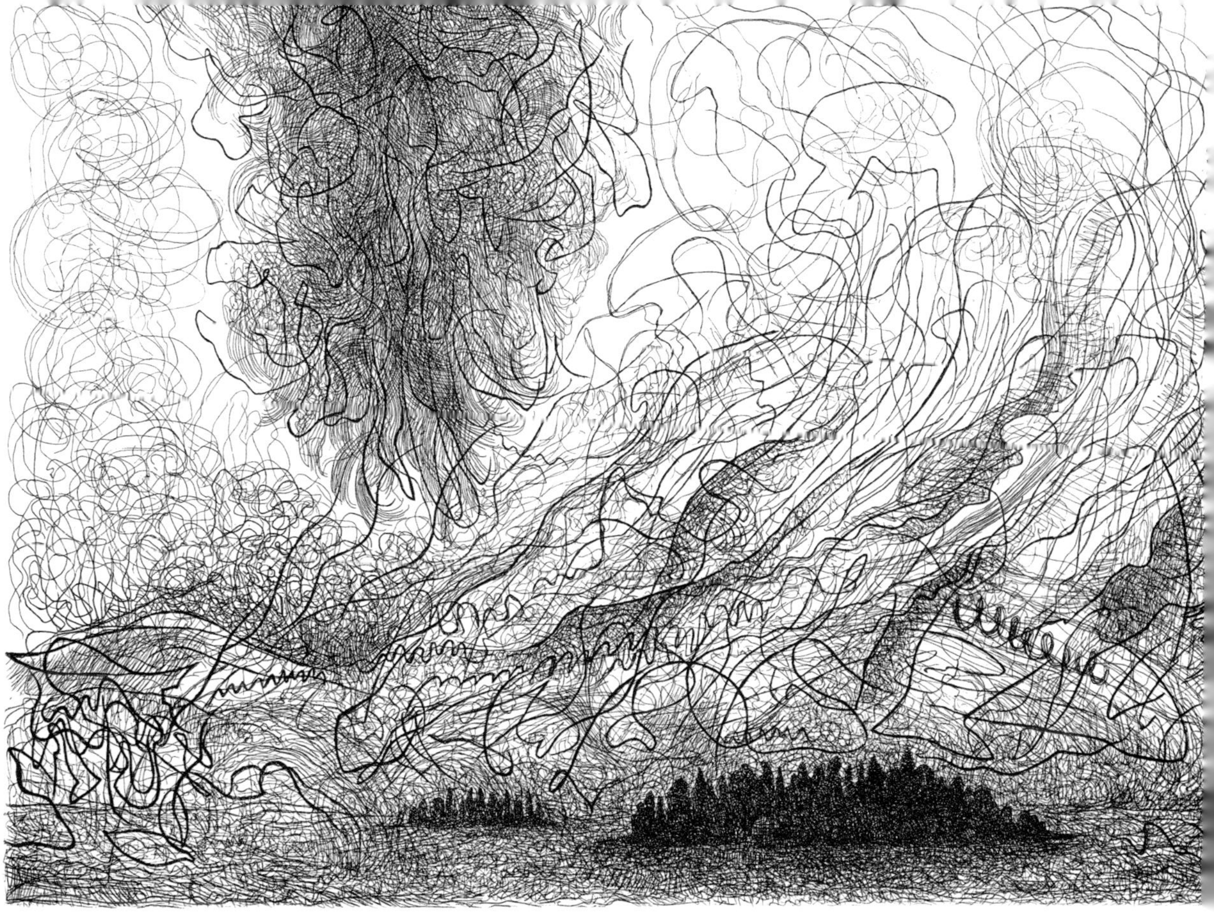

From far left: 'Sunset from Cadiz' (etching), 60cm x 80cm, edition of 40; 'Homage to Sarah Kane' (etching), 100cm x 50cm, edition of 40; 'Rain Approaching Isola Madre – Lake Maggiore' (etching), 30cm x 40cm, edition of 40

The Discerning Eye, the Royal Academy Summer Exhibition, the Courtauld Institute of Art, the Babylon Gallery in Ely and the Fitzwilliam Museum in Cambridge. Paul also has work in the collections of Aberystwyth University, the British Museum, The Queen's Collection and in the Metropolitan Museum of Art, New York.

He has twice won the Christie's Print Prize at the Royal Academy Summer Exhibition, and in 2017 was the recipient of the Urban Wildlife prize at the Wildlife Artist of the Year exhibition in London. Paul is a Fellow of the Royal Society of Painter-Printmakers (RE).
www.paulhawdon.co.uk

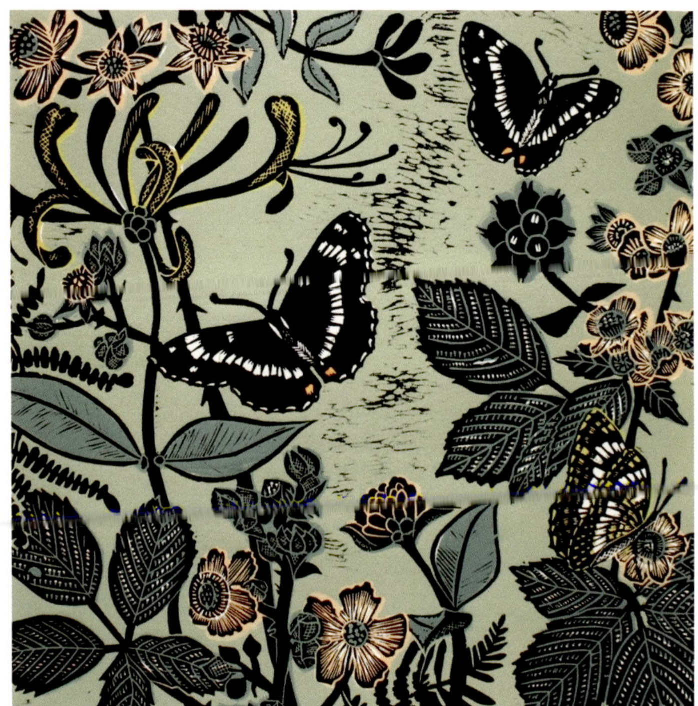

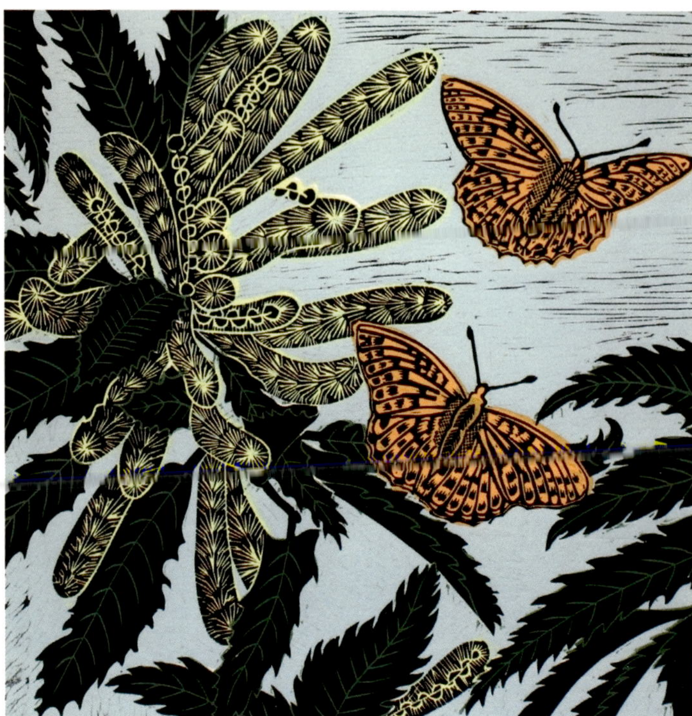

KATE HEISS

Kate Heiss is a modern British printmaker who is driven by her love of nature. She produces small, limited-edition illustrative prints depicting the flowers, birds and insects found in her garden and locally in the countryside of East Anglia, in particular the Norfolk Coast. The six prints shown here were commissioned by a private estate in Norfolk where several endangered species can be found.

After gaining an MA in Textile Design from the Royal College of Art in 1997, Kate worked as a textile designer across a wide range of fashion brands before setting up her own printmaking studio in 2011. Her style is influenced by her love of textiles, pattern and colour.

She loves the process of printmaking, particularly layering colour and texture to create pattern. "I love the element of surprise you always get when you pull the print through the press for the first time. Printmaking takes you on a creative journey, and you never quite know where you will end up." She works with a variety of printmaking techniques including linocut, screenprint and collage; often, her works combine more than one technique.

She exhibits throughout the UK, and continues to create personal commissions and work as part of collaborations with various companies that have licensed her designs. All of her work is handmade in her studio in Ashwell, Hertfordshire.
www.kateheiss.com

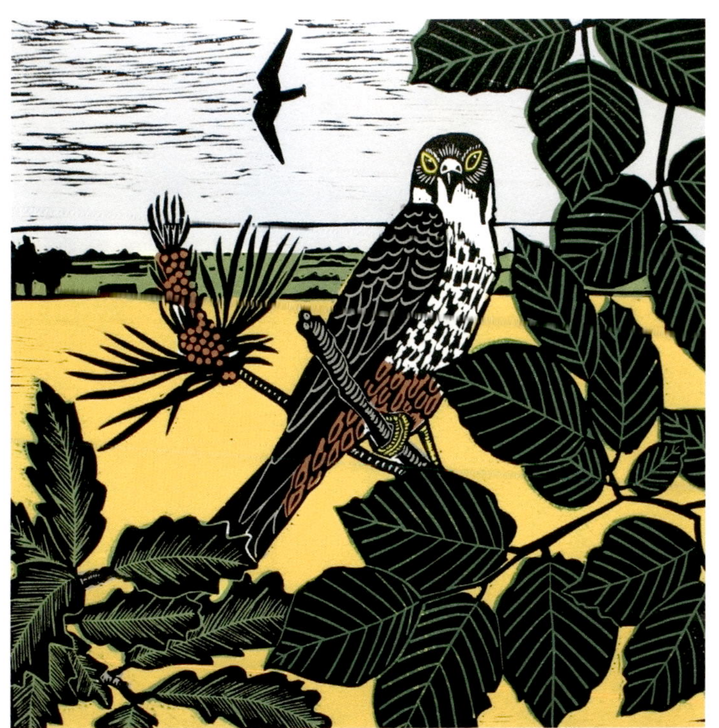

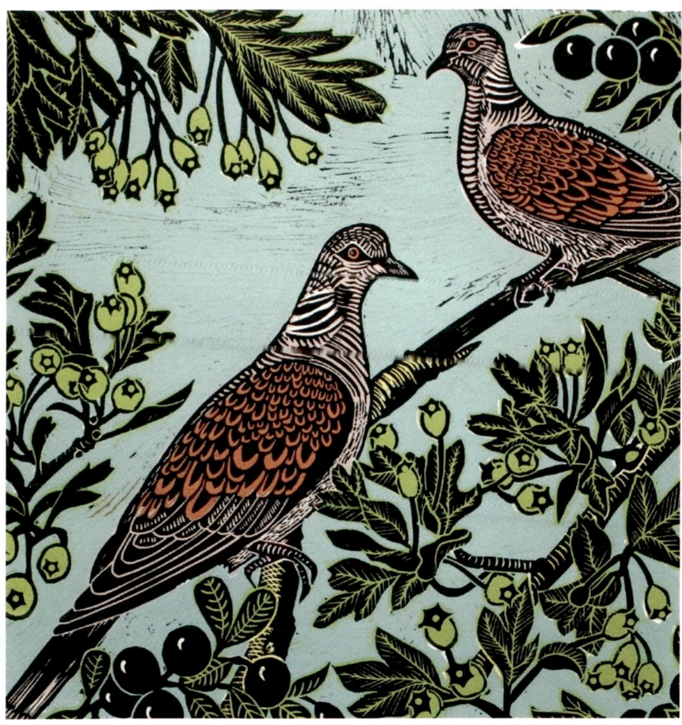

From far left: *'White Admirals in the Wood' (linocut), 30cm x 30cm, edition of 30*
"These beautiful butterflies fly for just a few weeks in the summer. I needed to find them so that I could photograph them in flight and observe their habitat. I was lucky to spot them in a small woodland clearing flying from the bramble flowers, where they were collecting nectar, then flying to the wild honeysuckle where they were looking for places to lay their eggs."

'Snettisham Sweet Chestnut' (linocut), 30cm x 30cm, edition of 30
"During early summer the strong fragrance of the Sweet Chestnut flower is so potent. When it is in bloom the branches look as though they are laden with candles. It is no wonder, then, that it attracts beautiful insects such as the Silver Washed Fritillary. I spotted this pair dancing among the leaves."

'Hobbies at Ken Hill' (linocut), 30cm x 30cm, edition of 30
"Here, two hobbies are seen flying across the cornfields looking for insects such as dragonflies. Hobbies are migratory birds and spend their summer in the UK."

'Two Turtle Doves' (linocut), 30cm x 30cm, edition of 30
"Two turtle doves are perched in a hawthorn bush. They have survived their migratory journey to spend the summer in the Norfolk countryside. The turtle dove is now the UK's fastest declining breed of bird. Between 1995 and 2004 the number of breeding birds fell by 93 per cent. This print is also featured in a new book, 'When Turtle Doves Fly', produced in conjunction with Operation Turtle Dove, a branch of the RSPB dedicated to saving turtle doves from extinction."

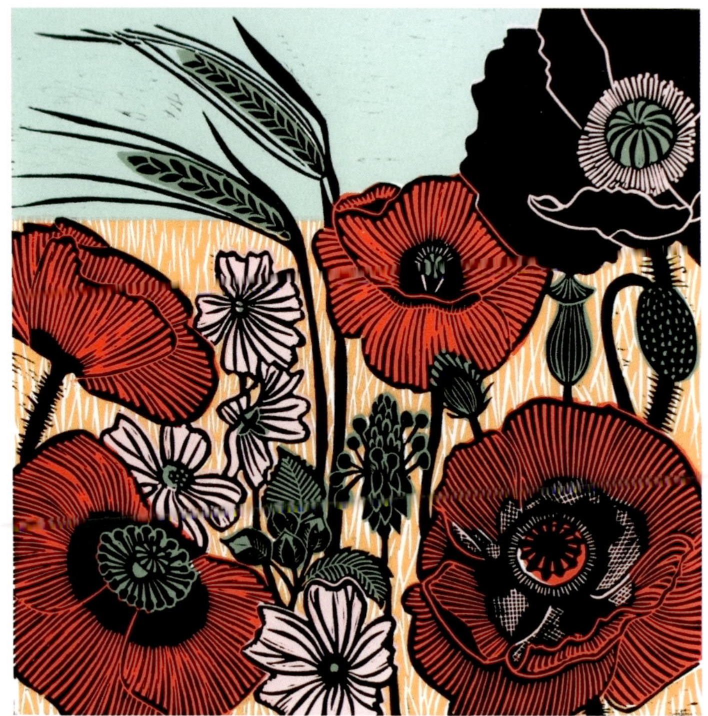

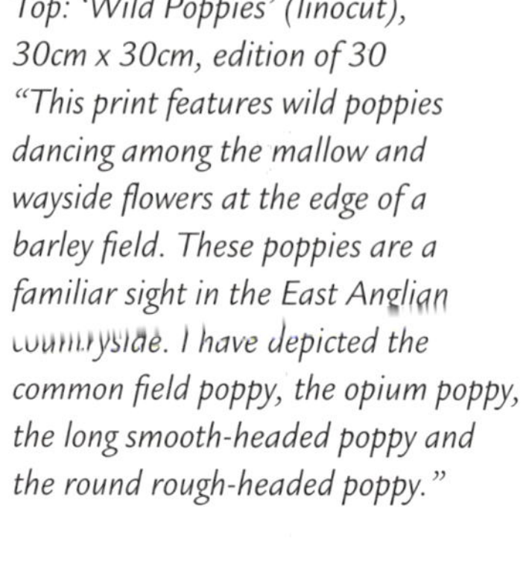

Top: 'Wild Poppies' (linocut), 30cm x 30cm, edition of 30
"This print features wild poppies dancing among the mallow and wayside flowers at the edge of a barley field. These poppies are a familiar sight in the East Anglian countryside. I have depicted the common field poppy, the opium poppy, the long smooth-headed poppy and the round rough-headed poppy."

Bottom: 'Yellow Horned Poppies' (linocut), 30cm x 30cm, edition of 30
"Yellow horned poppies are coastal plants found growing on shingle beaches, cliffs and sand dunes. Here, the yellow horned poppies dance alongside viper's bugloss and mullein flowers on the shingle bank at Snettisham Beach, with Ken Hill Wood in the background."

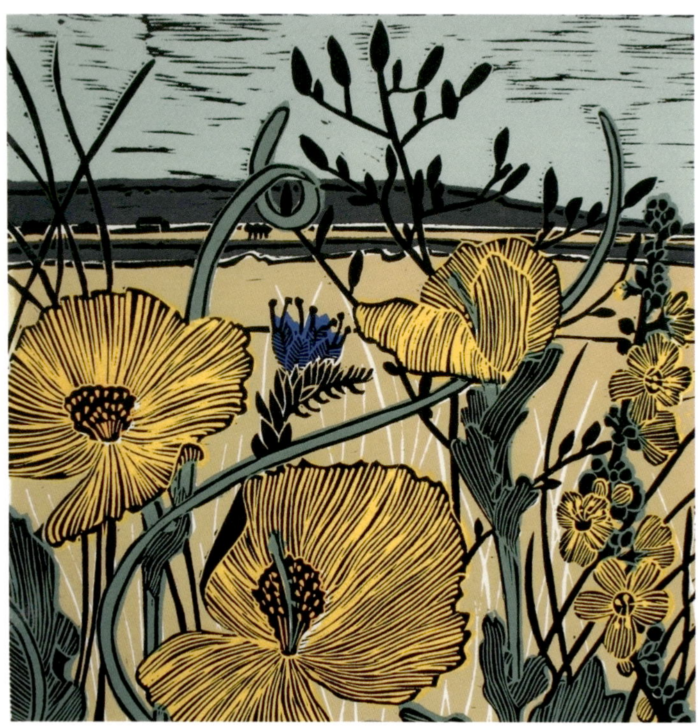

ANTHONY HOPKINSON

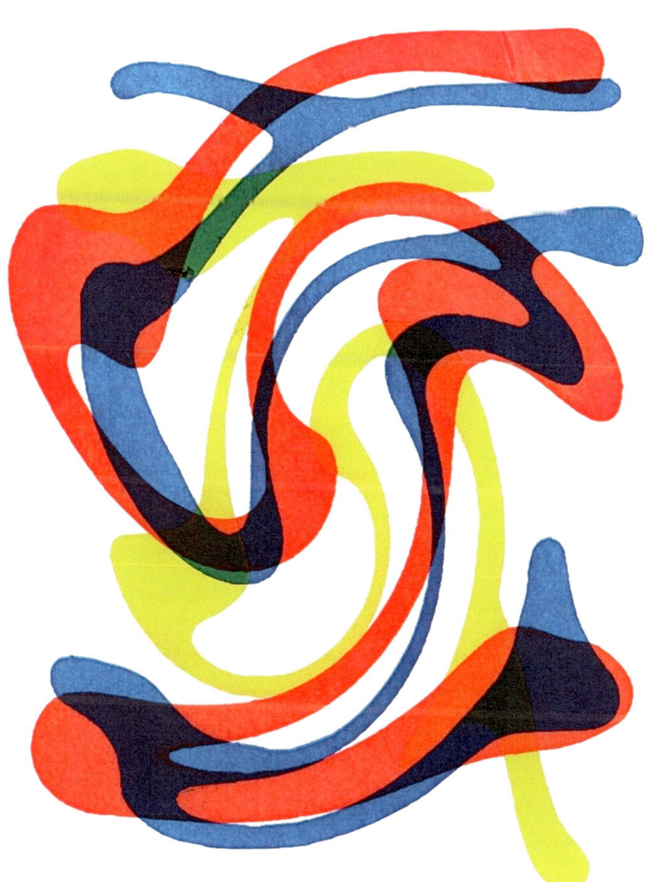

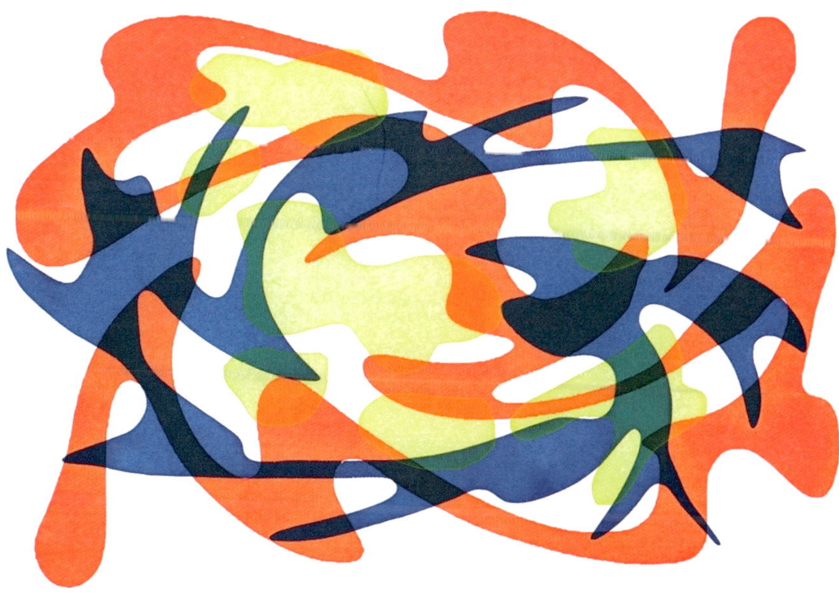

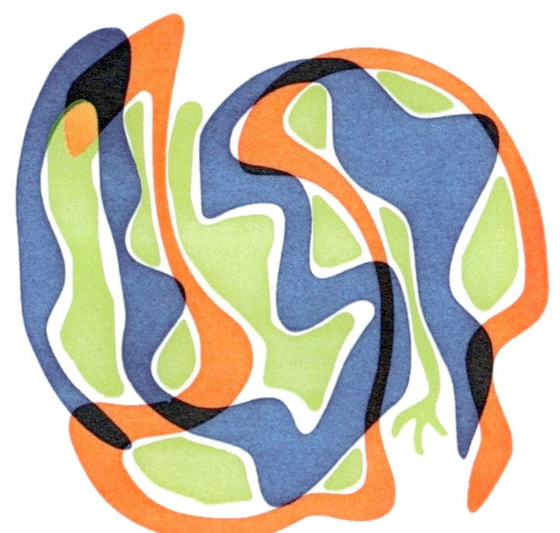

Anthony Hopkinson's work consists mainly of screenprints. He loves strong colours and bold shapes, created with paper stencils. "I am proud to have been one of the founders of Cambridge Original Printmakers as well as being involved for many years in the management of Cambridge Open Studios," he says. Anthony was also Treasurer and then President

From top left, clockwise: 'Antigone', 40cm x 30cm; 'Sun Dance', 30cm x 19cm; 'Hatchling', 17cm x 17cm – all screenprints and editions of 20

of the Cambridge Drawing Society.

"I must be one of the oldest players in the printmaking game, but I have no plans to give up. In fact, it's what keeps me going! Embarking on a new print is always an adventure."

His prints are sometimes representational; but he enjoys abstract, when he can indulge his passion for free-flowing shapes and colours.

Anthony works in his studio at the end of the garden – "a very short commute".

www.anthonyhopkinson.co.uk

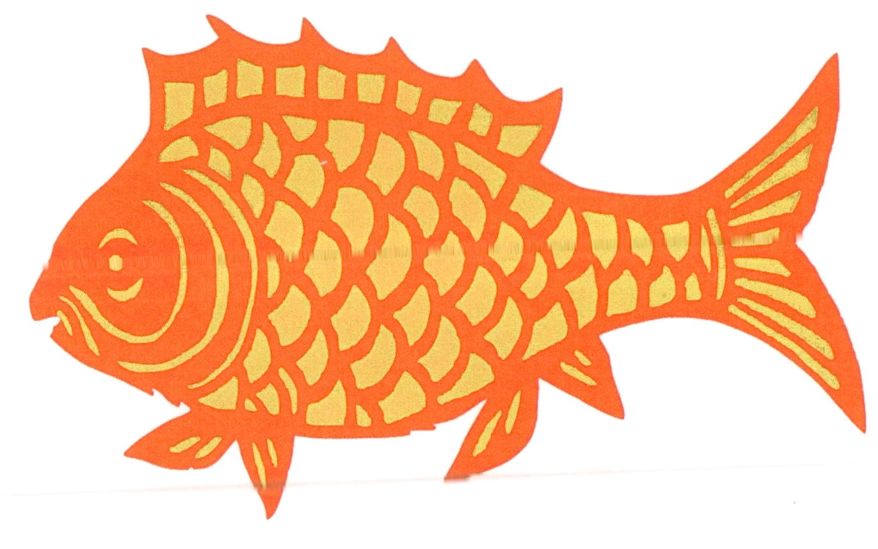

Above: 'Goldfish' (screenprint), 22cm x 14cm, edition of 20; Right: 'Renard' (screenprint), 40cm x 30cm, edition of 20

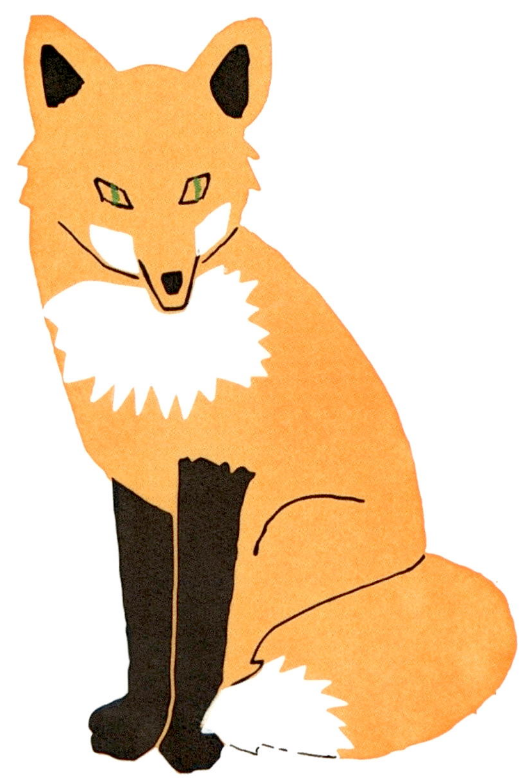

IONA HOWARD

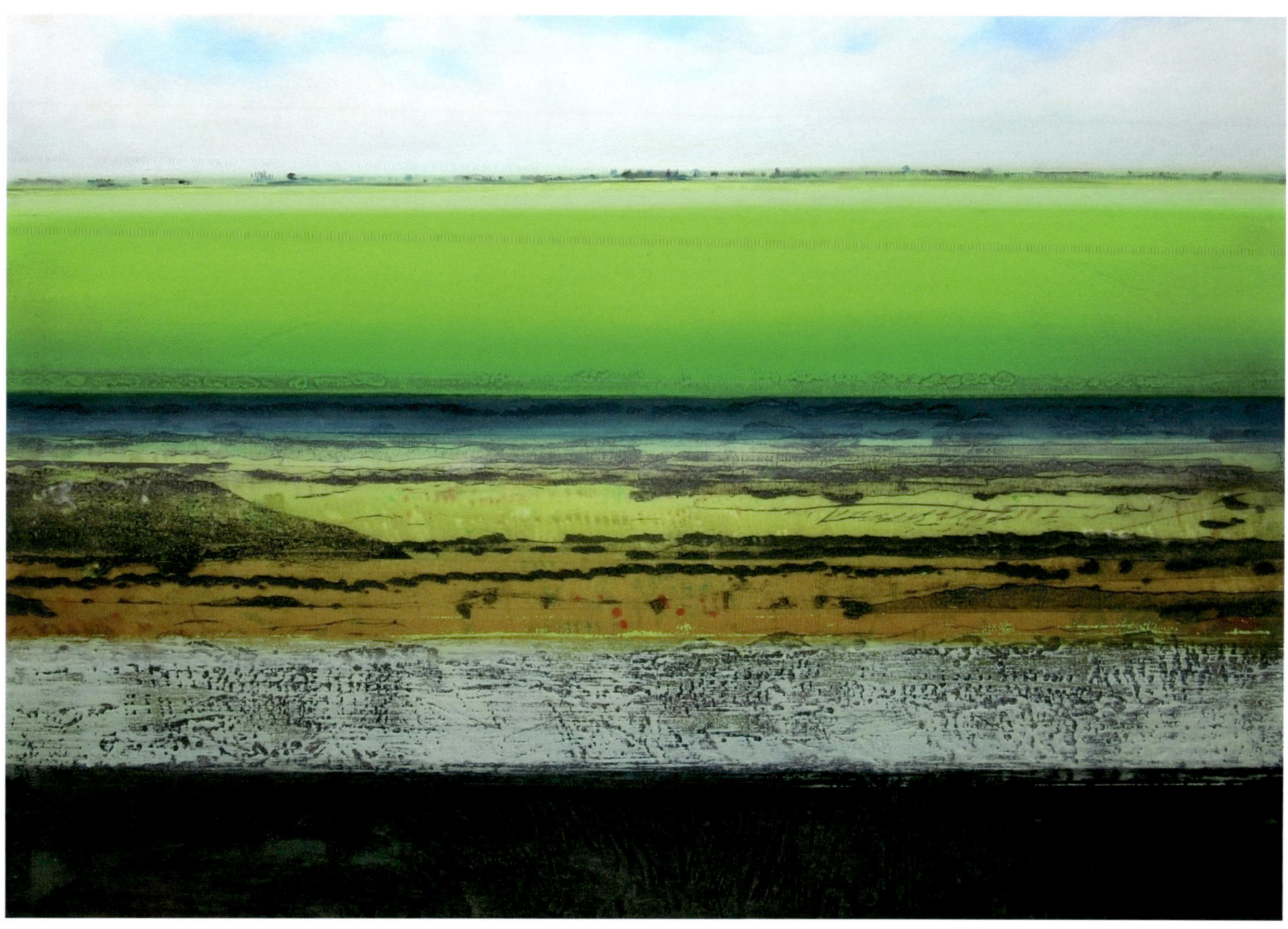

Above: *'Great North Fen in Summer VIII' (carborundum, monoprint and drypoint), 48cm x 69cm, unique*

Iona Howard describes her work as "exploring the notion of time and landscape through a contemplative exploration of surface".

The sources of her prints come from working in the open air or expressing landscape filtered through memory. The physicality of her approach to the printing process makes the subject spontaneous and vibrant while capturing an intimate connection with the landscape.

"I draw inspiration from sites that have a particular sense of place," she says. "Recent works of the Fens focus on the meeting point of land, horizon and sky, their flatness altering the perception of distance."

Her plates are predominantly

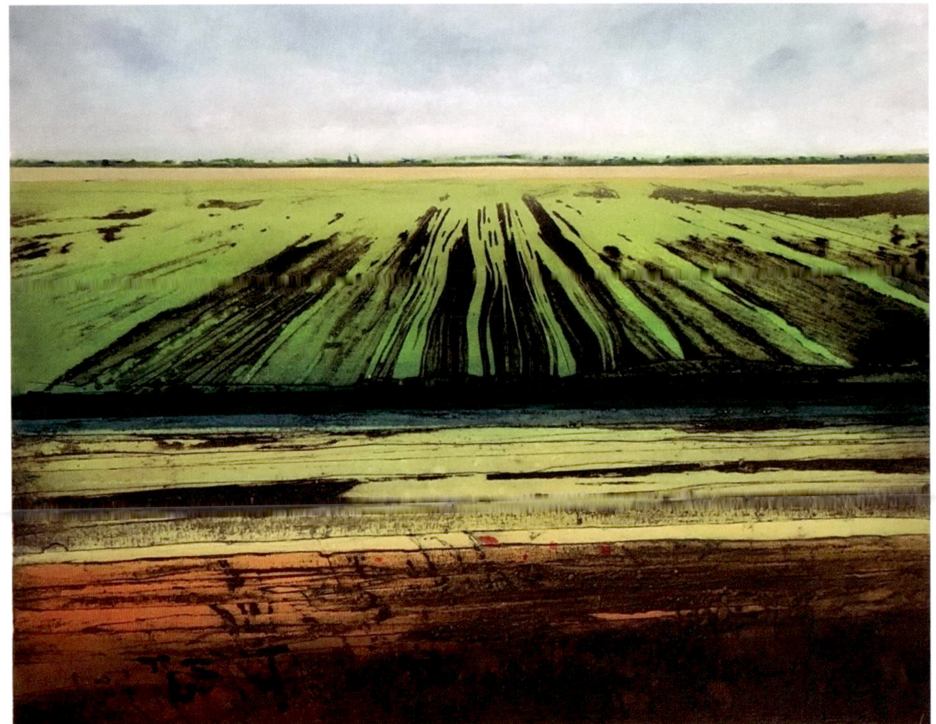

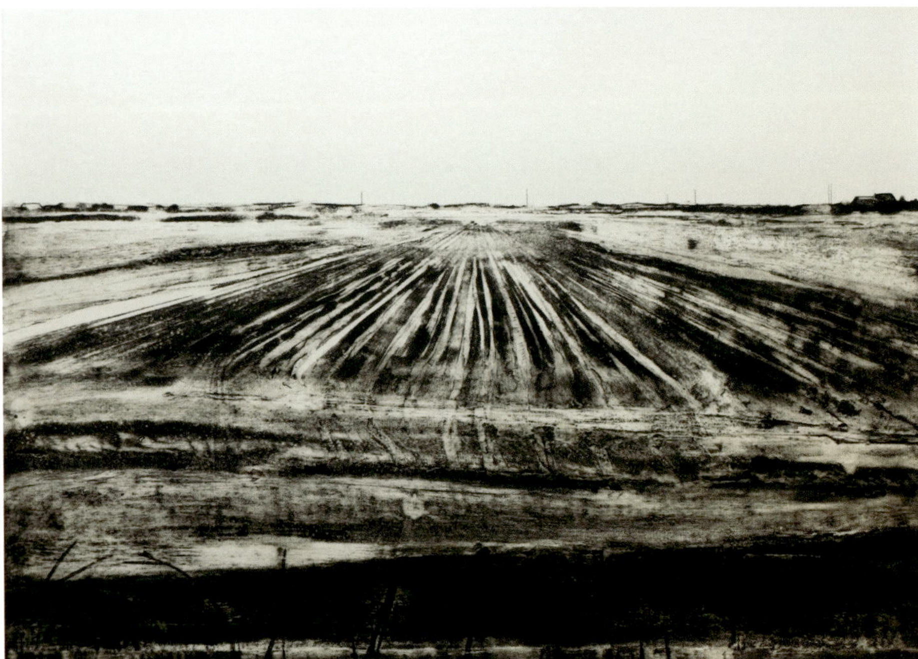

carborundum, a technique where a mix of a binder and carborundum grit is applied on to the surface of a plate and inked up. It provides highly embossed, velvety textures and rich, dense tones. This medium allows Iona the freedom to work on a large scale in the same way as approaching painting. To contrast the carborundum, drypoint is

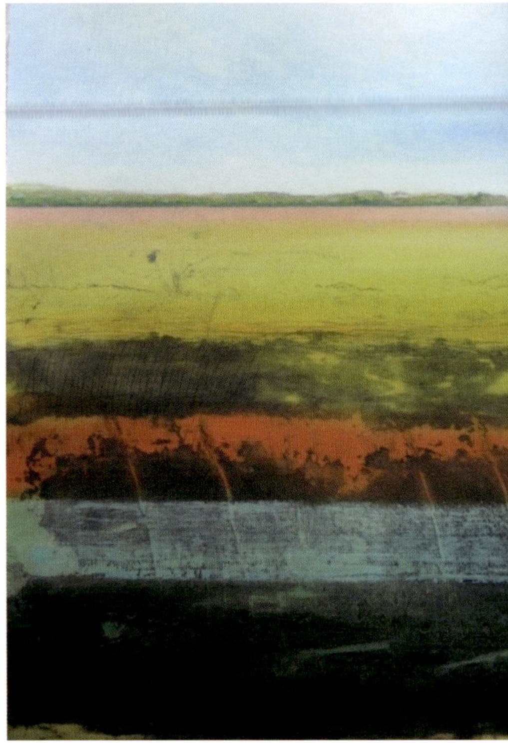

Top left: 'June Fen I' (carborundum, monoprint and drypoint), 40cm x 48cm, unique; Bottom left: 'November Fen' (carborundum, collagraph and drypoint), 39cm x 68cm, edition of 40; Above: 'Wicken Fen XIII' (carborundum, monoprint and drypoint), 69cm x 98cm, unique

added to produce an incised line, characteristically thin, linear and precise. Colour is introduced by layering carborundum plates; or, more often, realised though monoprint.

She prints to the edge of the paper to leave the composition as unconstrained as the landscapes from which she seeks inspiration.
www.ionahoward.com

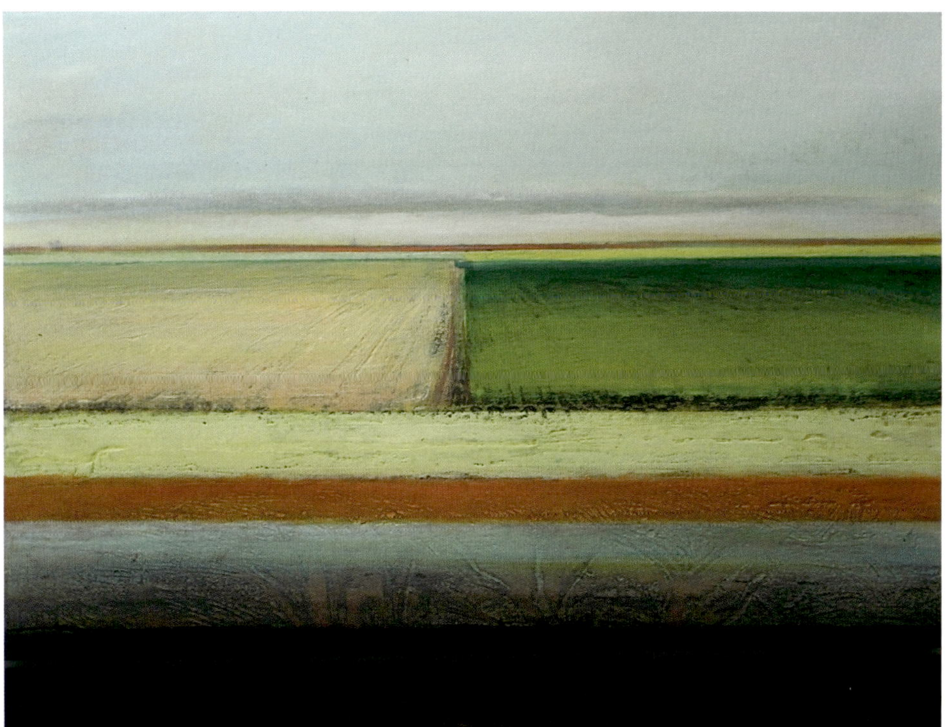

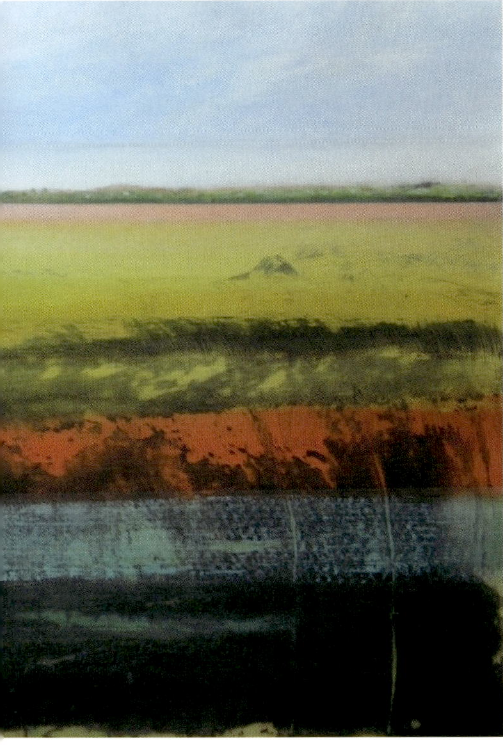

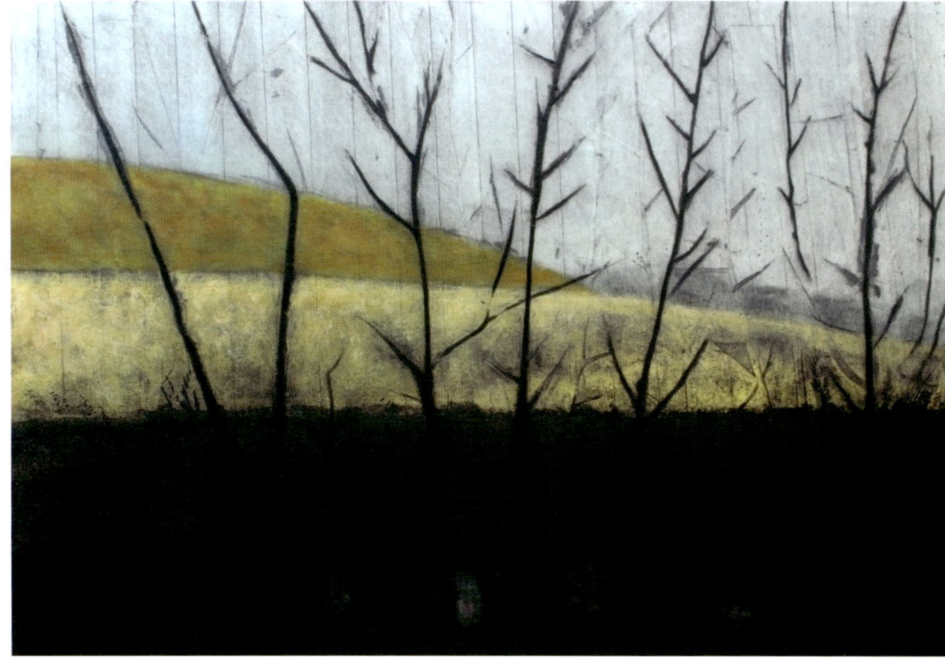

Top right: 'Spring Fen IV' (carborundum, monoprint and drypoint), 29cm x 39cm, unique; Bottom right: 'Goonhilly Downs' (carborundum and collagraph), 58cm x 78cm, edition of 40

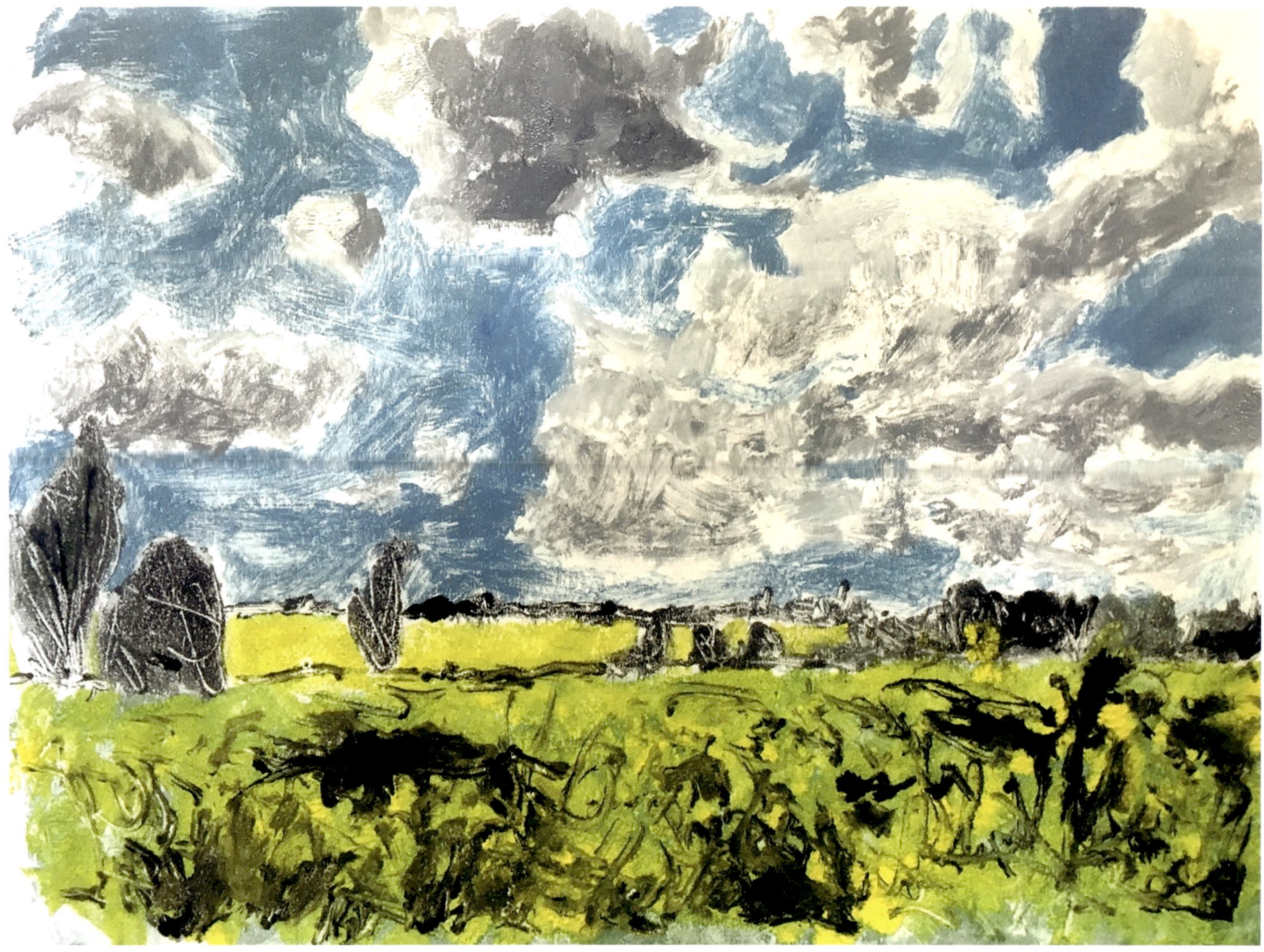

ROZ HOWLING

Roz Howling has been experimenting with printmaking for the past 10 years, inspired by the work of Elizabeth Fink, Andy Warhol and Franz Marc, who all incorporated animals, her main inspiration, within their work. Starting with linoprinting, she has since branched out, experimenting with collagraph, drypoint etching, aquatint, monoprinting and hybrid printing techniques.

"I'm attracted to printmaking because the process of pulling multiple prints from a single plate enables me to experiment with colour, mark-making and texture," she says. "I enjoy comparing the outcomes of various prints pulled from

This page: 'Bardfield' (monotype, single plate), 20cm x 26cm, unique; Opposite page, from top clockwise: 'Thoroughbreds' (linocut & etching), 20cm x 40cm, edition of 6; 'Mare and Foal' (hybrid print), 20cm x 16.0cm, 1 of 2; 'Coco' (monotype), 16cm x 18cm, 1 of 2

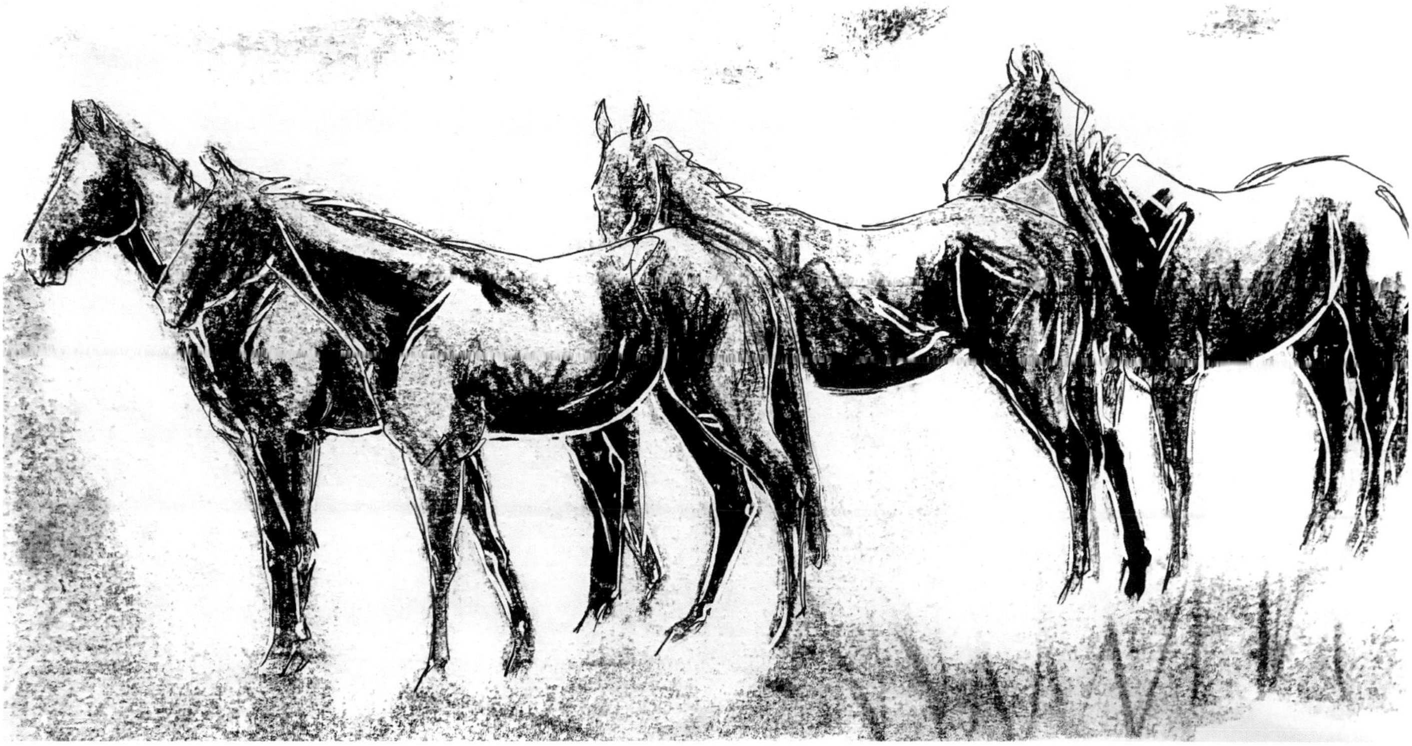

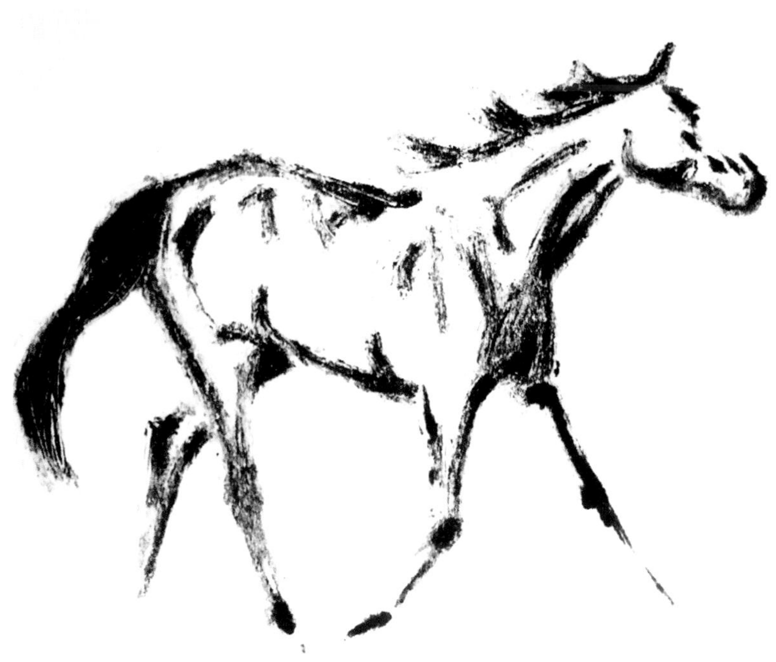

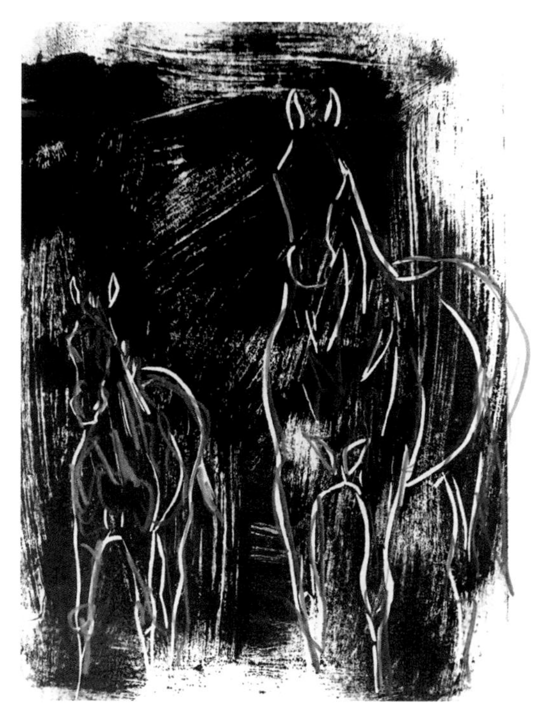

the same plate, eliciting which elements I prefer, and using this to inspire later works and further print editions."

Roz takes inspiration from the landscapes that surround her and, in particular, from the animals in her life. Living near Newmarket, the thoroughbred horse inspires her work to a huge extent. "Its speed, agility and elegance, combined with the energy and colour of a race, make for interesting compositions." The trees and agricultural landscape also feature in her work, often including scenery through which she has ridden.

"I enjoy experimenting, and am always evolving my technique and style in response to the subject of my inspiration." Her work is varied in both style and technique, although she often returns to the same subject matter and her number one passion, horses.
www.rozannaartist.co.uk

From top right, clockwise: 'Racing' (linocut), 24cm x 29cm, edition of 50; 'Elsie' (linocut), 15cm x 10cm, edition of 25; 'Swan' (monoprint), 24cm x 24cm, 1 of 2

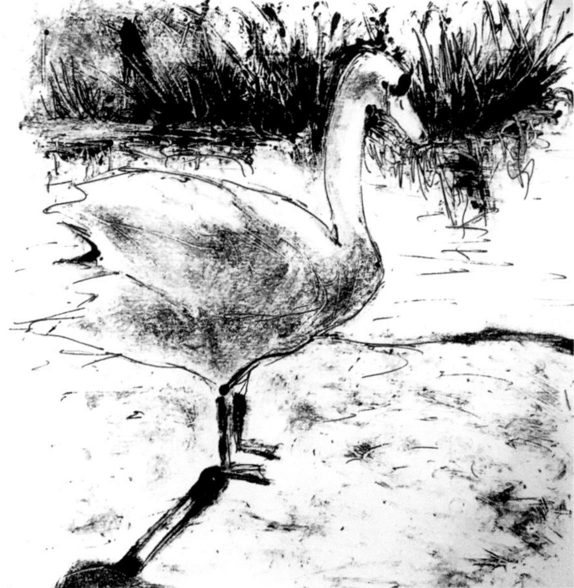

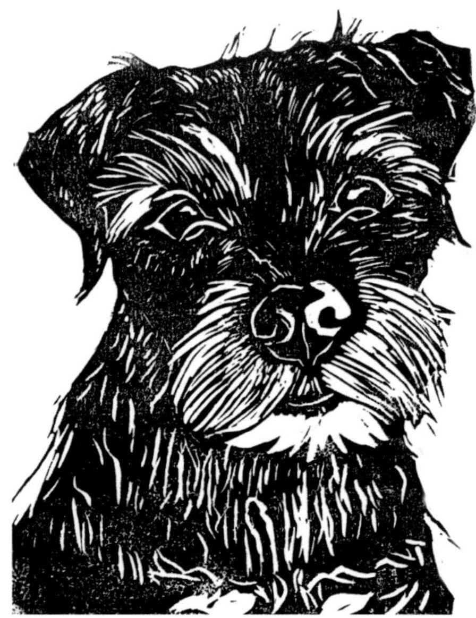

CONSTANCE JOHNSON

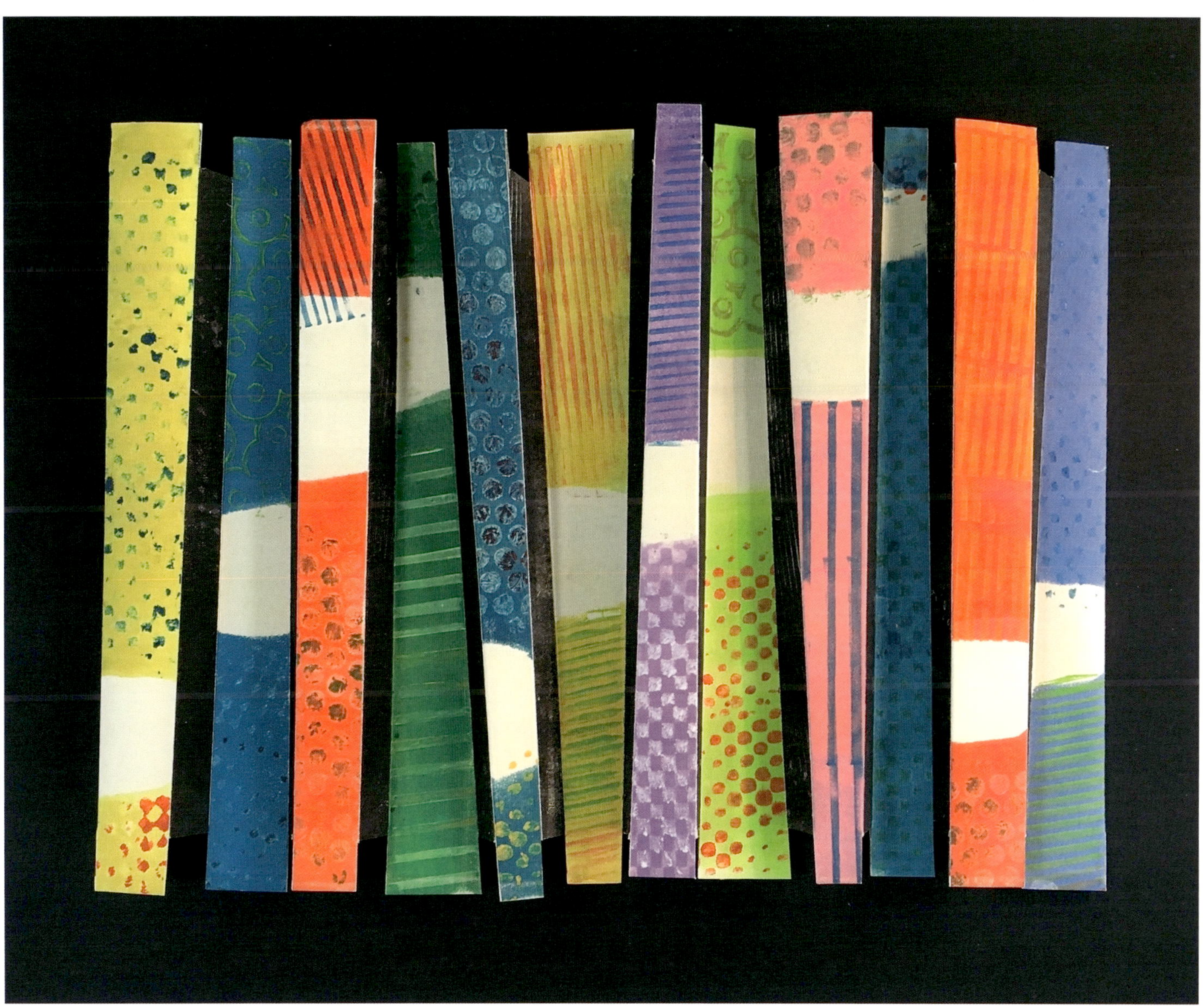

Above: 'Fanfare' (folded monotype), 28cm x 21cm, unique

Constance Johnson's art expresses itself in abstract designs that comprise layer upon layer of colour to capture depth and breadth.

"I'm an obsessive experimenter with the juxtaposition of contrasting and clashing colours," she says. "I fell in love with abstraction at a young age, and developed my interests through a degree in Fine Arts from

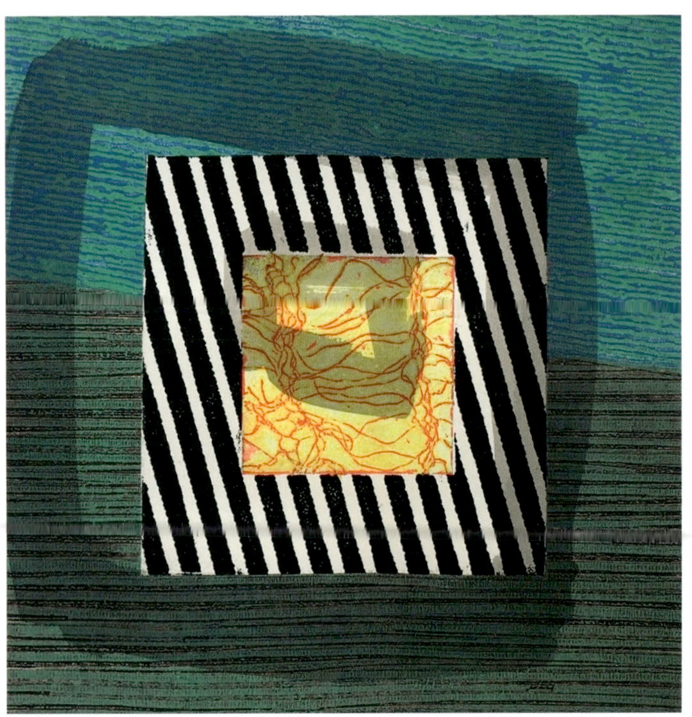

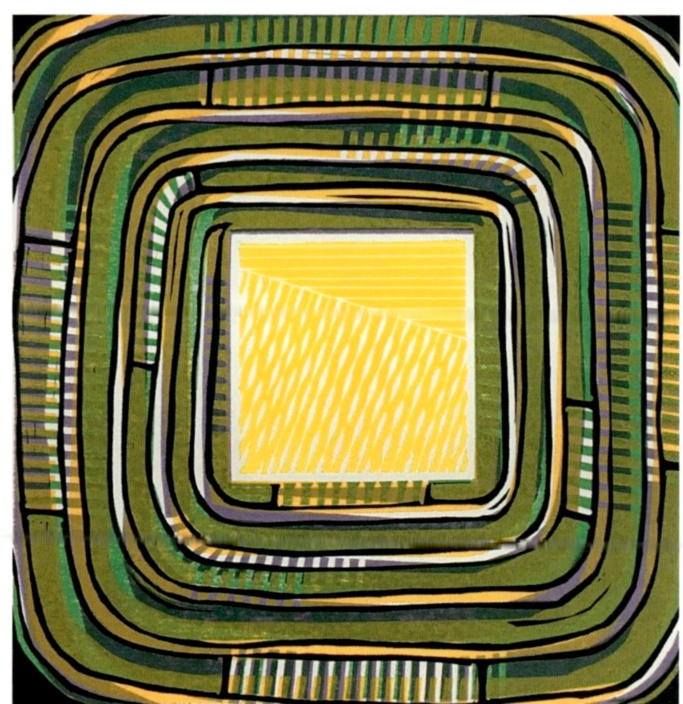

Washington State University. I also spent a year in Tokyo for further study on traditional dyeing techniques."

Her explorations with Japanese katazome involved paper stencils and a bean paste resist. Further experiments in printmaking have included clay monoprinting, which involves lifting colours from a leather-hard clay base on to canvas. Her experiments in design have recently extended to novel use of collagraph and linoprinting.

"Currently I'm really into abstract landscapes that are created with multiple nesting plates," Constance says. "I enjoy starting with a small format and creating an interactive design that captures an entire world." The finished effect of squares within squares features textures and patterns as well as diversity of colour.

Prints by nature are two-dimensional, but in some current work Constance pushes the boundaries of printmaking into three dimensions through folding, layering and overlapping. The resulting topographical display offers different perspectives depending on the angle of observation.

"These new prints are designed to break out from the flat surface of traditional printmaking," she says. "Ridges reflect light from different angles and involve the viewer in an interactive experience with the art."
http://connijohnson.weebly.com

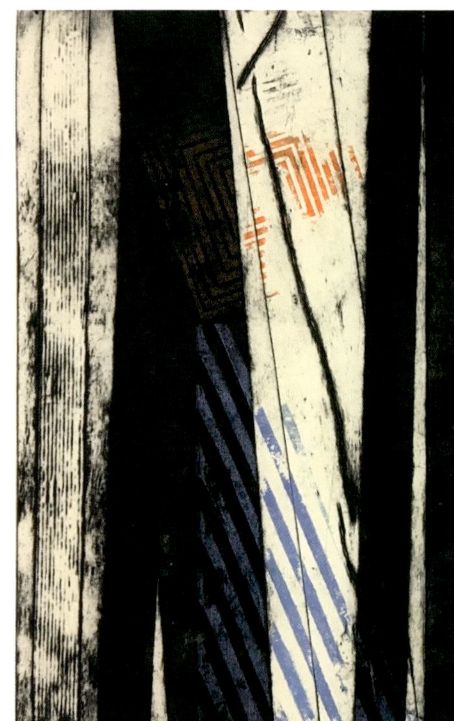

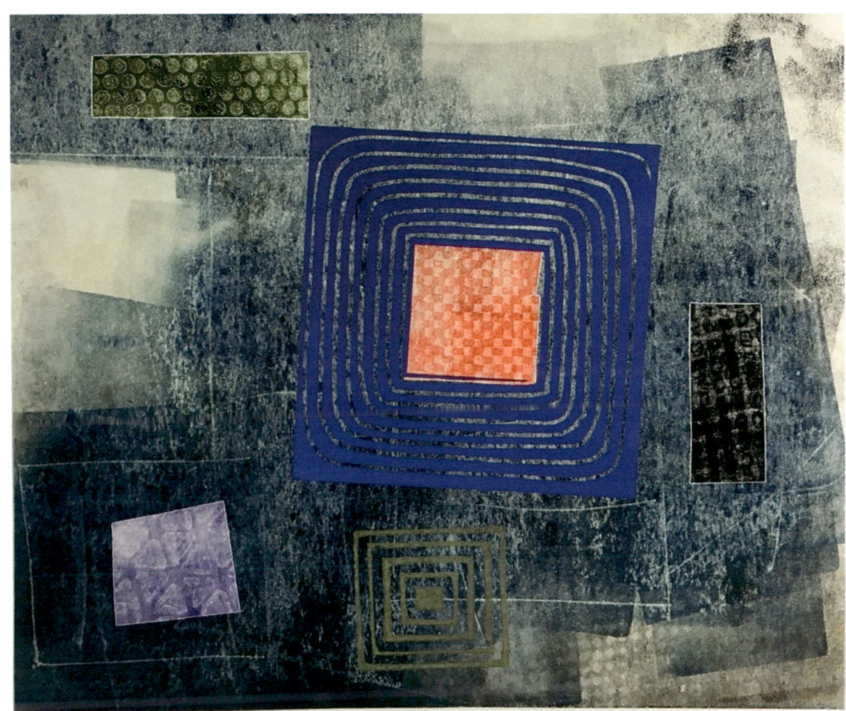

Top row, from left: 'Golden Light' (collagraph), 29cm x 29cm, unique; 'Forest of Change' (linocut), 15cm x 15cm, unique; 'Now Around the Edges' (monotype and linocut), 40cm x 35cm, unique; Bottom row, from left: 'Enchantment' (collagraph and linocut), 46cm x 35cm, unique; 'Snapped-off Perceptions' (folded monotype), 30cm x 21cm, unique

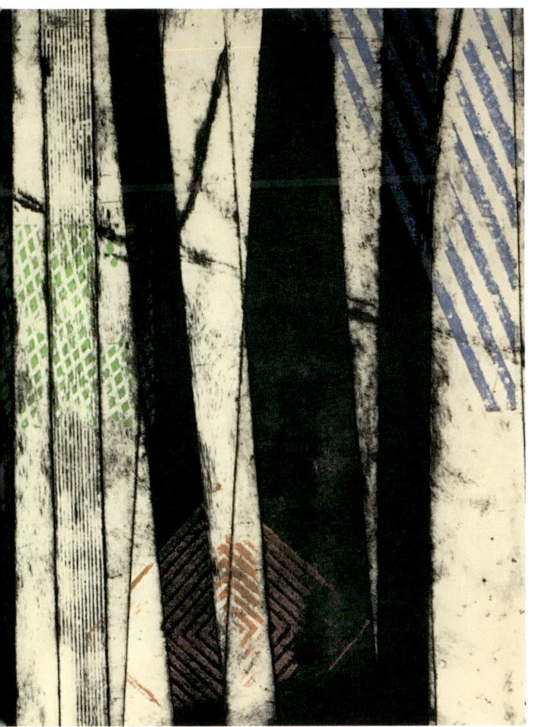

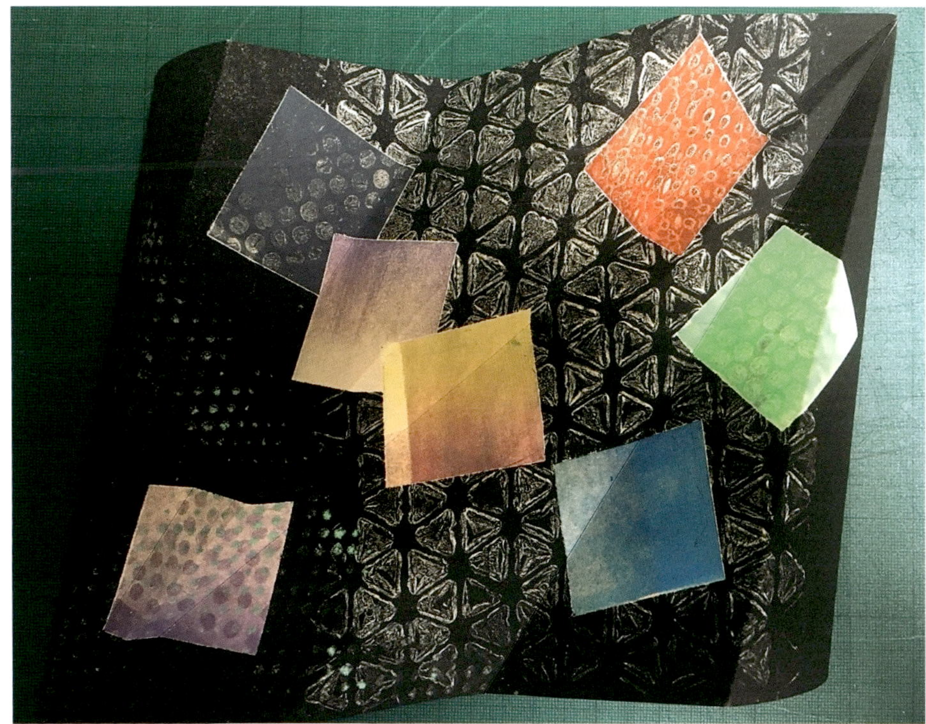

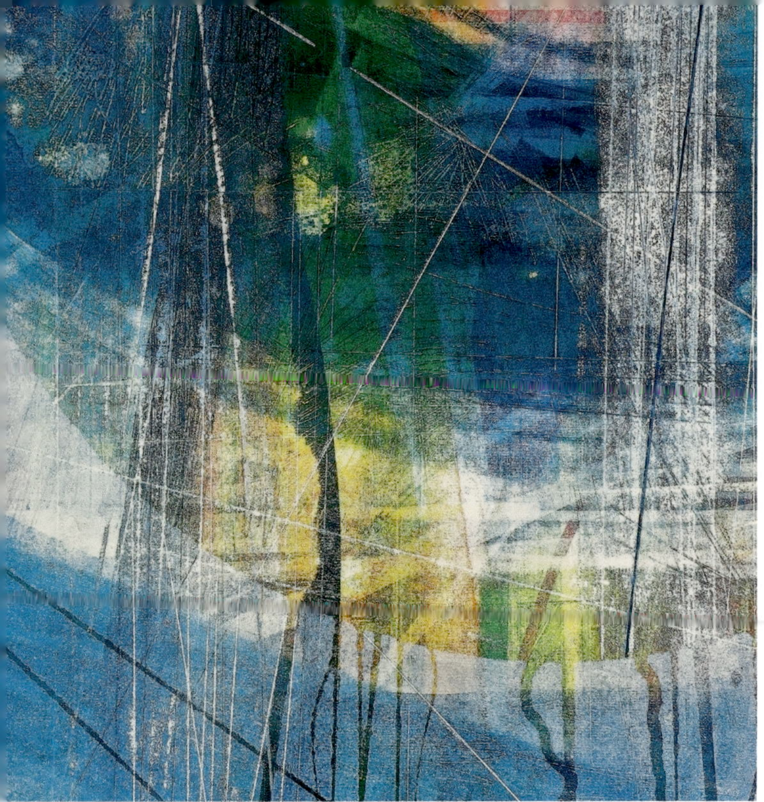

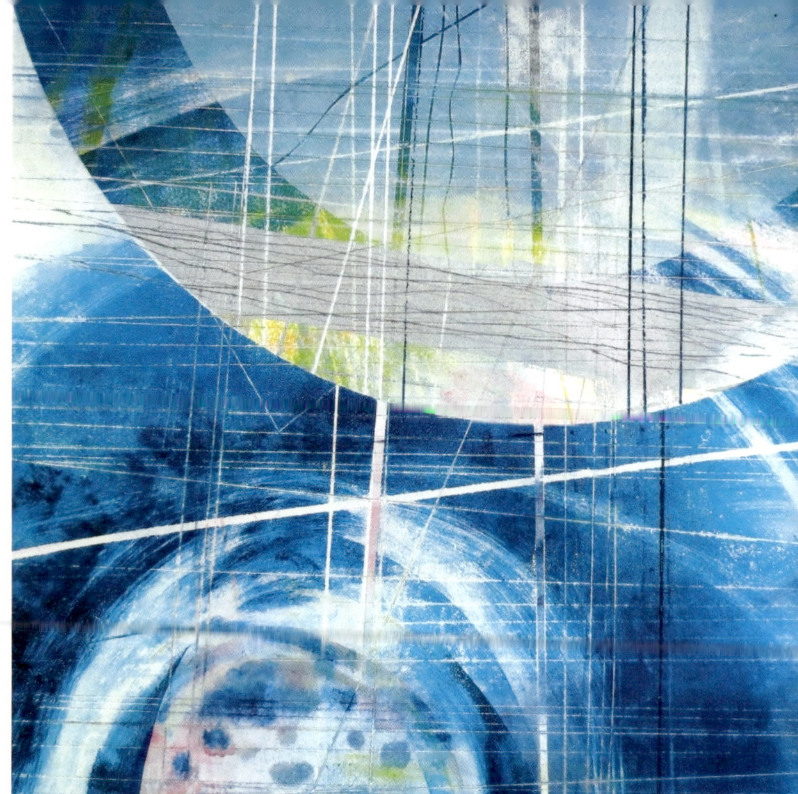

SUE JONES

Sue Jones is an artist, printmaker, tutor, co-founder of the Cambridge Original Printmakers Biennale, and passionate about print! Her abstract prints draw on the landscape, environment, chaos and control. "They are visual diaries documenting personal journeys, balancing the contrast of the manmade and organic, the painterly mark to the structured line," she says. "These are infused with a sense of mystery, drama, colour and space to create new, unseen emotional landscapes." Her monotypes are constructed of multiple layers and varying printmaking techniques, over long periods, "like a painting through print". Currently, Sue is working with monotypes, and developing her wood engraving skills.

She teaches printmaking workshops at the ACE Foundation, Stapleford Granary; Gainsborough's House, Sudbury; and is an Artist Facilitator with Kettle's Yard, Cambridge University. At Stoneman Press, her own studio at Wimbish, Saffron Walden, she delivers a variety of printmaking workshops. Sue has taught at The British

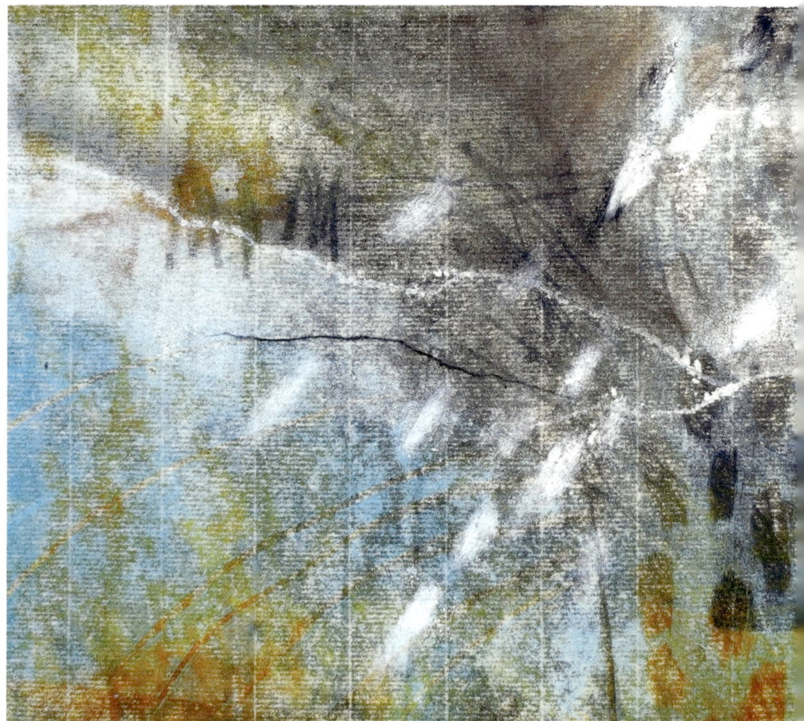

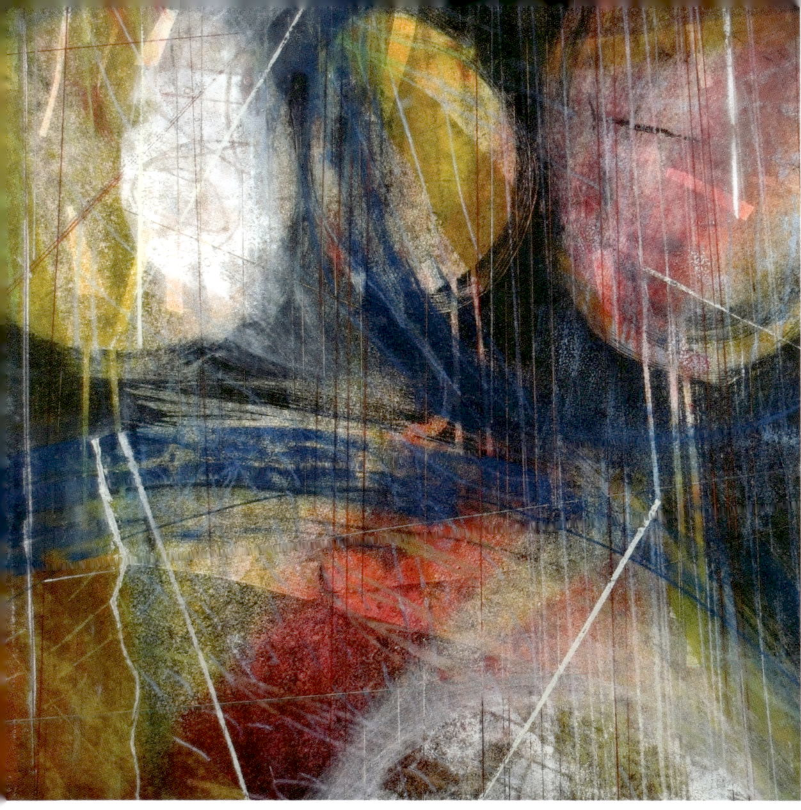

Top row, from left: 'Moon Dance I'; 'Moon Dance V'; 'Moon Dance VII' (all monotype, 45cm x 45cm, unique); Bottom row, from left: 'Softer Lines II' (monotype), 26cm x 18cm, unique; 'Lunar Moth' (photopolymer with chine-collé), 24cm x 24cm, edition of 5; 'Elements I' (lithograph), 24cm x 24cm, edition of 5

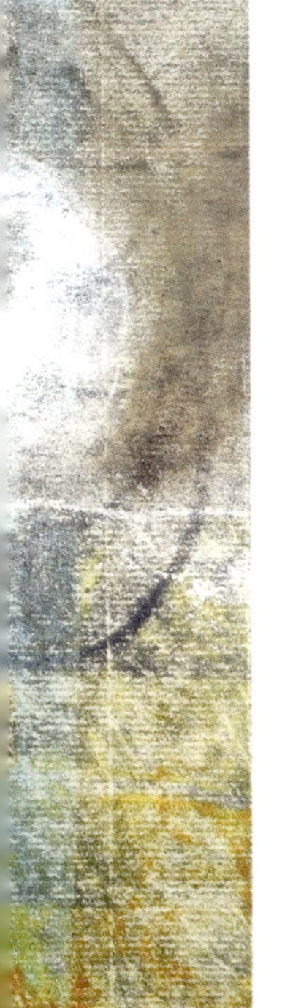

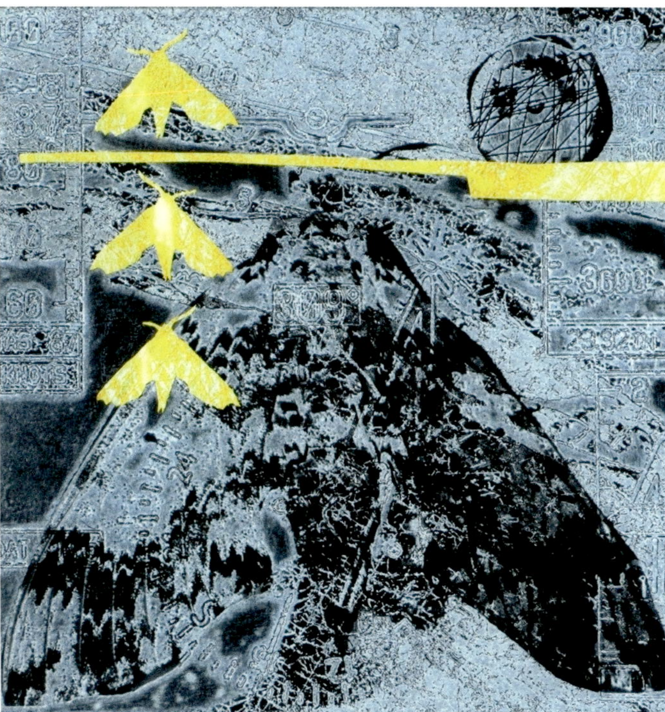

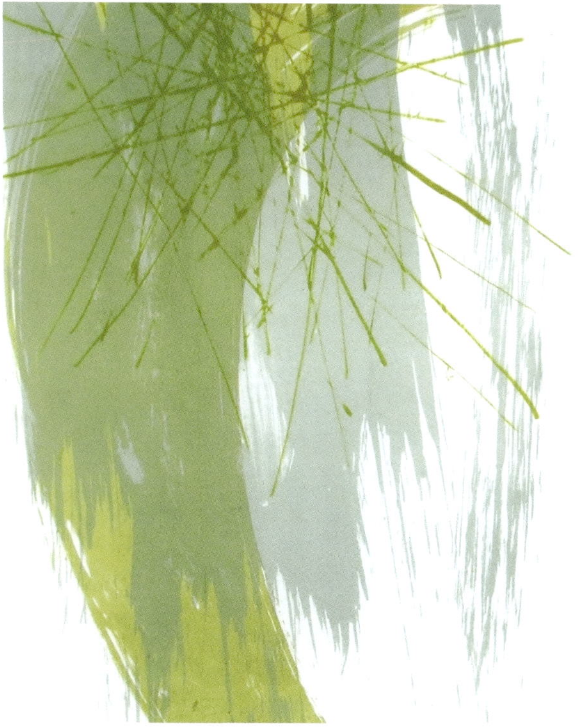

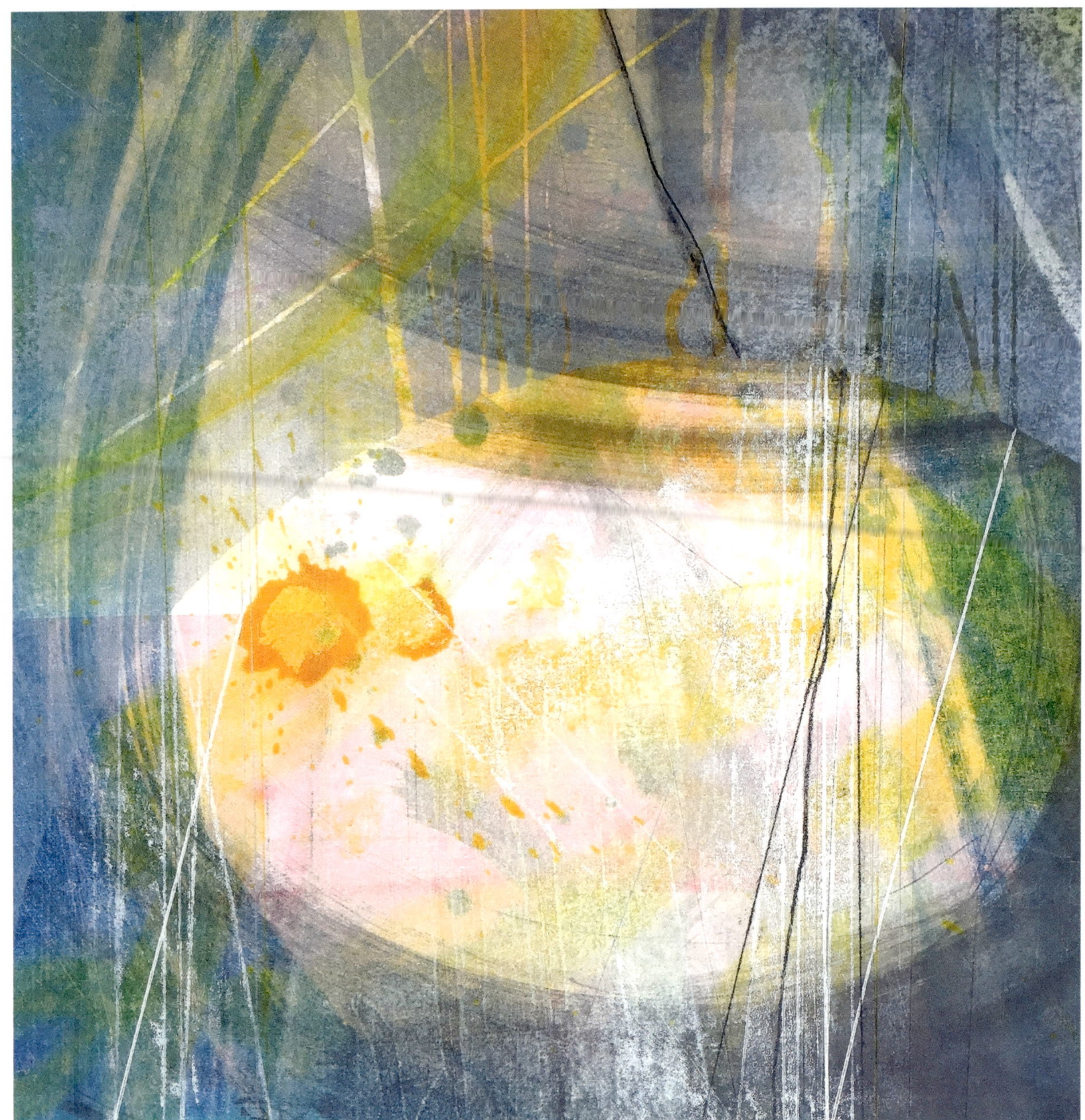

Museum, Blenheim Palace, the Fitzwilliam Museum, Museum of Anthropology and Archaeology, Museum of Zoology, and Kettle's Yard; and has 17 years' experience as Lead Tutor and Studio Manager at the Curwen Print Study Centre.

She exhibits with Church Street Gallery in Saffron Walden, and with Cambridge Contemporary Art. *www.printsuejones.com*

Above: 'Moon Dance II' (monotype), 45cm x 45cm, unique

THOMAS LEMON

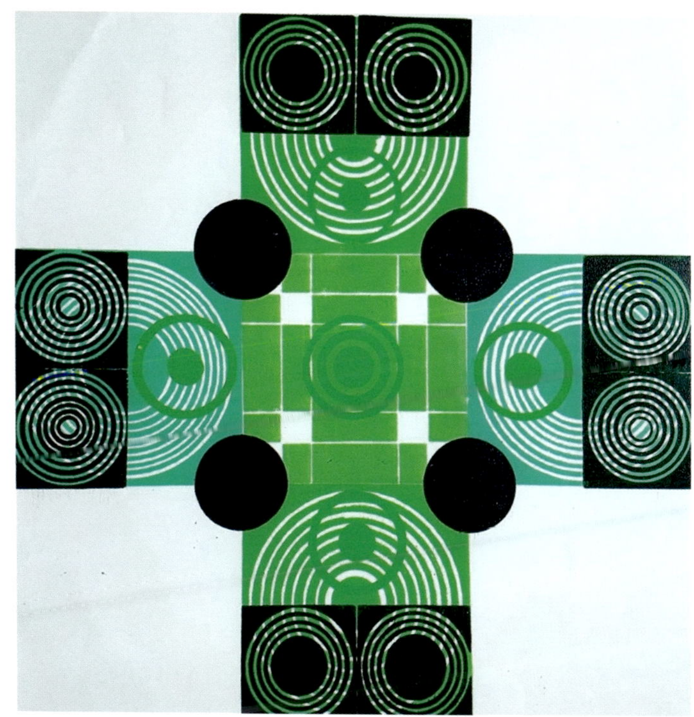

Thomas Lemon developed his method of block printing during his degree, when he experimented with various techniques before settling on a refined woodblock method.

"Victor Vasarely and his Alphabet Plastique work was a big inspiration to me because of his use of formulae and methodical compositions. I also draw inspiration from Wassily Kandinsky and Hélio Oiticica with regard to their abstract compositions and bold use of colour."

Thomas describes his prints as an "exploration of colour, shape, design and precision". He uses oil- and water-based inks, paper, his woodblocks and a handmade jig. "This method affords me endless possibilities of composition and

All prints untitled, 18" x 18" (woodblocks), each unique

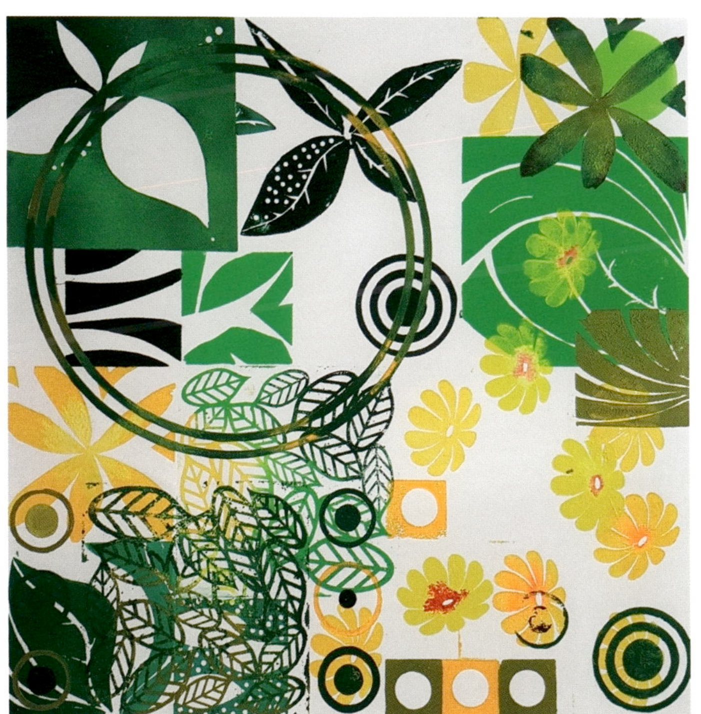

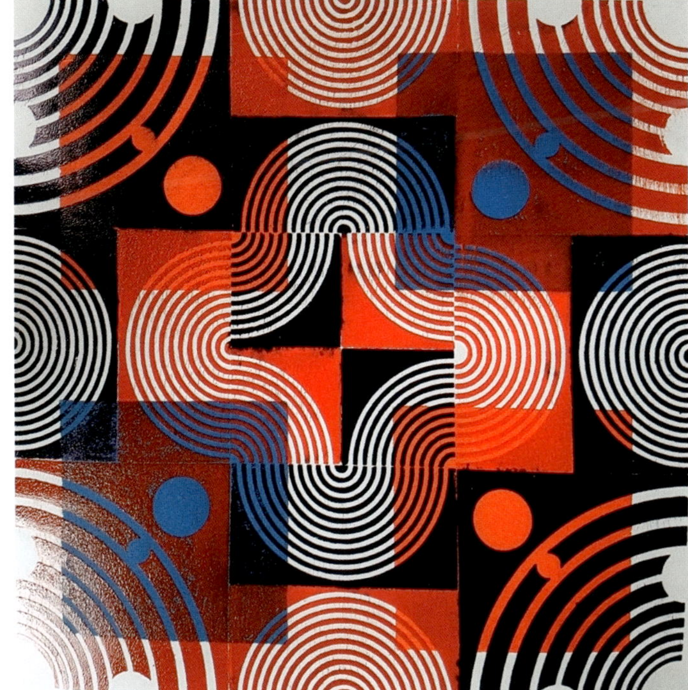

colour combinations by reconfiguring the blocks in the jig. By carving out motifs and patterns into individual woodblocks, I build up layers of contrasting colour and shapes to deliver a powerful visual experience."

He often uses geometric and concentric repeating patterns, as well as more traditional shapes such as circles and squares, to focus on the structure and colour theory within each series. "By overlaying blocks, designs and pigments, I create pieces that I hope surprise, intrigue and enthral."

www.thomaslemonart.com

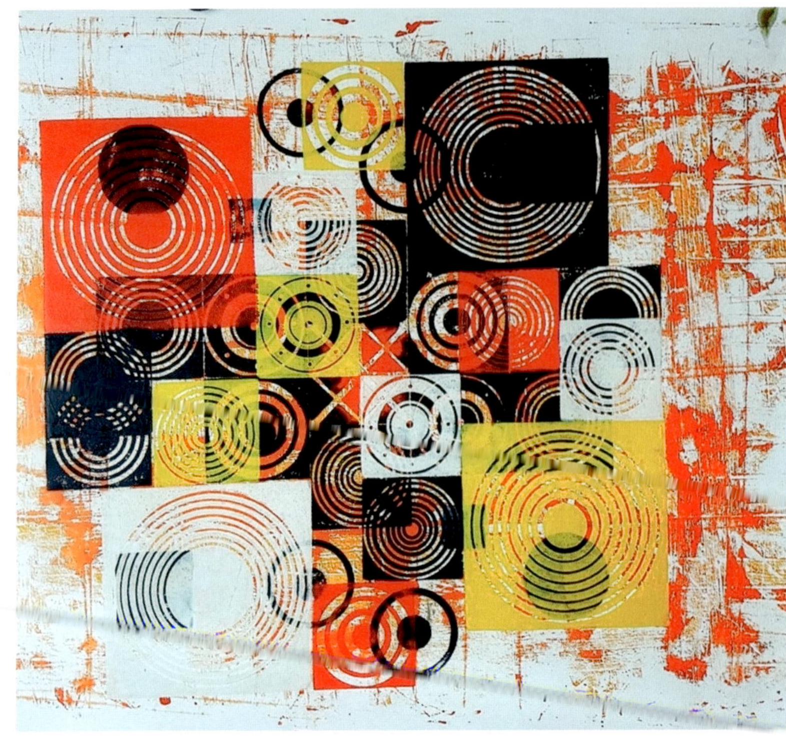

All prints untitled, 18" x 18" (woodblocks), each unique

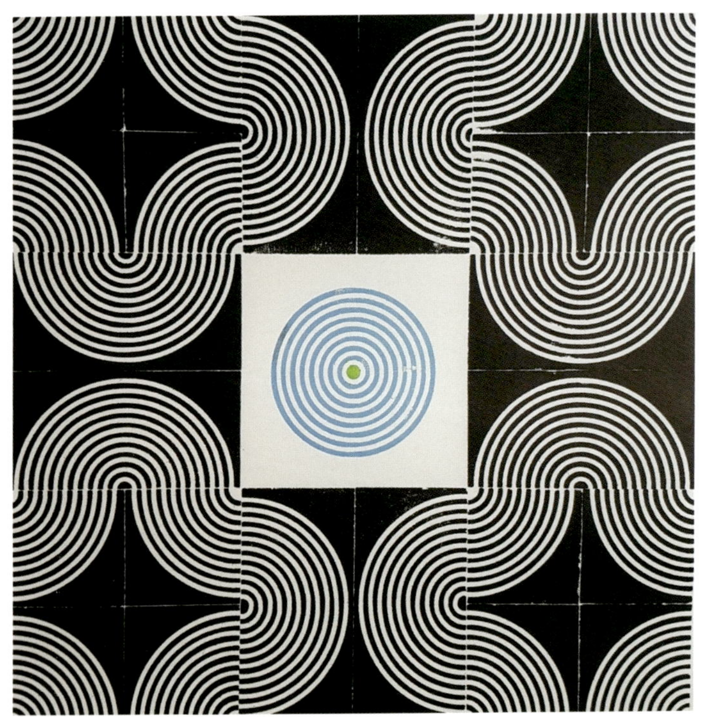

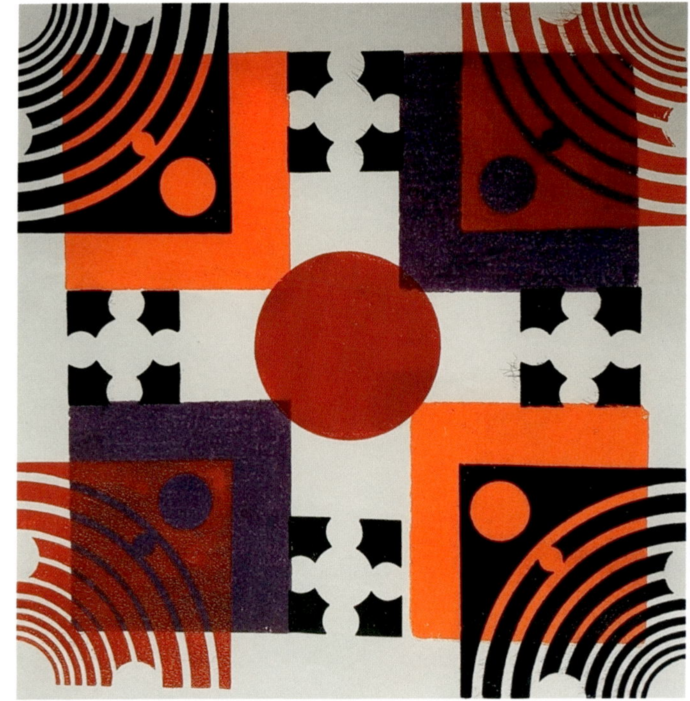

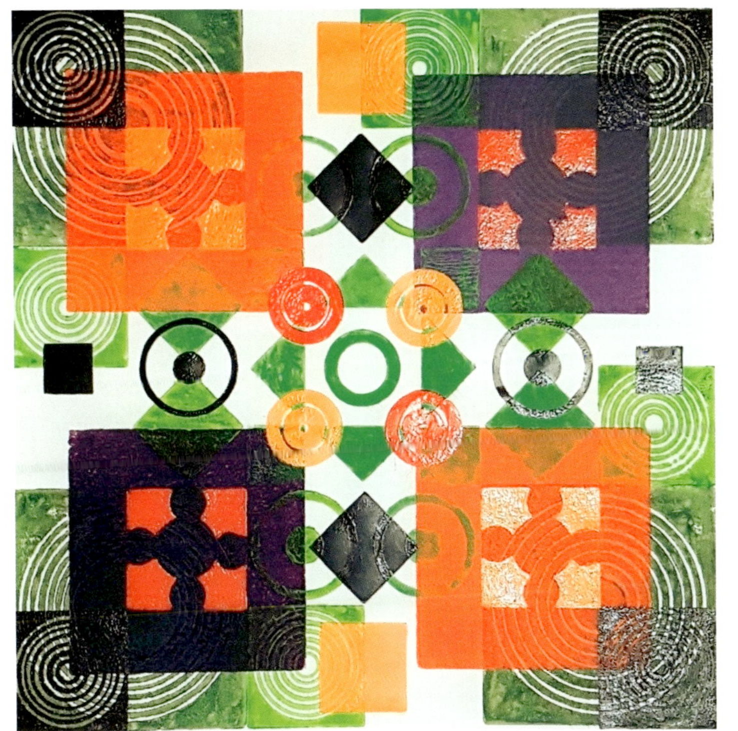

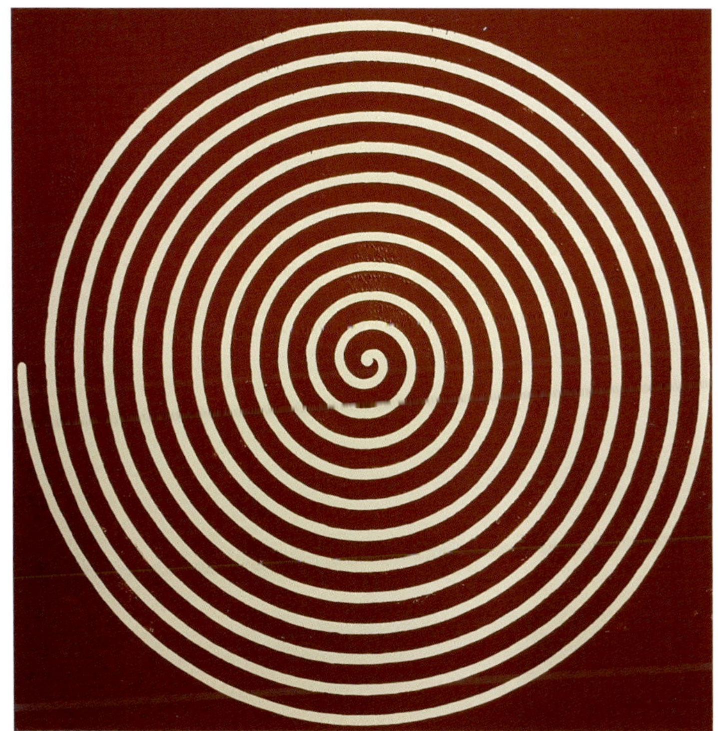

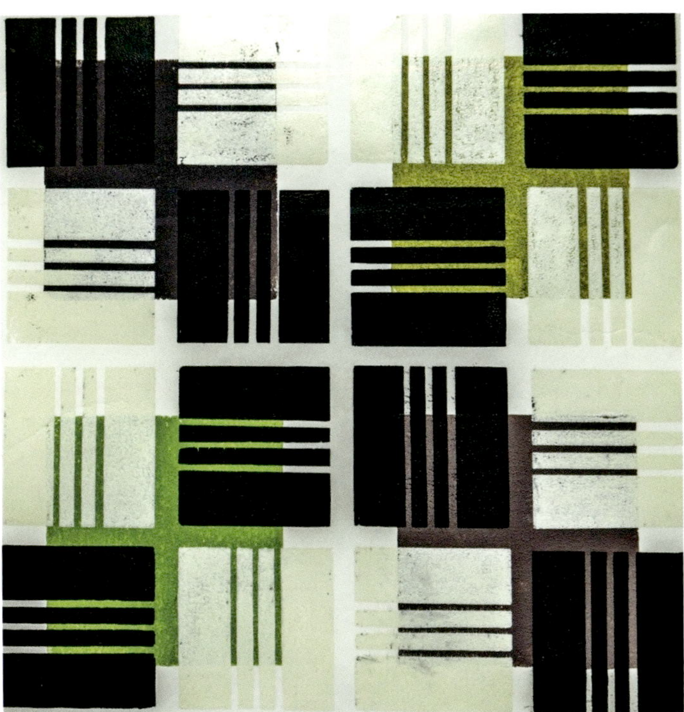

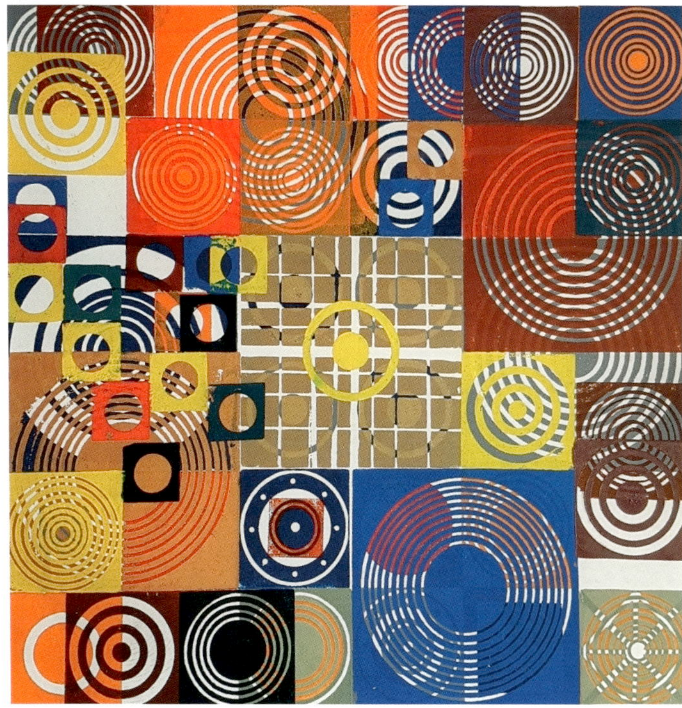

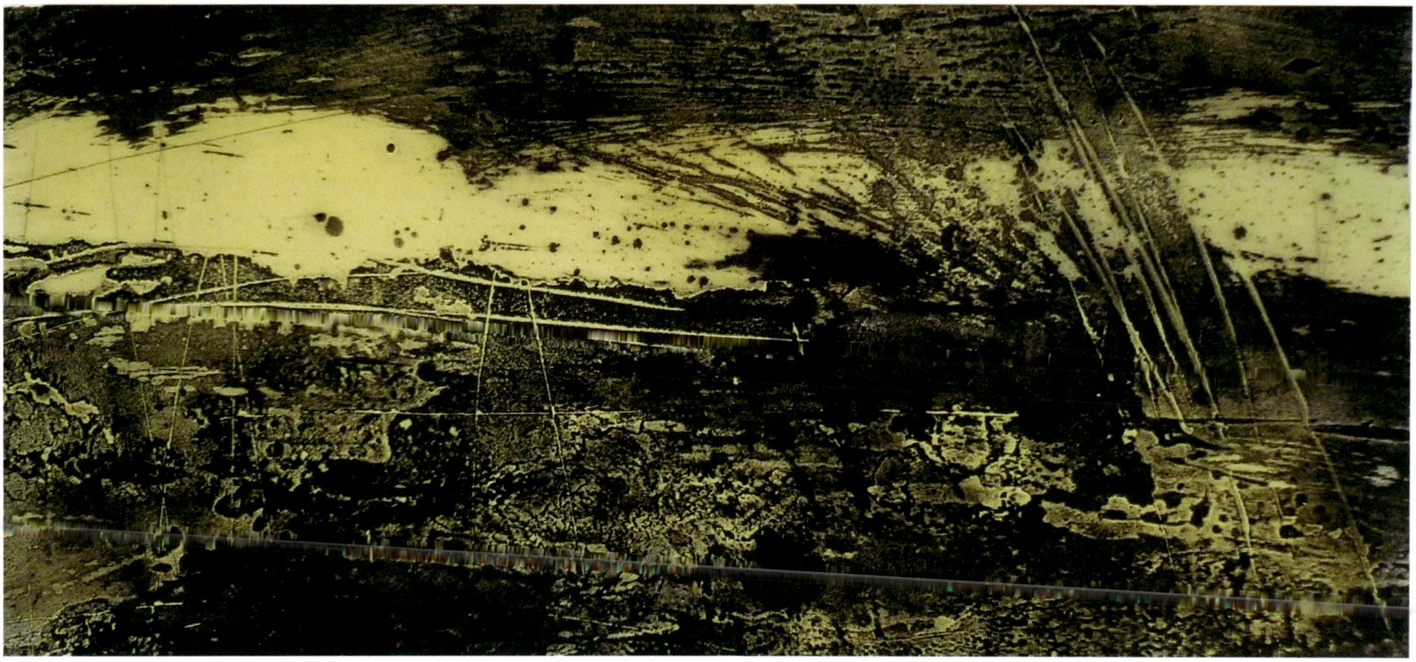

ROSS LOVEDAY

Printmaker, painter and sculptor Ross Loveday aims to convey "an atmosphere – the essence of the place" in his work, irrespective of which medium he is using. "I want to capture the mood and light of a particular moment, rather than its topography. The subjects are only the starting points; sometimes a

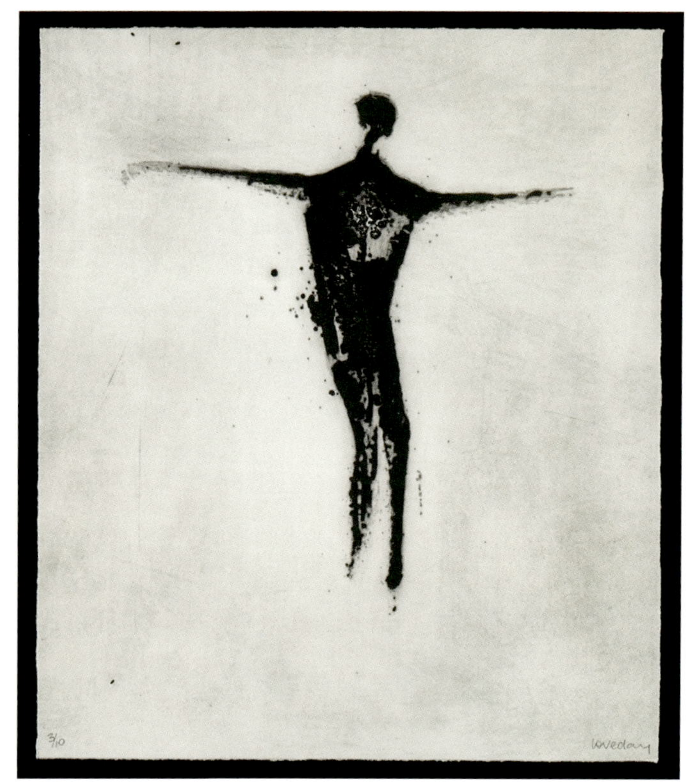

This page, from top: 'Storm on the Marshes', 34cm x 72cm, edition of 10; Untitled, 52cm x 46cm, edition of 10; Facing page: 'Prologue', 53cm x 52cm, edition of 5 – all drypoint and carborundum

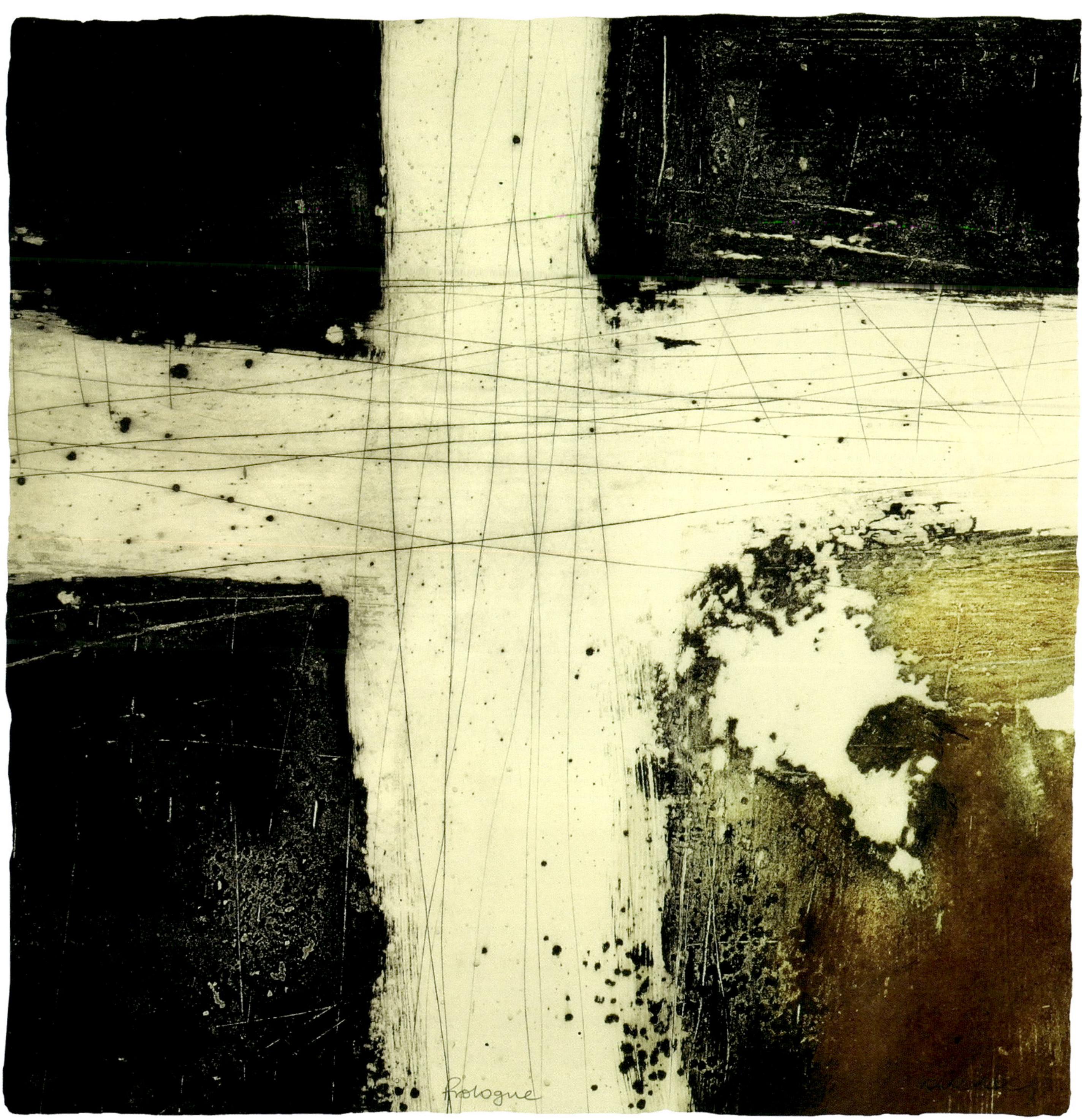

small, insignificant detail or texture – a thorn bush by a path, or twigs poking through the snow, can trigger a new work."

Ross prints all his own work in small editions using the drypoint and carborundum technique, "which gives the painterly quality that I like. Chance and accident in my work are embraced and enjoyed. I don't draw much or plan anything out, and when I start a work I am never quite sure where it will take me."

Although his prints are inspired mainly by landscape, his emphasis is on abstraction and texture. "I use natural earth colours to suggest the unique feel of a place, to capture a fleeting moment."

Ross exhibits with Eames Fine Art in Bermondsey, London, and at the Bircham Gallery in Holt, Norfolk. *www.rossloveday.com*

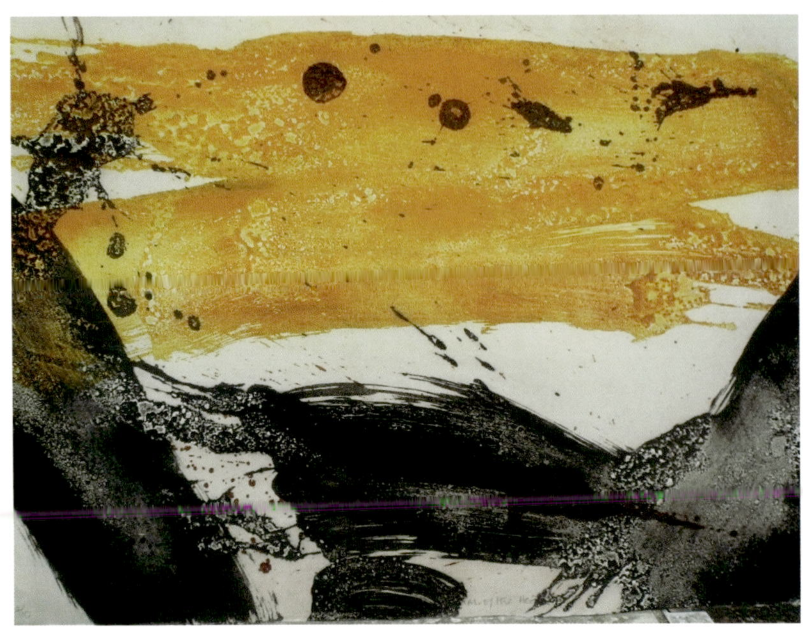

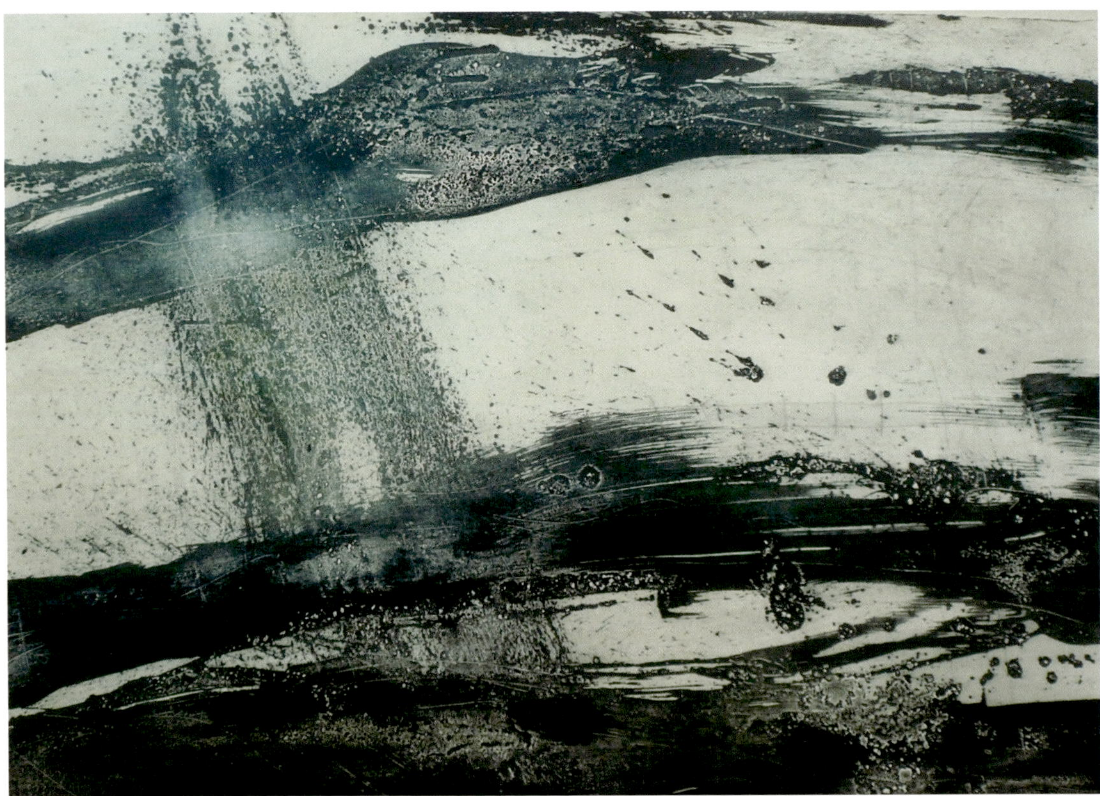

From top: 'Rhythm of the Heat', 56cm x 76cm, edition of 10; 'Ebb and Flow', 76cm x 111cm cropped, edition of 3 – both drypoint and carborundum

KIM MAJOR-GEORGE

Kim Major-George stumbled into printmaking while she was an illustrator, and was captivated by the vast array of raw mark-making that collagraph printing can produce. "I still find it exciting to explore unusual combinations of materials, breaking them down with heat, mixing up the ordinary and extraordinary to create unusual plates and prints," she says.

Her strong, contemporary images – often with an illusionary, even other-worldly, look – come from her interests in ancient civilisations, their philosophies, poetry and the role of man on the planet. Many of her collagraphs have contemporary connected poems by the poet Steve Thorp, creating thought-provoking touring exhibitions.

Kim teaches collagraph from her studio, and says that her students "seem to be attracted to the images and know I break the rules, mixing many different materials, techniques, diverse ways of loading inks and presenting the finished image. This maverick method of working has also kept me interested in this fascinating field, and is reflected in *Collagraph: A Journey Through Texture* and *All Cracked Up*, the technical printing books I have written along the way."
www.majorgeorge.co.uk

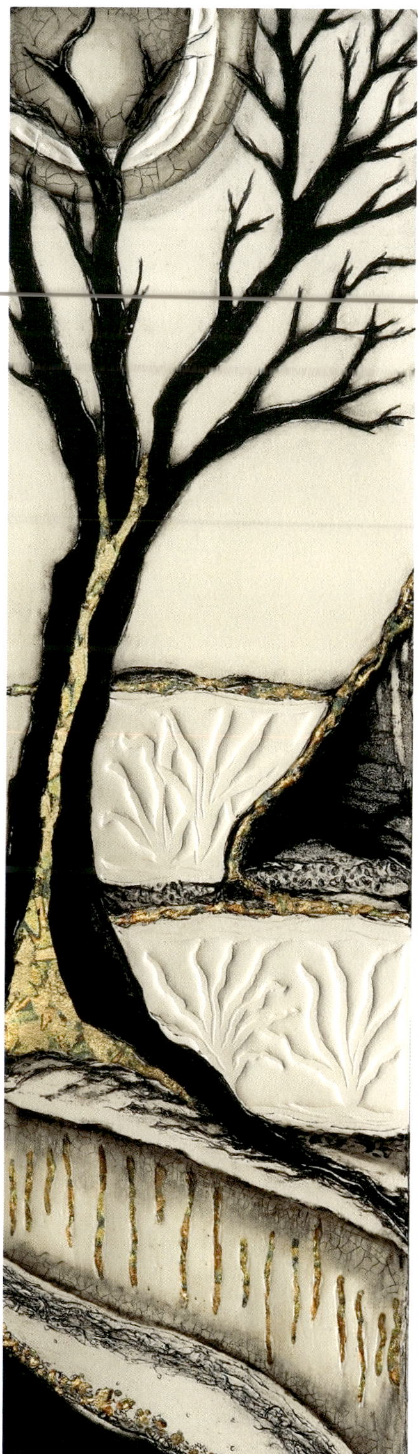

Right: 'Ancient Whispers' (collagraph), 24cm x 80cm, edition of 10; Far right: 'Whispering Trails' (collagraph), 24cm x 80cm, edition of 10

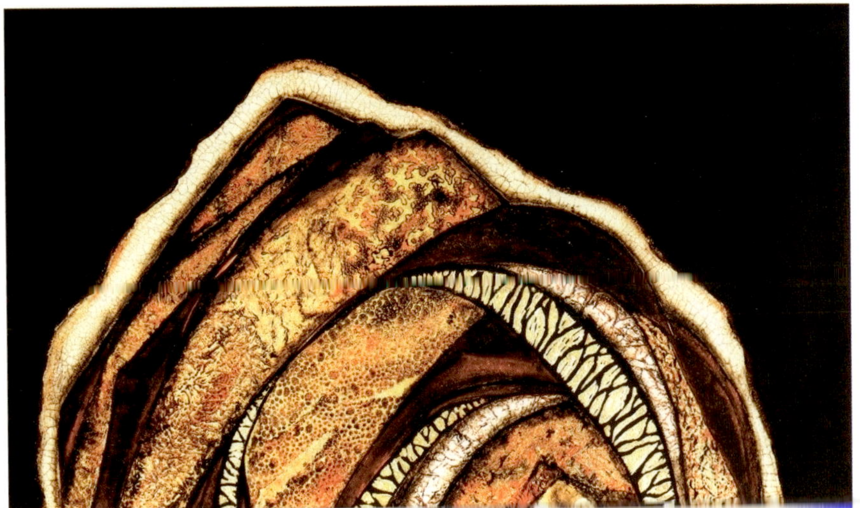

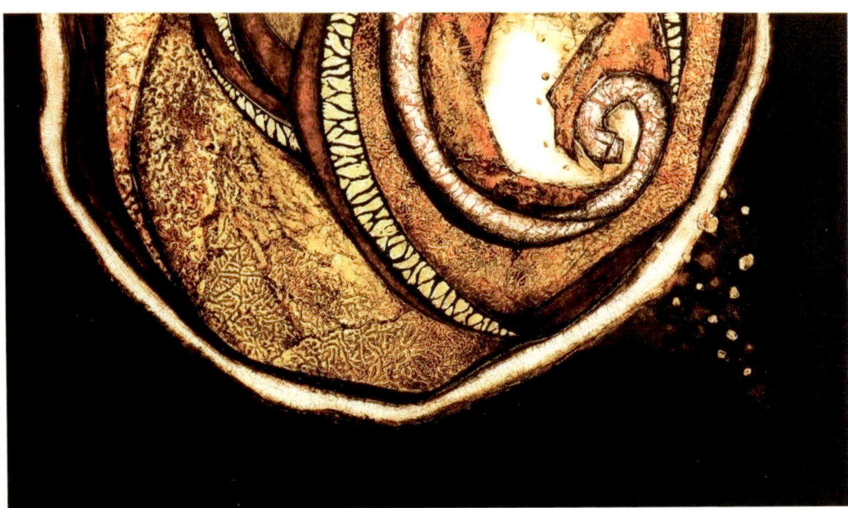

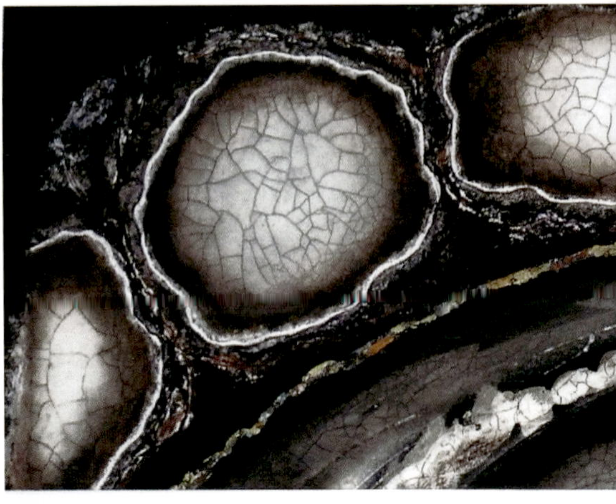

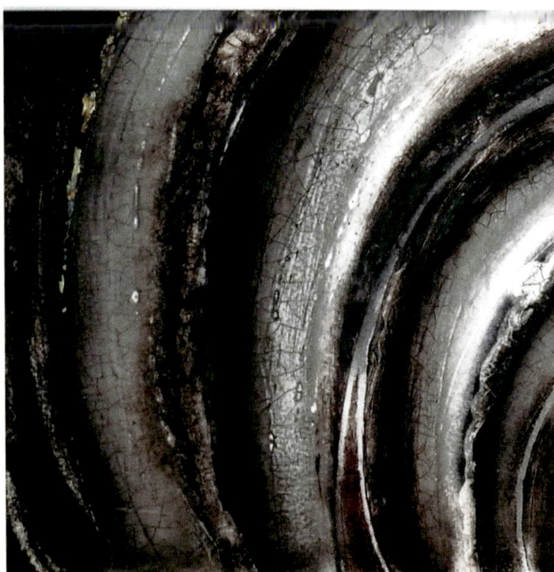

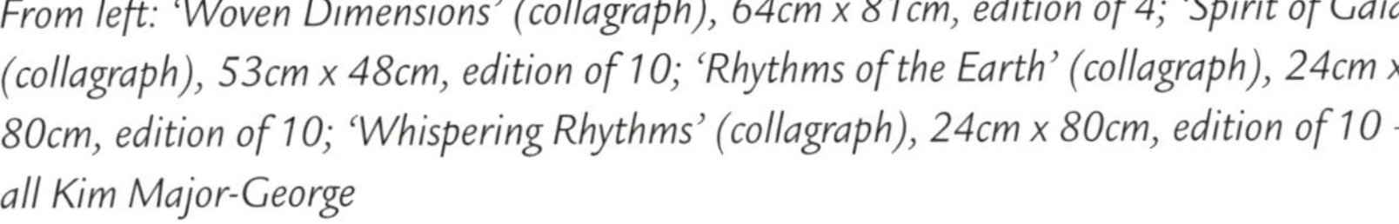

From left: 'Woven Dimensions' (collagraph), 64cm x 81cm, edition of 4; 'Spirit of Gaia' (collagraph), 53cm x 48cm, edition of 10; 'Rhythms of the Earth' (collagraph), 24cm x 80cm, edition of 10; 'Whispering Rhythms' (collagraph), 24cm x 80cm, edition of 10 – all Kim Major-George

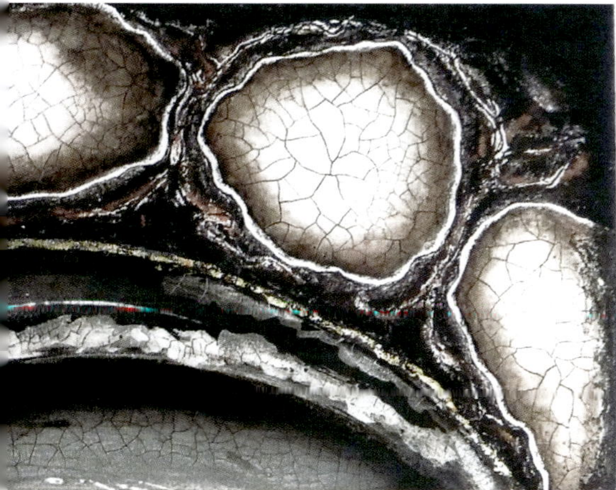

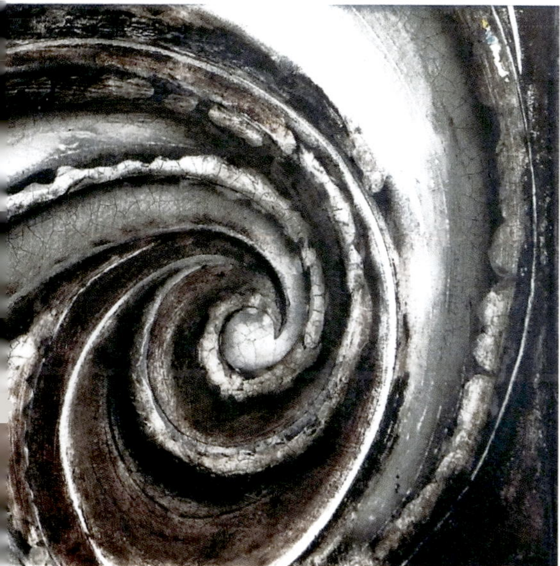

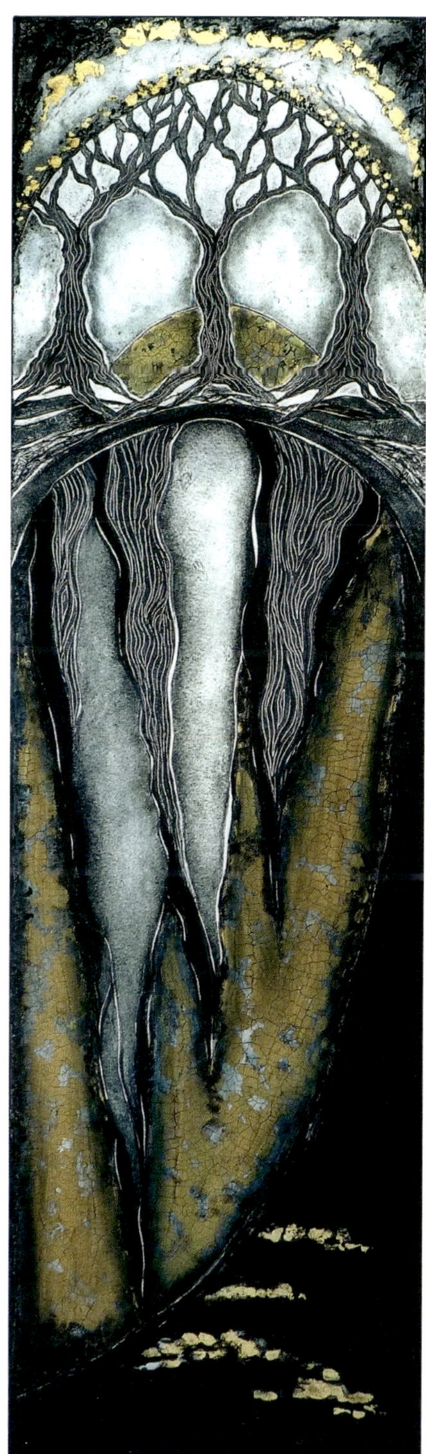

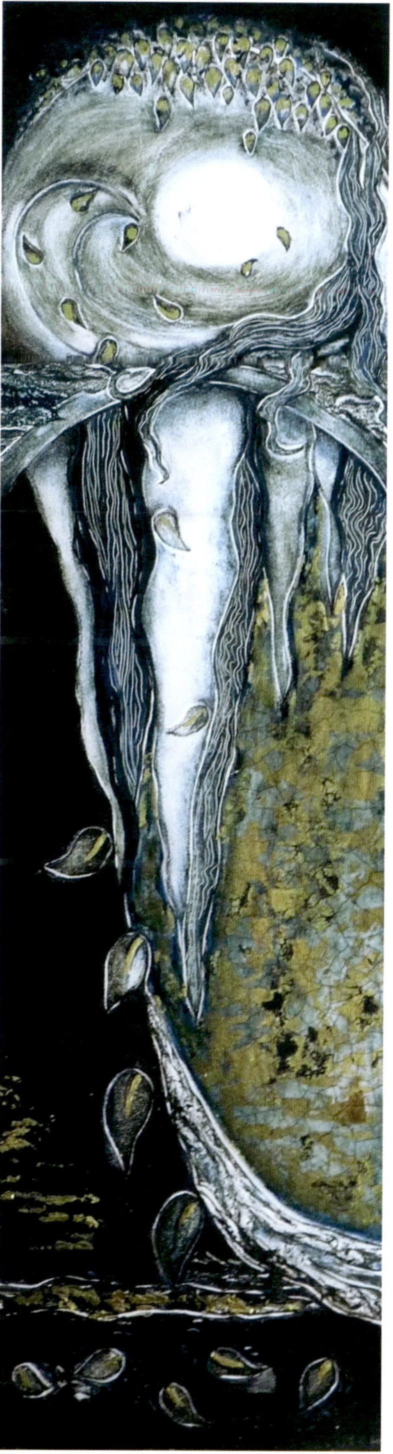

ANDY McKENZIE

Andy McKenzie gains inspiration from observing everyday objects and things that surround him, often pre-loved or discarded technology. "I acknowledge my respect for contemporary and mid-century artists and designers whose work informs my creativity," he says. "I also have an imagined life for my bird creations."

He draws, sketches, doodles or creates monoprints before interpreting ideas into the printmaking process. "I really enjoy the process itself, and like to experiment with colour and scale. I am aware of the inherent marks or 'mistakes' created, and consider whether they enhance the image before producing samples for my limited-edition hand-pulled screenprints. Sometimes I add watercolour for a softer effect, recycled paper collage for texture or reconsider

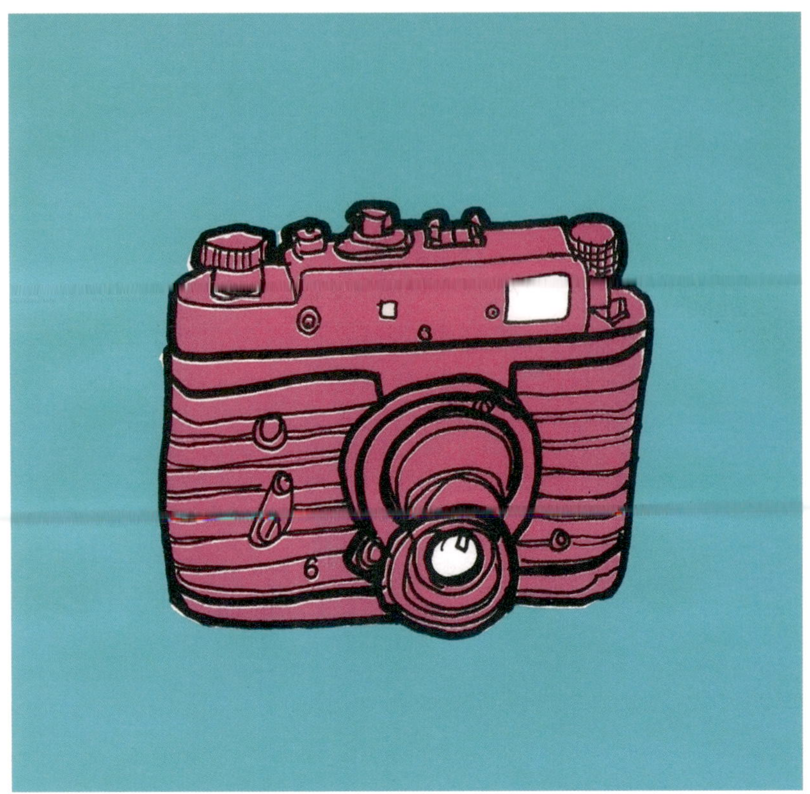

Top row, from left: 'Pink Z' (screenprint), 19cm x 21cm, edition of 12; 'City Bright Spot' (screenprint), 15cm x 23cm, edition of 15; 'Puffin Green' (screenprint), 15cm x 24cm, edition of 10; 'Blue Penguin' (screenprint with watercolour), 15cm x 24cm, edition of 10; Bottom row, from left: 'Rouge Radio' (screenprint), 16cm x 16cm, edition of 14; 'The Pink' (screenprint), 18cm x 18cm, edition of 9

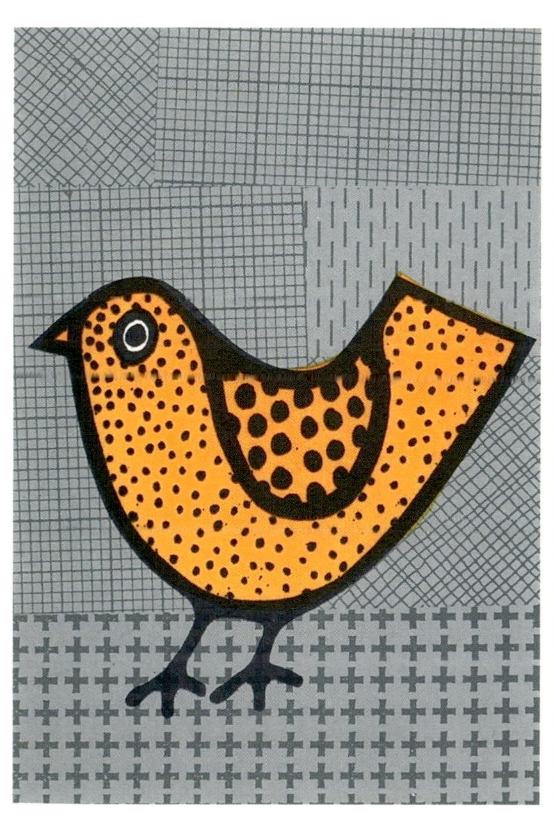
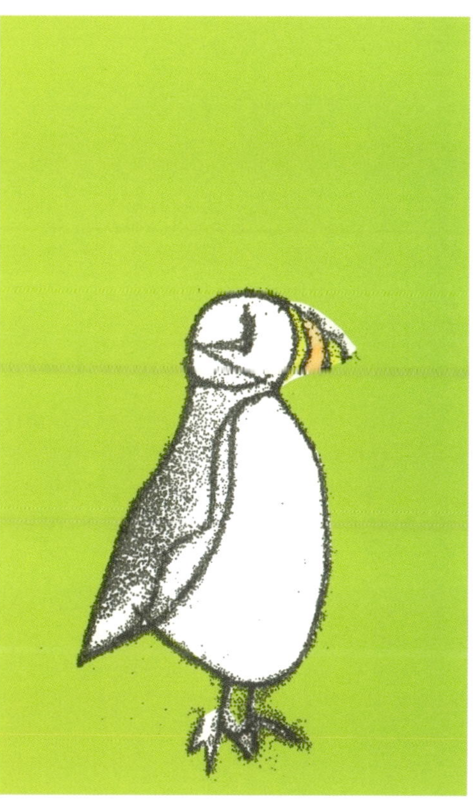
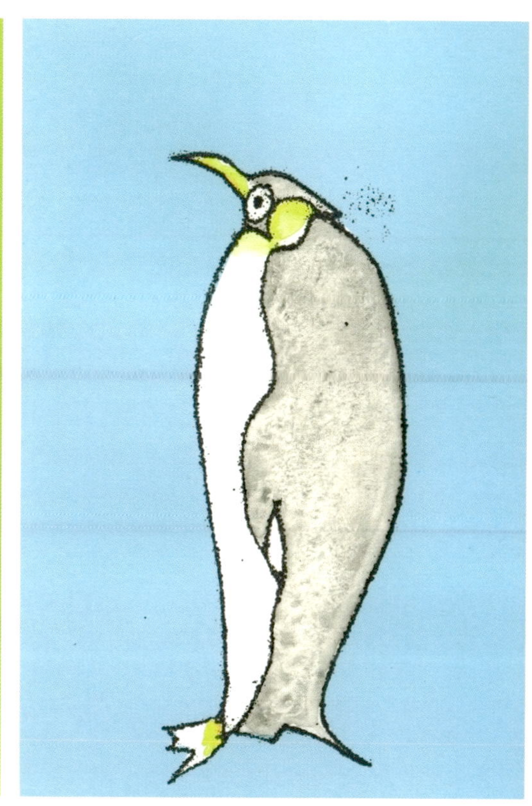
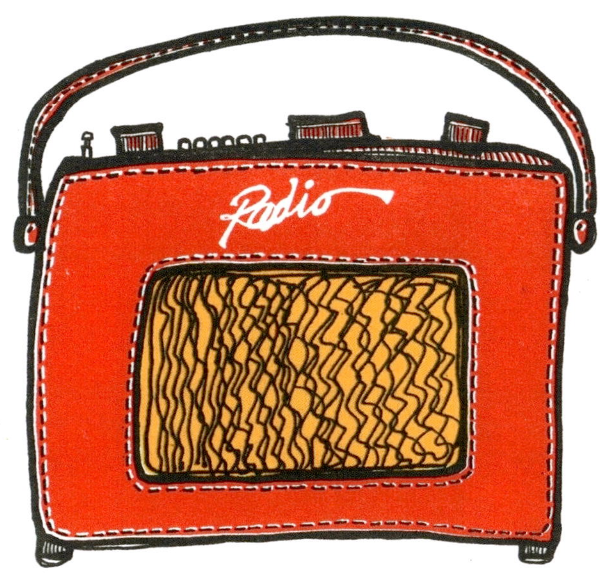
Radio
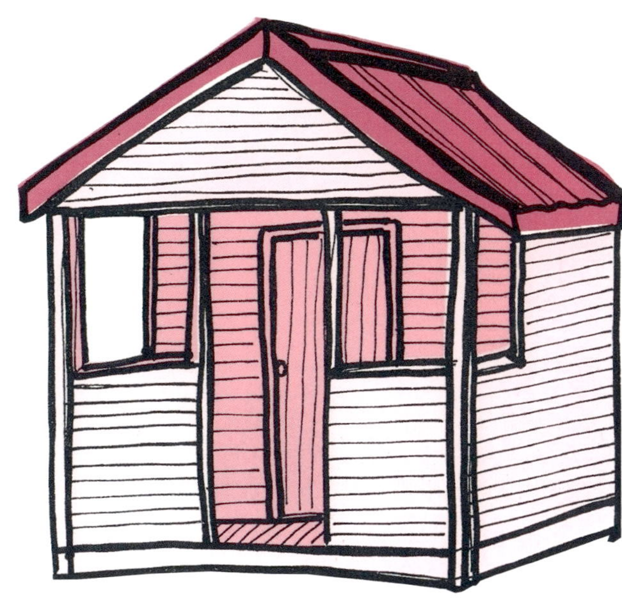

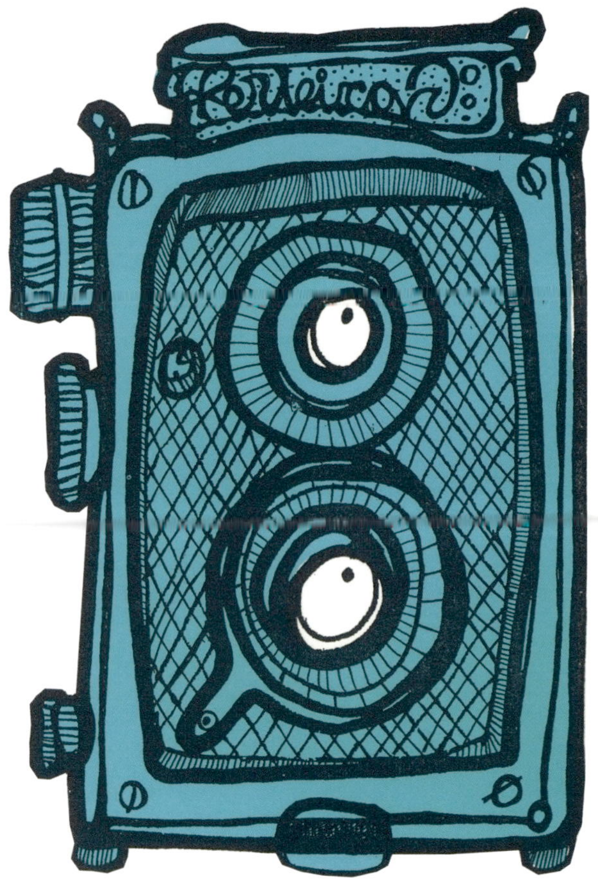

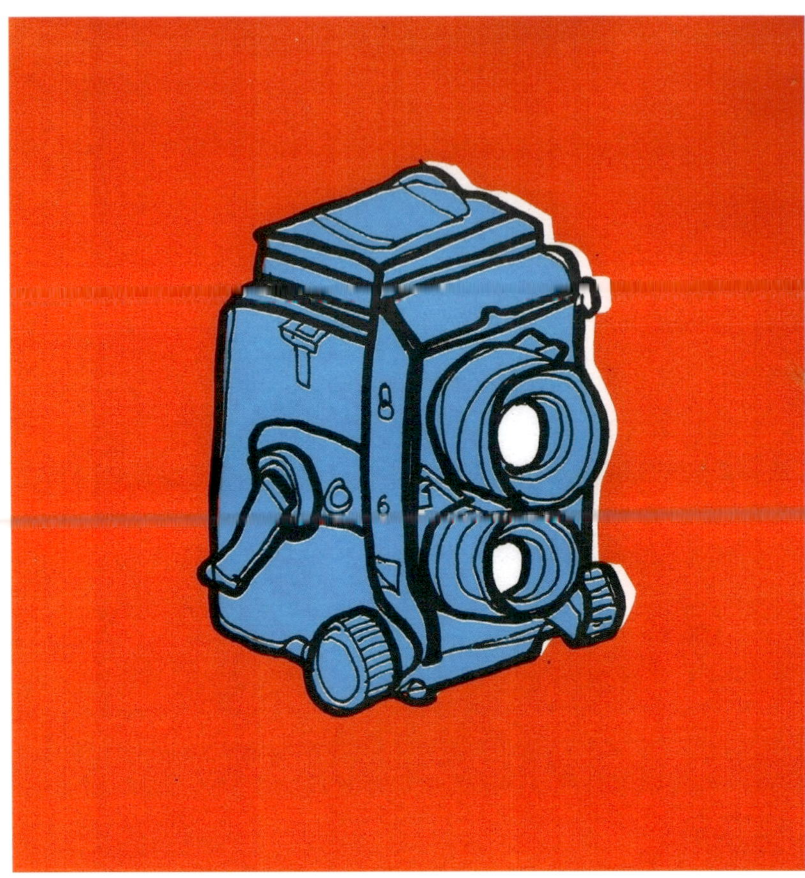

previous work to offer a new perspective."

Andy has taught printmaking for a number of years to FE students, teenagers and adults. He has a BA Honours degree in Two Dimensional Design from the University of Hertfordshire, and an MA in Fine Art Printmaking from the Cambridge School of Art at Anglia Ruskin University.

He exhibits regularly around Cambridge in Open Studios and with the Cambridge Drawing Society, and shows in selected galleries in the UK and at International AAF Art Fairs.
www.andymckenzieprint.uk

Above, from left: 'Blue Cord' (screenprint), 15cm x 22cm, edition of 8; 'Ortucam' (screenprint), 20cm x 21cm, edition of 11

SUSAN MEALING

Printmaker Susan Mealing works in both 2D and 3D, using a combination of traditional printmaking techniques such as etching, screenprinting and collagraph as well as contemporary giclée digital printing. Her work incorporates various materials, including glass, plaster and textiles.

"My main interest lies with the flawed; my work embraces imperfection and impermanence. The wabi-sabi belief that nothing lasts, nothing is finished and nothing is perfect is fundamental to my philosophy and aesthetics. A strong component of these concerns draws me towards both entropy and the accidental, aspects integral to my approach and method of working."

The Flotsam series, which focuses on the plight of refugees and lost identity, is among her recent work.

Susan has a studio at Cambridge Artworks, and exhibits widely across the UK. She has also recently qualified as an Art Therapist, and is working with children and adolescents in Cambridge, Essex and Hertfordshire.
www.susanmealing.com

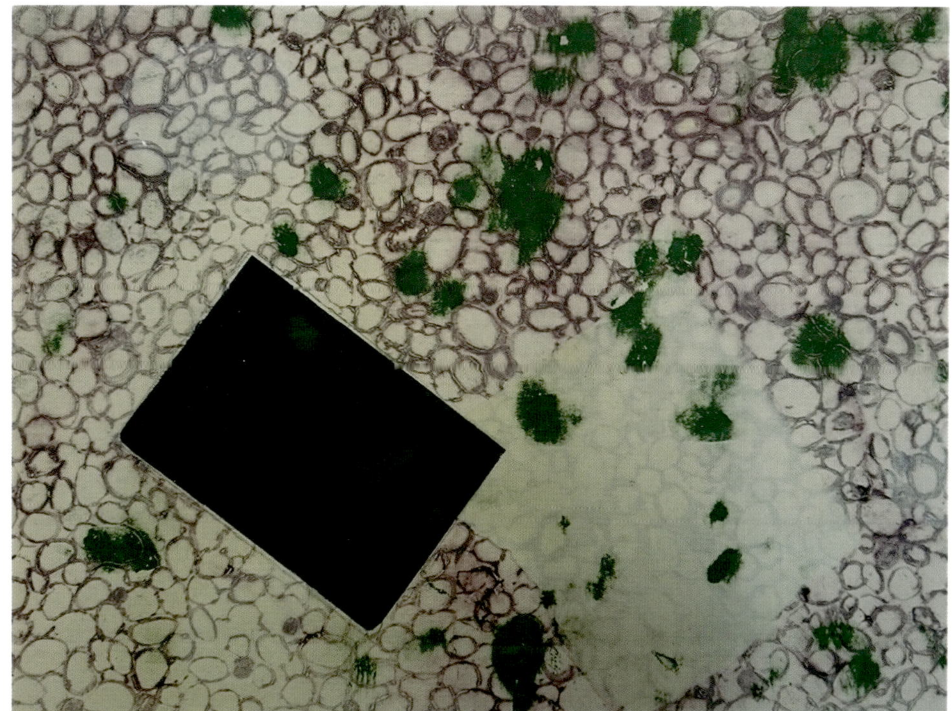

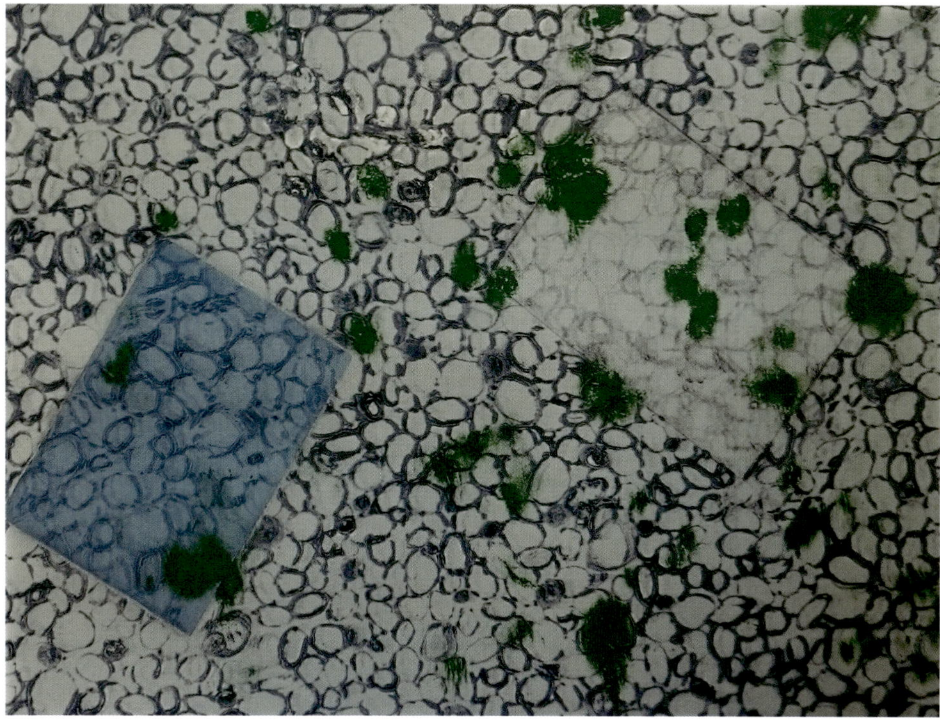

From top: 'Flotsam II' (collagraph, relief, chine-collé), 50cm x 40cm, unique; 'Flotsam III' (collagraph, relief, chine-collé), 50cm x 40cm, unique

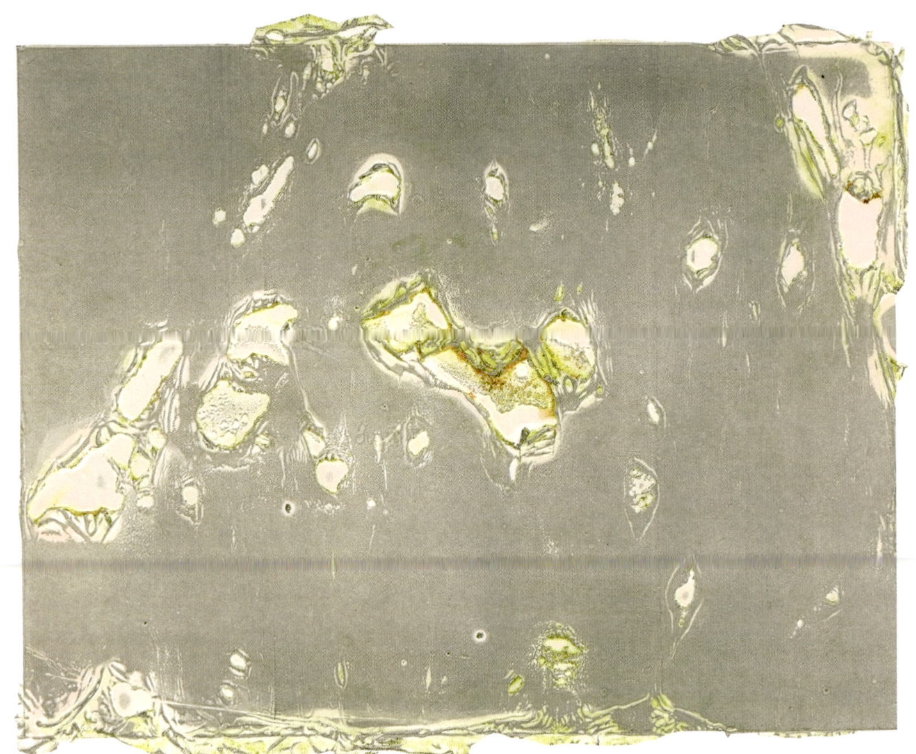

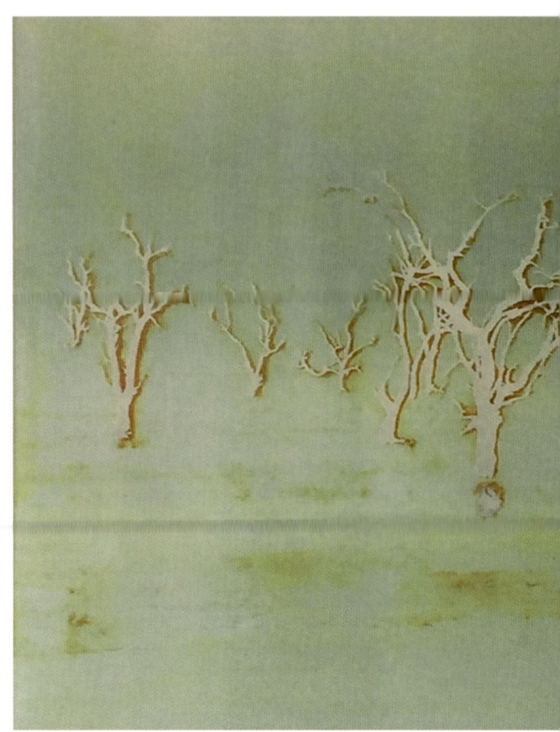

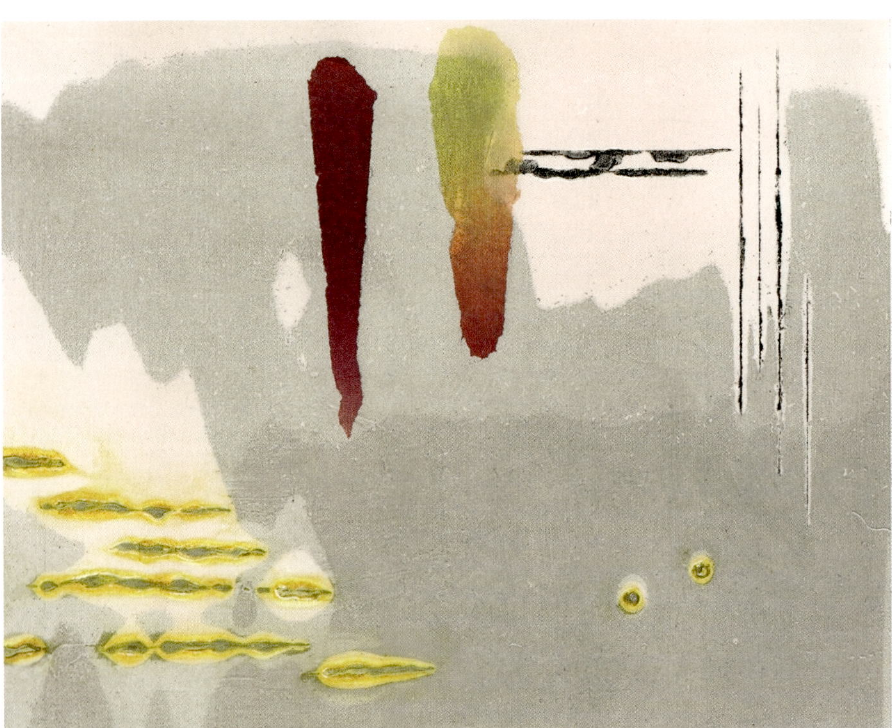

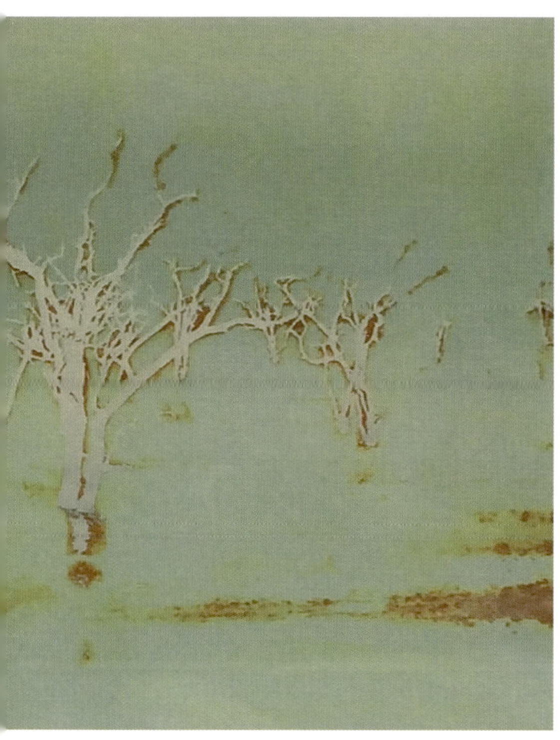

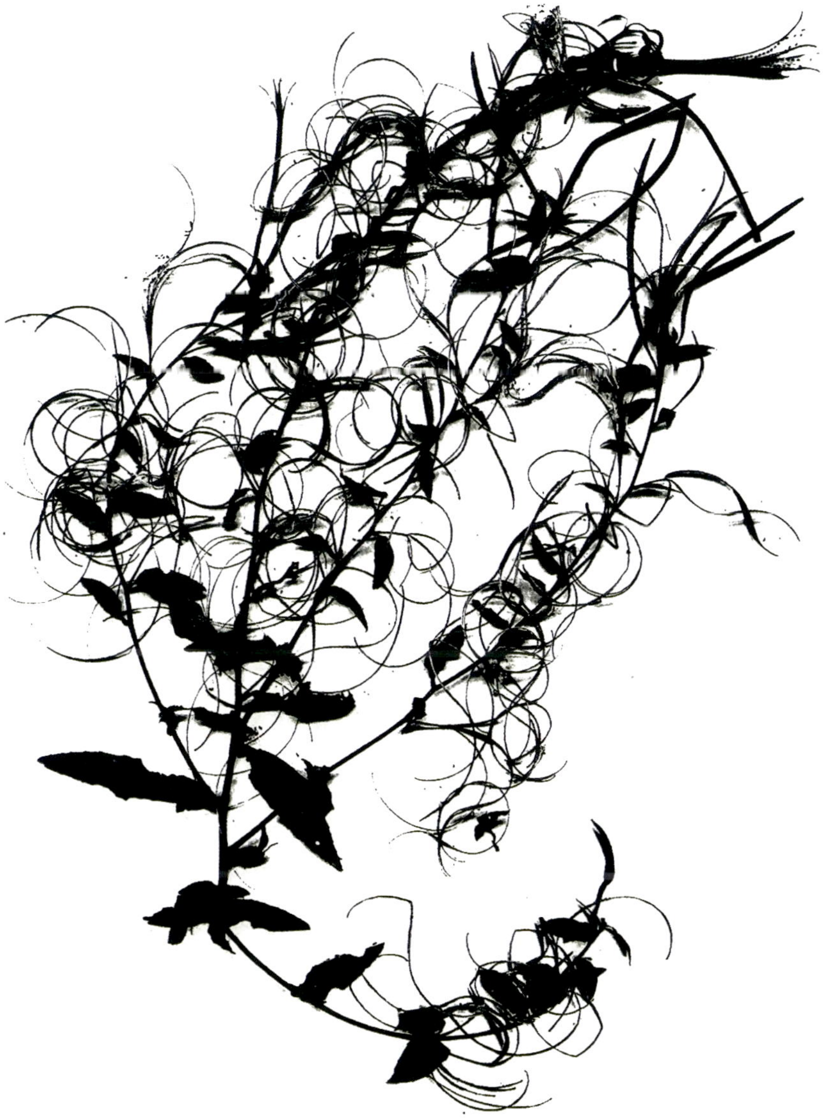

Top left: 'Varanasi II' (collagraph and chine-collé), 55cm x 48cm, unique; Top centre: 'Selous II' (collagraph and screenprint), 53cm x 38cm, unique; Bottom left: 'Varanasi IV' (collagraph), 55cm x 48cm, unique; Right: 'Rosebay' (screenprint), 50cm x 70cm, edition of 25 – all Susan Mealing

JILL OGILVY

Jill Ogilvy began her career as a natural history illustrator and children's book designer in the UK, and while living in France for several years she returned to her love of painting in the landscape. "The regimented rows of vines and vegetables were a source of inspiration as I filled my sketchbooks and canvases." Later, an MA in Authorial Illustration at Falmouth College of Art rekindled her interest in monoprint and monotype.

"I love the freedom of spontaneous mark-making; it encourages risk-taking, and over the years has enabled me to become much bolder in my interpretation of the subject – quite different to the meticulous botanicals I used to paint! Now, I find myself drawn back to the landscape and to the sea and coastline of my native Scotland. I also like to make images of 'tablescapes' using vases, containers and everyday objects."

Jill paints using mixed media, and likes to play with colour and pattern in her still-life work. In her encaustic paintings she incorporates drypoint and wax prints with her own hand-made stamps on Japanese paper. These are layered along with other collage materials. She also makes stencils and masks for her encaustics and monotypes, with each process informing the other.
www.jillogilvy.co.uk

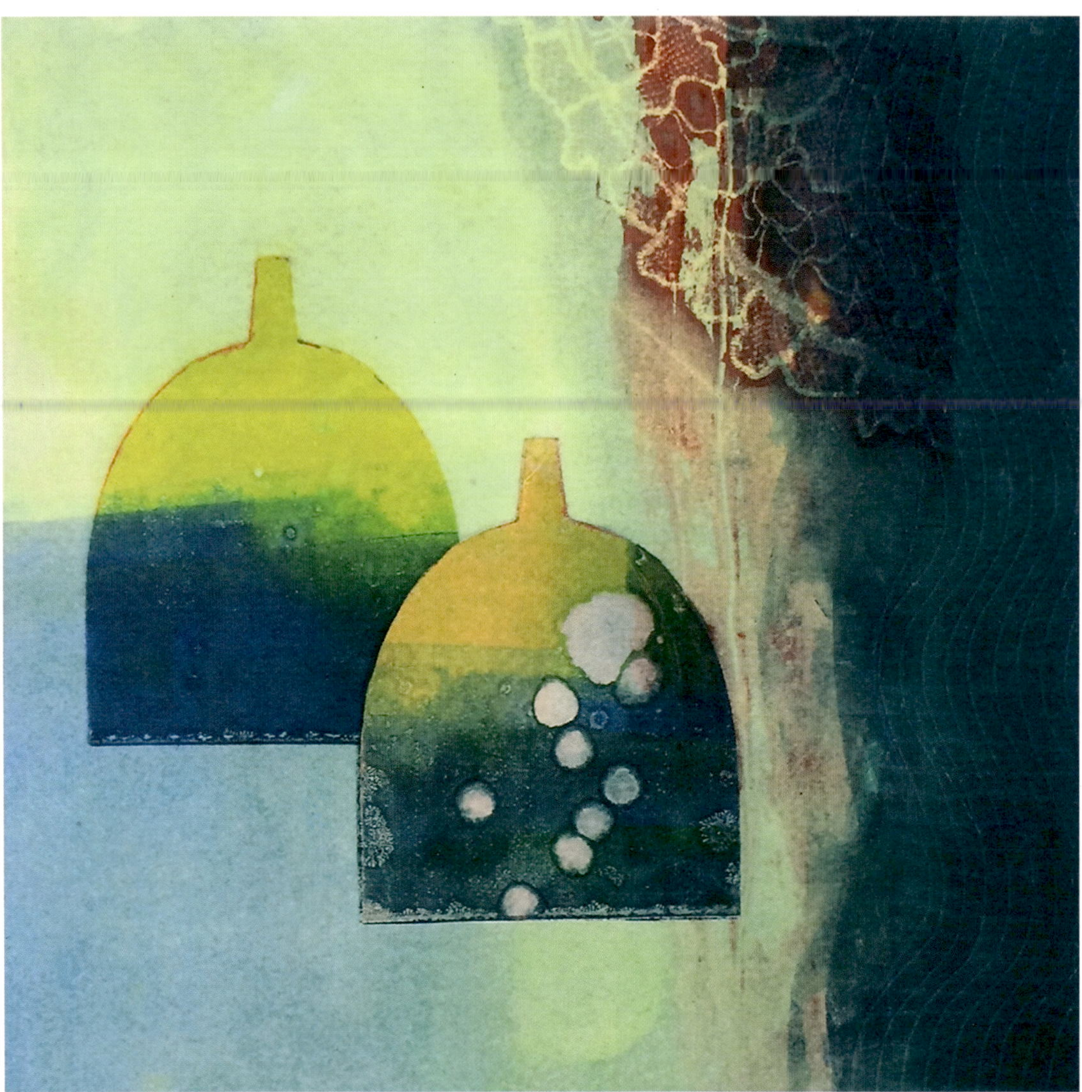

Above: 'Heaven Scent' (monotype), 30cm x 30cm, unique; Facing page: 'Orange Jug' (monotype and drypoint), 30cm x 30cm, unique

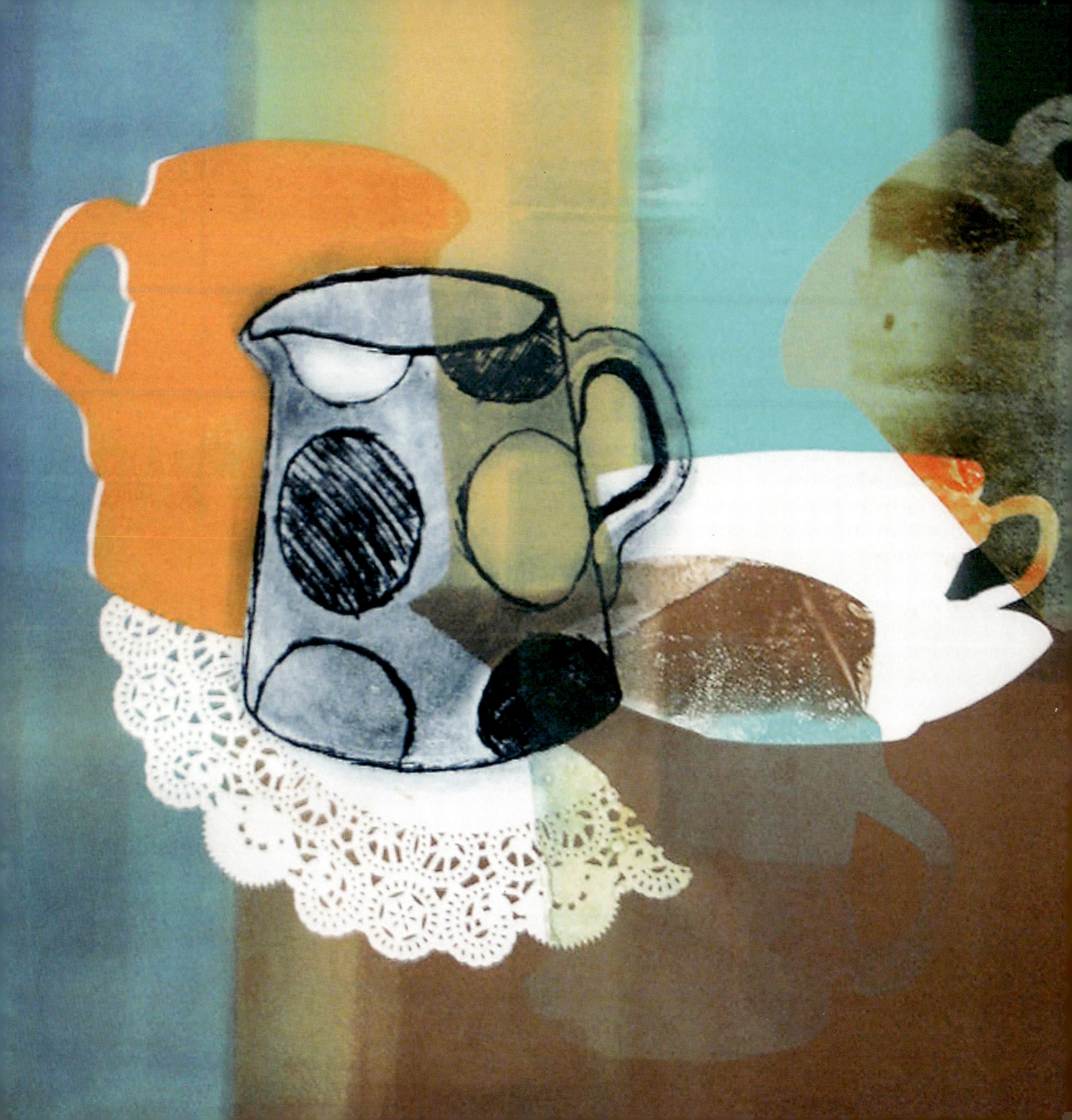

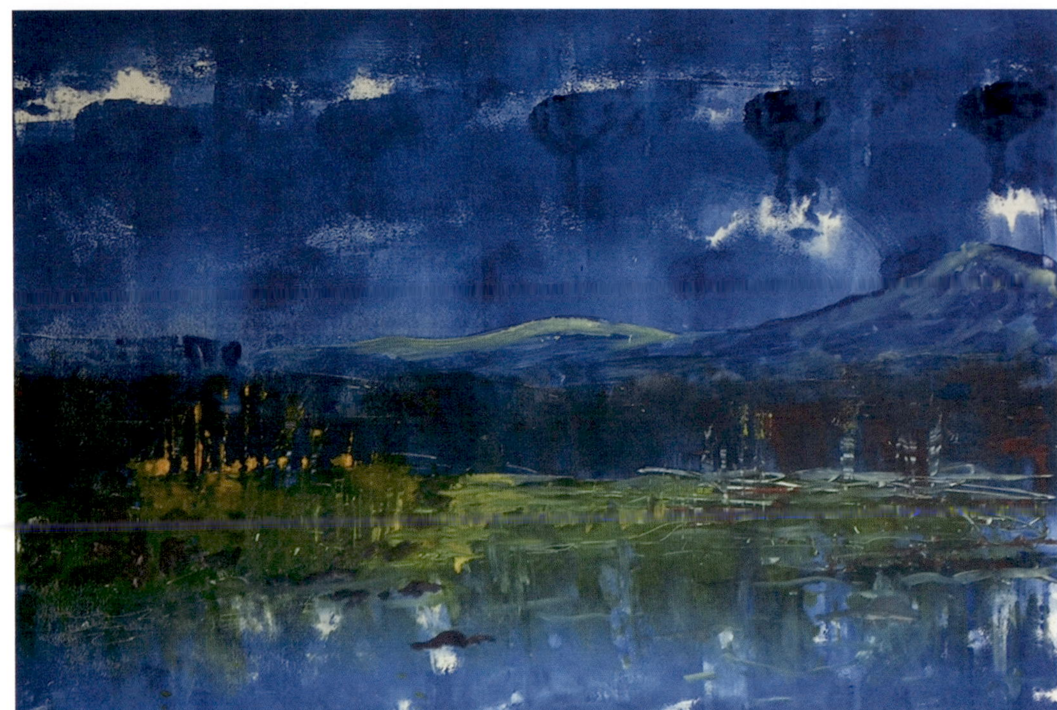

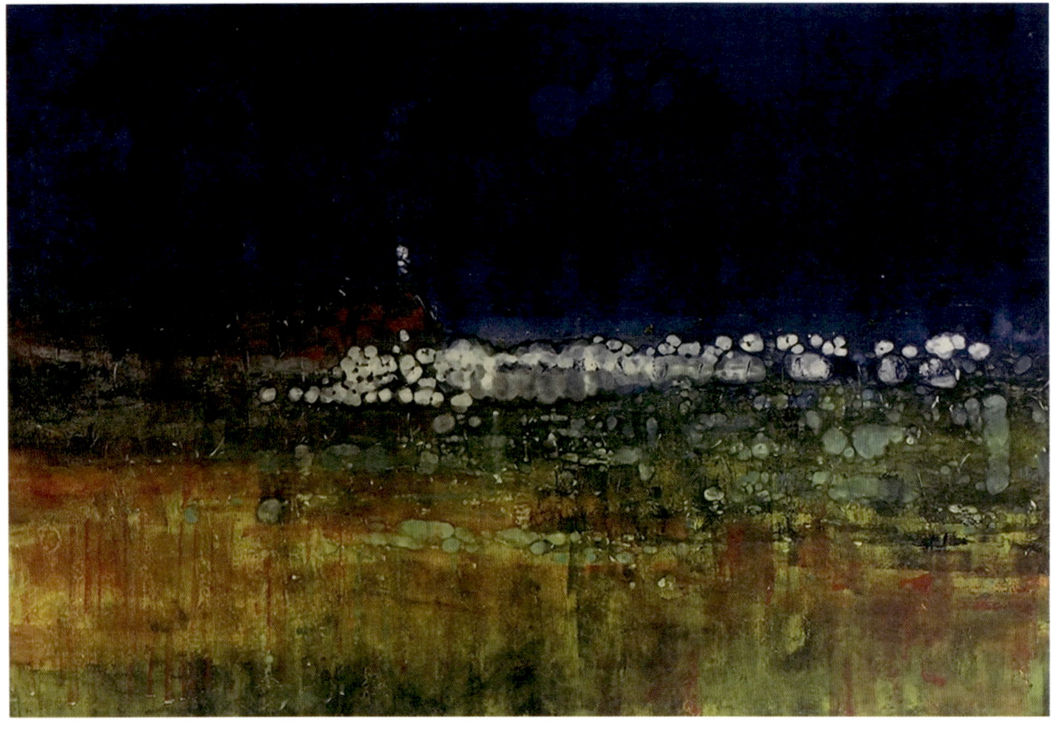

From top: 'Harbour Lights' (monotype), 40cm x 59cm, unique; 'Stormy Shore' (monotype), 40cm x 59cm, unique – Jill Ogilvy

RUTH OINN

Ruth Oinn is interested in "how the layering process that is central to printmaking echoes how language and music contain many layers of meaning". Work in recent years has arisen from Shakespeare's plays, the operas of Benjamin Britten and poetry about birds. Her current work is a response to Schubert's great song cycle, Winterreise.

"There is a particular challenge in searching for the essence of a piece of music or work of literature and re-visualising it on paper," she says. "Although music and literature inspire me, to interpret them I instinctively go to the natural world for the subjects of my prints.

"It is important to me that the prints I create are

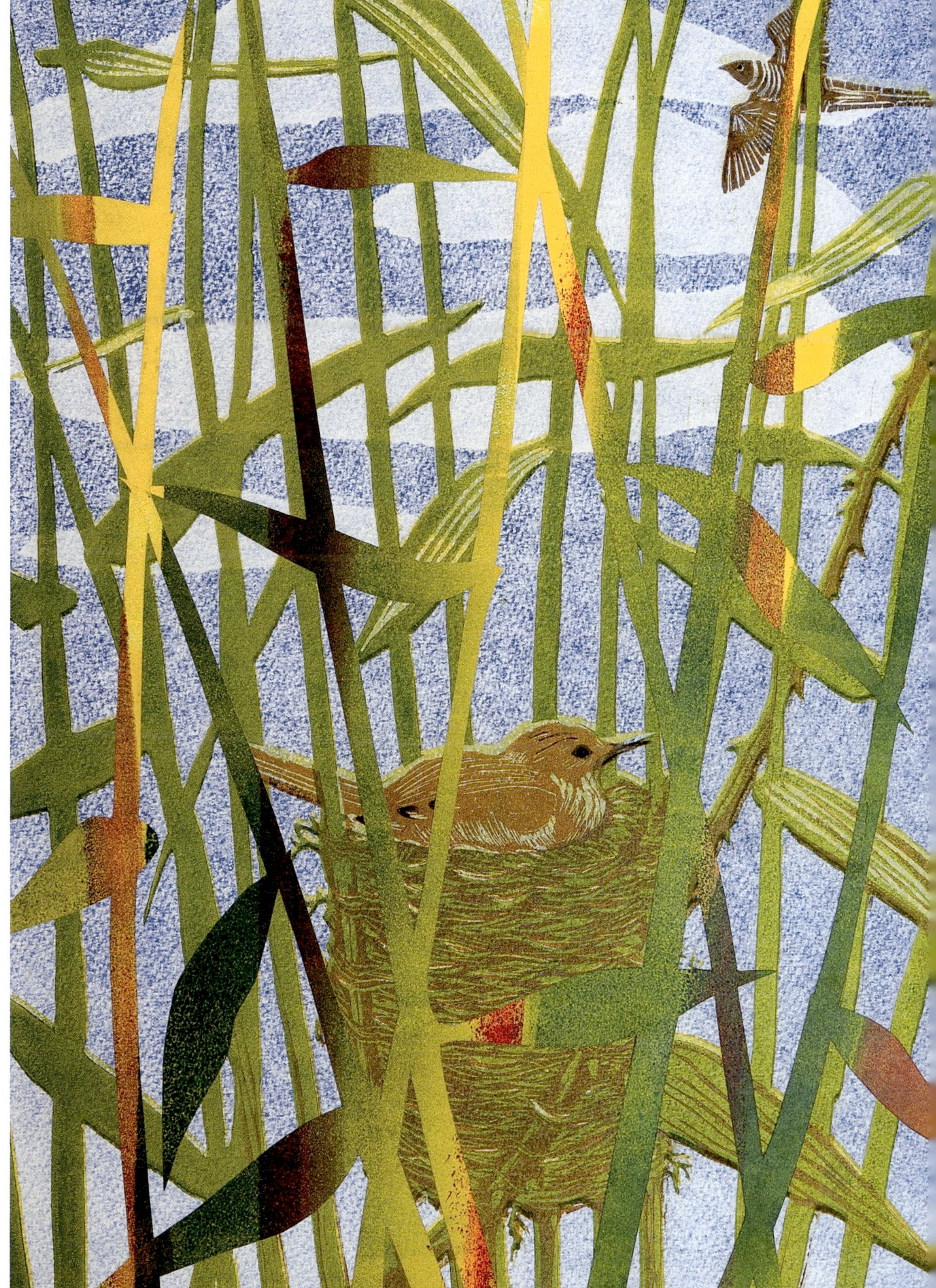

Right: 'Loud Sing Cuckoo' (monotype, linocut and collage), 42cm x 30cm, 1 of 4 CV

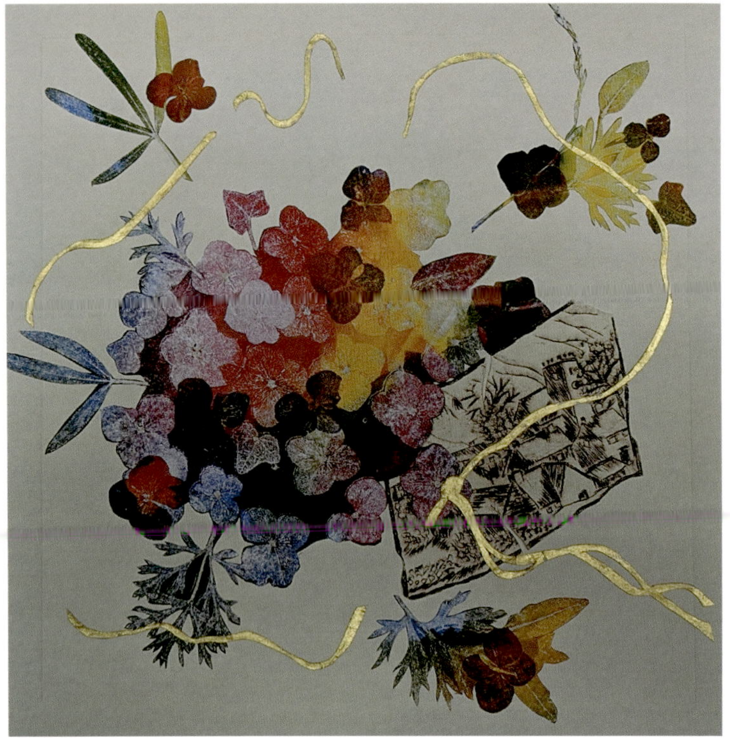

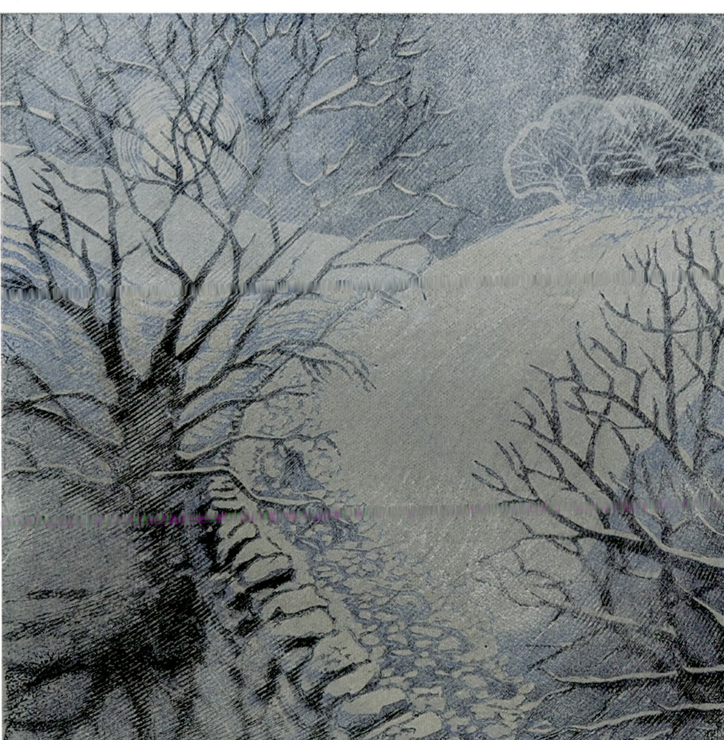

interesting and thought-provoking, and I hope they are also beautiful. As I often employ several different techniques in one print, each is generally unique."

Ruth trained as a printmaker at the Curwen Print Study Centre, Cambridge, qualifying in 2011, and since then has had a number of solo exhibitions throughout East Anglia. She works from her studio in Saffron Walden, Essex.
www.printsbyruth.com

Top row, from left: 'Manchem Blumenstrauss' (monotype, drypoint and collage), 32cm x 32cm, unique; 'Ein Mondenschatten' (reduction linocut), 30cm x 30cm, 1 of 3 CV; 'Blumen im Winter' (monotype, drypoint and collage), 32cm x 32cm, unique; 'Kalt und Unbeweglich' (reduction linocut and collage), 30cm x 30cm, unique – all part of a series of prints in response to Schubert's song cycle Winterreise

Bottom row, from left: 'Spring Fever' (monotype and linocut), 30cm x 30cm, unique; 'Hedgerow' (monotype and collage), 30cm x 30cm, unique

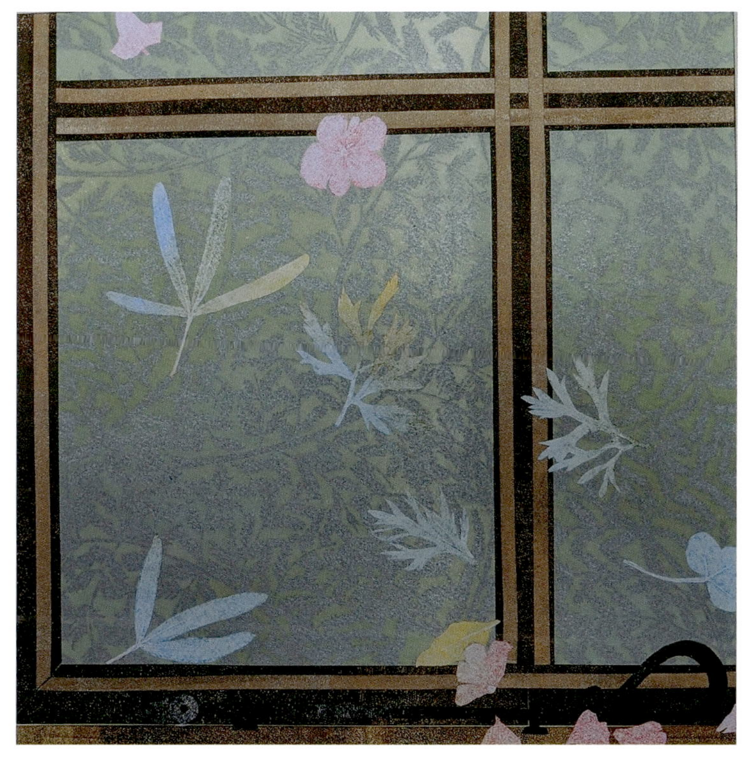
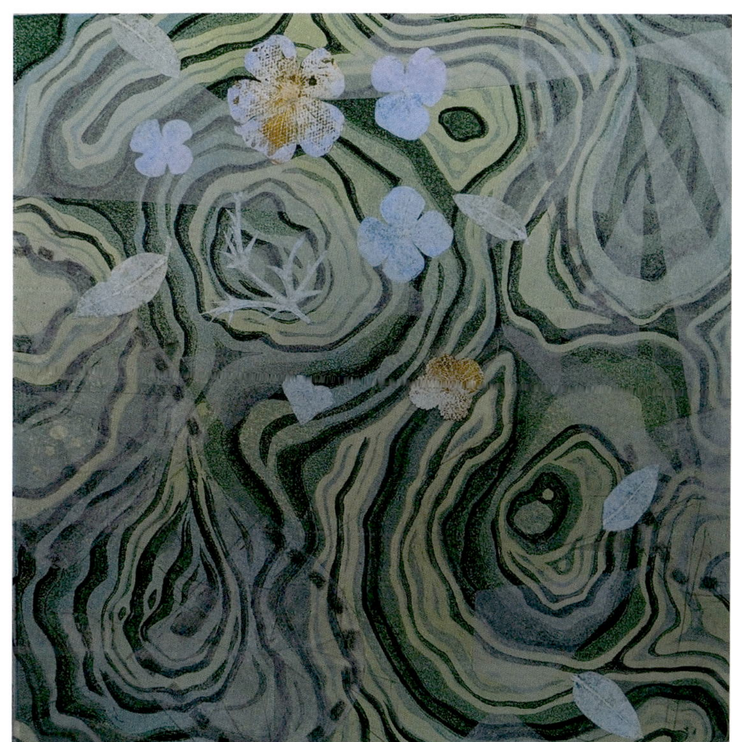
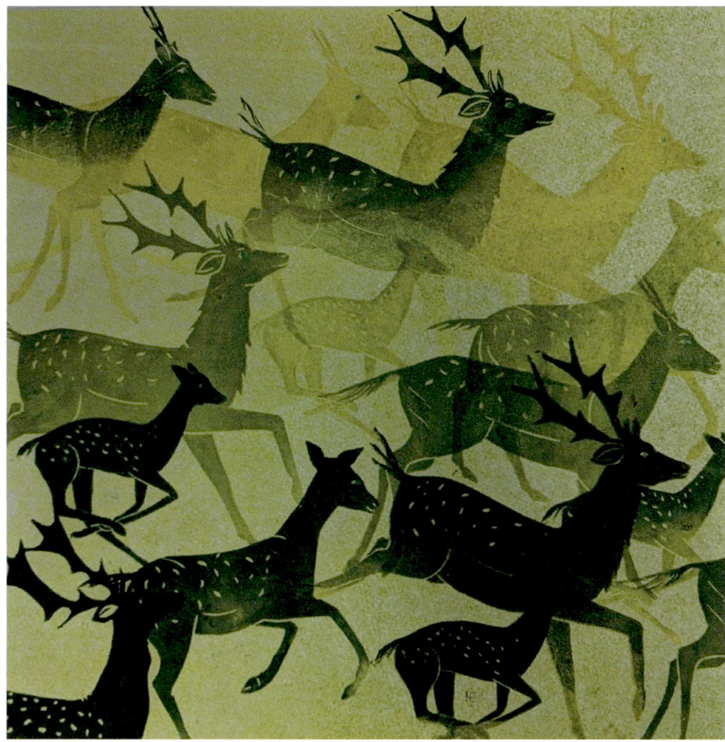
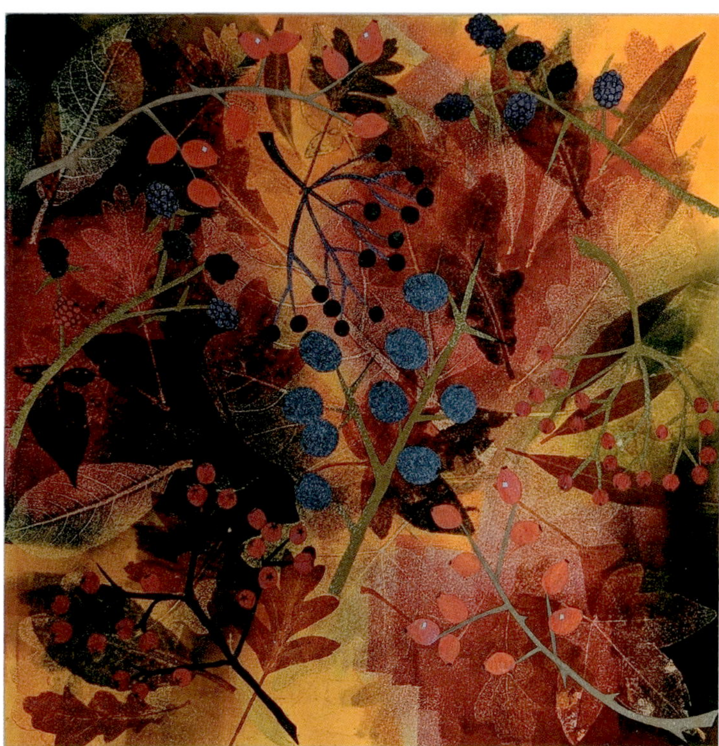

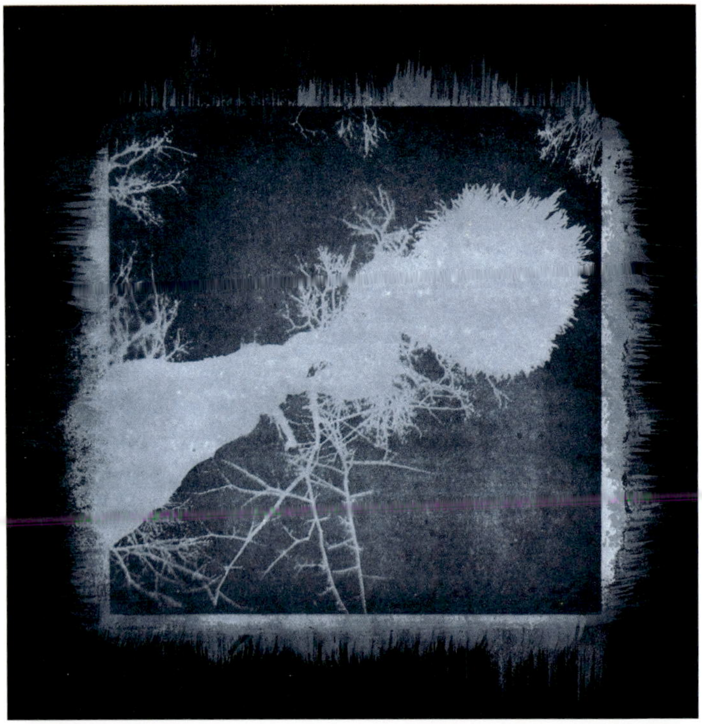

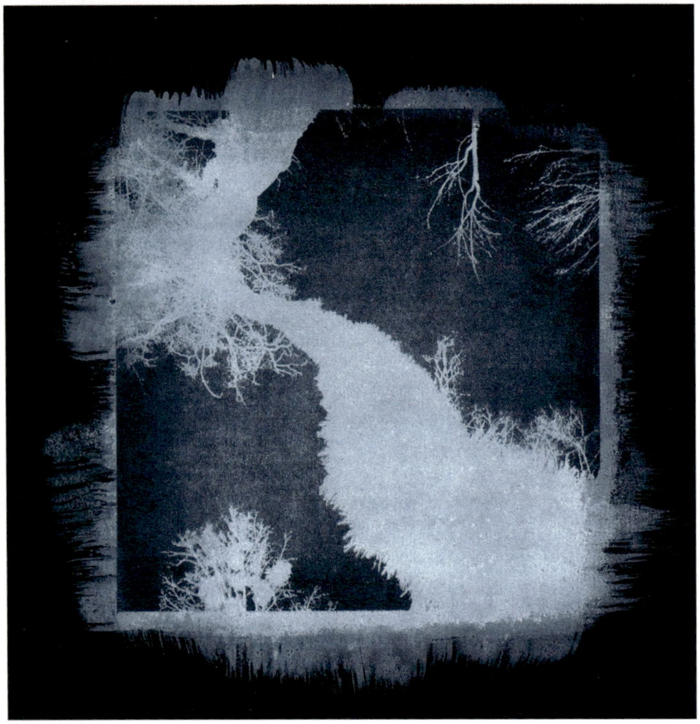

PAVLA ONDROVA

Czech-born photographic artist and printmaker Pavla Ondrova takes her inspiration from natural rhythms and occurrences, as well as from Zen philosophy, specifically the concept of wabi-sabi.

"Transience and impermanence, two key principles of wabi-sabi, are themes present throughout my work, which tends to be minimalistic."

Following Pavla's studies in photography, she began to experiment with alternative photographic processes. "I'm fascinated by photographic dichotomies," she says. "Positive and negative, analogue and digital. My practice explores their interceptions by combining the latest technologies with pioneering photographic techniques. I either scan objects or take digital images, then print them using cyanotype or gum bichromate."

It is the hands-on process that appeals to Pavla. "I really enjoy all the practical elements – mixing pigments and solutions, coating paper, and so on – but, more importantly, the process itself adds a sense of authenticity. Each print made is unique. There is beauty to be found within each small imperfection, and the occasional unexpected outcome also adds an extra depth of interest. Not just for myself as a maker, but also, I hope, for the viewer."
www.pavlaondrova.com

Top left: 'Untitled 3', from the series Variables (gum bichromate), 20cm x 20cm, unique; Bottom left: 'Untitled 4', from the series Variables (gum bichromate), 20cm x 20cm, unique; Facing page: 'Untitled 1', from the series Infinite Possibilities (cyanotype), 30cm x 30cm, edition of 12

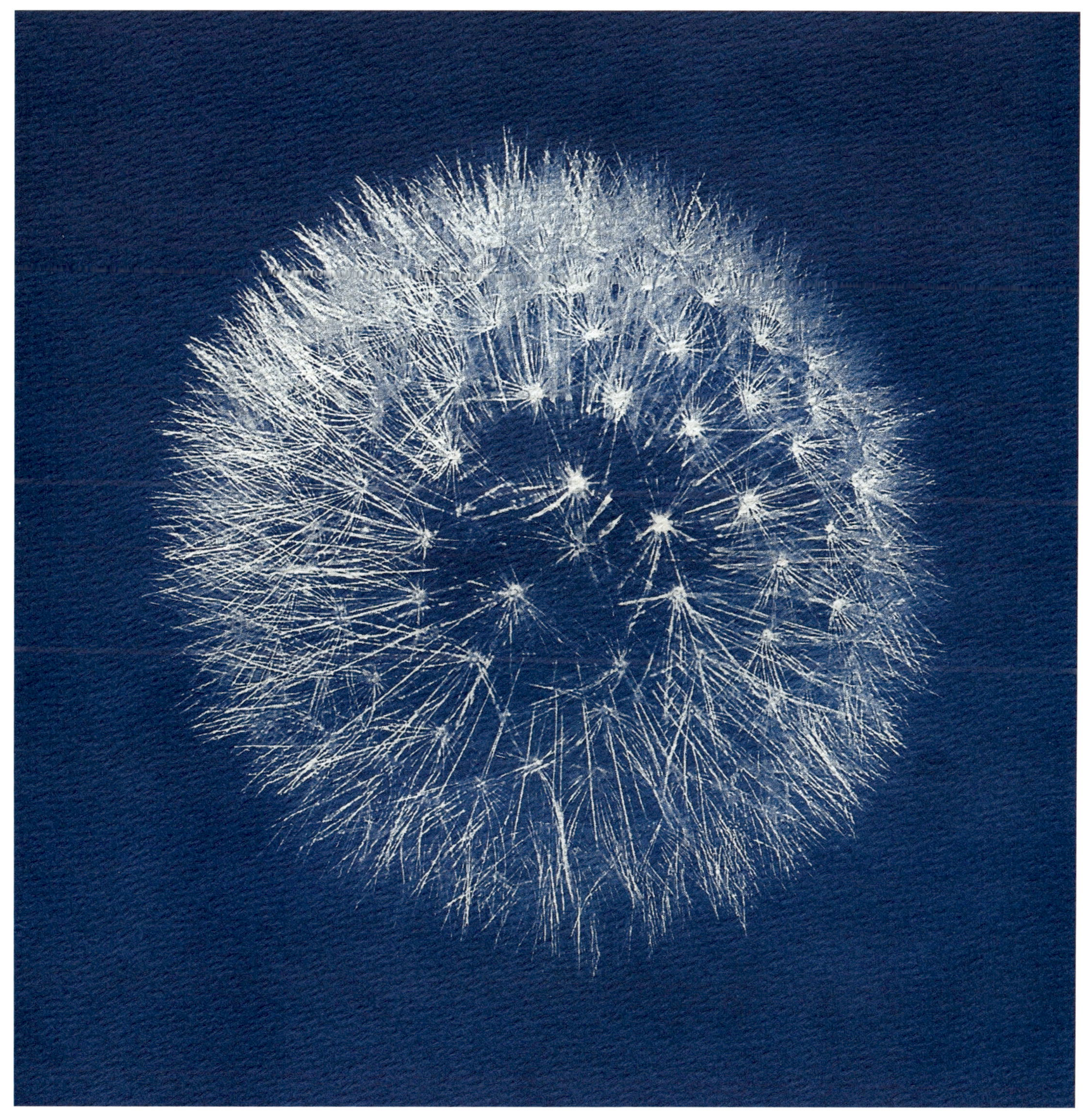

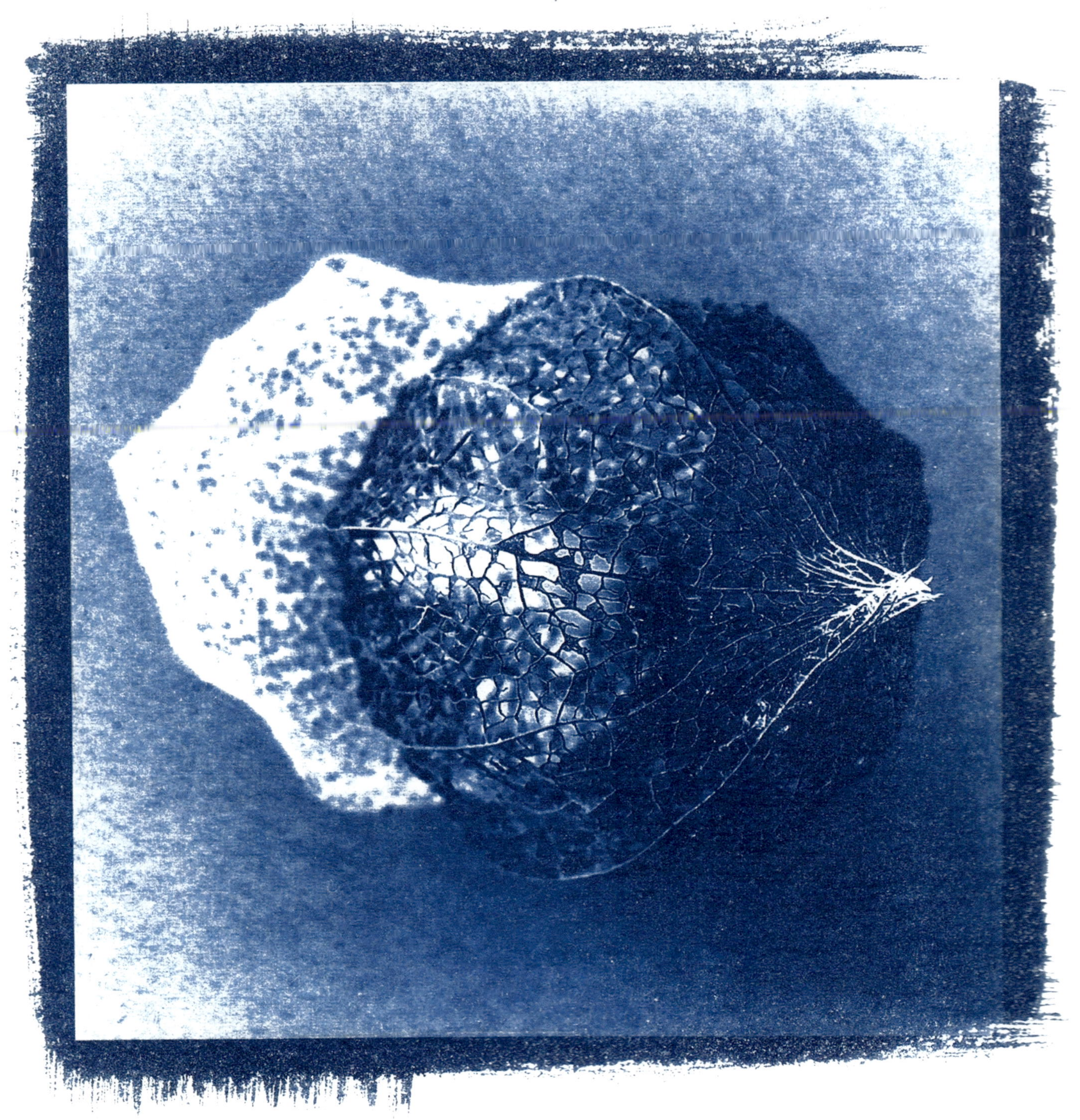

Above: 'Untitled 4', from the series Lanterns (cyanotype), 22cm x 22cm, edition of 9 – Pavla Ondrova

NAOMI ONSLOW

Naomi Onslow's favourite printmaking technique is collagraph, and she uses this to respond to the landscape around her in rural Suffolk. "I'm drawn to places that have a link with the ancient past, in particular pathways and crossing places.

"I begin collecting ideas through observational watercolour sketches that I work into with oil pastels and by taking panoramic photos. I translate the marks and textures from my sketches into marks on the collagraph plate with PVA glue, Polyfilla, textured mediums, carborundum and materials ranging from wallpaper to cabbage leaves.

"I particularly like working in monochrome, in warm blacks and rich turquoise that feature the textured surface, and I aim to create a sense of space in the landscapes and draw the viewer in. Sometimes my pieces take on a more realistic response to the landscape; and sometimes more abstract, where I work into the inked plate with a solvent and print to the edges of the paper."

Naomi achieved a Certificate in Fine Art Printmaking at the Curwen Print Study Centre, Cambridge, in 2016. She studied Fine Art at the University of Gloucestershire, achieving a First Class Honours Degree in Visual Art and English Literature in 1994.

Email: naomi.onslow@btinternet.com

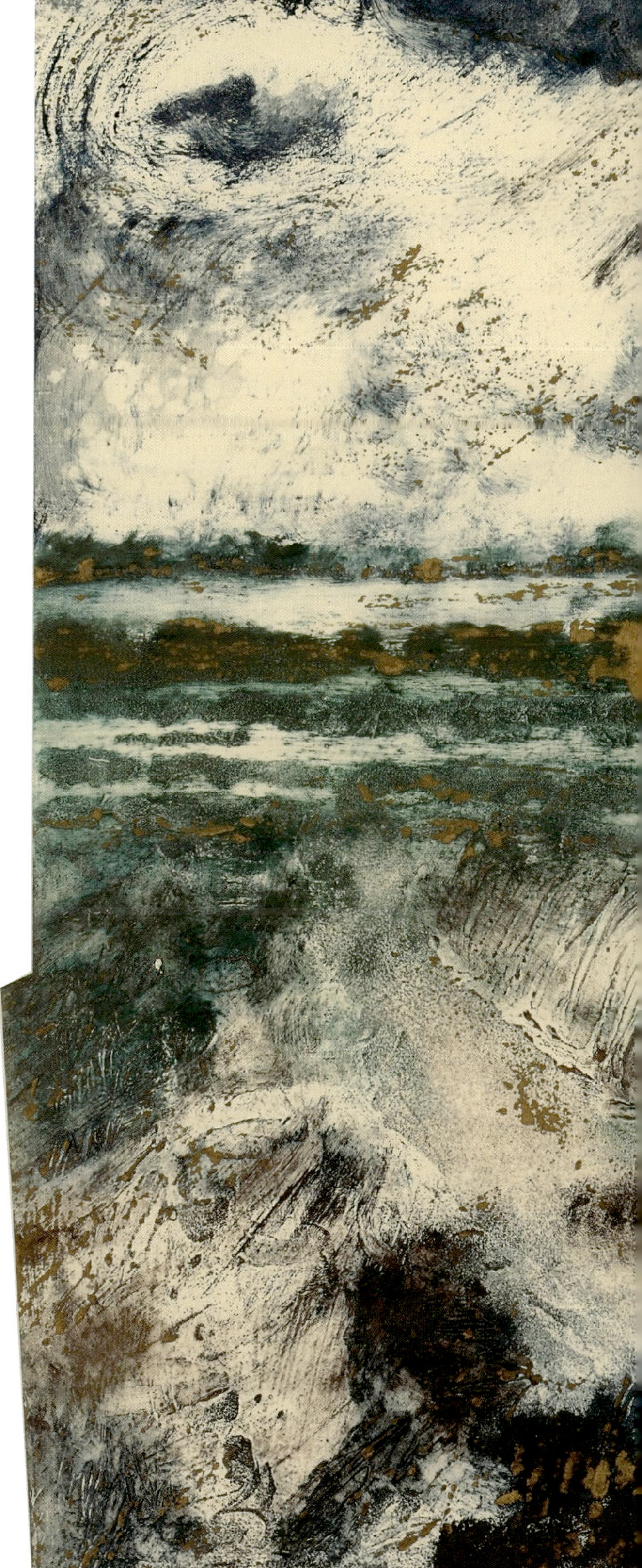

Right: 'Sospirando' (collagraph), 76cm x 30cm, edition of 6

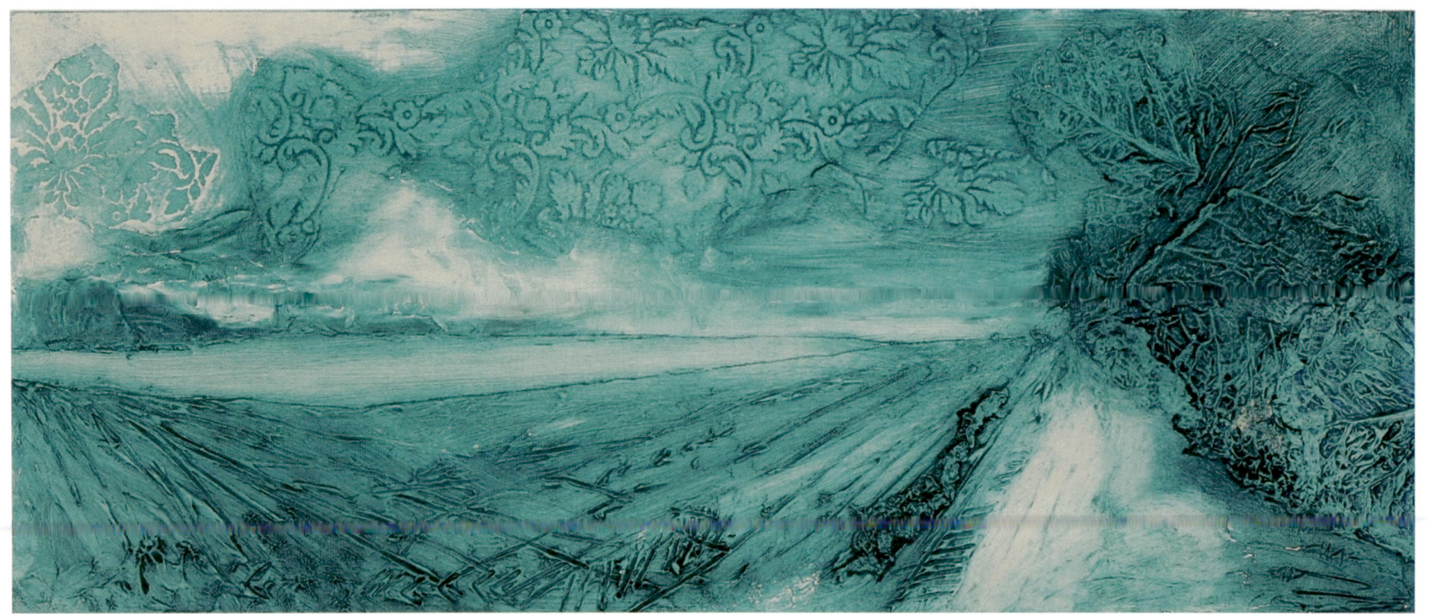

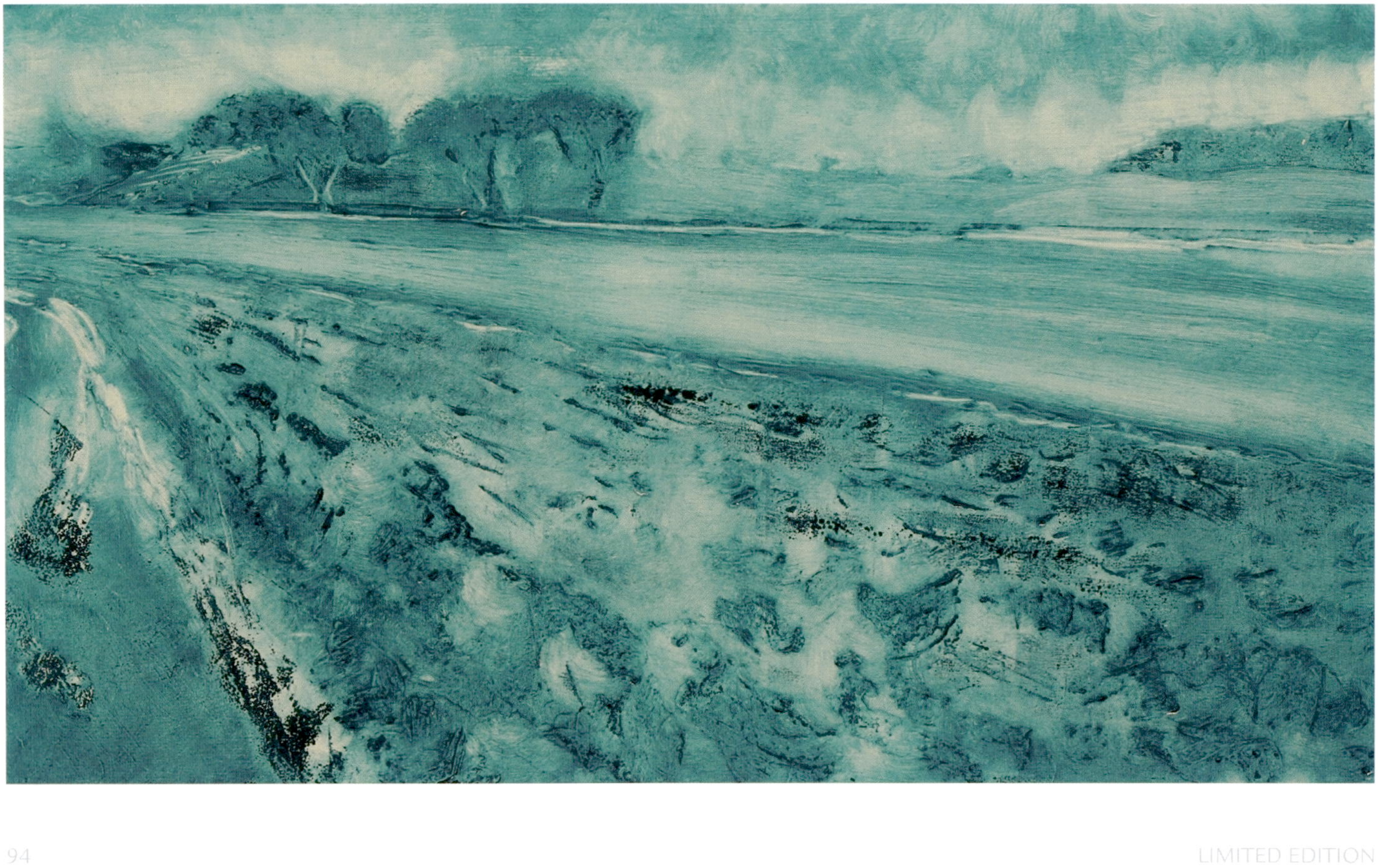

Facing page, from top: 'Clare to Cavendish 1' (collagraph), 69cm x 28cm, unique; 'Sillion Shine' (collagraph), 65cm x 35cm, unique

Right, from top: 'Sudbury Willows and Setting Sun' (collagraph), 46cm x 31cm, unique; 'Scherzando' (collagraph), 57cm x 42cm, edition of 6 – all Naomi Onslow

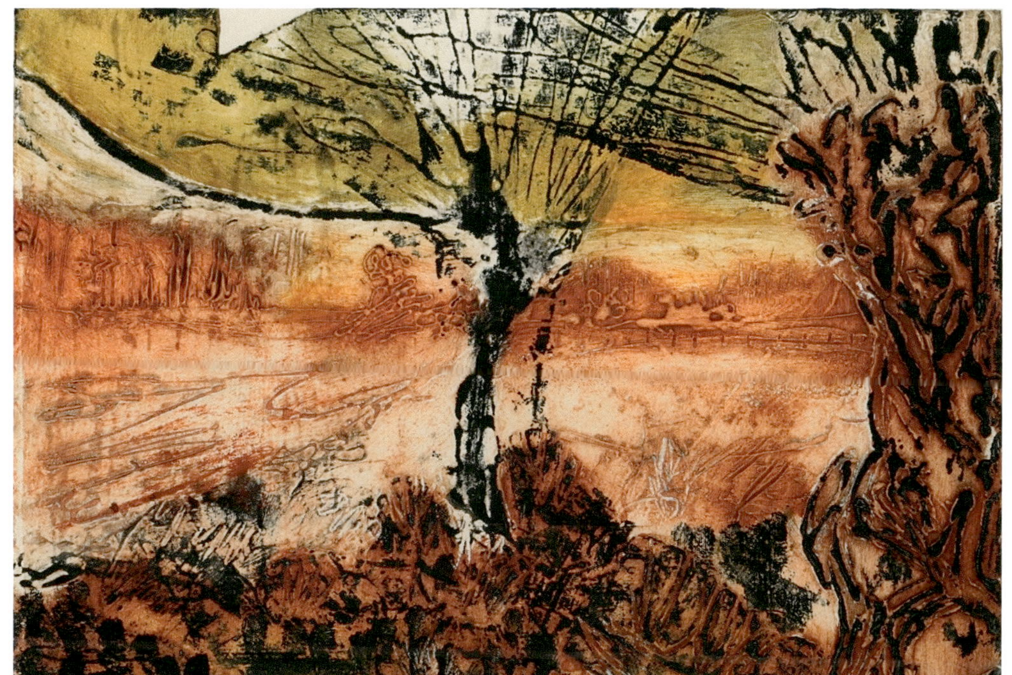

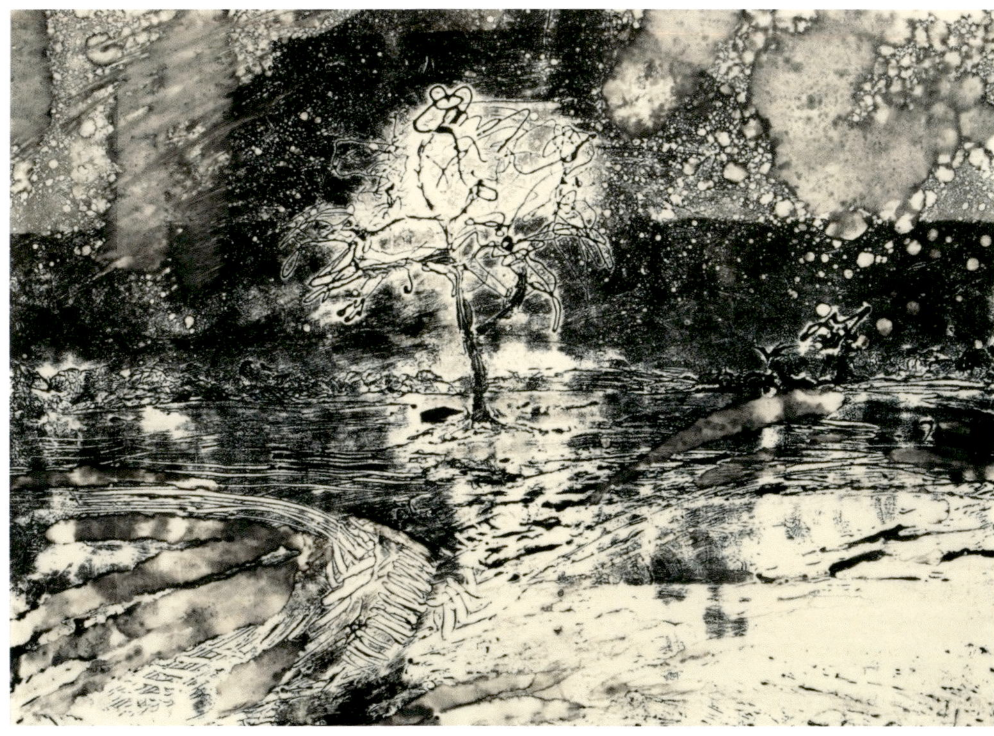

ANTONIA PHILLIPS

The starting point for the work of painter and printmaker Antonia Phillips is nature, and the inspiration for the prints shown here was a photographic study into undergrowth.

The work drills into and peels away layers, exposing the chaos and fractals of the natural world. These are continuously reinterpreted through this

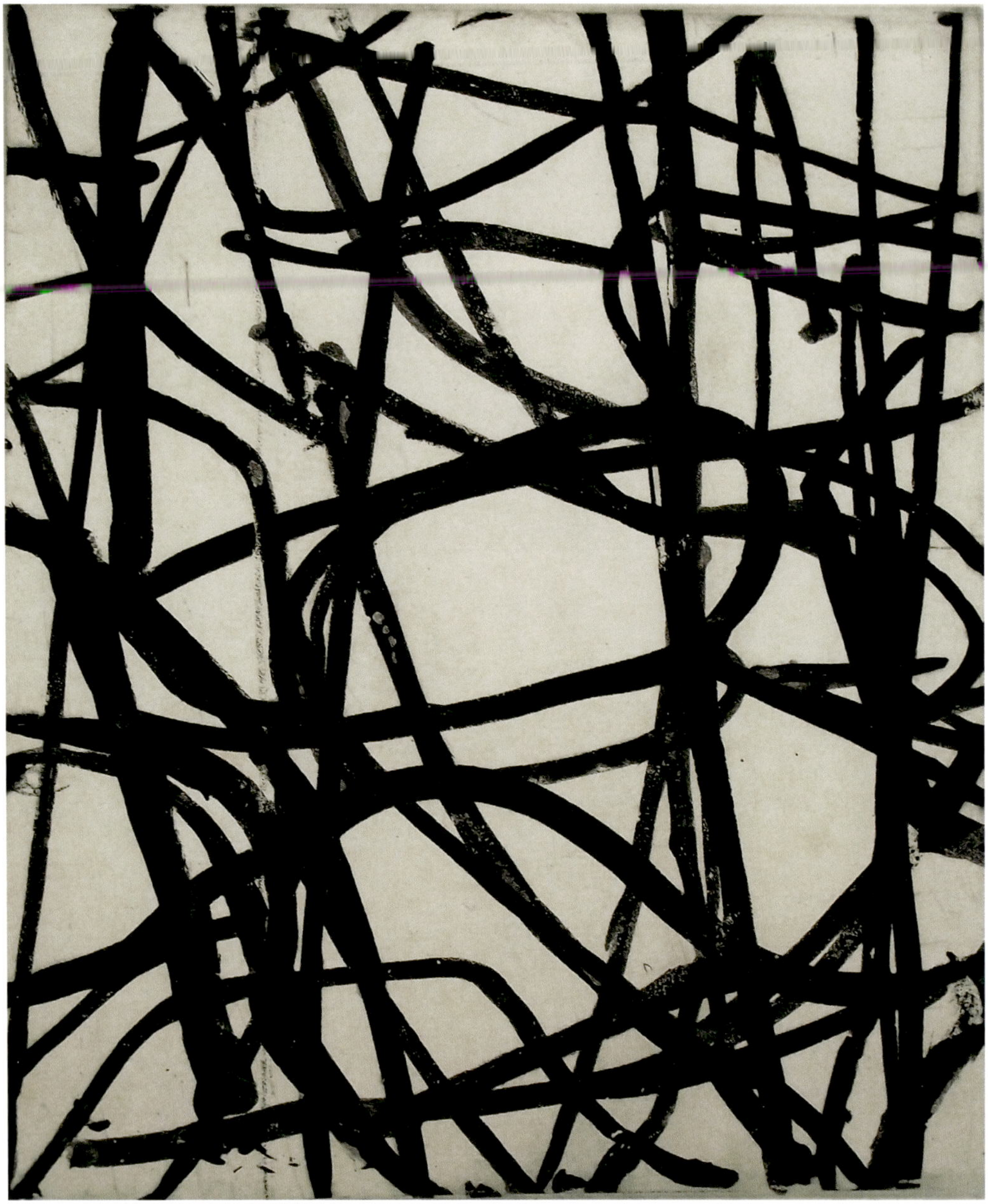

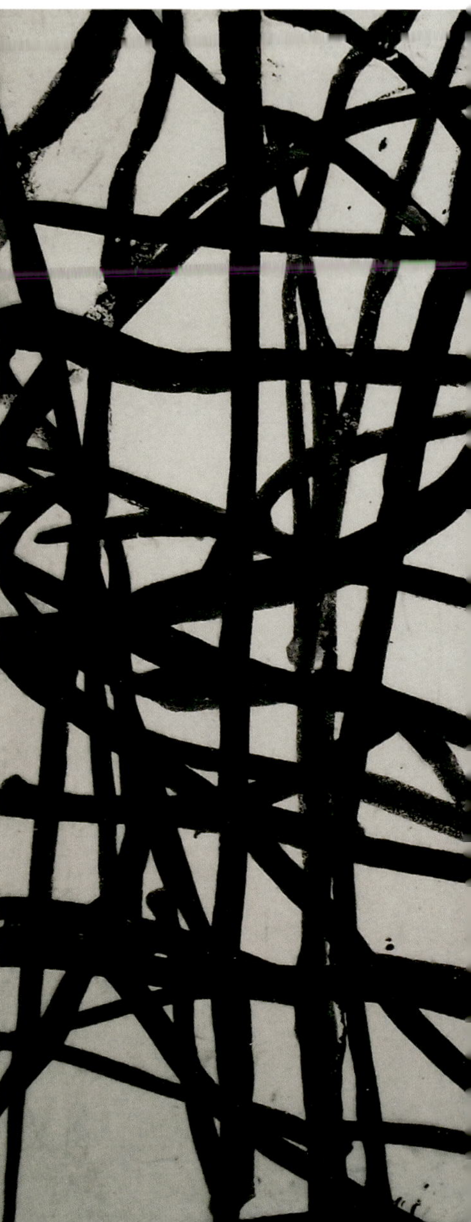

'Tangle I, II, III' (all copperplate etching with aquatint), 26cm x 32cm each, edition of 3 each

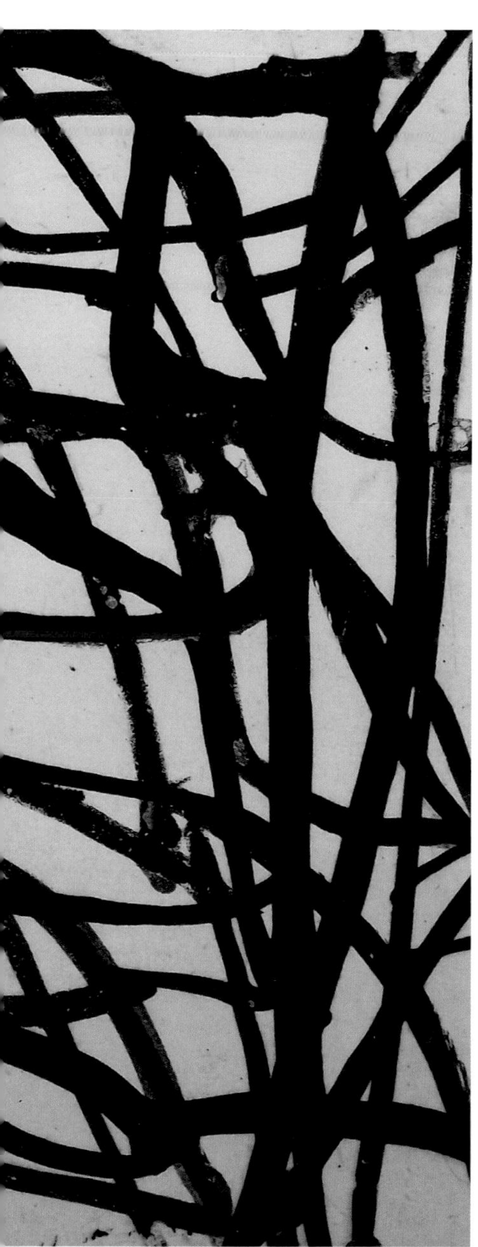

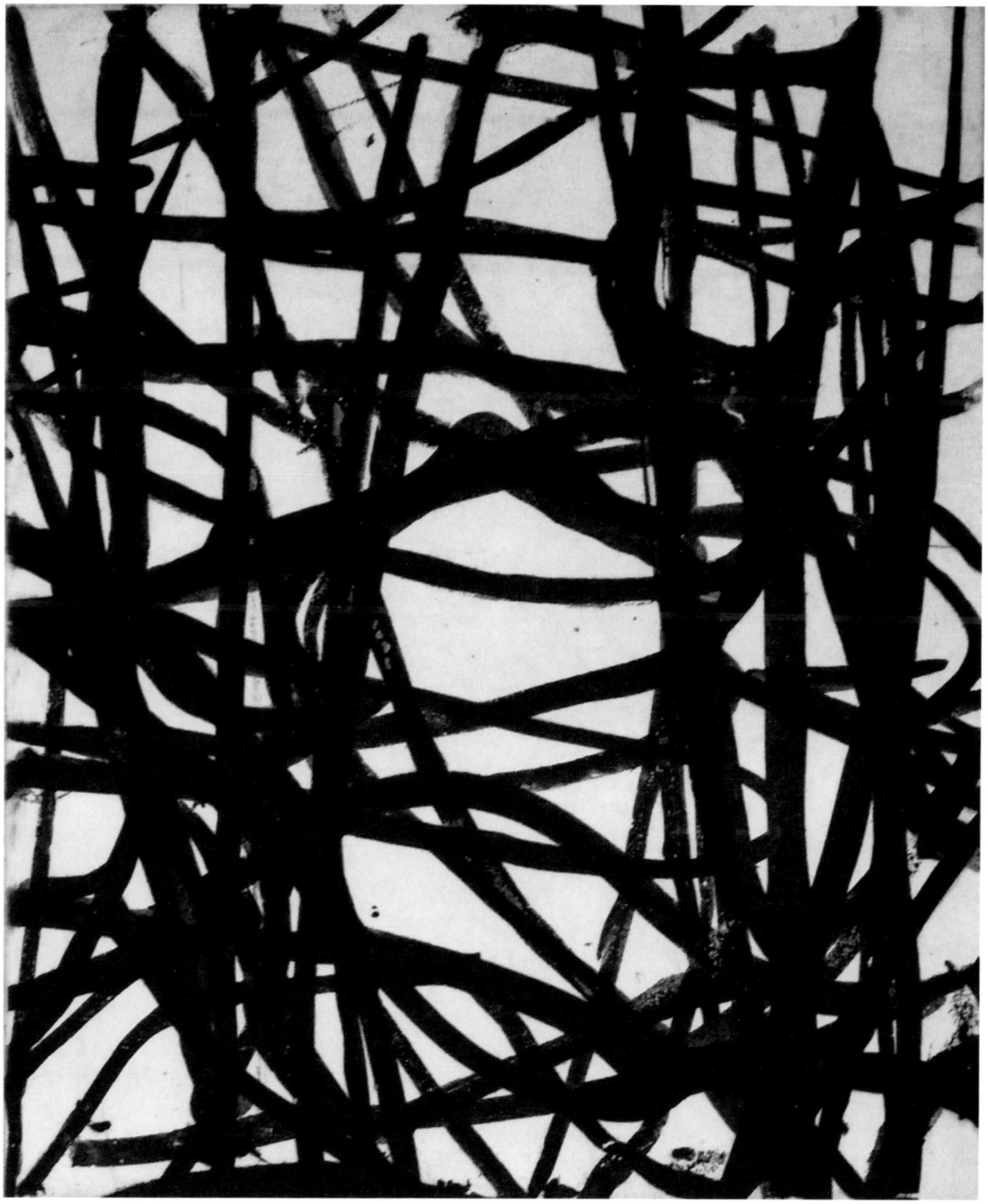

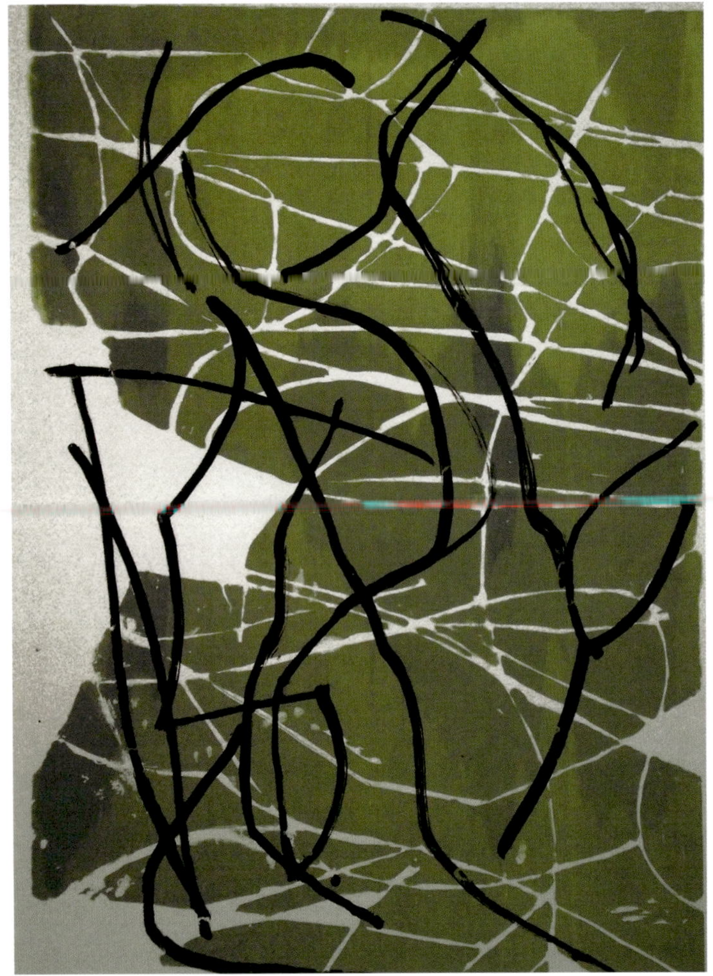

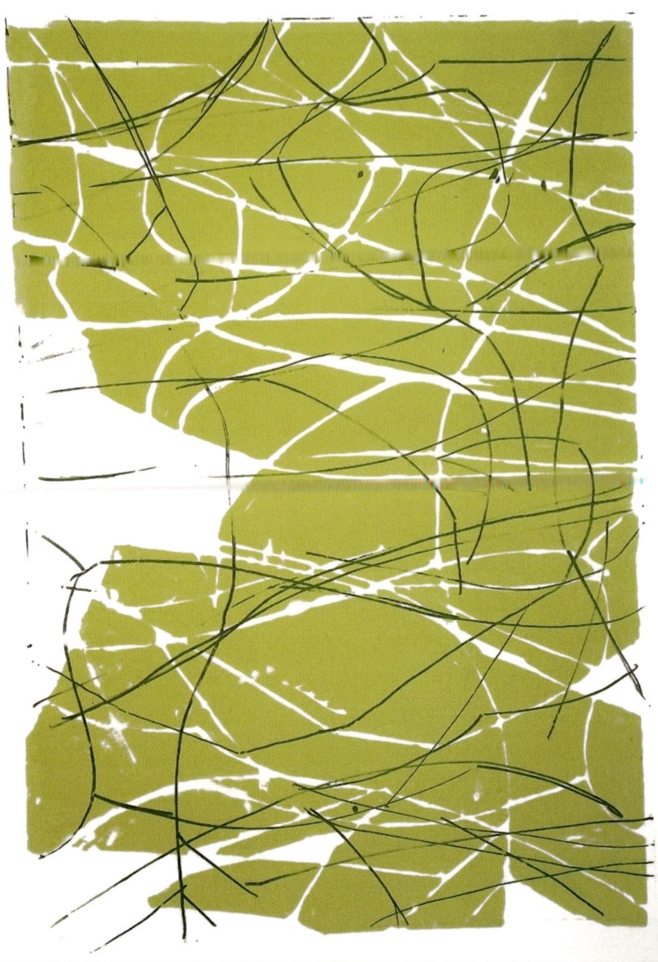

From left: 'Deviation' (screenprint), 97cm x 67cm, unique; 'Afterwards' (screenprint), 97cm x 65cm, unique

suite of prints. The works take a snapshot of a static place but breathe energy and flow into them; and printmaking allows Antonia to express this openly.

"By emphasising negative space, the freedom and movement of the line is implied by space, and space is created by line," she says. "The pared-down nature, the scale and use of colour, forces the viewer unconsciously to perceive the work as a whole before the brain dissects the marks."

Email: antoniafield@btinternet.com

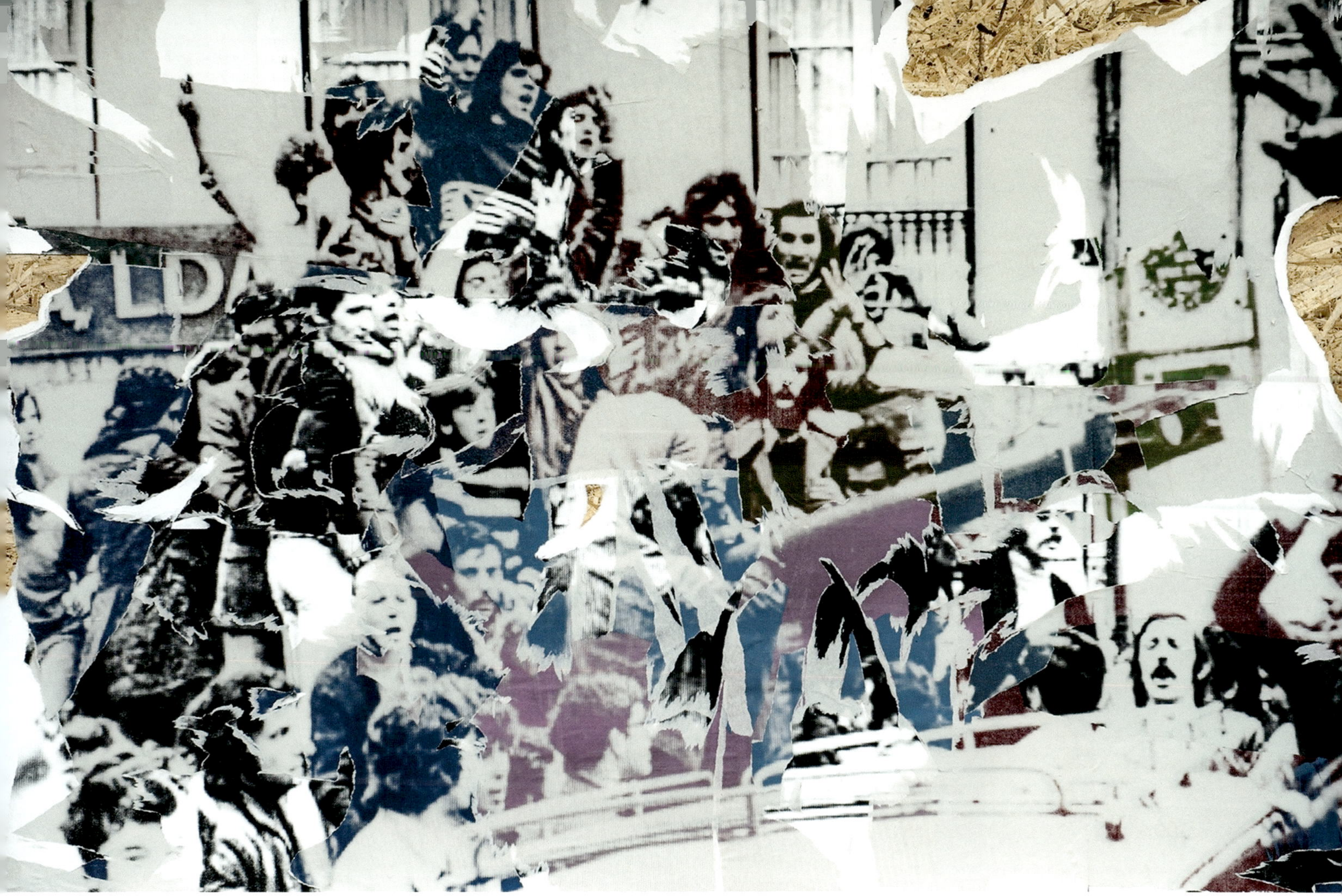

RICARDO PIMENTEL

Ricardo Pimentel is a printmaker firmly rooted in the mode of experimentation. Screenprinting is his preferred medium, often incorporating elements of his photographic work which are half-toned screenprinted and also have additional freehand elements. As a result, each piece has a unique look and feel.

As the son of Portuguese immigrants to the UK in the 1960s, his work not only draws heavily on the cultural, political and literary influences with which he grew up, but also reflects a life made in England. The result of this cross-fertilisation of influences and a Fine Art degree from Central Saint Martins is a body of work that resists pigeon-holing. “My aim is

Above: ‘2U5IT4NIA (i)’ (monoprint décollage on board), 100cm x 150cm, unique

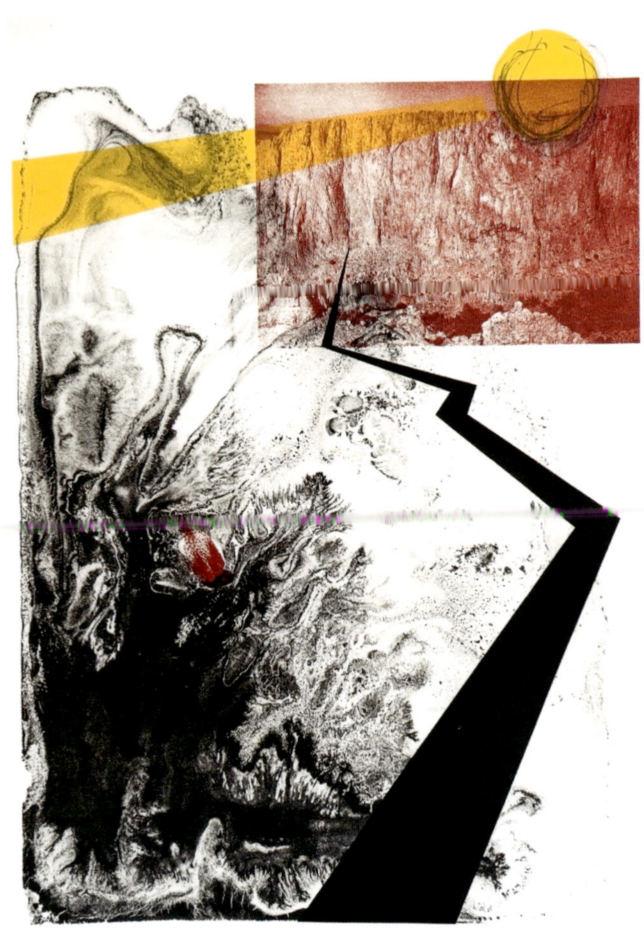

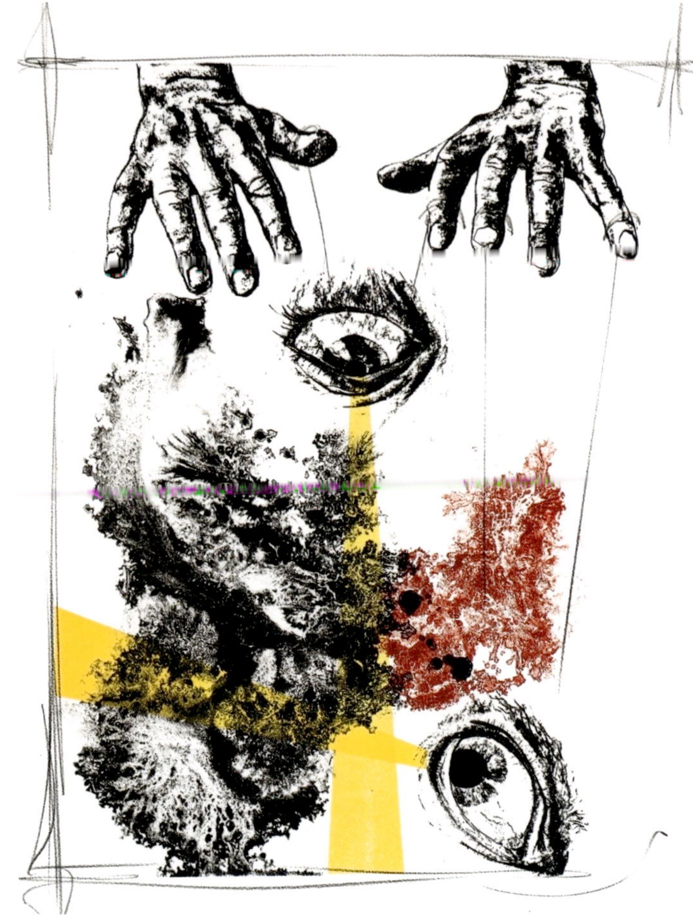

not primarily for my work to be aesthetically pleasing, although the results sometimes are, but to invite the viewer to engage with its subject matter."

Ricardo's latest project, of which some pieces are being shown for the first time at the Cambridge Biennale, is an interpretation of Dante's Inferno. Transposed to 21st-century Britain, it follows each of the original Cantos in theme but incorporates additional references to contemporary British society.
www.ricardopimentel.co.uk

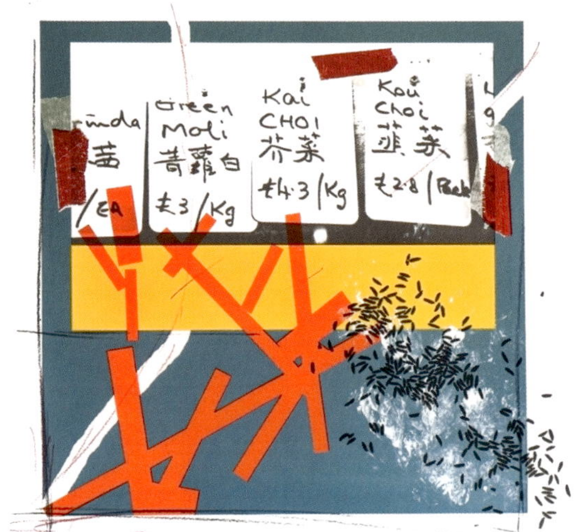

Top, left to right: 'Inferno – Canto I' (screenprint), 76cm x 56cm, edition of 15; 'Inferno – Canto II' (screenprint), 76cm x 56cm, edition of 15; 'Cultural Consequences (one)' (screenprint, acrylic, graphite, masking tape), 48cm x 67cm, edition of 12

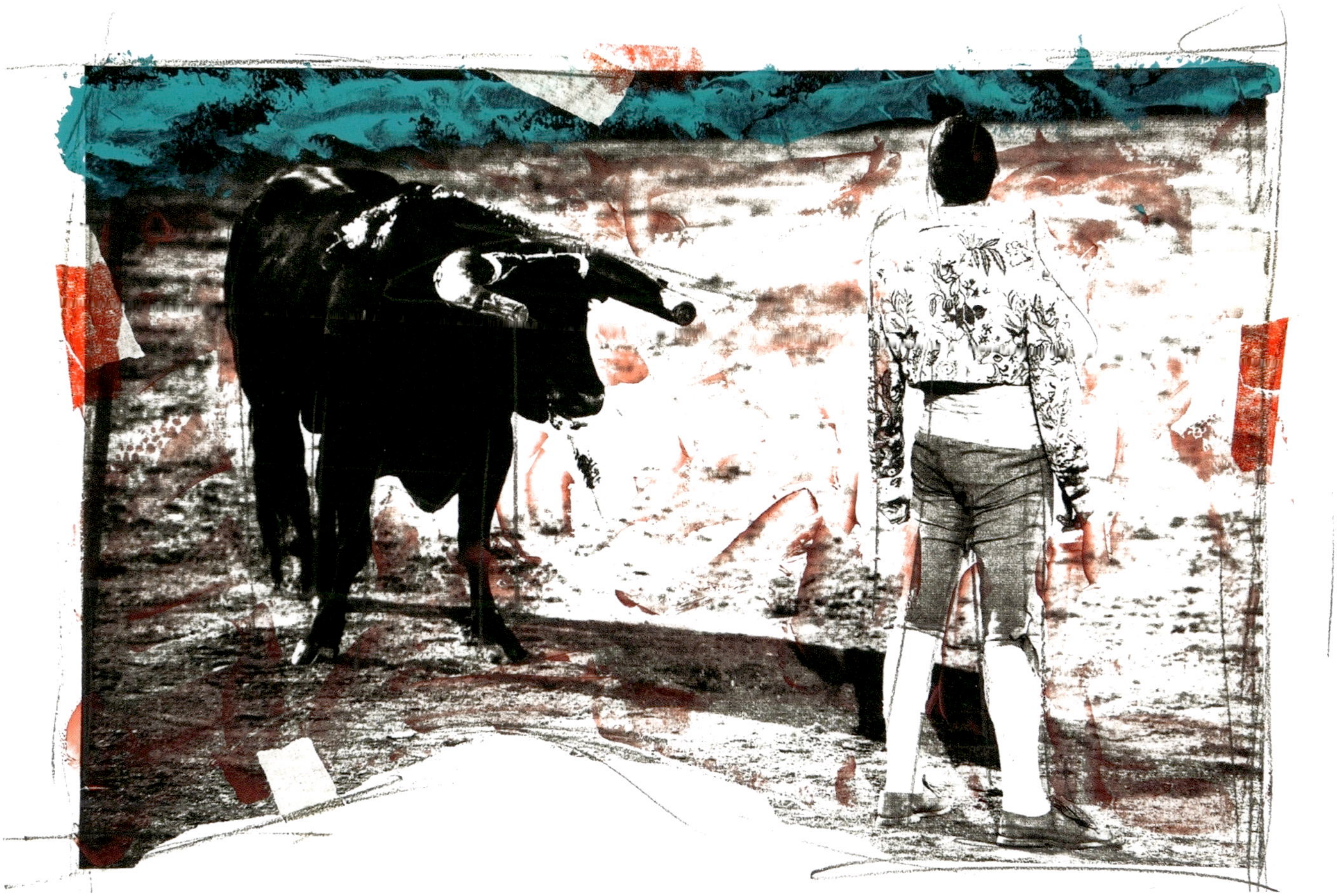

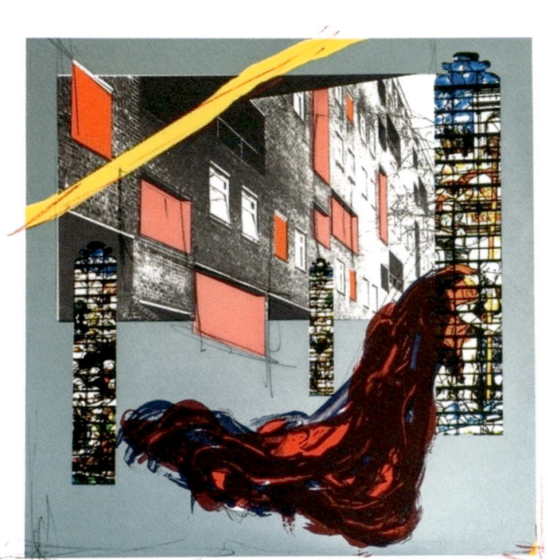

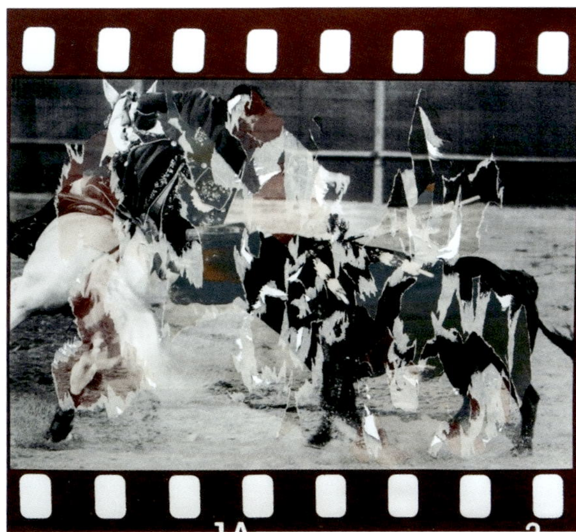

Bottom, from far left: 'Transient Passage (four)' (screenprint, charcoal, pastel, masking tape), 56cm x 46cm, edition of 10; 'Transient Passage (three)' (screenprint, charcoal, pastel), 56cm x 46cm, edition of 4; 'Cultural Consequences (two)' (screenprint décollage), 70cm x 82cm, edition of 8

JOHN PRESTON

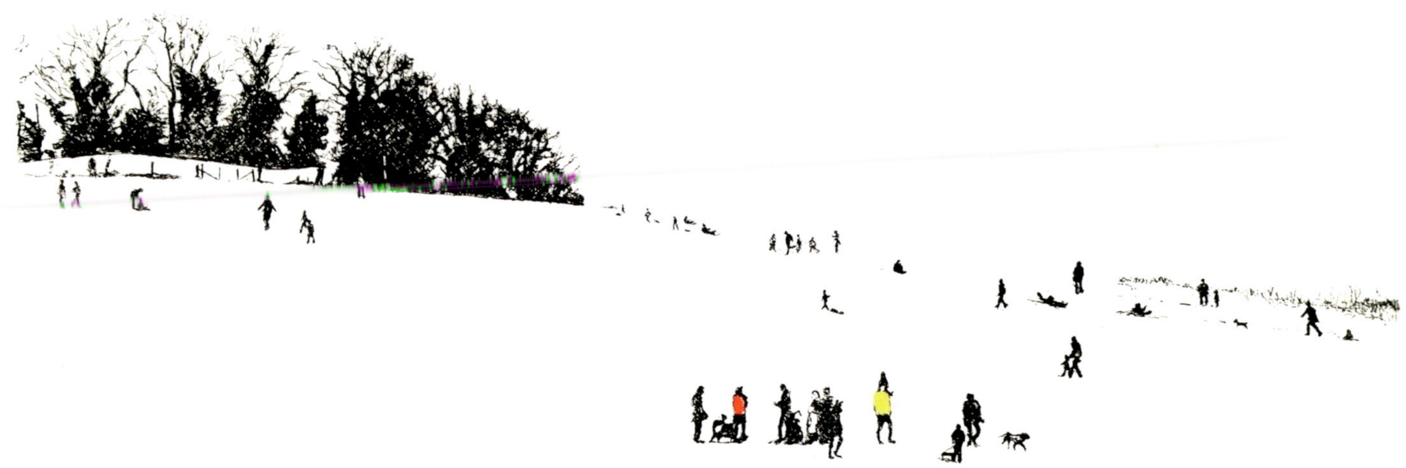

John Preston was a student at, and is a long-term resident of, Cambridge. He is both an artist and a champion of the city's heritage; his professional interest in buildings has always informed his art.

He starts an etching "with an idea, based on what I see; the key choices are about what to leave out". Creating the image is a process of give and take: "Acid can be unpredictable, and the plate often has a mind of its own. I respond to what happens, and adjust my ideas at every stage of the process."

When possible, John draws plates on the spot: using drypoint, or drawing through a wax ground, then etching the plate in the studio. To create tone, he uses aquatint (resin dust heat-sealed on to the plate), a process like watercolour but in

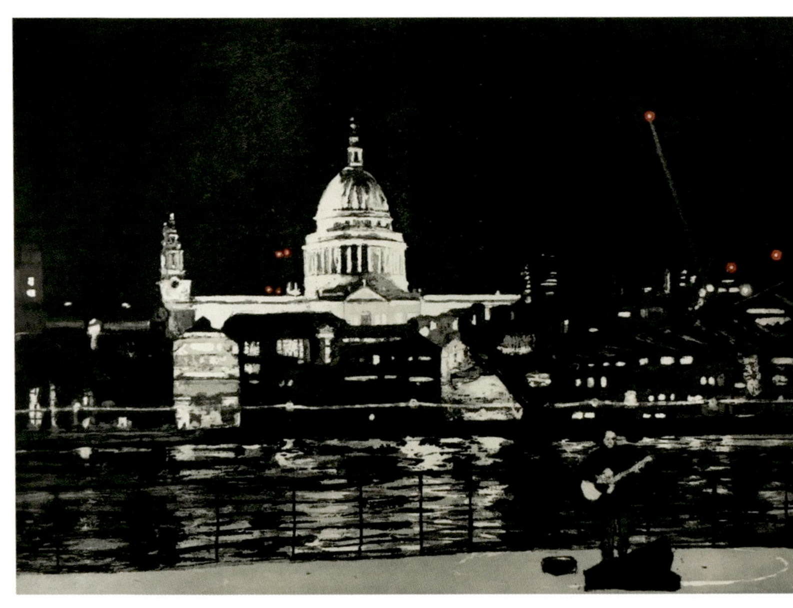

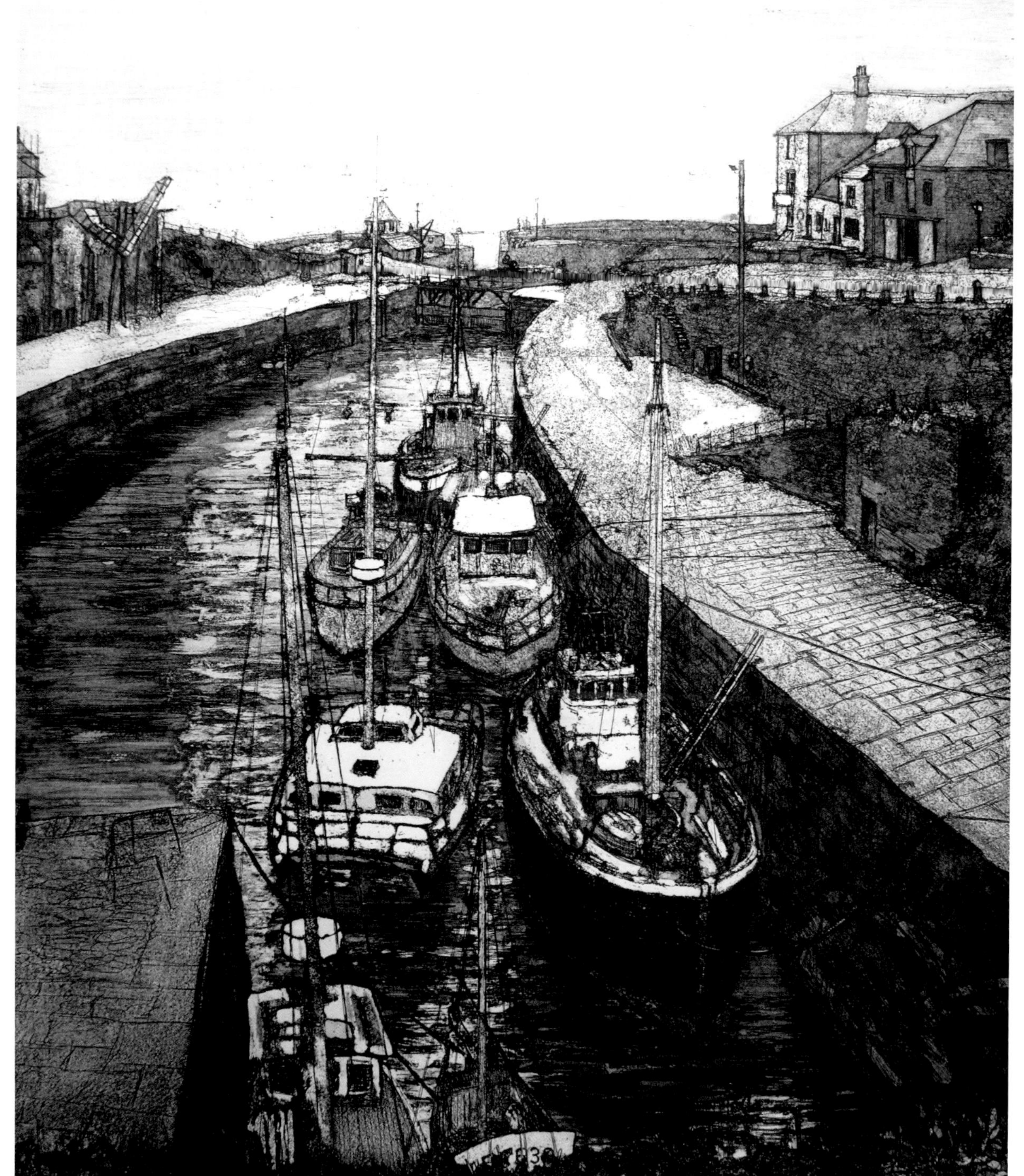

Facing page, from top: 'Tobogganing on the Gogs' (hand-coloured etching), 25cm x 50cm, edition of 50; 'Bankside into the Night' (sugarlift aquatint), 30cm x 40cm, edition of 50; This page: 'Charlestown' (steel etching), 50cm x 40cm, edition of 250

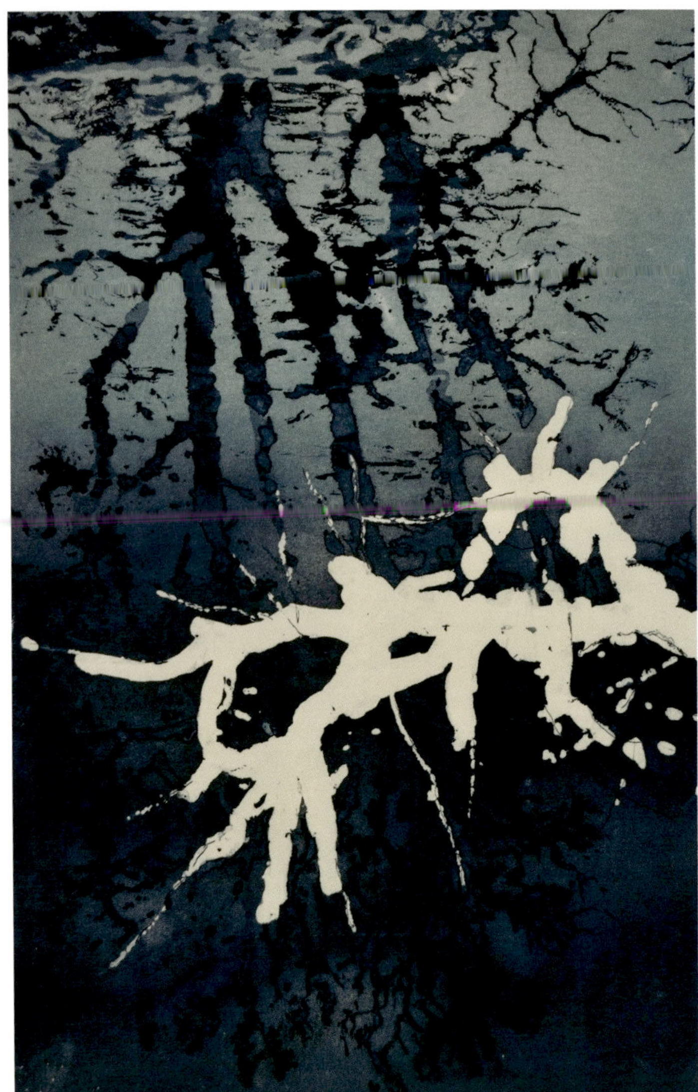

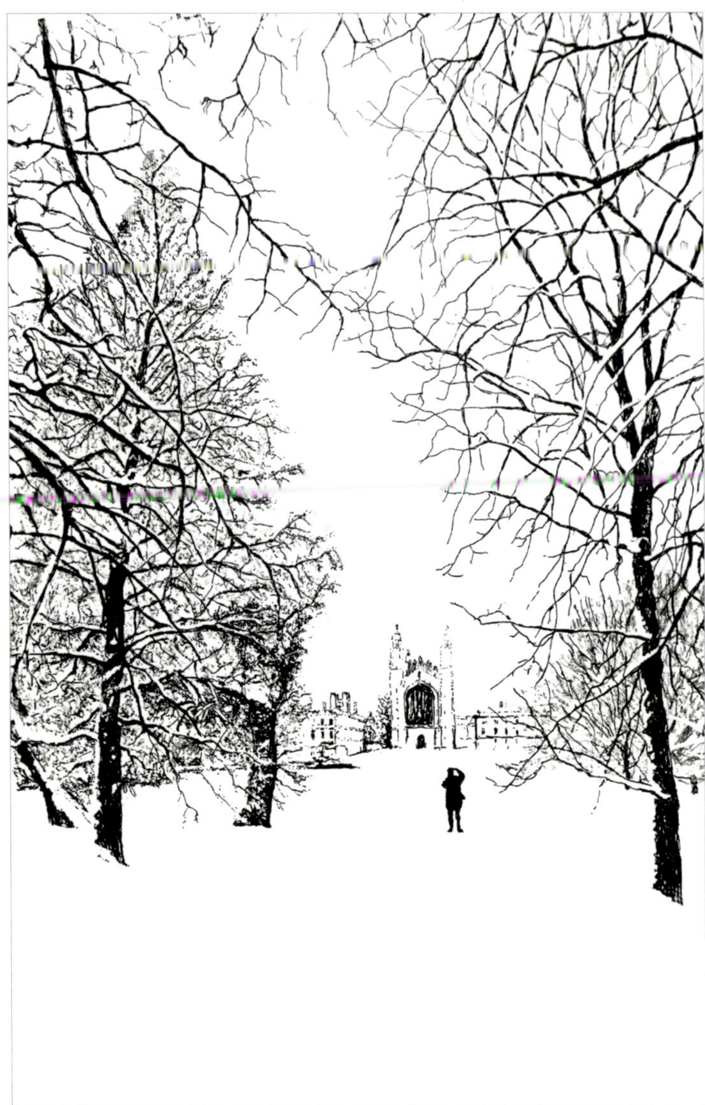

reverse and very much slower. For greater directness, he often uses 'sugar lift', beginning by painting the image in saturated sugar solution.

John started printmaking at an evening class. Advised to try etching, he instantly loved its combination of line and tone, which he uses to create atmospheric images. Favourite themes include buildings, trees and landscape, with Cambridge and Italy (particularly Venice) featuring strongly.

One of John's aquatints was selected by Norman Ackroyd RA for 'The Masters: Etching' at the Bankside Gallery in 2016. He has twice had work hung in the Royal Academy Summer Exhibition, and has been shortlisted on nine other occasions. *www.cambridgedrawingsociety.org*

From left: 'Snow and Water' (sugarlift aquatint), 40cm x 33cm, edition of 50; 'An Image of King's' (etching), 46cm x 30cm, edition of 50

ANNA PYE

Growing up on a farm in south Cambridgeshire, Anna Pye was immersed in nature and the countryside. This continues to inspire her work which, in retirement, has become focused increasingly on printmaking.

"I enjoy linocutting, screenprinting and monoprinting – I love the tools, processes, materials and colours involved in printmaking, both on paper and on fabric. For linocuts I use a beautiful old book binding press, and a new etching press for my monoprints."

Her current work is a playful approach with monoprinting; celebrating a lifetime love of nature, textiles and sewing. Anna first sewed and pressed flowers when she was a child, and now these lifelong interests are reflected in the colours, materials and textures she uses in her printmaking.

She holds linocutting and monoprint workshops in her studio in Steeple

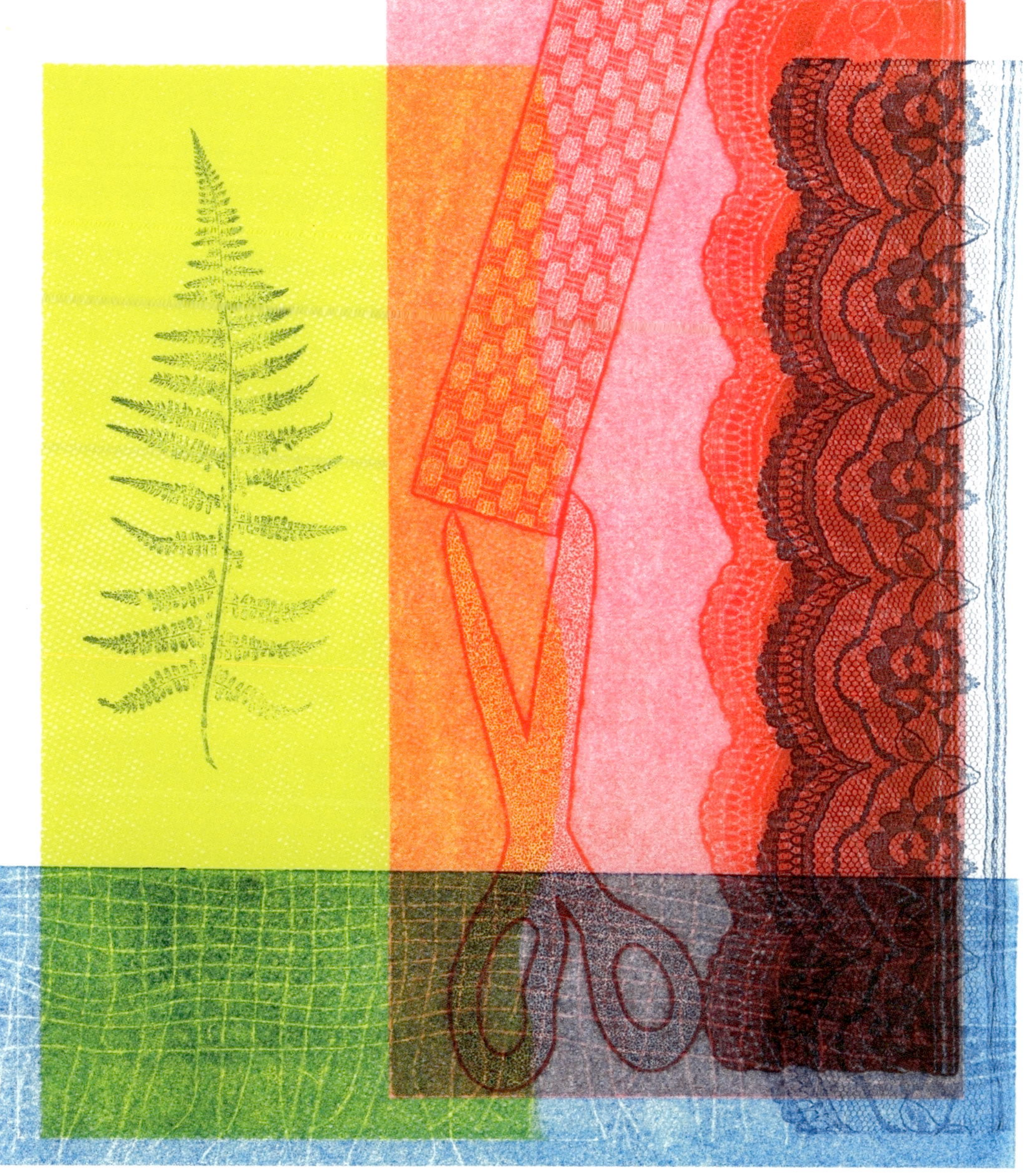

Above: 'Fern' (monoprint), 30cm x 28cm, unique

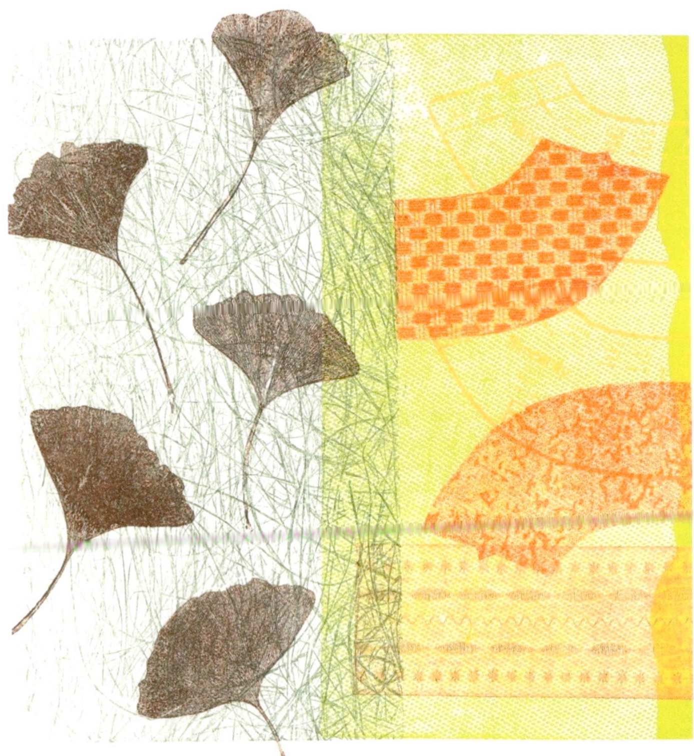

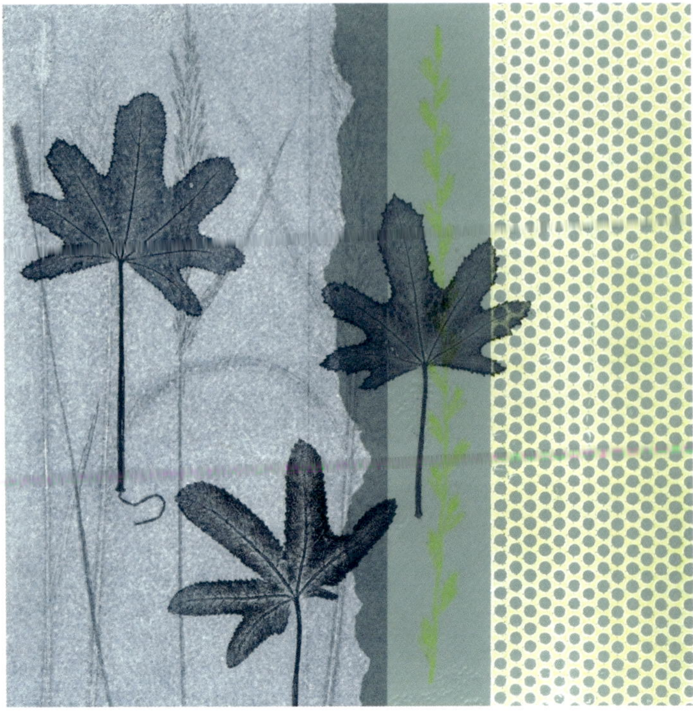

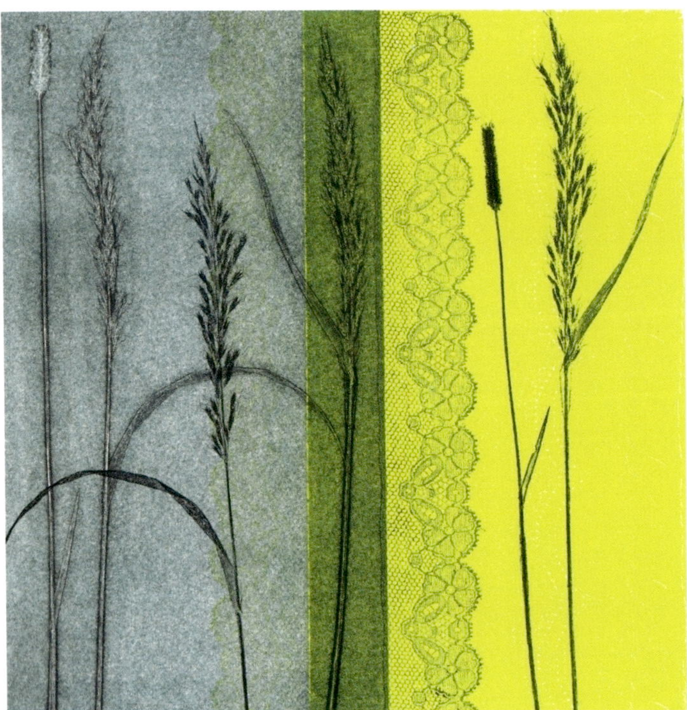

Morden, Cambridgeshire, and at other venues including Art Van Go, The Settlement and Oxford Summer School. She exhibits widely and with the Cambridge Drawing Society, Royston Arts Society, The Wynd Gallery and Cambridge Open Studios. "I have also enjoyed being part of the team organising the Cambridge Original Printmakers Biennale 2018 exhibition."
www.annapye.com

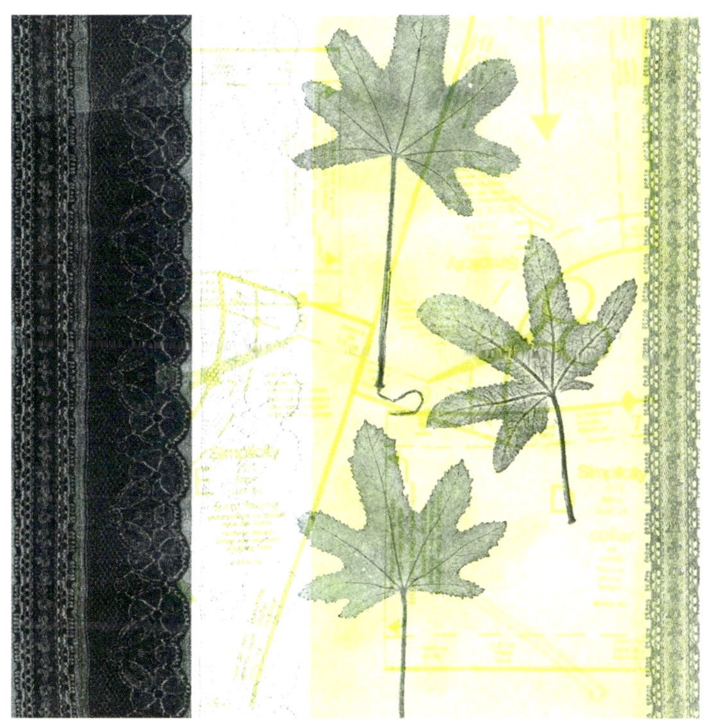

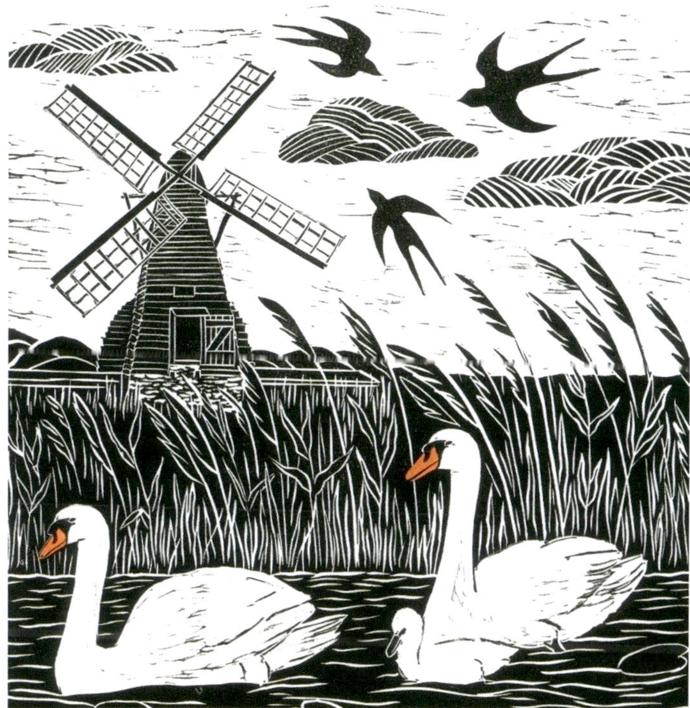

Top, left to right: 'Textures 1' (monoprint), 28cm x 30cm, unique; 'Hollyhock Leaves 1' (monoprint), 28cm x 29cm, unique; 'Lace and Leaves 1' (monoprint), 28cm x 29cm, unique; 'Wicken Fen' (linocut), 30cm x 30cm, edition of 50

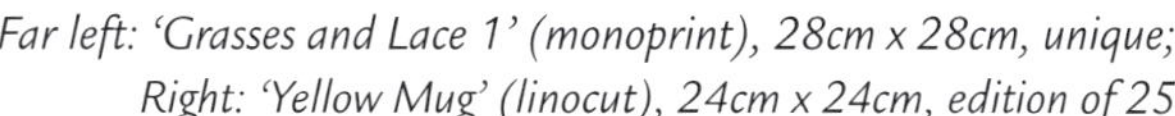

Far left: 'Grasses and Lace 1' (monoprint), 28cm x 28cm, unique;
Right: 'Yellow Mug' (linocut), 24cm x 24cm, edition of 25

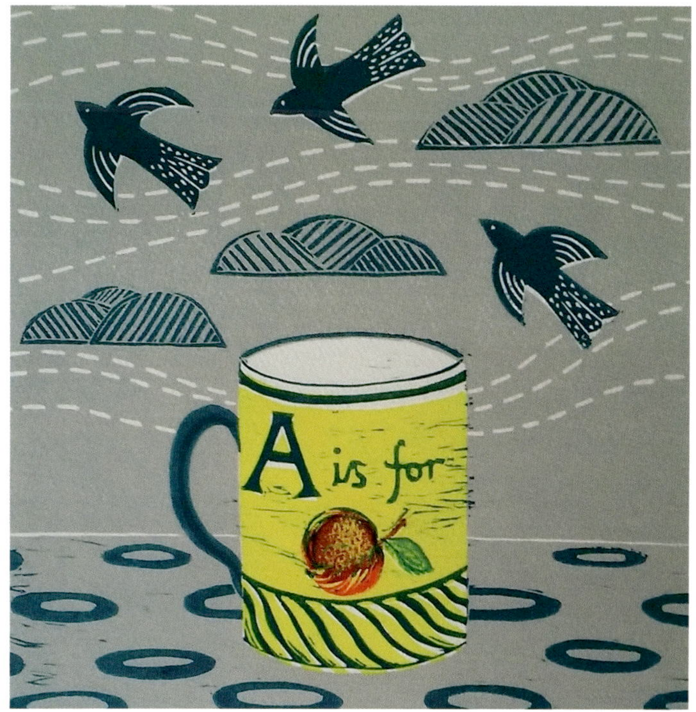

SHERRY REA

Sherry Rea's keen interest in biodiversity is expressed in her printmaking. She grew up on the Kent coast, studied for a PhD at Oxford University, and now tutors biological sciences. Her art often centres on the flora and fauna of rural Cambridgeshire, where she now lives and works, as well as on plants and creatures from her seaside roots and travels farther afield. Sherry focuses on texture and its resonance with the subject.

She enjoys collagraph and linocut. Her collagraphs may incorporate areas of drypoint, chine-collé or monoprint to achieve the effect she is after. "What some may throw in the recycling or on the compost heap, I squirrel away and hoard for creative use. I glue my finds on to pieces of cardboard and acetate, which I have strategically cut to shape, scratched into, and adorned with sticky varnishes and PVA glue. This assembly is the humble collage of refuse from which I print.

"Ink is painted on and then polished back to reveal the texture of the plate and to create highlights in the artwork. The contours of my collagraph plate mould the ink as it presses into the paper."

www.sherryrea.co.uk

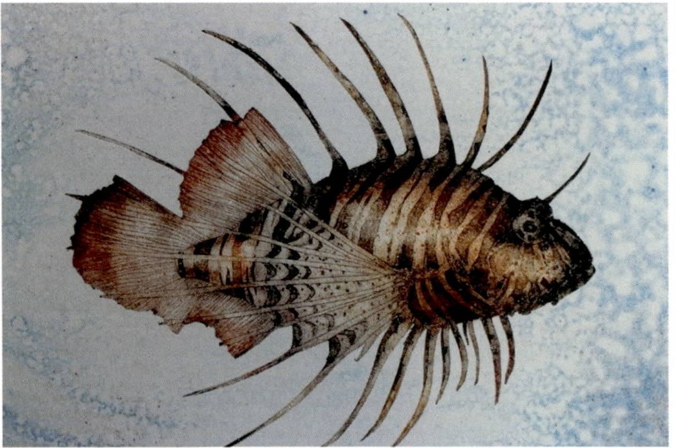

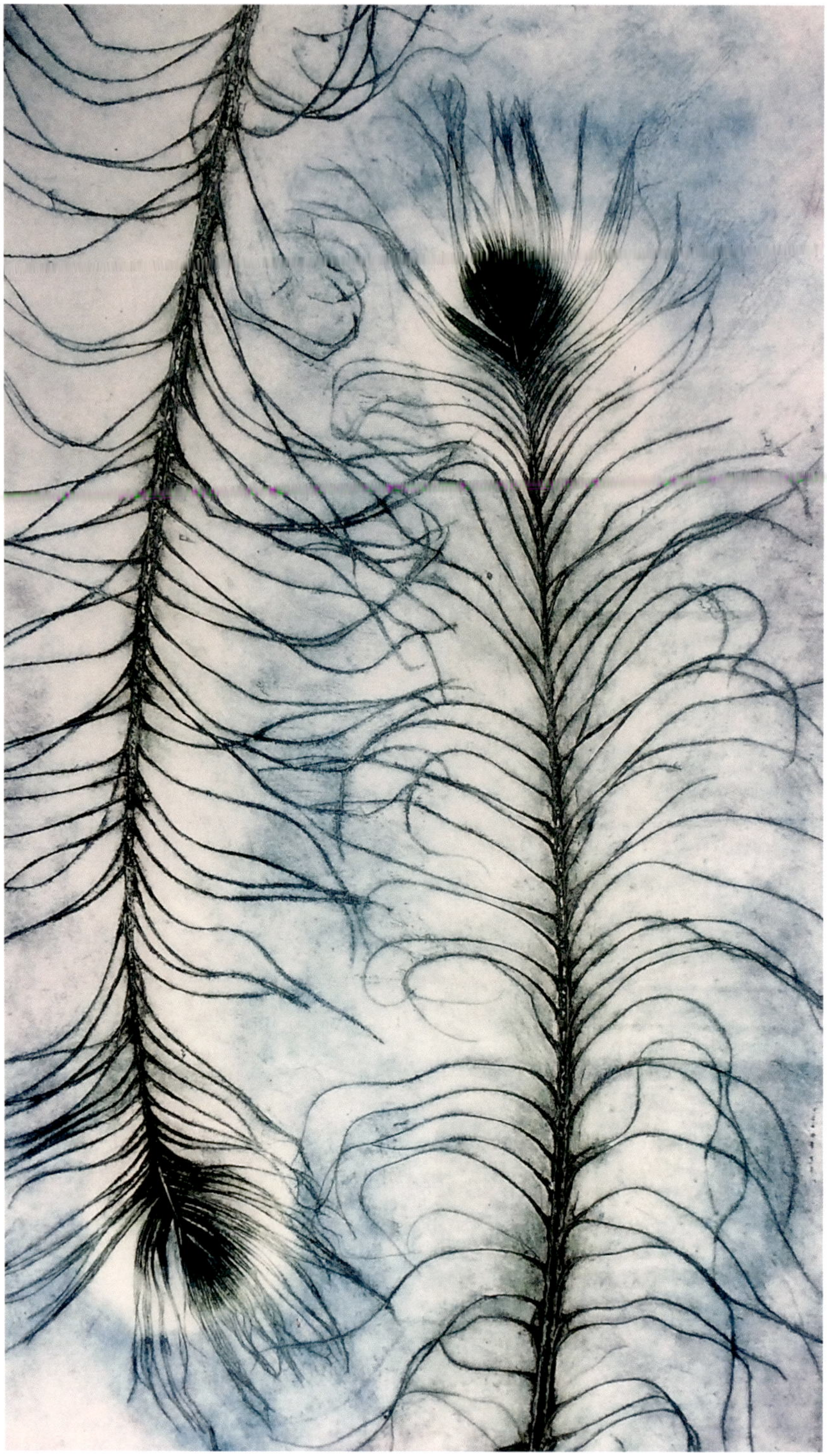

Above: 'Of the Ocean' (monoprint), edition of 12; Right: 'Top to Tail' (collagraph), edition of 12; Facing page, from left: 'Kismet' (collagraph), unique; 'Master of Disguise' (collagraph), edition of 6

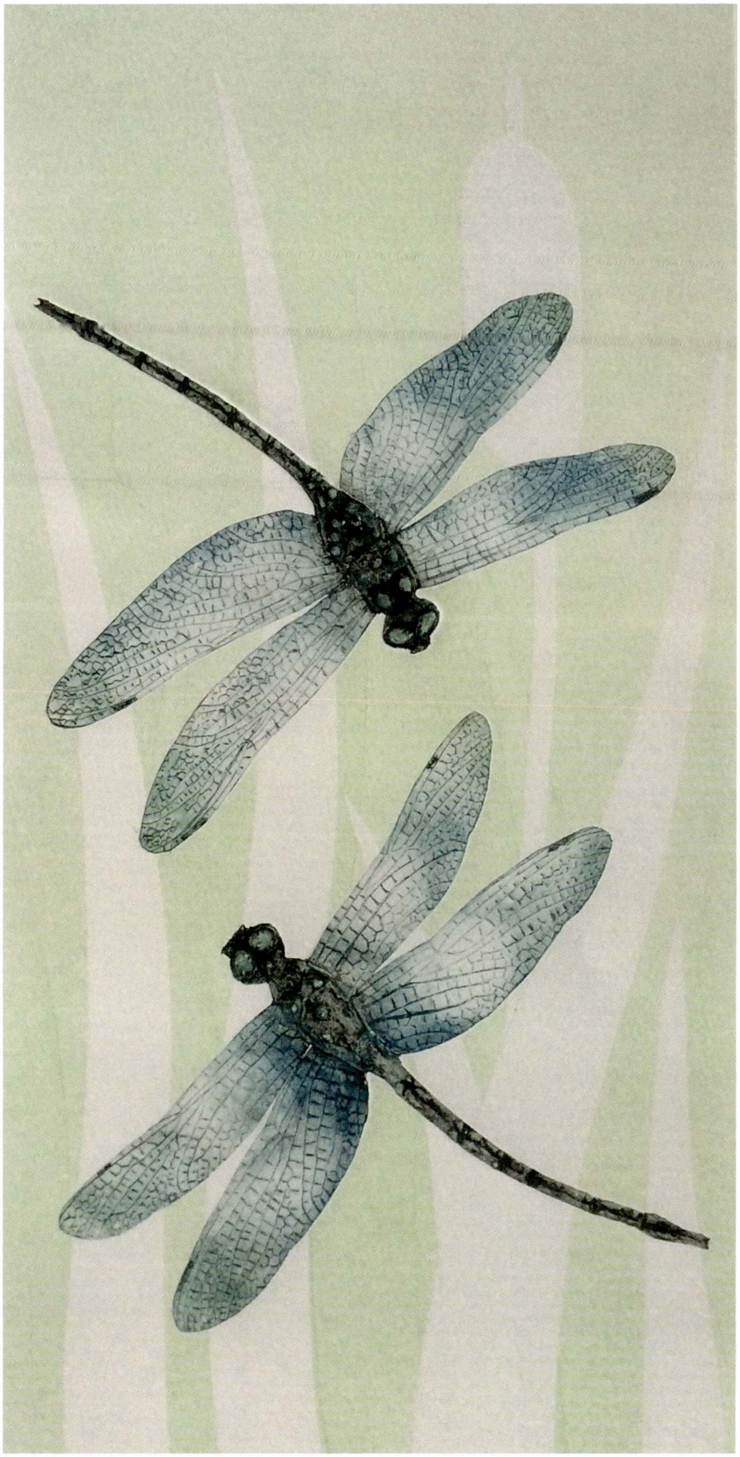

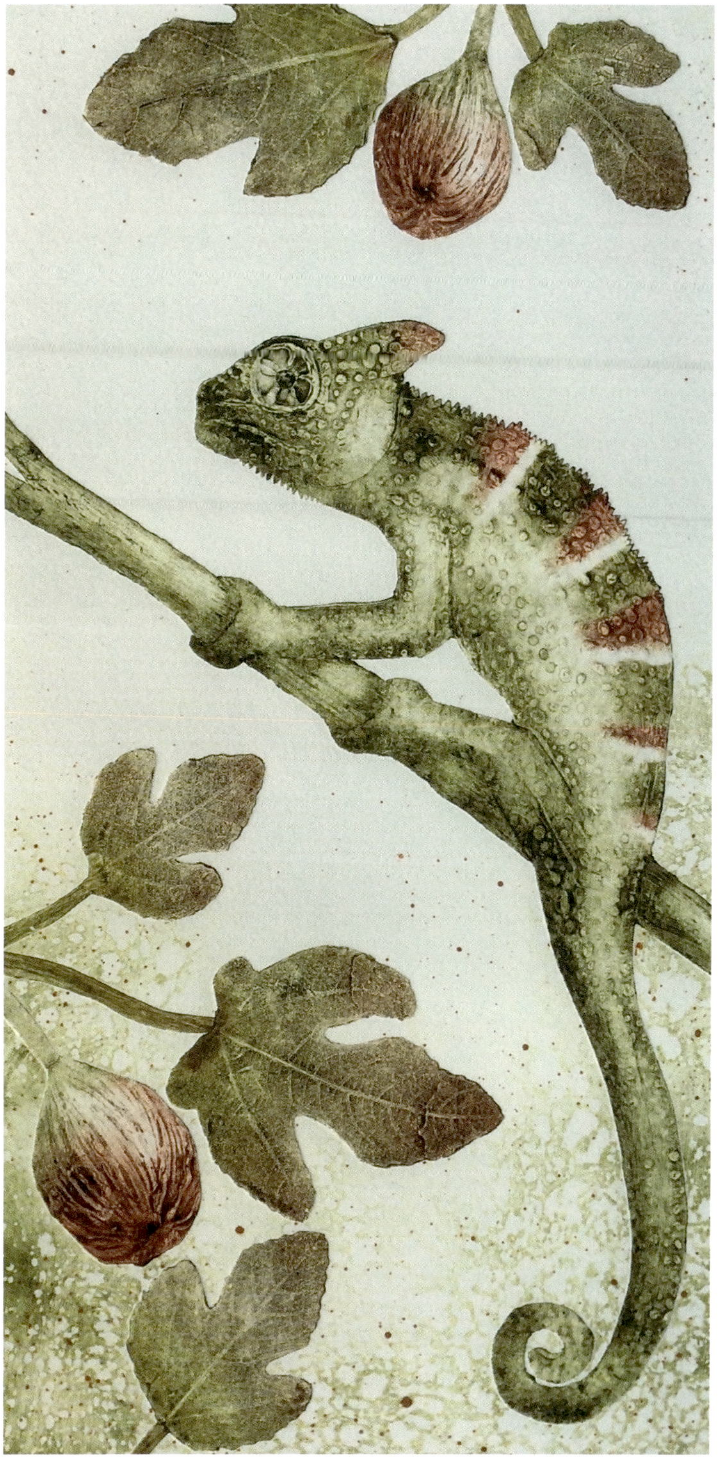

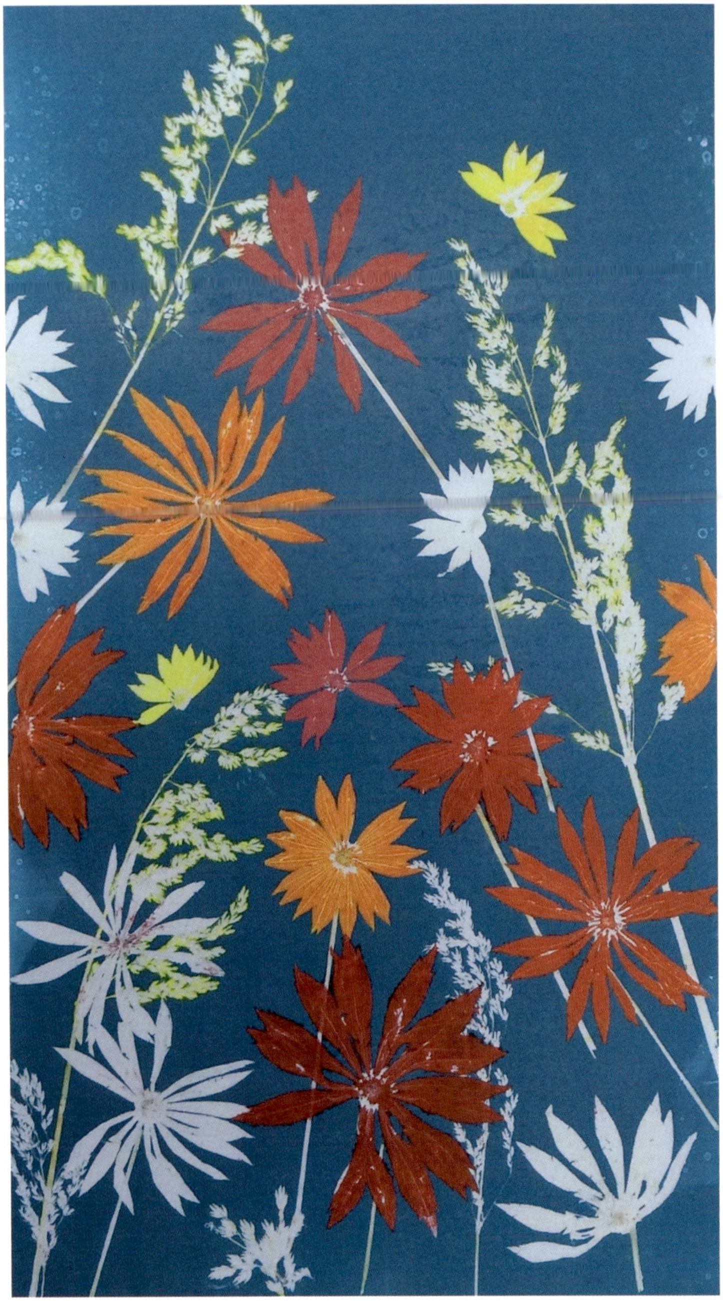

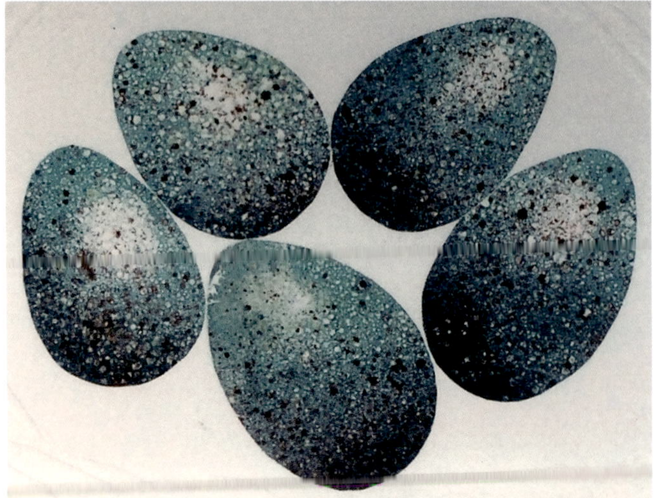

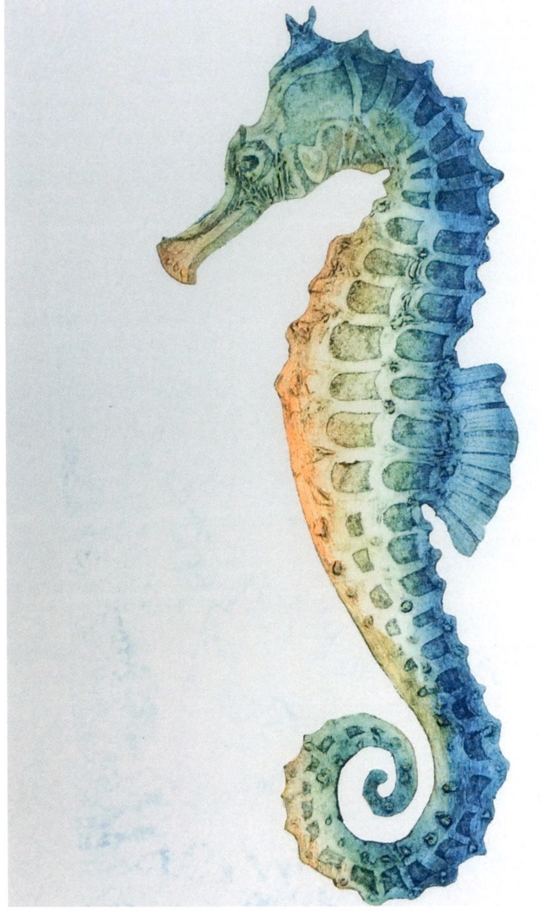

Above: 'Summer Blaze' (monoprint), unique; Top right: 'Redstart's Nest' (monoprint), unique; Right: 'Equus' (collagraph), edition of 12

NINA SAGE

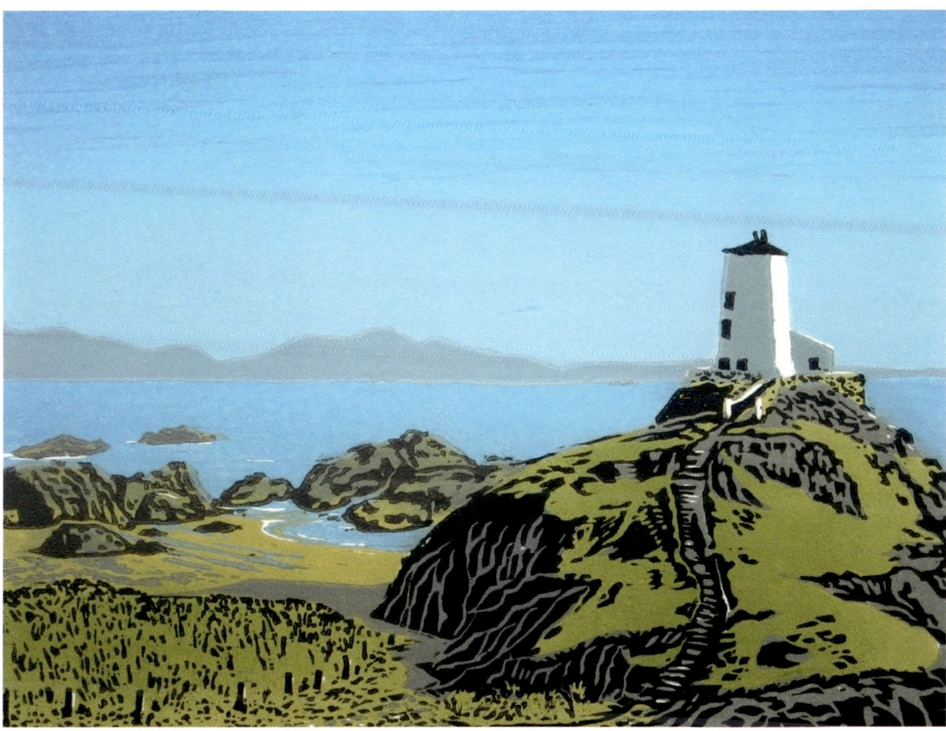

Ecologist-turned-printmaker Nina Sage takes her inspiration from a lifelong love of the natural world and her experiences working in the water industry. “It is no surprise that water and the life within it is a recurring theme in my work, and many of my prints feature the wildlife habitats and species I worked with in the field.”

She specialises in relief methods and monoprint, creating colourful, multi-layered prints in small, variable editions. “I find it hugely satisfying creating a beautiful image from a humble floor tile! I use both reduction and multi-block methods, sometimes combining both to get the images I want. I love colour, and spend ages mixing to get the balance

Above: ‘Path to the Old Lighthouse’ (woodcut), 30cm x 22.5cm, edition of 25;
Right: ‘By the Ford’ (linocut), 10cm x 30cm, edition of 20

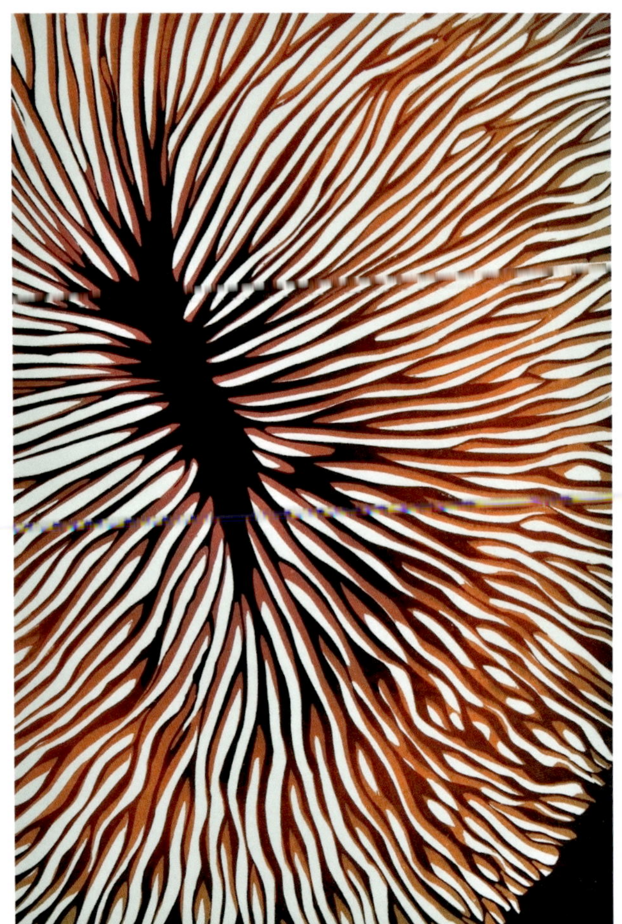

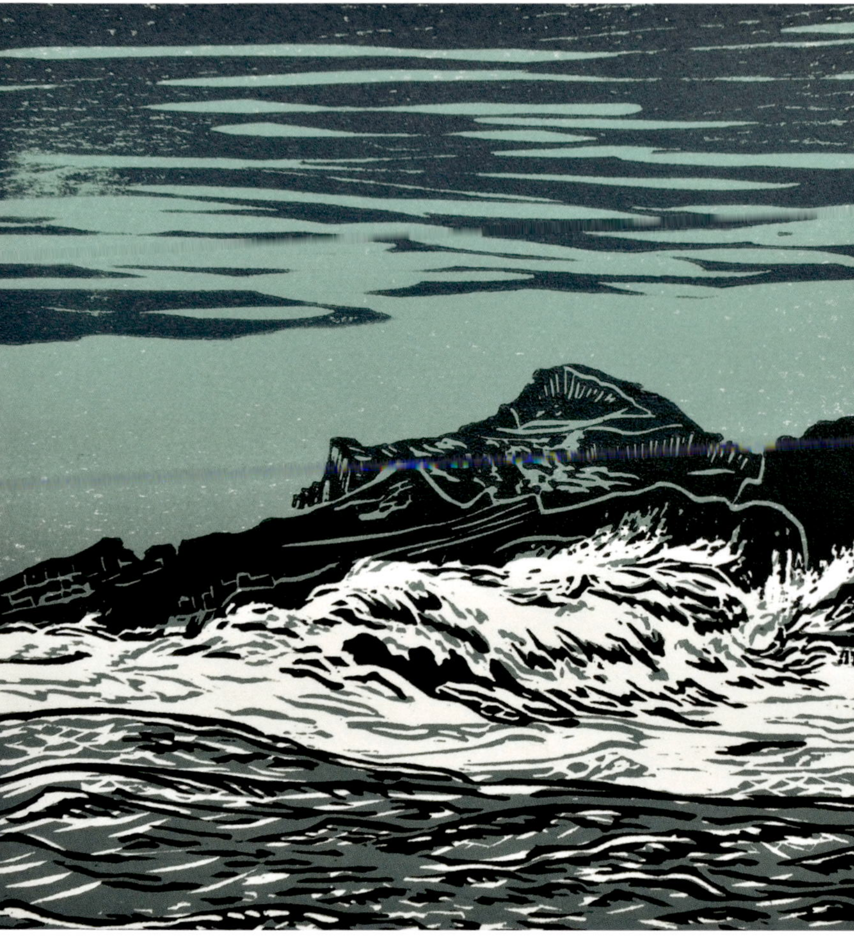

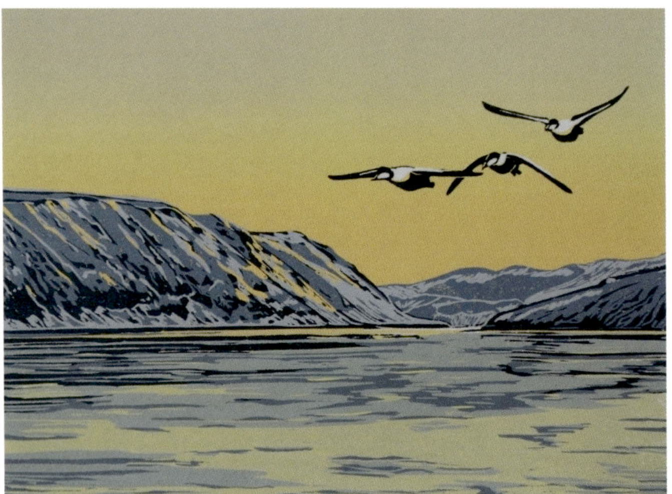

right, often using three to four colours per layer." Currently her work is focused on lino and woodcuts inspired by the coast of Britain and Norway.

Nina completed her formal training as a printmaker at the Curwen Print Study Centre in 2012. "My husband bought me a Rollaco press for our wedding anniversary that year, and I haven't looked back since!"

She exhibits locally, is a member of Cambridge Open Studios and the Cambridge Drawing Society, and enjoys teaching evening classes and workshops.

www.ninasage.co.uk

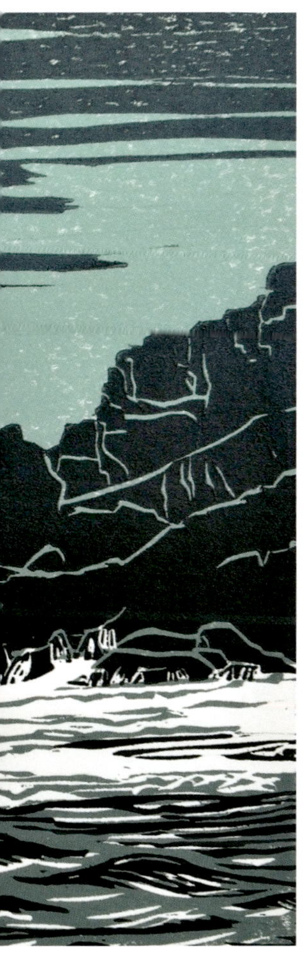

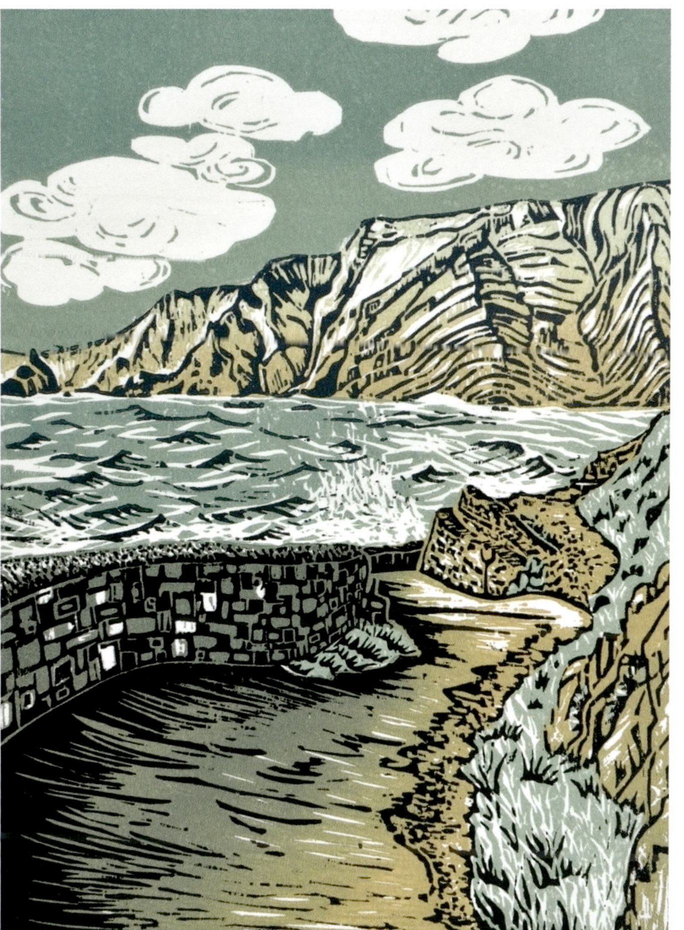

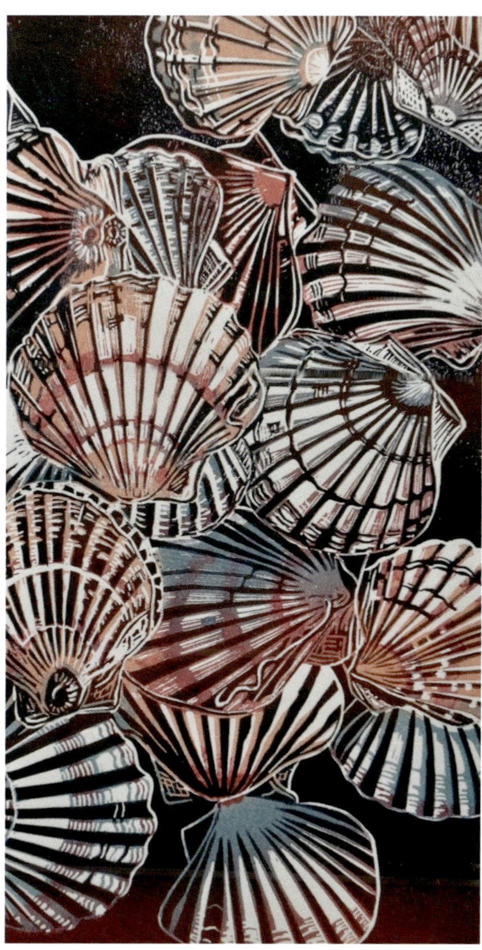

From far left, top: 'Mushroom Coral' (linocut), 20cm x 30cm, edition of 24; 'On the Rocks' (woodcut), 22.5cm x 30cm, edition of 23; 'Down to the Quay' (woodcut), 22.5cm x 30cm, edition of 17; 'Red Scallops' (linocut), 20cm x 30cm, edition of 23; Bottom left: 'Eiders Wing North' (reduction linocut), 30cm x 22.5cm, edition of 25; Right: 'End of the Day' (linocut), 30cm x 22.5cm, edition of 25

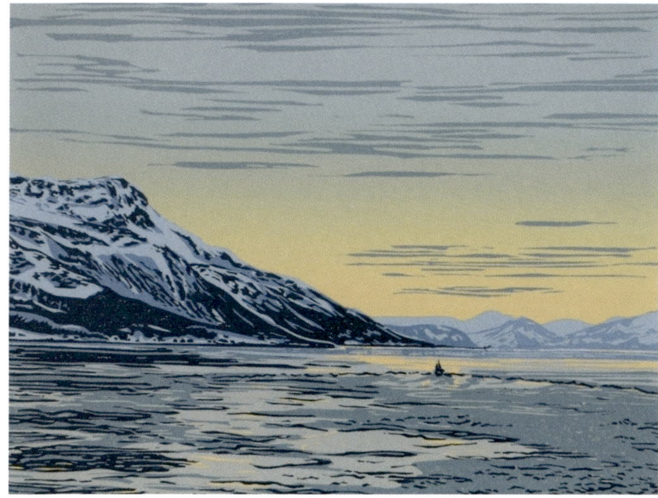

LOUISE STEBBING

Louise Stebbing has been mesmerised by printmaking techniques since attending an Art Foundation Course at Cambridge followed by a degree course in Sheffield and Postgraduate Printmaking at Camberwell, London. In her Norfolk studio she uses a variety of techniques, but mostly lino printing and etching.

She draws inspiration from her environment, and tries to capture the essence of a place. "My images usually start with a sketch, and I like the print to evolve as I create it – not working out too much detail in advance, but using my many years of experience to let the image develop in the direction it happens to take me at that particular time."

Louise has exhibited extensively in the UK, including at the Summer Exhibition at the Royal Academy, Mall Galleries, Affordable Art Fair Battersea and Hampstead. She has won prizes for her prints and been published in several art books. She is a member of The Printmakers Council and West Norfolk Artists Association; and a Core Team Member for the Cambridge Original Printmakers Biennale 2018.
www.louisestebbingprintmaker.com

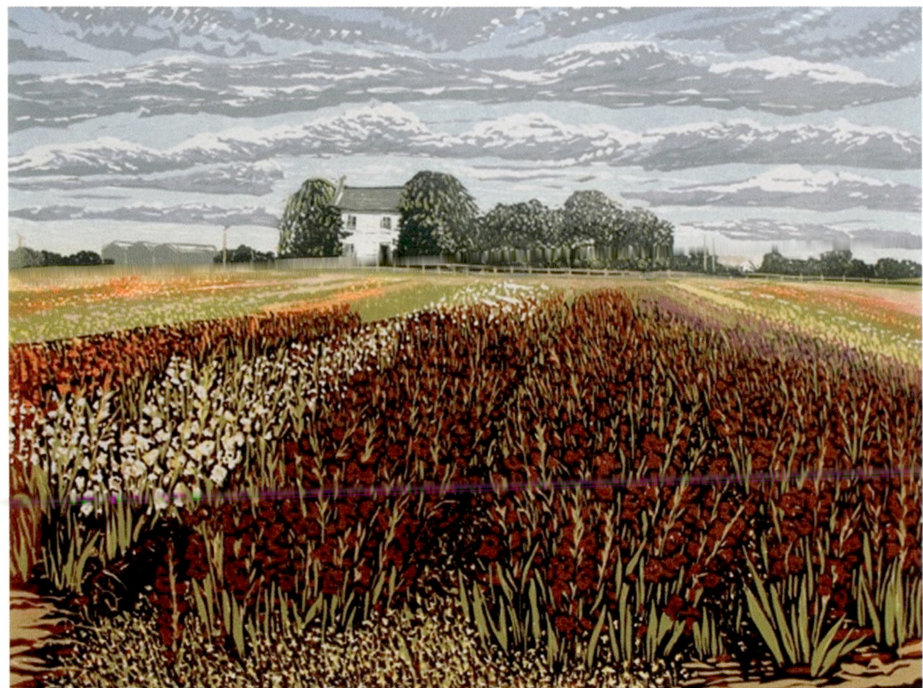

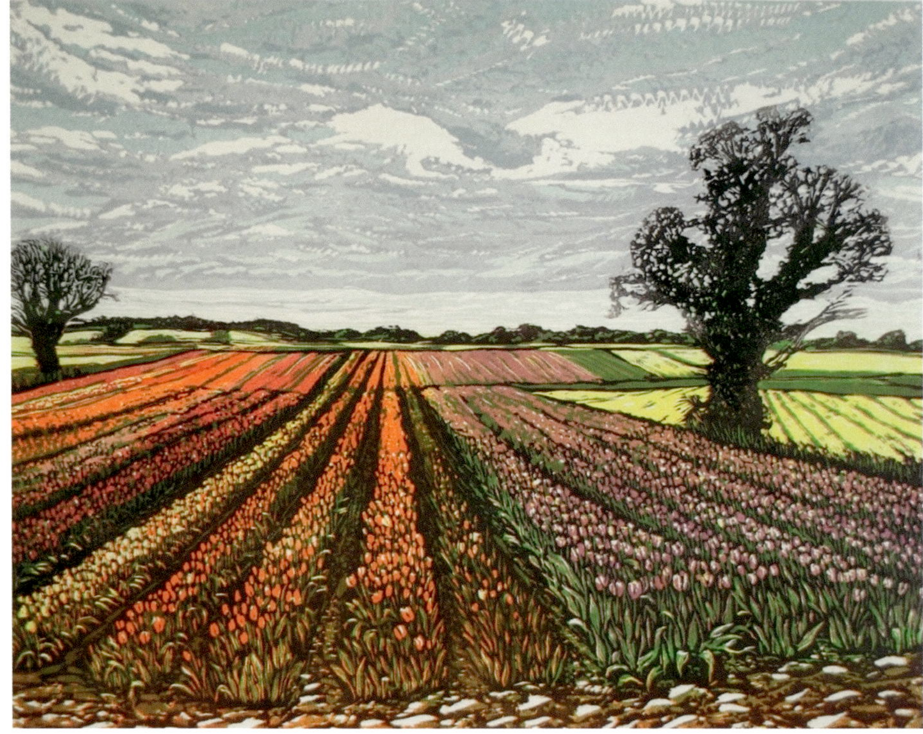

This page, from top: 'Return of the Gladioli' (linocut), 50cm x 40cm, edition of 14; 'Tulip Fields in Norfolk' (linocut), 50cm x 39cm, edition of 14; Facing page, from top: 'Attracting the Gulls' (linocut), 18cm x 39cm, edition of 14; 'Hunstanton Cliffs' (linocut), 54cm x 28cm, edition of 8

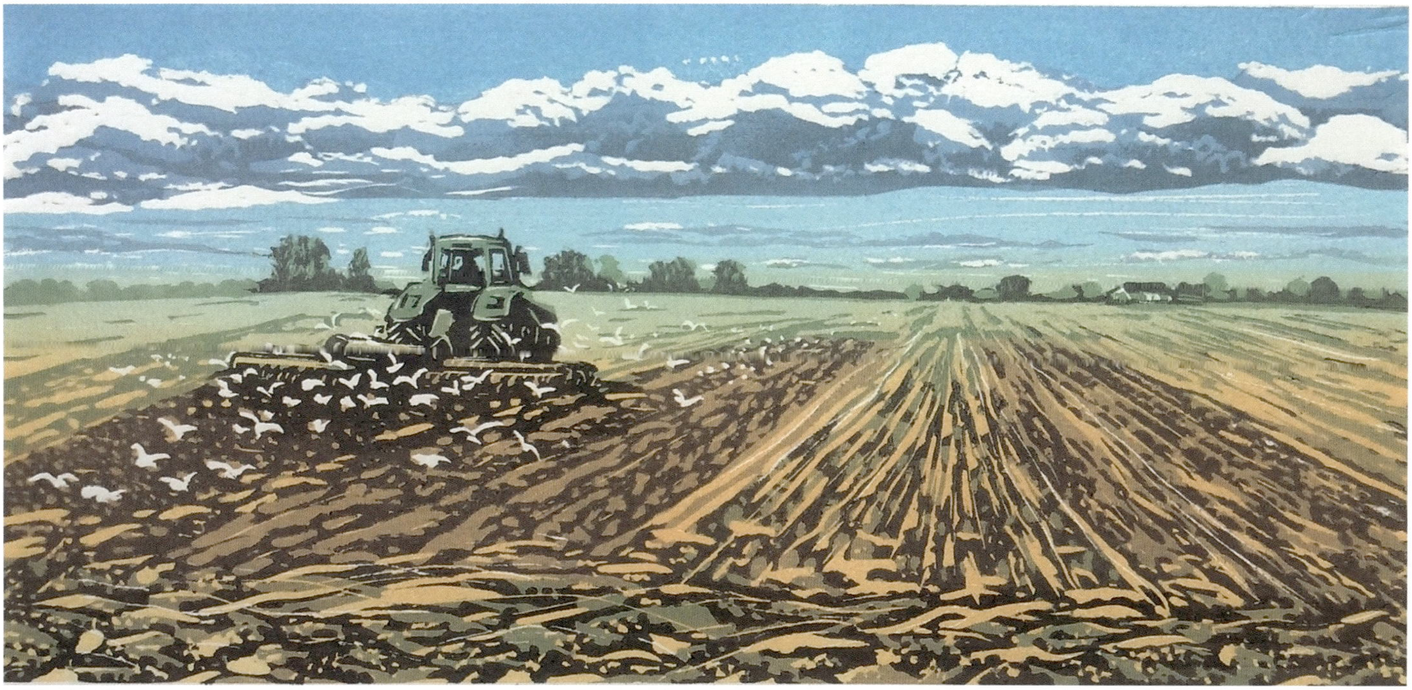

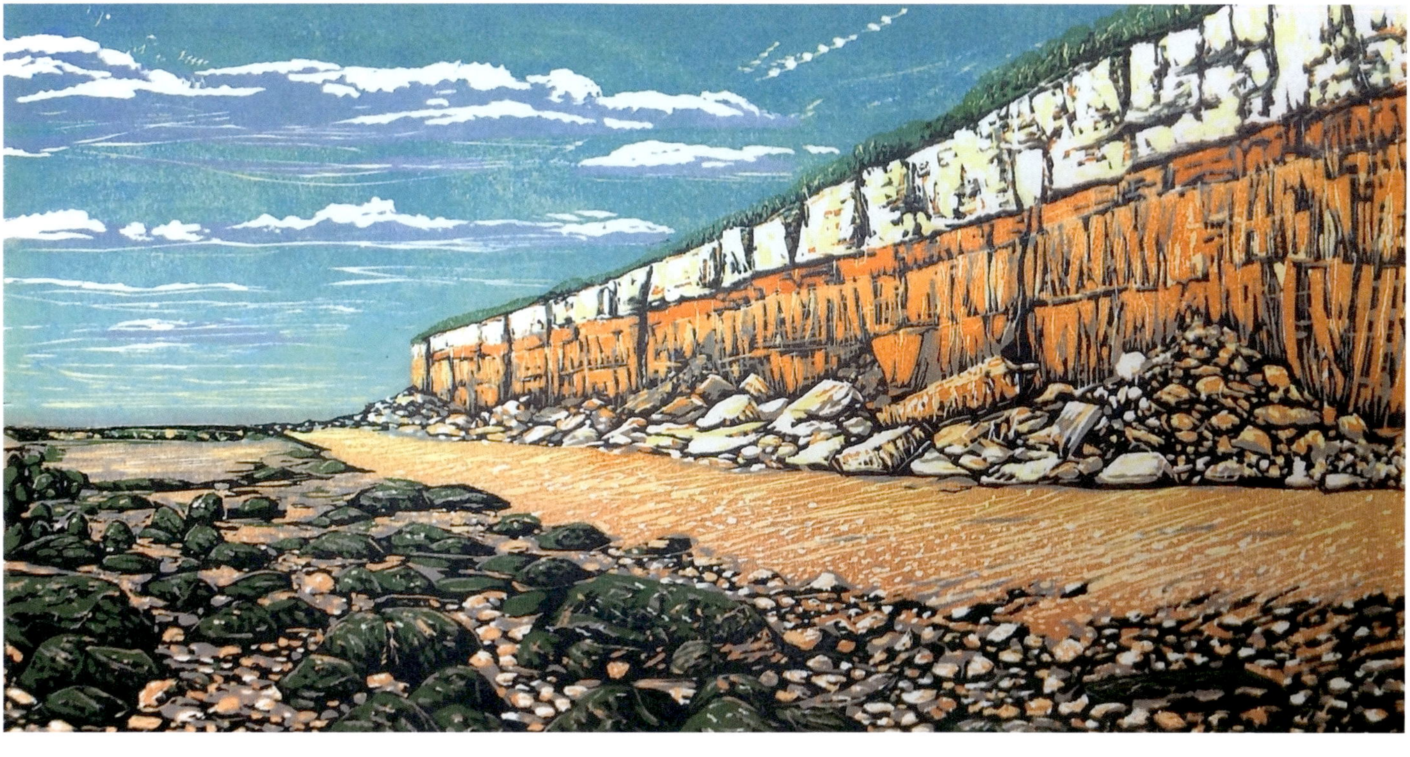

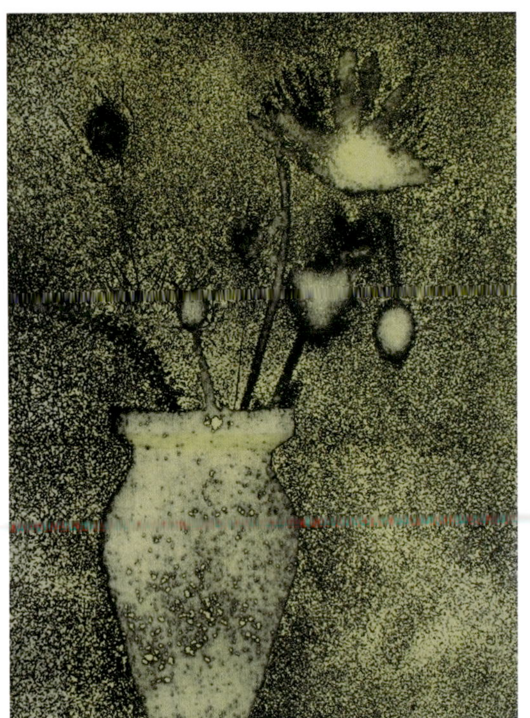

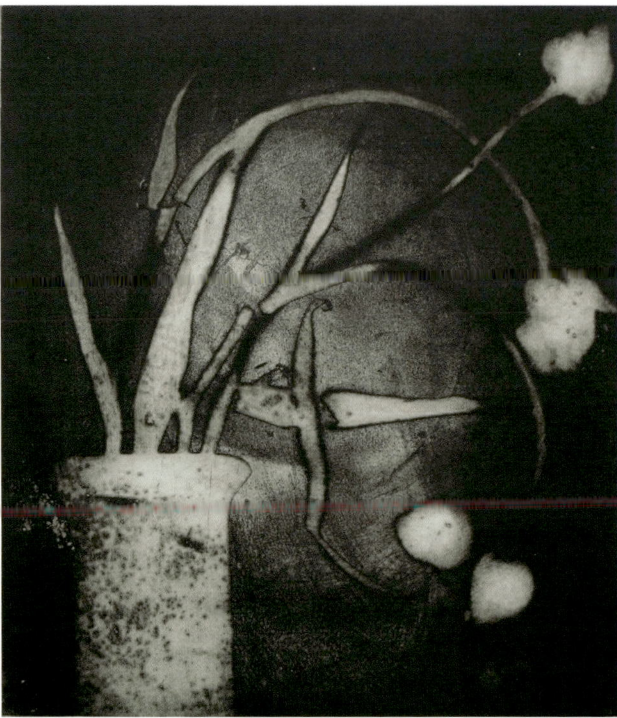

Far left: 'Serene' (aquatint), 30cm x 23cm, edition of 50; Left: 'Tulips' (aquatint), 30cm x 25cm, edition of 50; Bottom left: 'River Trail' (linocut), 18cm x 39cm, edition of 14 – all Louise Stebbing

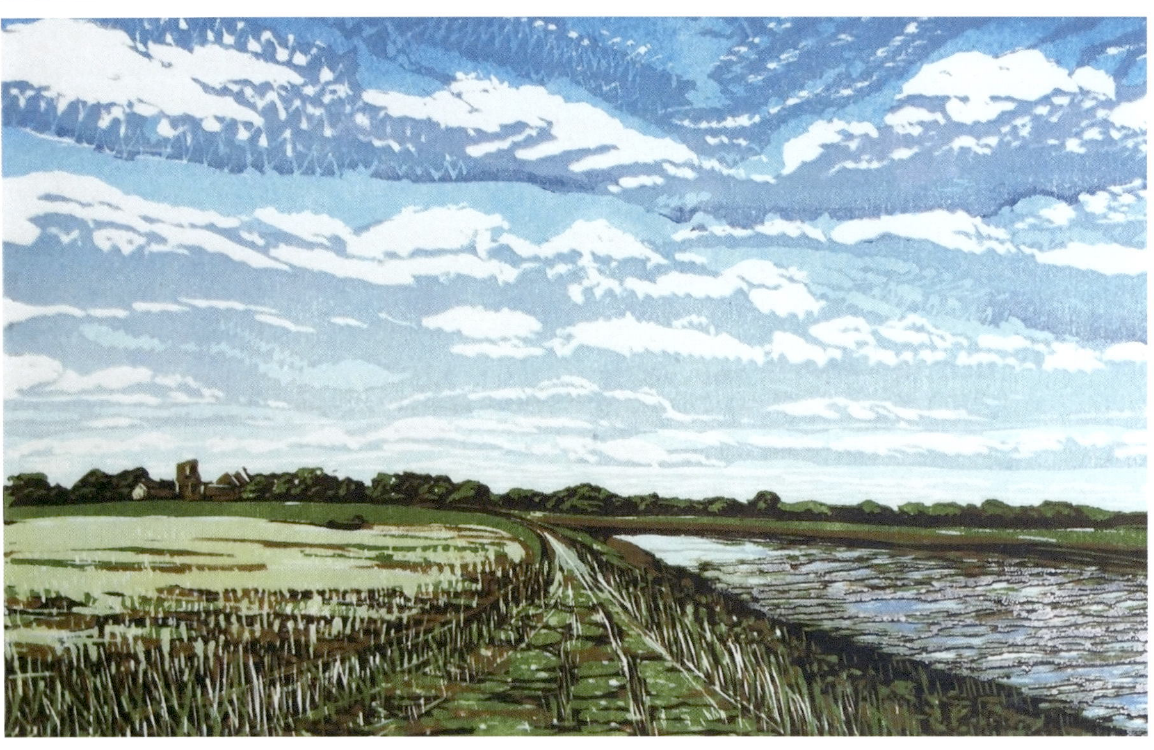

RUTH TILLYARD

Linocut printer Ruth Tillyard trained in Glasgow but recently moved to Cambridge. "I generally depict places I like," she says, "and seek to capture the essence of locations by, often, combining visual elements from original sketches in a playful or whimsical way."

Ruth has a BA Honours (1st class) in Visual Arts. Prizes include the Glasgow Print Studio Prize (for her degree show) and the Millennium Award for Best in Show (Milngavie Art Club).

She sells through galleries including the Lillie Art Gallery in East Dunbartonshire and the Fairfax Gallery in Holt, Norfolk. *www.ruthtillyardartist.co.uk*

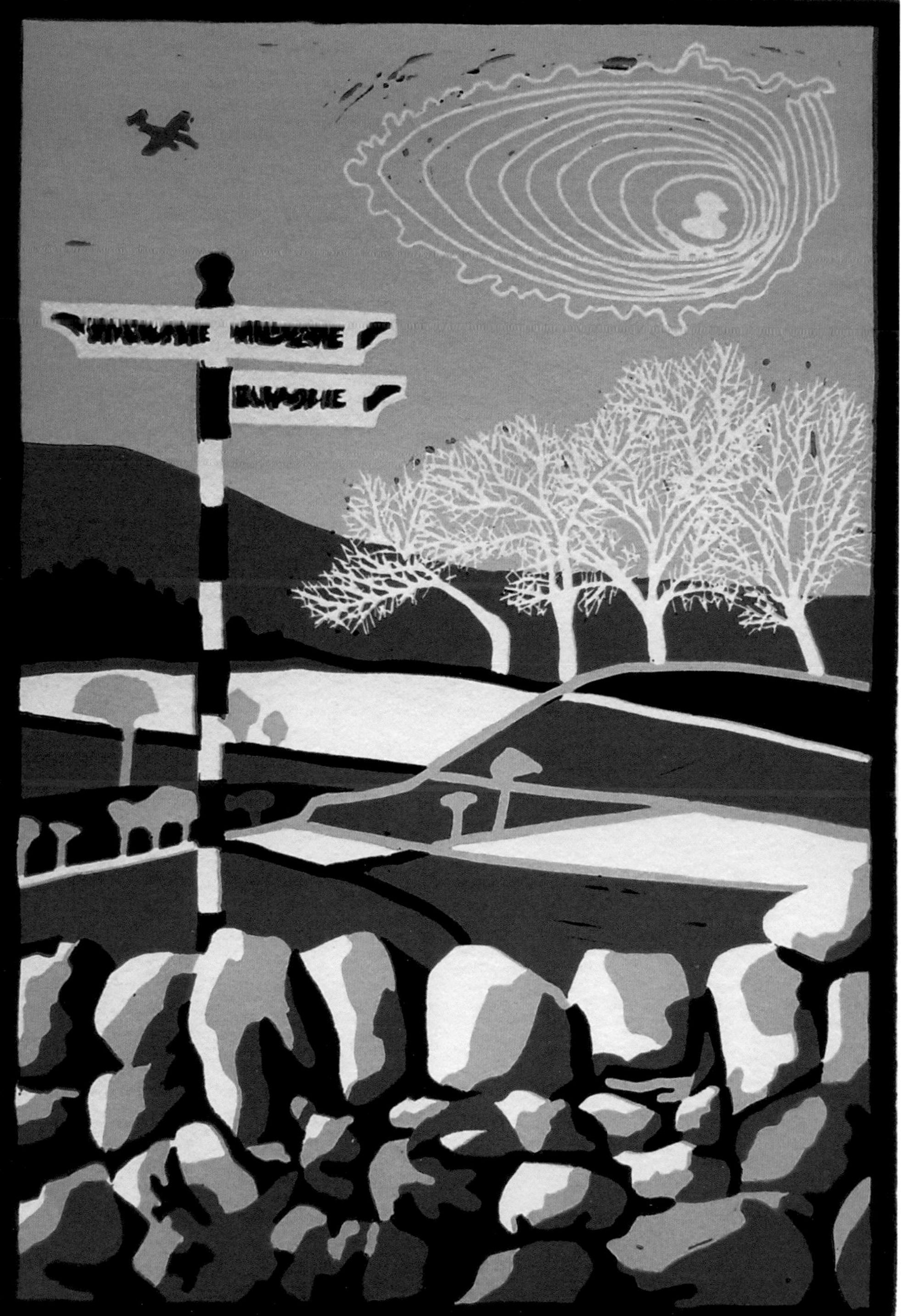

Right: 'Baldernock 2' (three-colour reductive linocut), A4, edition of 25

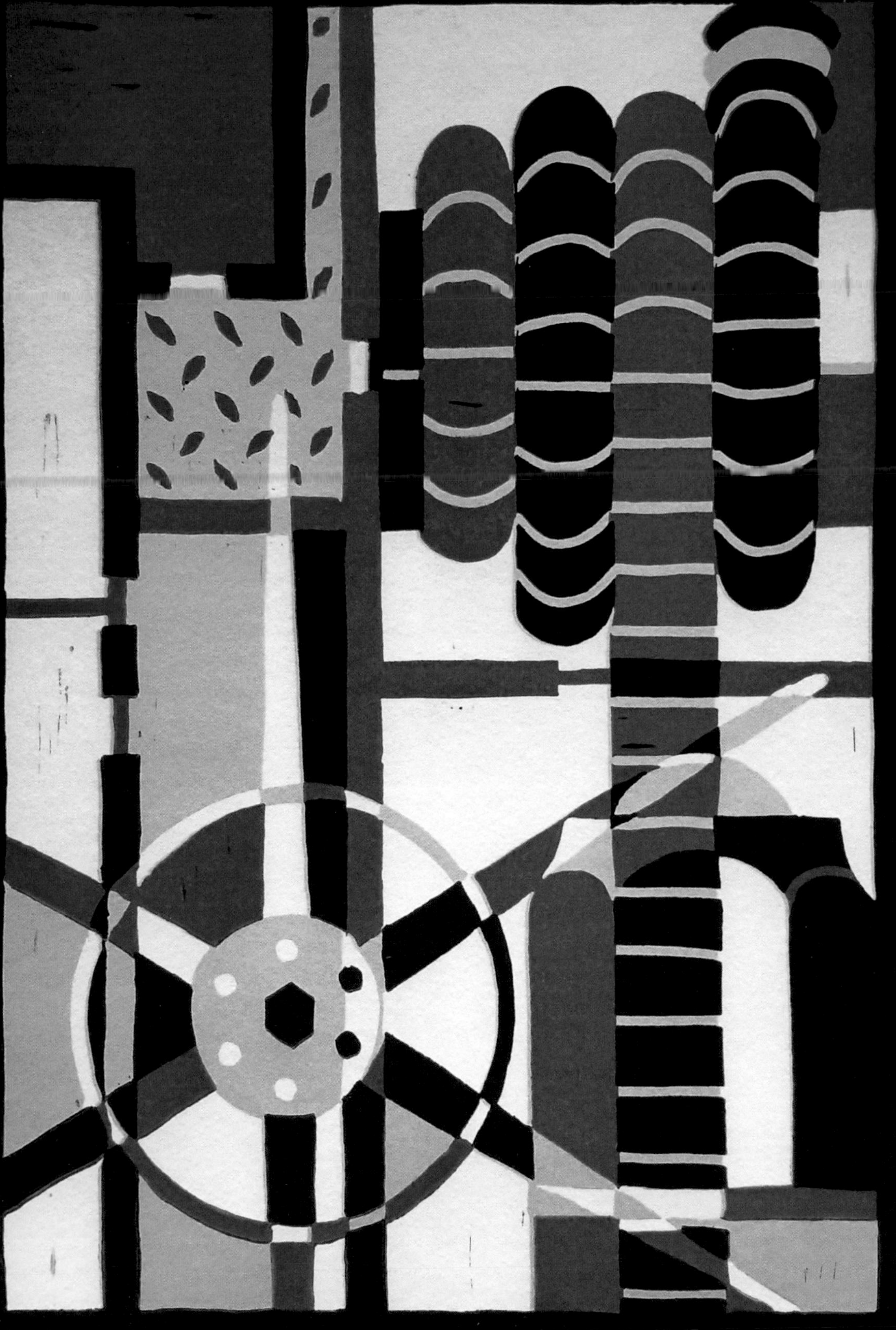

Left: 'Studio 2' (3-colour reductive linocut), A4, unique – Ruth Tillyard

From top: 'Mackerel' (3-colour reductive linocut), A4, edition of 24; 'Blakeney – Who's Watching?' (3-colour reductive linocut), A4, edition of 26 – Ruth Tillyard

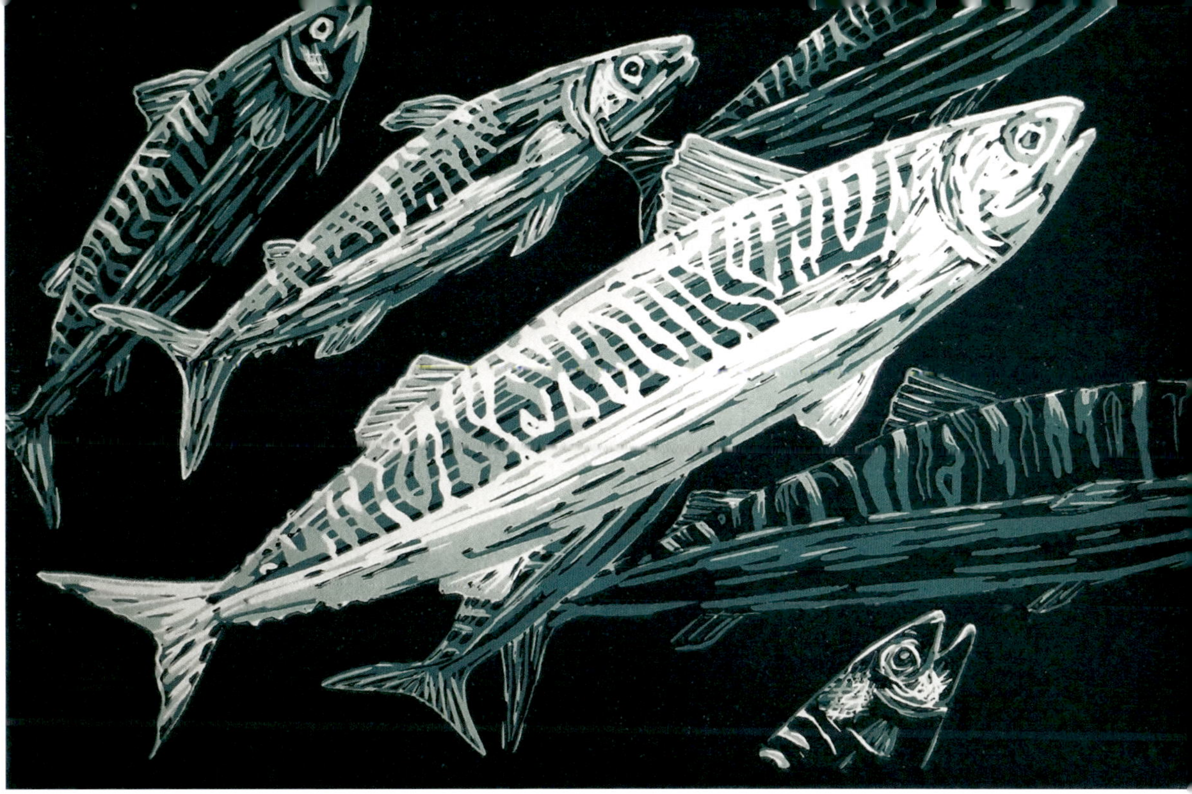

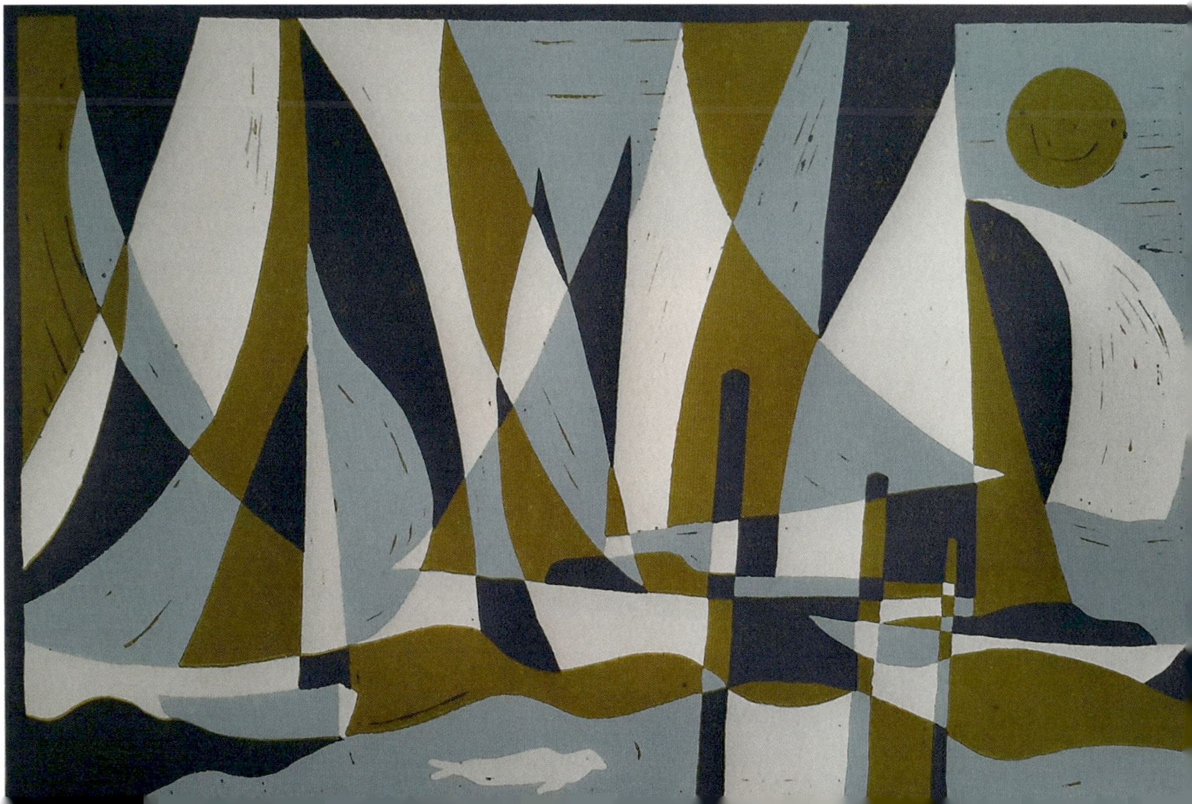

JO TUNMER

Visual artist Jo Tunmer is a Cambridge Original Printmakers co-founder. Her interest in printmaking was piqued while studying for the certificate in advanced printmaking at the Curwen Print Study Centre in 2012.

Originally from East London, she is drawn to explore the juxtaposition of urban and rural life in her work. Her landscapes usually feature large skies, often devoid of people and buildings. In contrast, her urban scenes tend to focus on solitary figures. Jo's work evokes a sense of calm, and her aim is to encourage viewers to look for the unexpected. They might discover incorporated text, or be left intrigued by her use of blended colour that leaves them wondering what lies beyond what is immediately visible.

She works predominantly with relief Solarplate etching. However, her recent studies for her Masters in Printmaking at Cambridge School of Art have provided a platform for her to venture into new printmaking techniques. She is currently working on large installation woodcut prints, marrying these with digital printmaking processes.

Jo's Cambridge Walkabout series of Solarplate etchings are exclusive to Cambridge Contemporary Art. In addition to running her art practice, she is also a private art educator and an artist facilitator for Kettle's Yard.

www.jotunmer.com

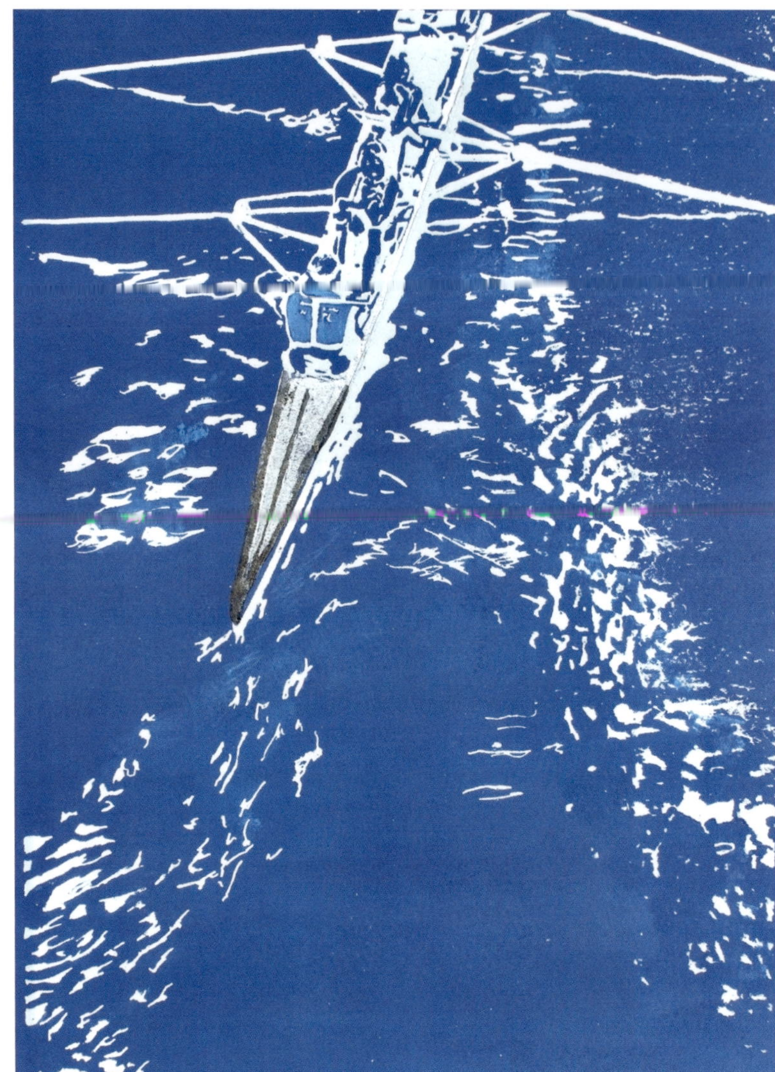

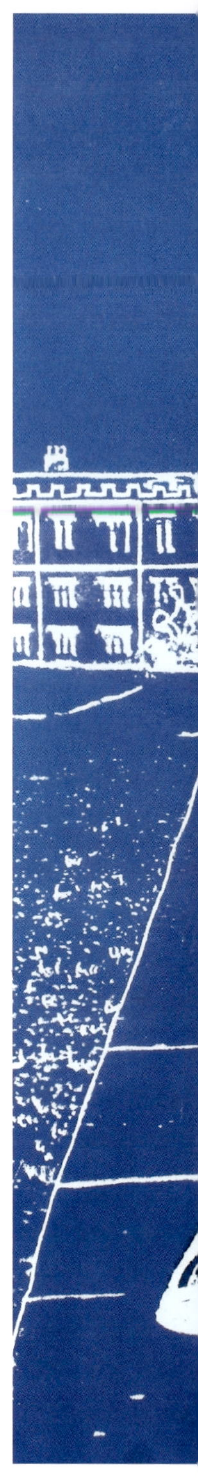

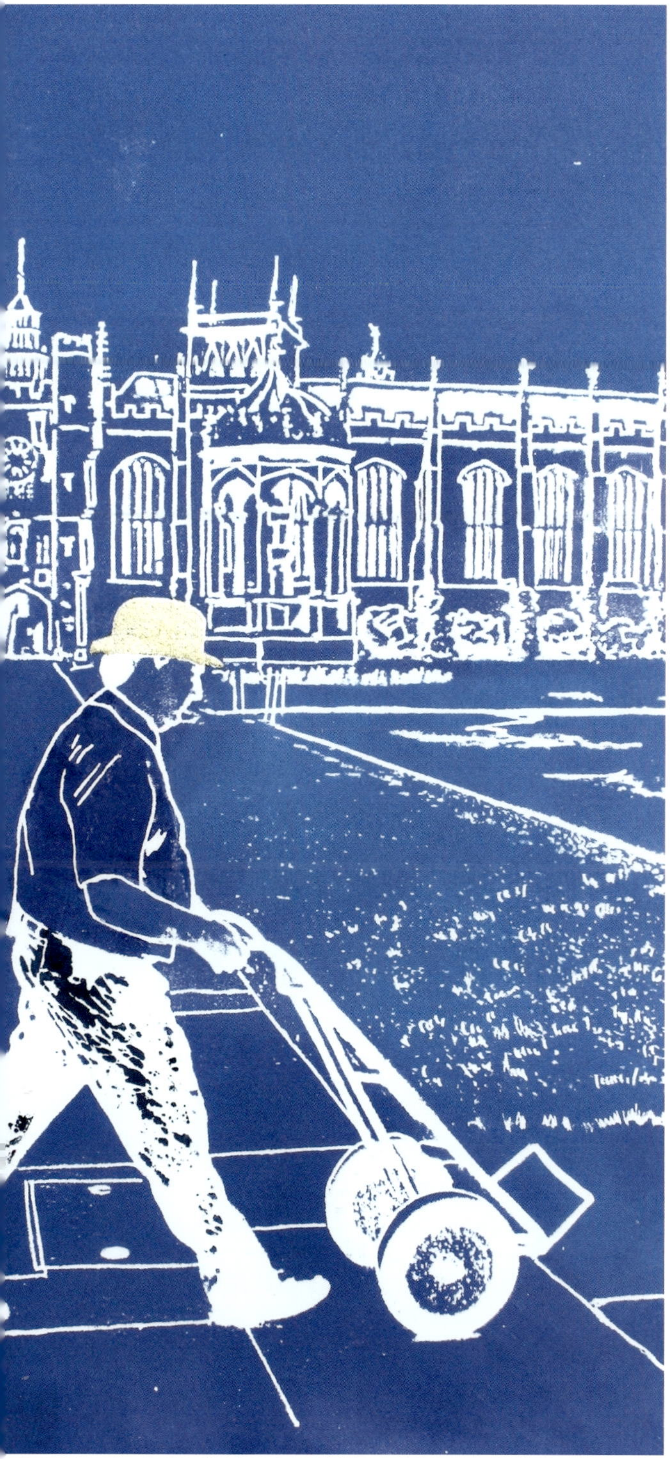

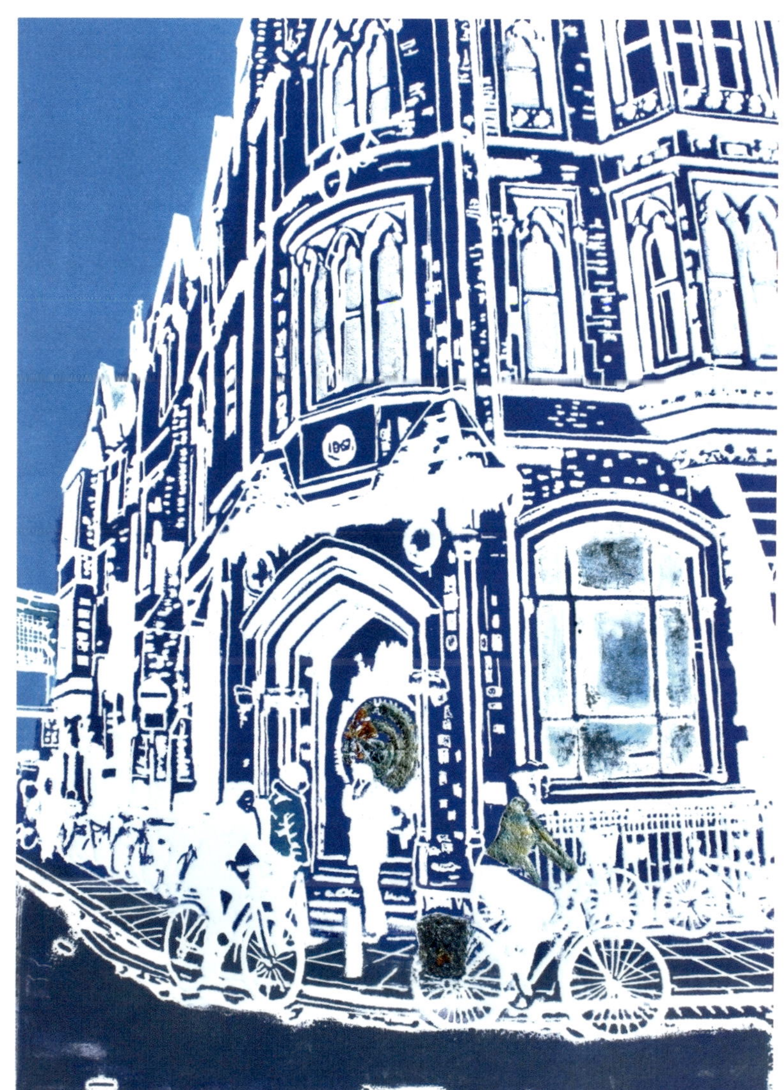

From far left: 'Out of the Picture'; 'Another Day at the Office'; 'Passing Time' (all relief Solarplate etchings), A4, editions of 40

From right, clockwise: 'Silent Study' (relief Solarplate etching), A3, edition of 30; 'Dappled' (Solarplate etching with variegated gold leaf), 15cm x 15cm, edition of 25; 'In Motion' (relief Solarplate etching), 10cm x 10cm, edition of 25

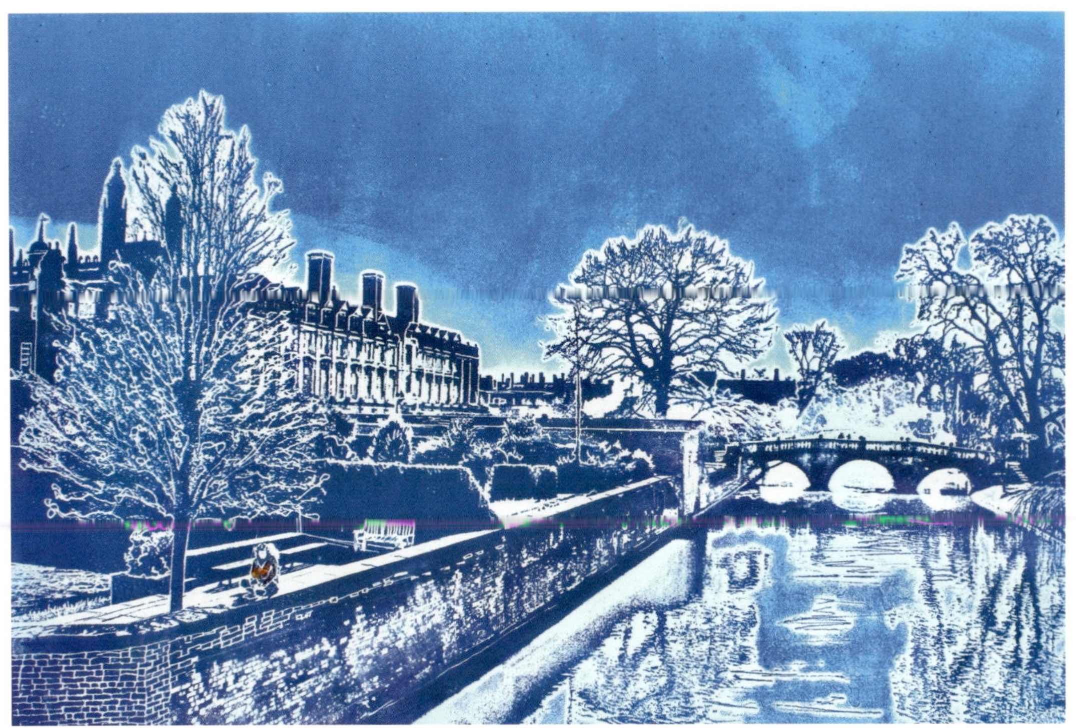

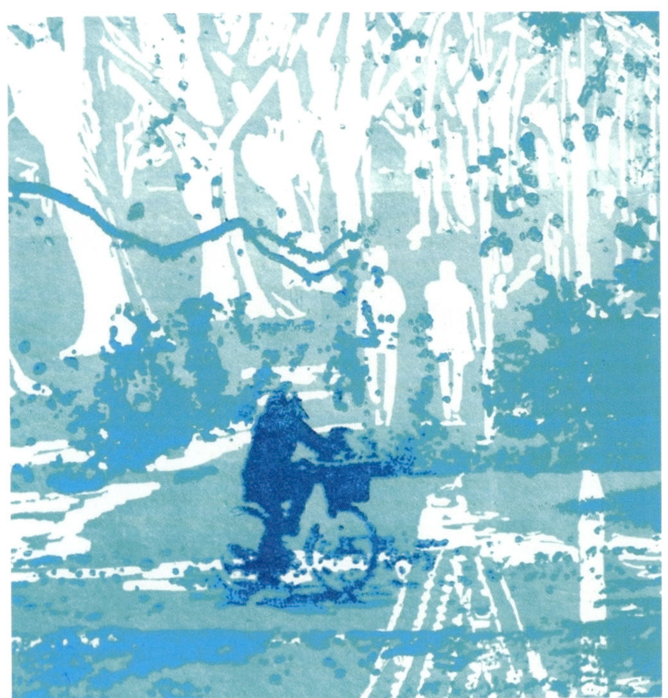

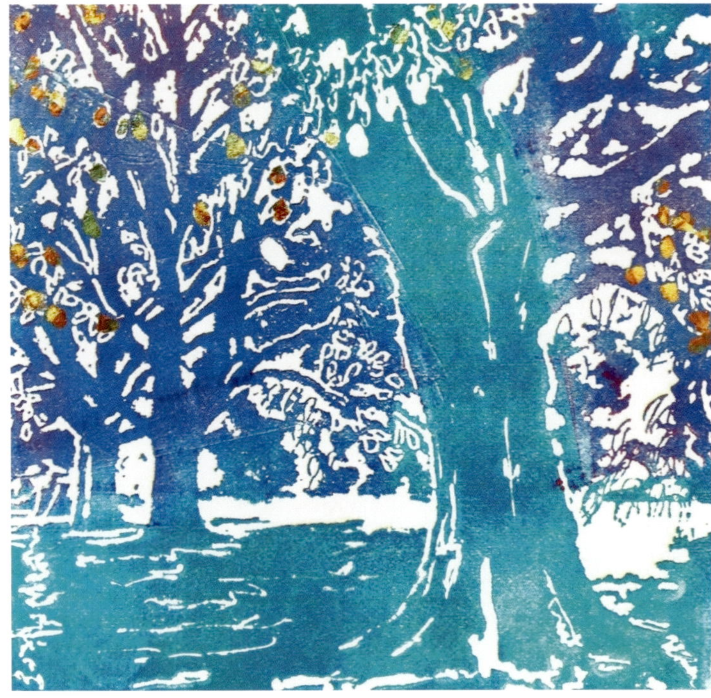

BREN UNWIN

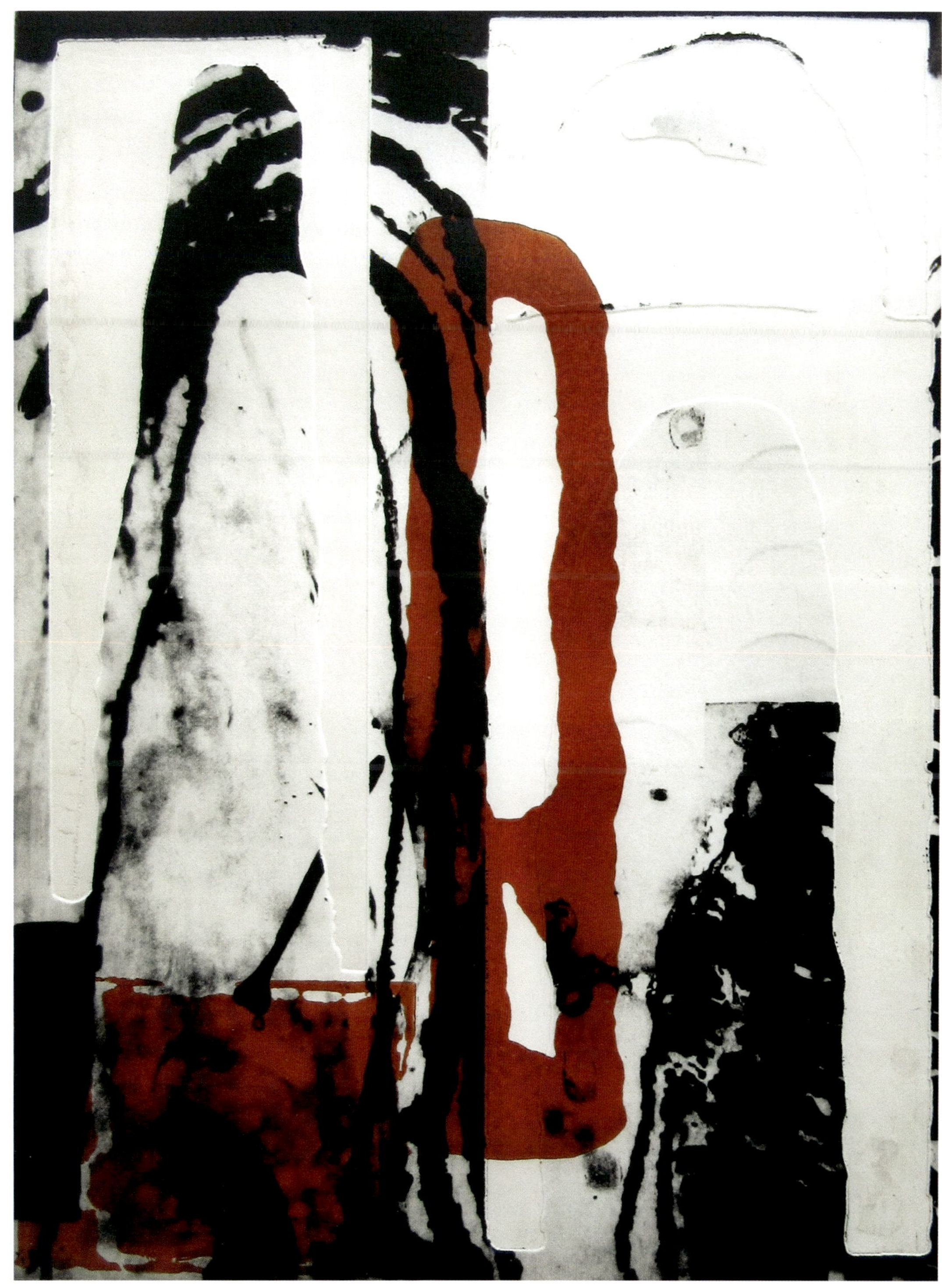

Artist-printmaker Bren Unwin's work reflects her interest in relationships that exist between an active perceiver and their dynamic environment. Materials, actions and ideas are explored in association with the mediated character of experience. Developing notions and themes over decades, her prints provoke a response that is both charged and complex. Relationships between place and perceiver, materials and objects, invoke a human presence and ambiguities of meaning.

Her prints are usually unique, rather than editioned, with each series beginning with a newly etched plate that is then used in many different ways, incorporating both new and past imagery, plates and techniques. Her processes include intaglio and relief etching, collage and chine-collé, together with embossed

Right: 'Minsden Sanguine, 5th State' (etched brass, etched and embossed copper, intaglio Solarplate), 30cm x 40cm, unique

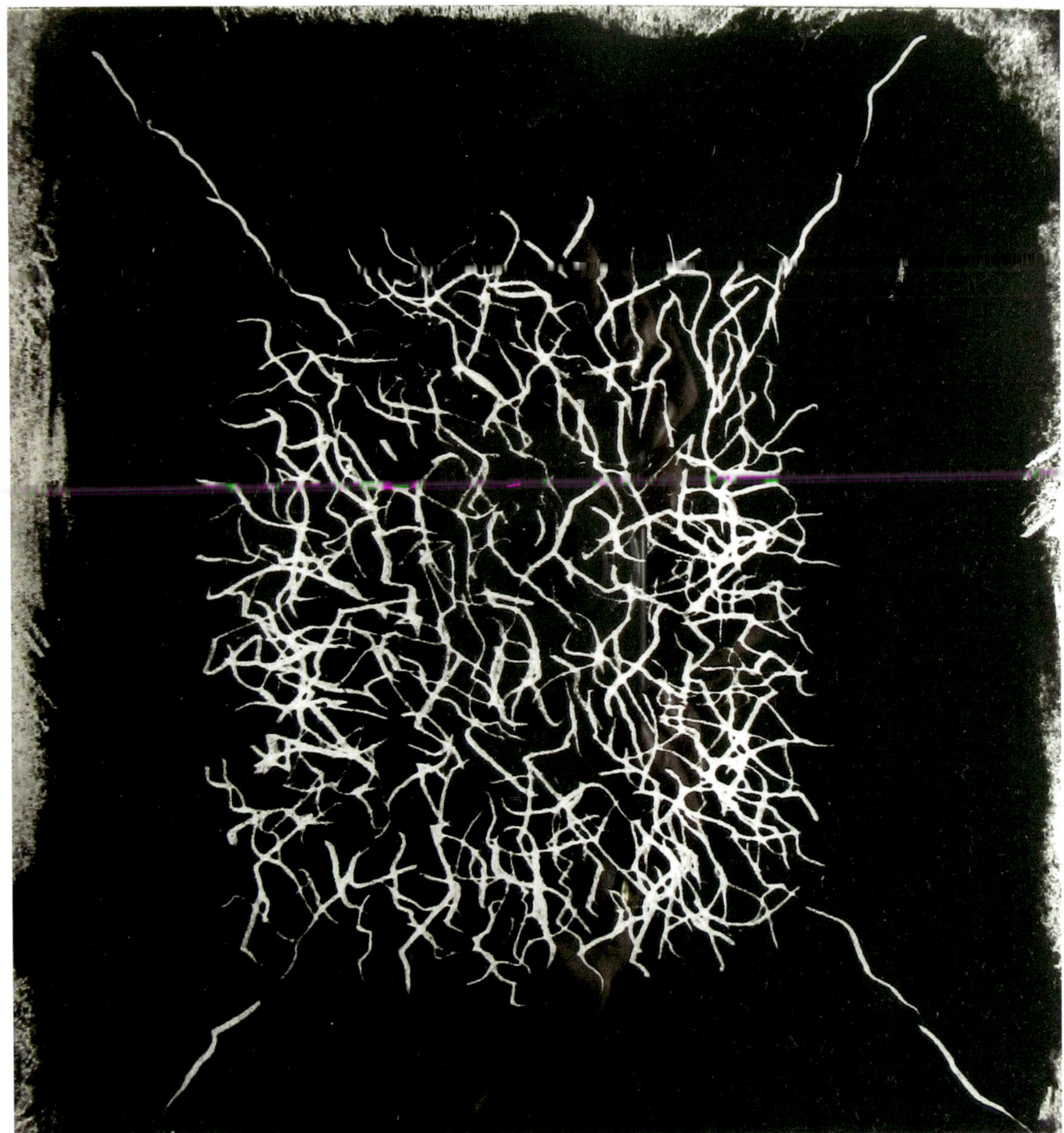

Left: 'True Loyals, Frogmore' (intaglio Solarplate), 25cm x 25cm, edition of 15; Facing page: 'Strait of Malacca, 2nd state' (etched brass, etched copper, collage, embossed, copper wire), 60cm x 60cm, unique

materials and the use of Solarplate technology.

Bren's work is held in national and international collections, including the Ashmolean Museum, Oxford; the British Museum, London; the Fitzwilliam Museum, Cambridge; and The Royal Collection of Her Majesty The Queen. In 2008 she was awarded a PhD and the Chancellor's Medal for outstanding doctoral research by the University of Hertfordshire. Her thesis was entitled 'Phenomenology and landscape experience: a critical analysis for contemporary art practice'. *www.brenunwin.com*

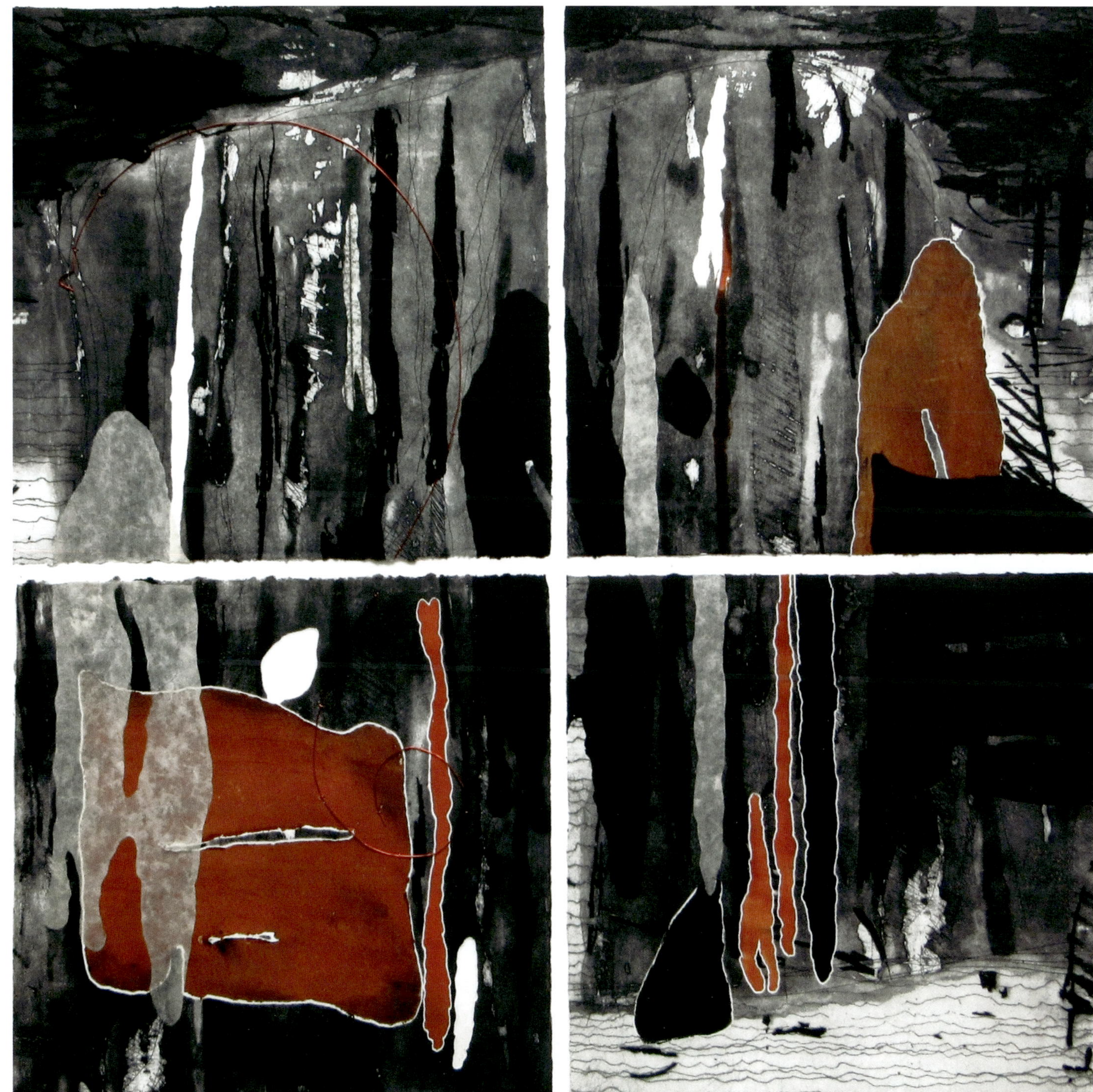

SARAH VIGLIOTTI

Born in London but later growing up in South Cambridgeshire, printmaker and photographer Sarah Vigliotti is inspired by both the rural and urban landscape, with an interest in the past and in changes taking place.

Much of her work depicts her local environment on the outskirts of Cambridge, including areas that may be overlooked, focusing on pattern, texture, surface and detail. There is normally an absence of people, but often a suggestion of their presence.

Sarah's current work includes both monochrome and colour reduction linocuts, with material taken from

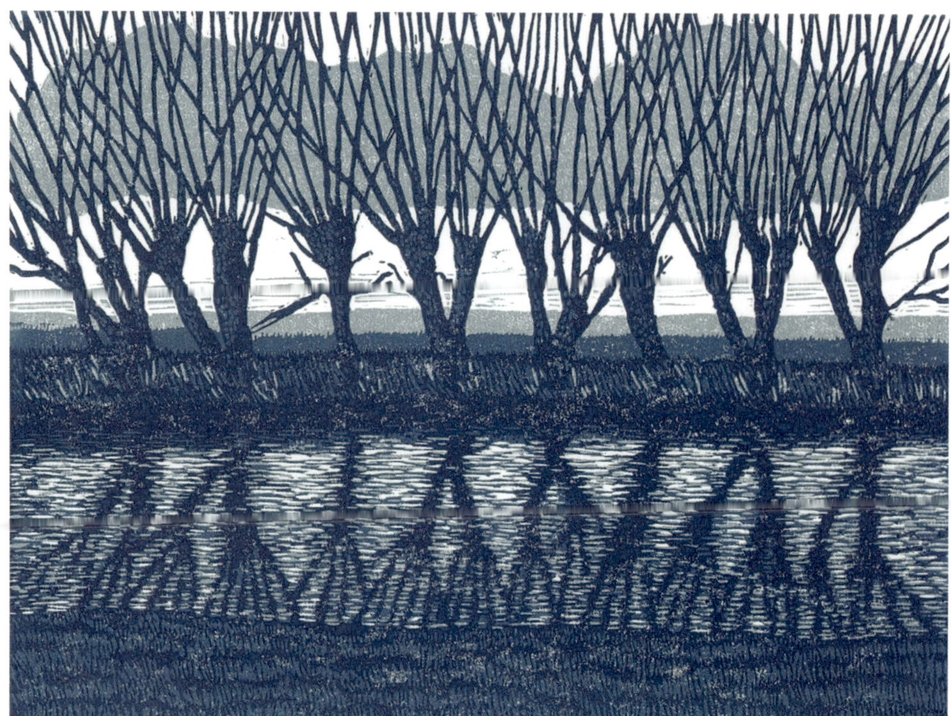

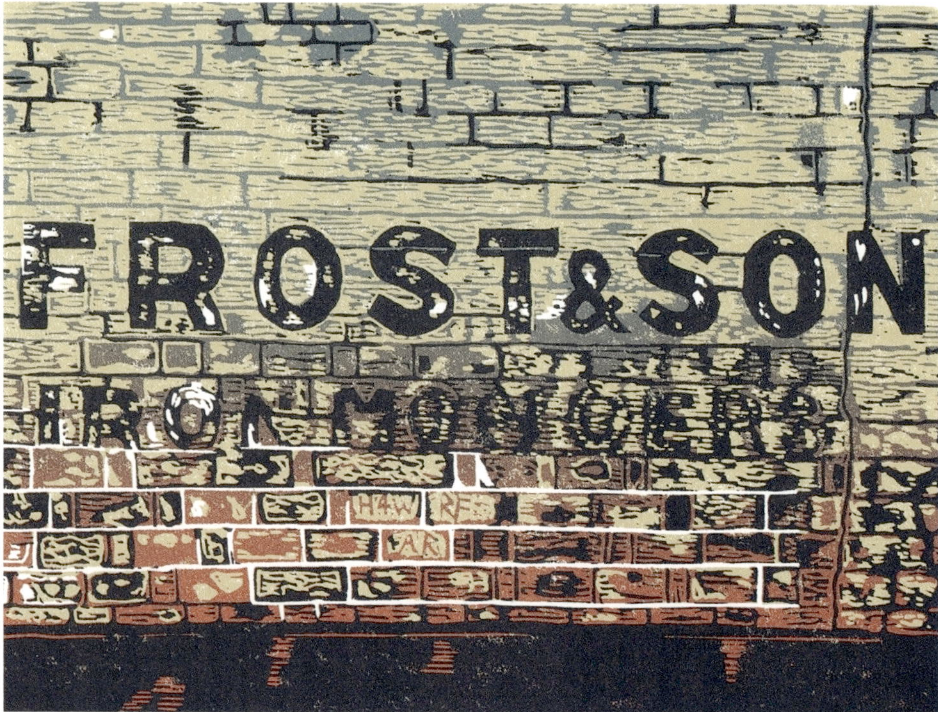

From top: 'Willows, Grantchester' (reduction linocut), 20cm x 15cm, edition of 5; 'Frost and Son' (reduction linocut), 20cm x 15cm, edition of 7

sketches and photographs. Her love of drawing is reflected in her style of linocutting, and she enjoys the problem-solving aspect of translating a drawn image into a print.

"Many of the mark-making decisions are left to the cutting stage, working with the lino in a spontaneous way. Colour reduction prints are built up in layers, adding to the risk and uncertainty of the finished print. My work is constantly evolving as I try new ideas and methods."

Sarah has a BA in Fine Art and Graphic Design from Camberwell College of Arts, and regularly takes part in Cambridge Open Studios.
www.sarahvigliotti.co.uk

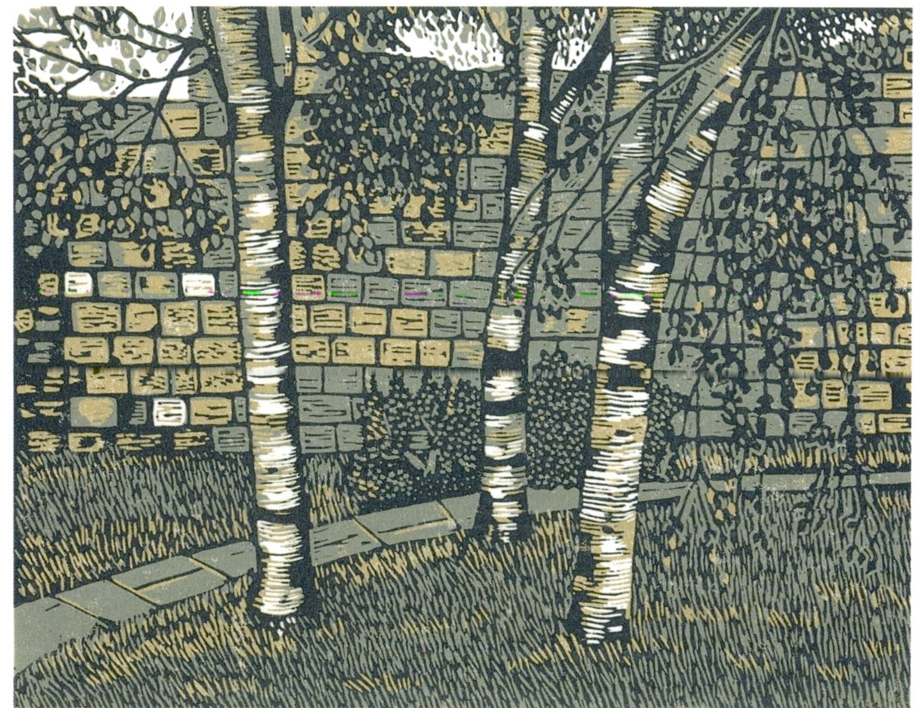

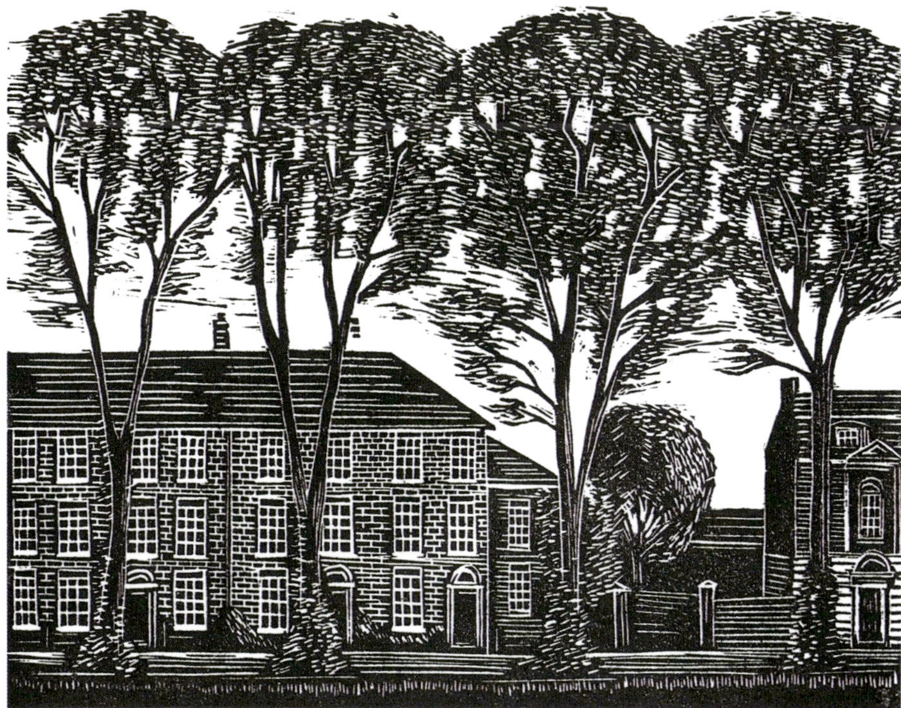

From top: 'Three Birches, York' (reduction linocut), 20cm x 15cm, edition of 7; 'Parker's Piece, Cambridge' (linocut), 20cm x 15cm, edition of 15

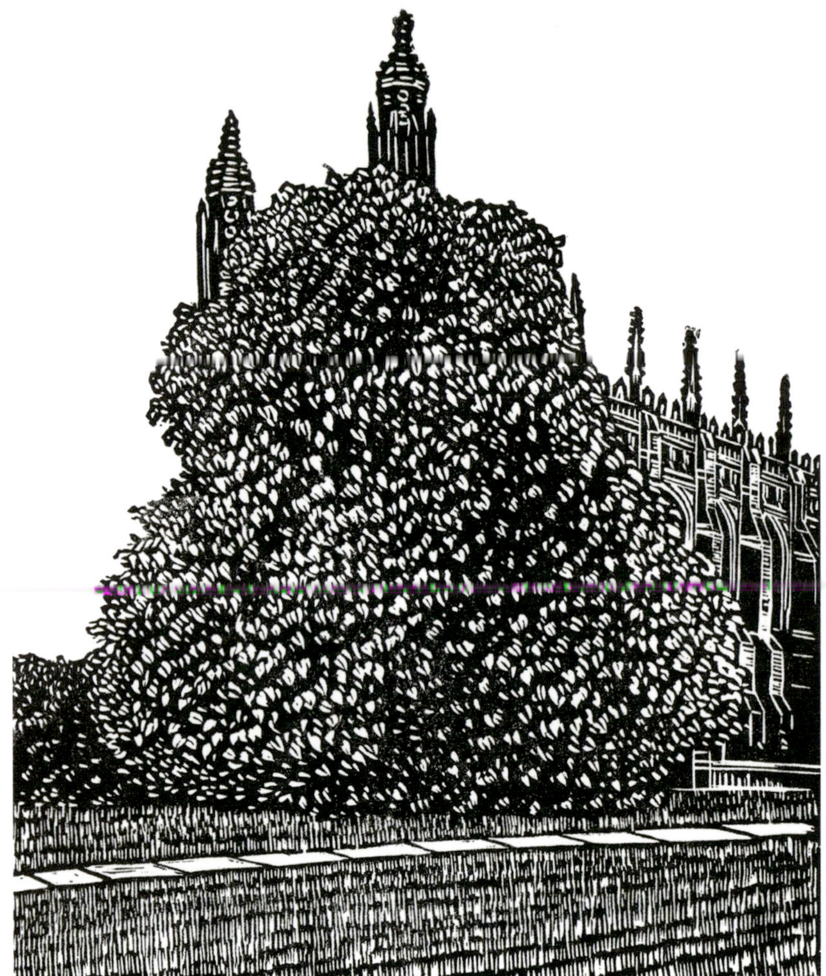

Top left: 'Horse Chestnut, King's College' (linocut), 15cm x 20cm, edition of 10; Bottom left: 'Walled Garden Wimpole' (reduction linocut), 20cm x 15cm, edition of 6; Bottom right: 'Busway' (reduction linocut), 20cm x 15cm, edition of 5 – all Sarah Vigliotti

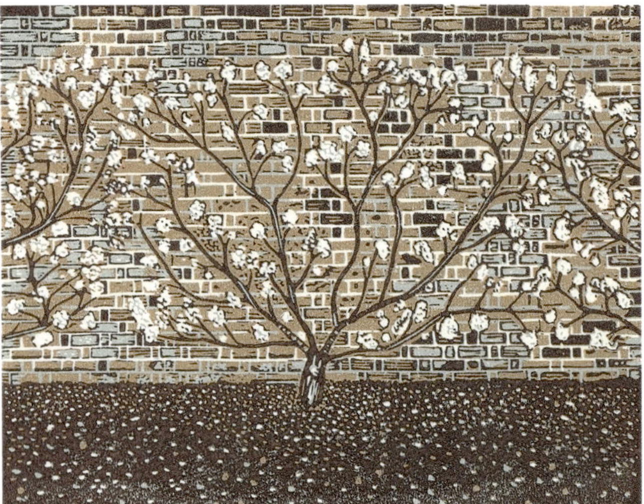

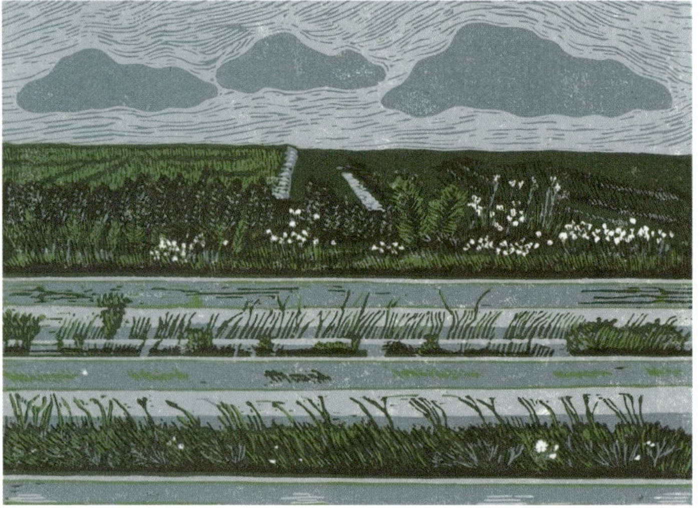

GERI WADDINGTON

Member and past chair of the Society of Wood Engravers (SWE), Geri Waddington engraves on traditional endgrain woodblocks, and sometimes on resin blocks, producing limited editions on a Victorian hand press. She also creates book illustrations.

"I'm drawn to subjects such as natural forms and architecture, and I'm currently exploring the meeting of the natural with the man-made in a series of engravings of 'Uninvited Guests' found in a French farmhouse," she says. In 'Logs 1 and 2' (overleaf), Geri ponders: "Are they mice or rats? Either way, as long as they stay in the woodstore we can grudgingly cohabit!"

Other works shown here include 'Petra' (right), in which the artist recalls "a very special birthday visit to the rose-red city – this engraving had to be in colour!"; 'The Drying Room' (overleaf), showing the 'sechoir', or paper drying room, at the Moulin du Verger near Angouleme; and 'Oundle' (p131), a celebration of the buildings in Geri's local town, where Northamptonshire limestone turns golden when the sun shines.

As well as being a member of the SWE, Geri is a 'brother' of the Art Workers' Guild, and a founder member of the International Academic

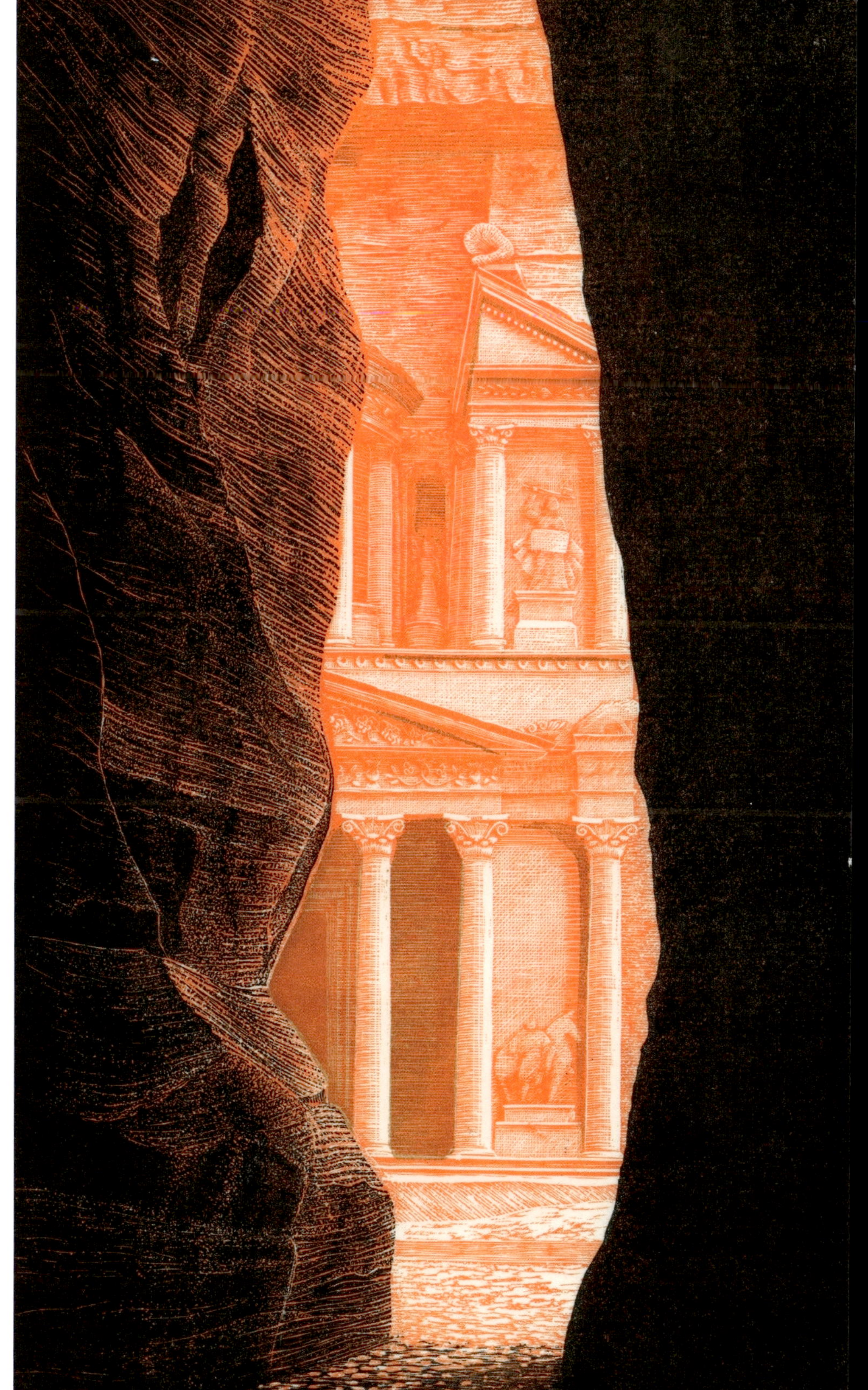

Right: 'Petra' (resingrave engraving), 16.3cm x 15.2cm, edition of 50

Below: 'Logs 1 and 2' (resingrave engraving), 5cm x 15.5cm, edition of 100; Right: 'Summer Visitors' (wood engraving), 12.5cm x 10cm, edition of 60; Bottom: 'The Drying Room' (resingrave engraving), 12.5cm x 23cm, edition of 100; Facing page: 'Oundle' (wood engraving), 23.0cm x 16.0cm, edition of 150

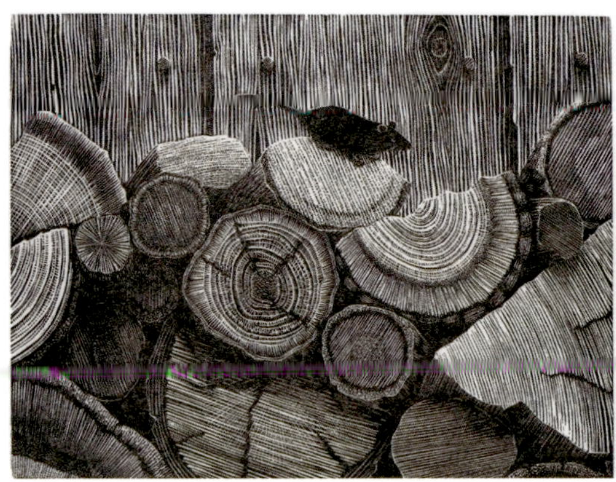

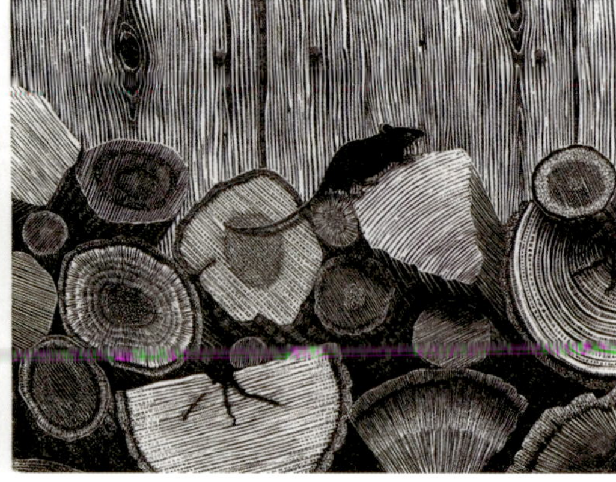

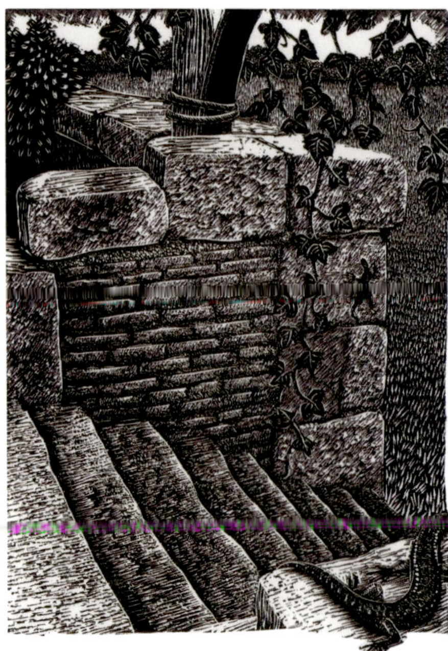

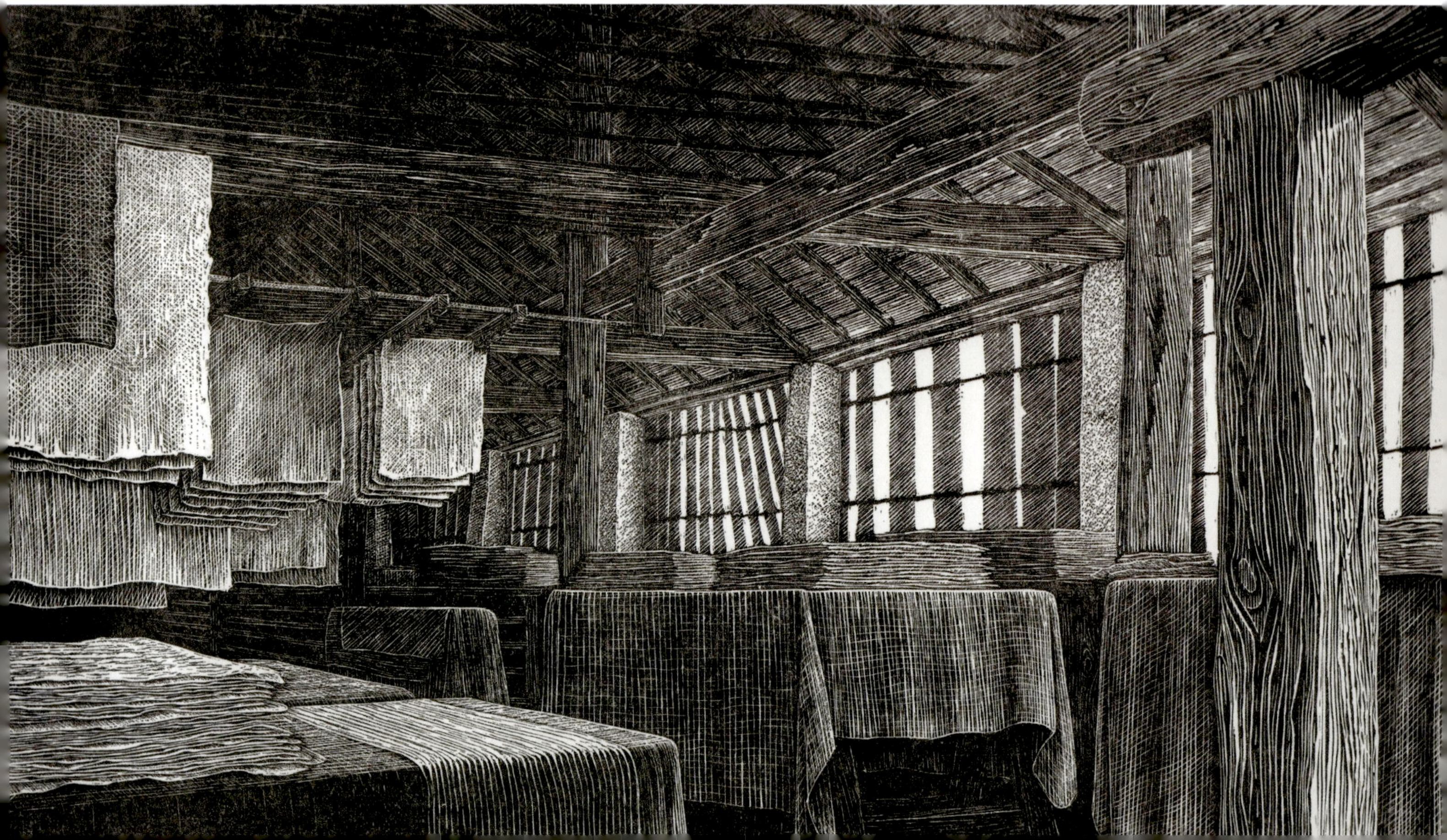

Printmaking Alliance. She exhibits extensively across the UK, and as far east and west as China and the USA.

Her work is in public and private collections, including the Ashmolean Museum, Bristol Museum and Art Gallery, the Hunt Institute for Botanical Documentation in Pittsburgh, and the Central Academy of Fine Arts in Beijing. She trained at the Slade.
www.geriwaddington.com

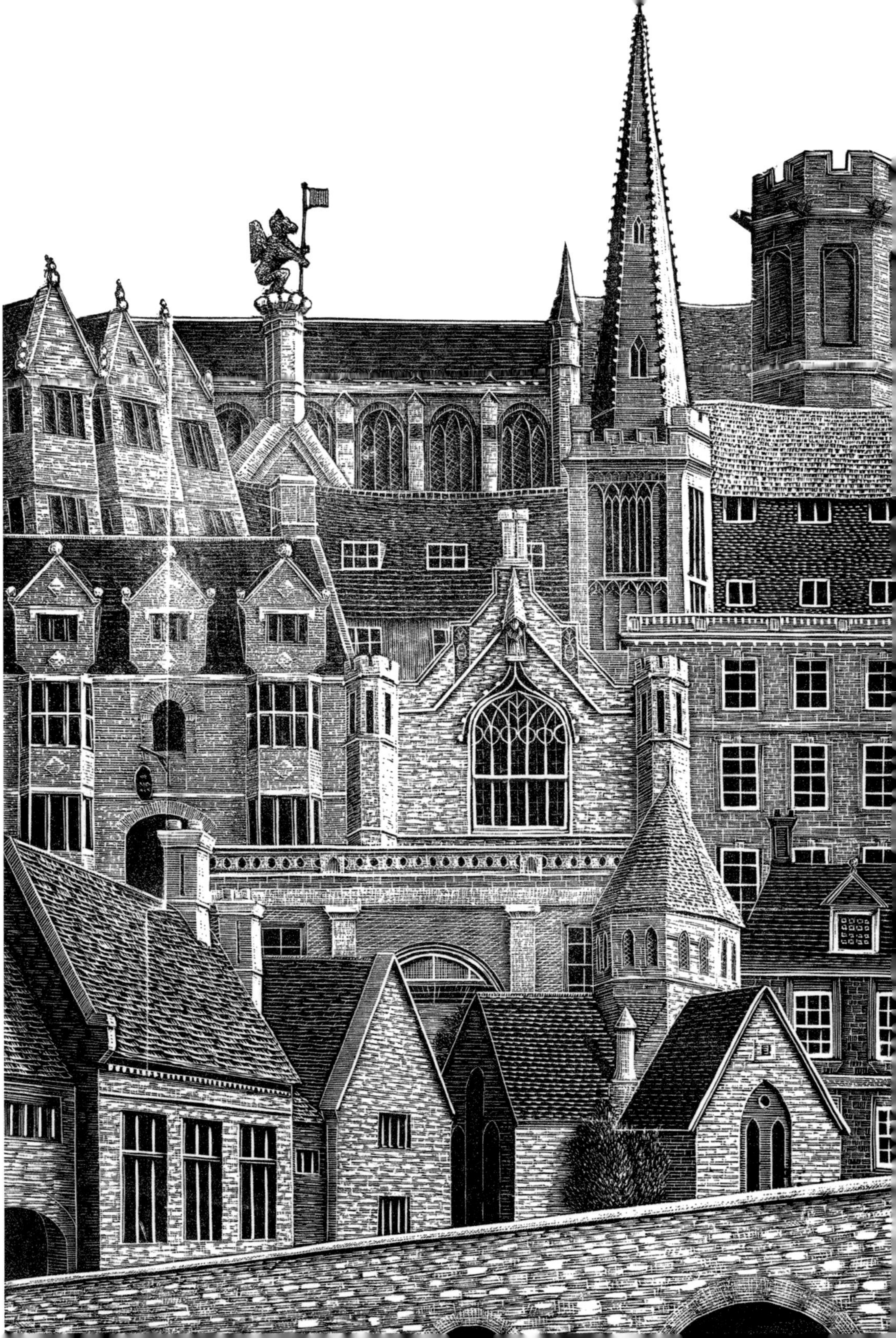

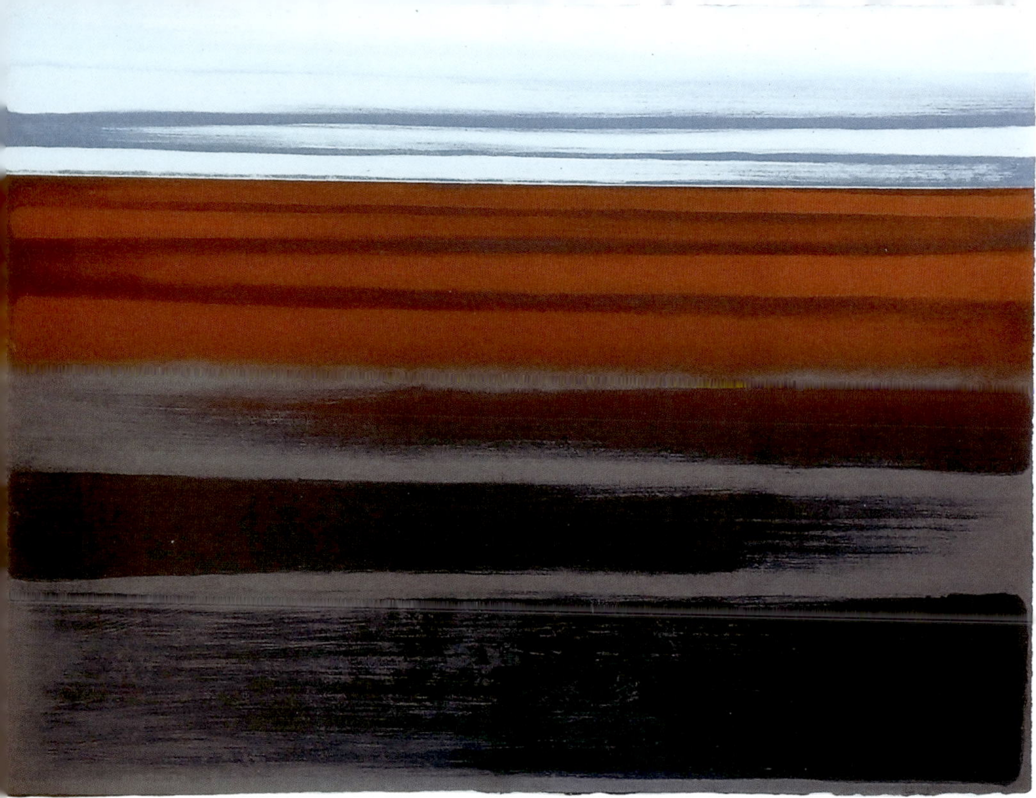

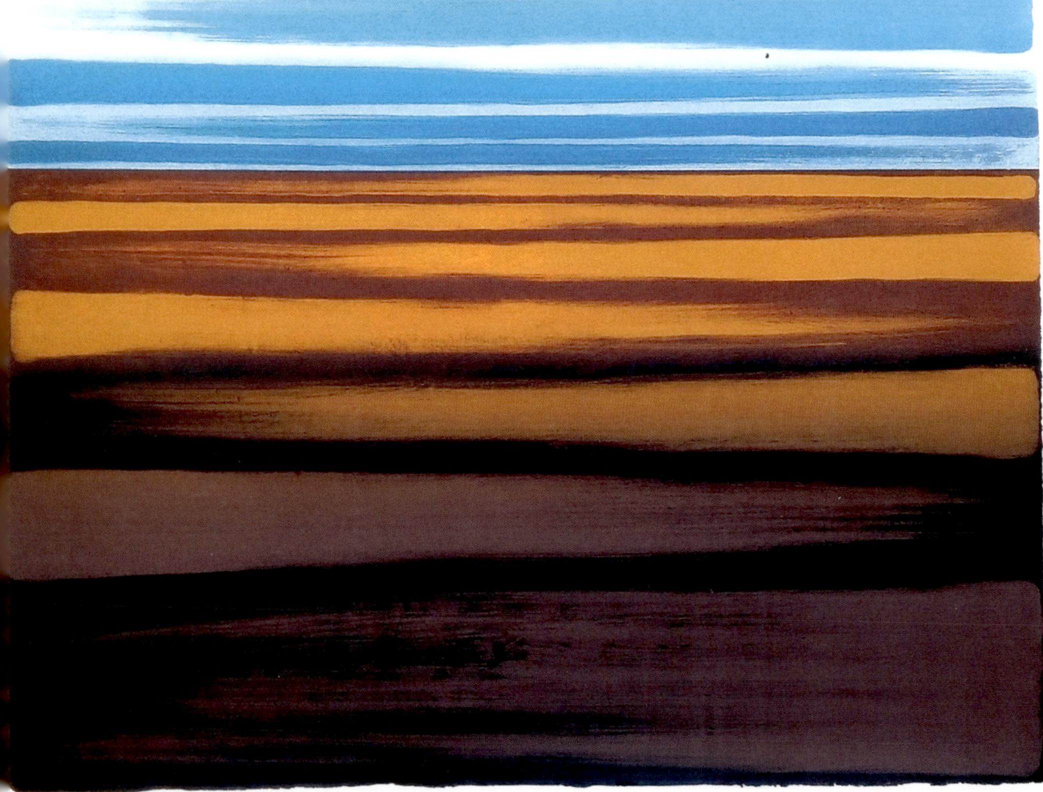

EDWIN WILSON

Ed Wilson's prints are founded on rhythms and asymmetrical intervals inspired by often ignored everyday objects, places and events.

"I develop my ideas primarily through relief and intaglio processes. Within my practice lies the desire to create as simple a statement as possible. I wish to celebrate intuitively the printing processes as a response to developing ideas, and the unique qualities print brings to the surface of the final image. My work is a combination of both the idea and the craft involved within the process of creating a print; they are of equal importance. The techniques exploited are an integral component of the process of creating a print, as well as my response to the subject matter that stimulated that process. Considered selection of shape, colour, form and mark-making is paramount, and is influenced by contemporary events and historical precedent."

Ed trained at Winchester School of Art (1968-69) and Cardiff College of Art (1969-72). He exhibits in the UK and Europe, and has work in public and private collections in England, Wales, France, Germany, Norway, Denmark, Estonia, USA, Canada, Hong Kong, Japan and Australia.
www.edwilsonartist.co.uk

Facing page, top and bottom: 'Furrows I' and 'Furrows II' (both relief and carborundum), 56cm x 76cm, each an edition of 4; This page, from top: 'Night Whispers' (relief and carborundum), 21cm x 29cm, edition of 5; 'Secret Whispers' (relief and carborundum), 56cm x 76cm, edition of 3

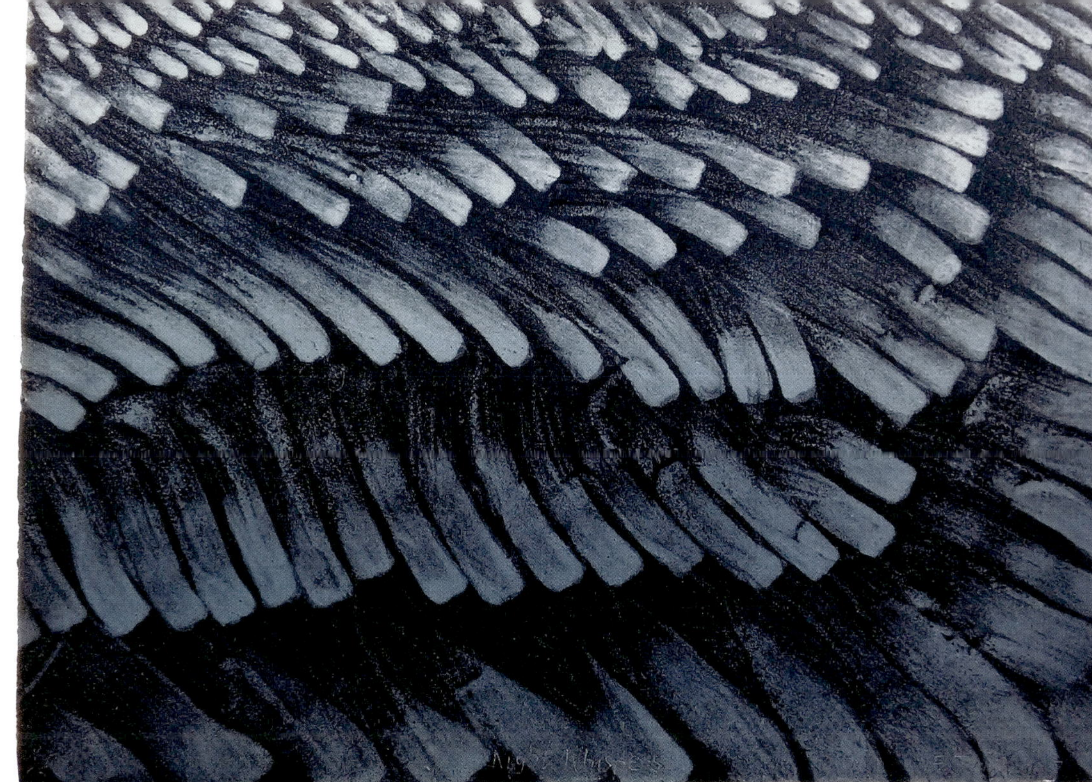

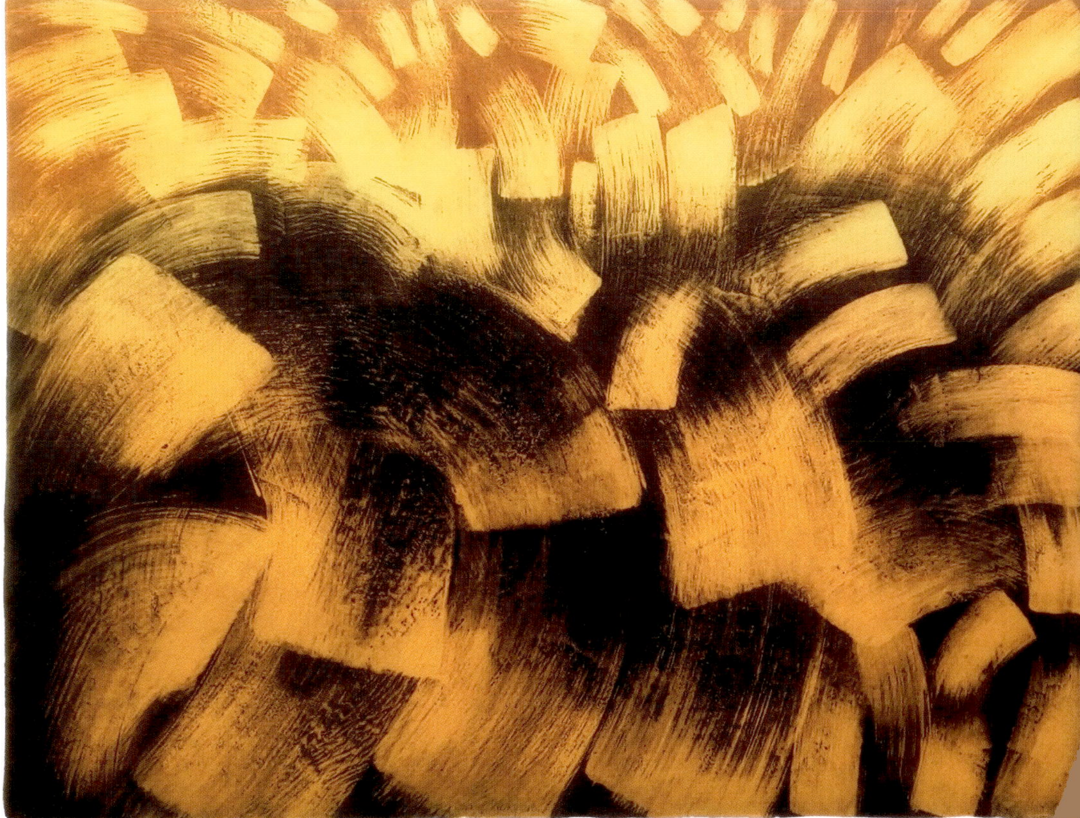

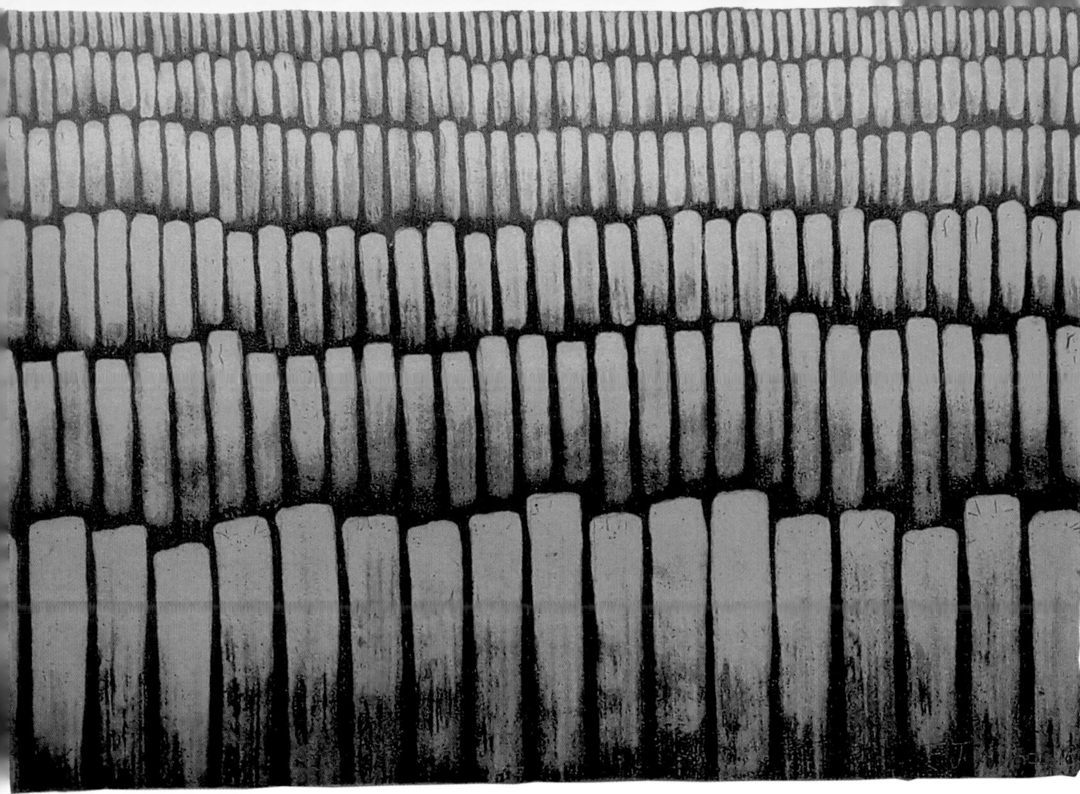

Left: 'Quiet Stalks' (relief and carborundum), 29.5cm x 21cm, edition of 8; Below: 'Whispering Grass' (relief and carborundum), 29cm x 21cm, edition of 5 – both Edwin Wilson

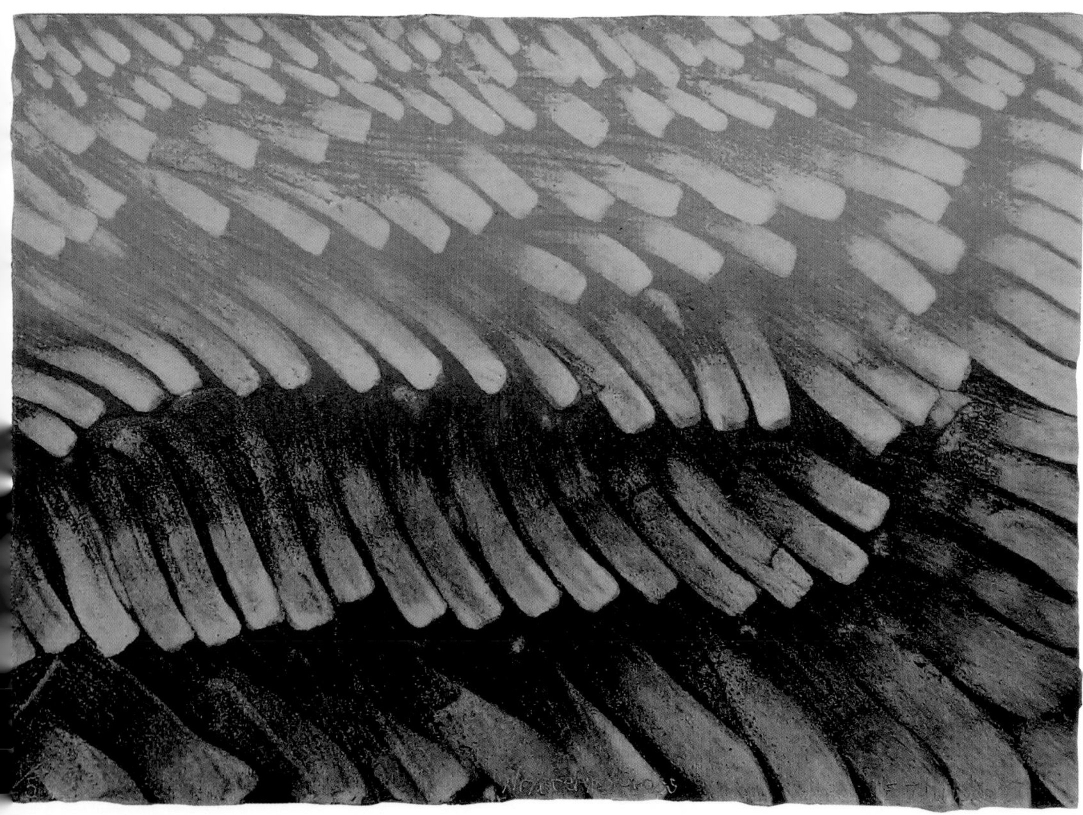

CLARE MARIA WOOD

Trained originally as a painter, Clare Maria Wood has taught printmaking for 15 years. She creates monoprints and small, variable edition collagraphs such as those on the right.

As a painter, it seems natural to Clare to take an inventive approach to printmaking. She begins by building up layers of texture on card using brushes, card and sticks. This can be carborundum, pumice, acrylic gel and plaster. She often burns back into these plates, allowing the process to dictate the outcome to an extent while retaining control of the feel of the shape. This allows her to create organic-feeling assemblages such as 'Fossil Flower' (p137).

Using an intaglio method of printing, Clare creates heavily embossed prints with deep, velvety tones, which contrast with bright colour rubs that she layers on top. She incorporates rust imprints, pure copper and silver leaf, creating areas of intense light and interest under the printed surface.

Her most recent monoprints are inspired by familiar landscapes and seascapes around Cornwall and the Cambridgeshire Fens. Bold organic shapes take centre stage in Clare's printmaking, suggesting ancient rock formations, weather-worn fragments and woodland.

She exhibits nationally, and has work in collections around the world.

www.claremariawood.co.uk

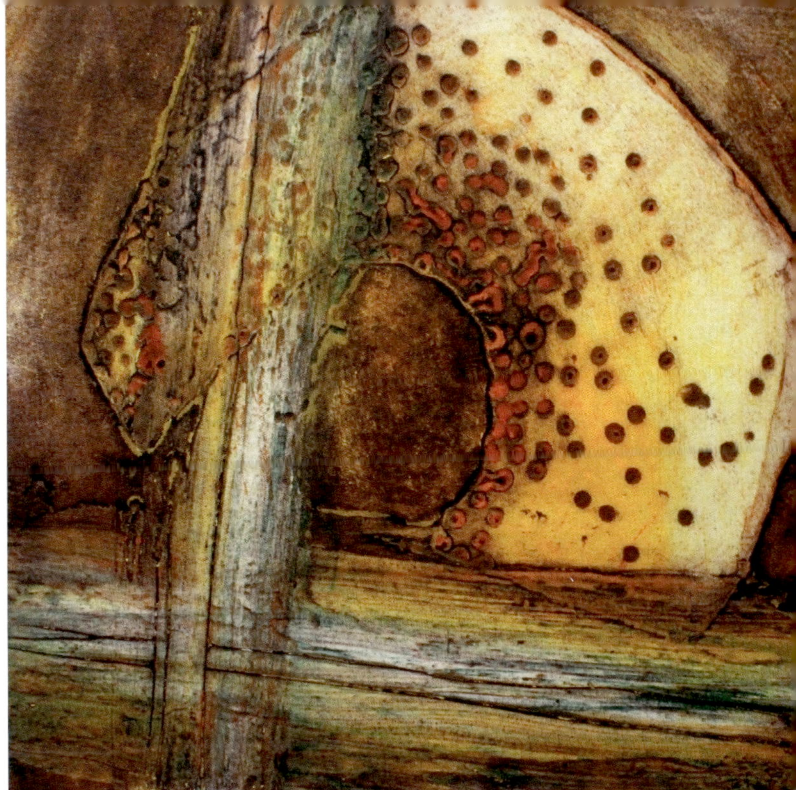

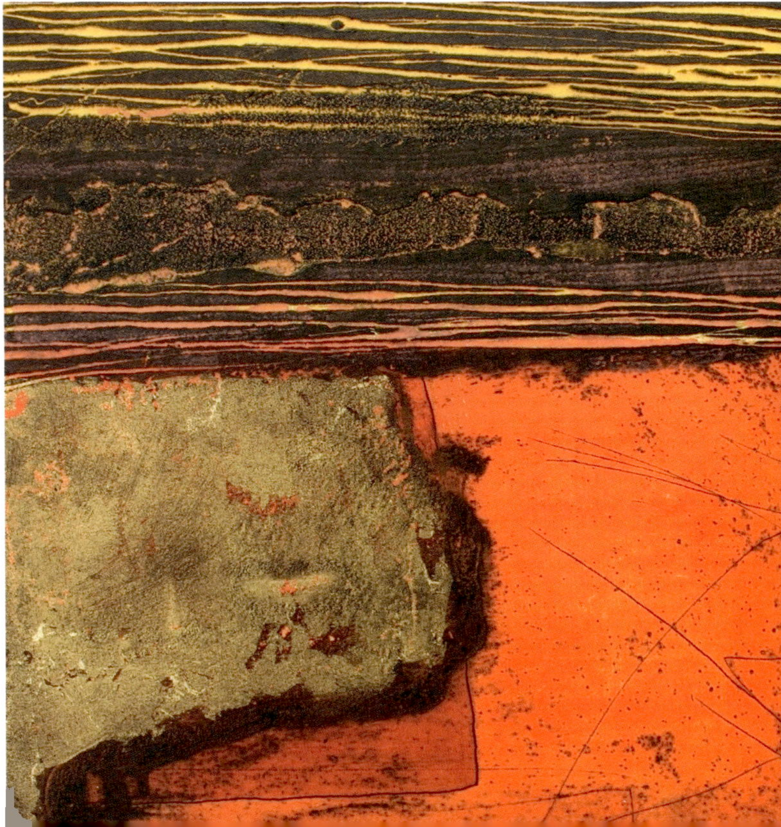

From top: 'Entwined' (collagraph), 28.5cm x 28.5cm, variable edition of 50; 'Moorland Trace' (collagraph with gold leaf), 28.5cm x 28.5cm, variable edition of 50

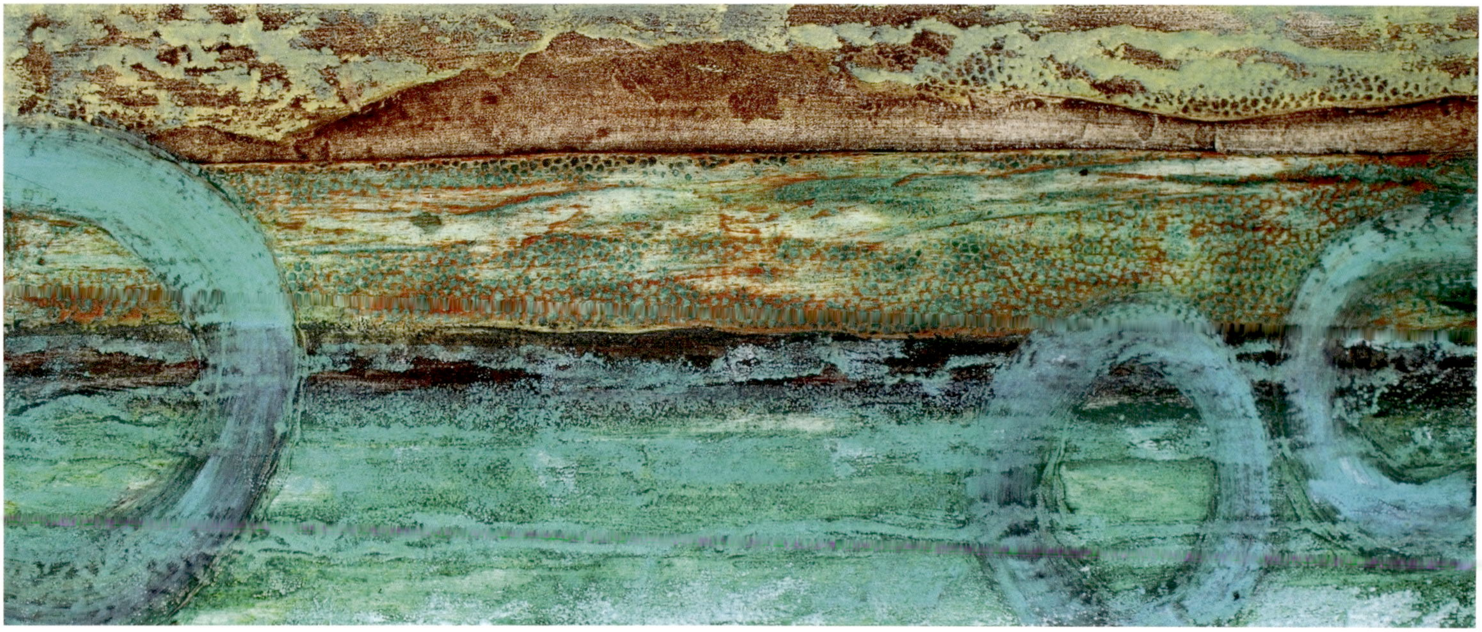

From top: 'Sea Drift' (collagraph), 21cm x 52cm, variable edition of 50; 'Phoenix' (collagraph with gold leaf), 42cm x 54cm, variable edition of 50

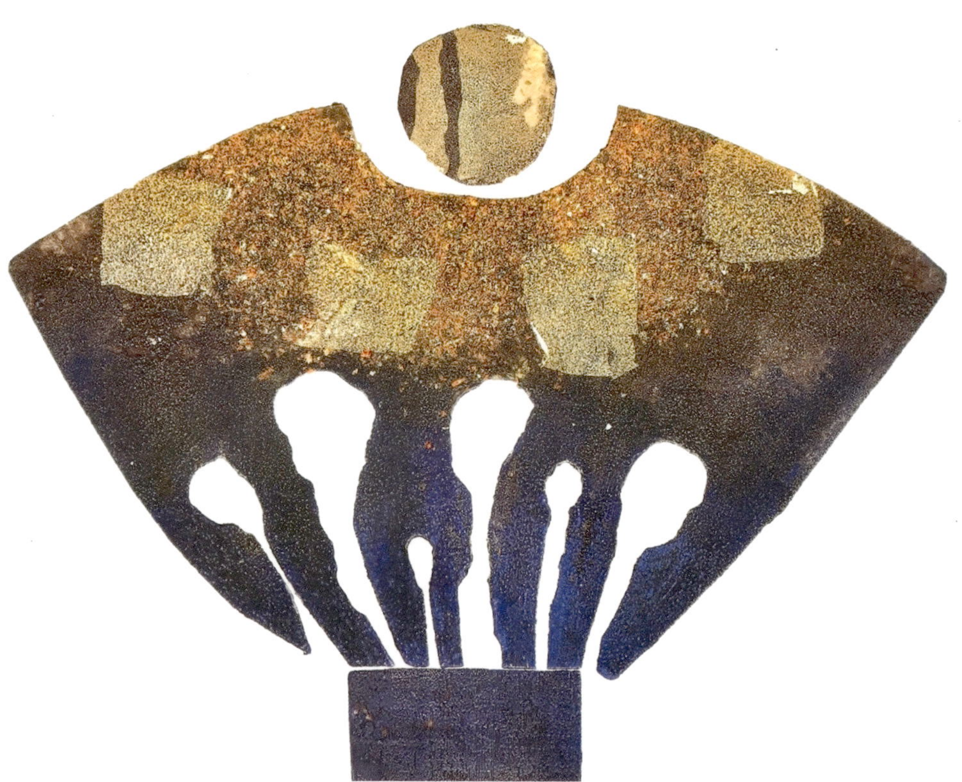

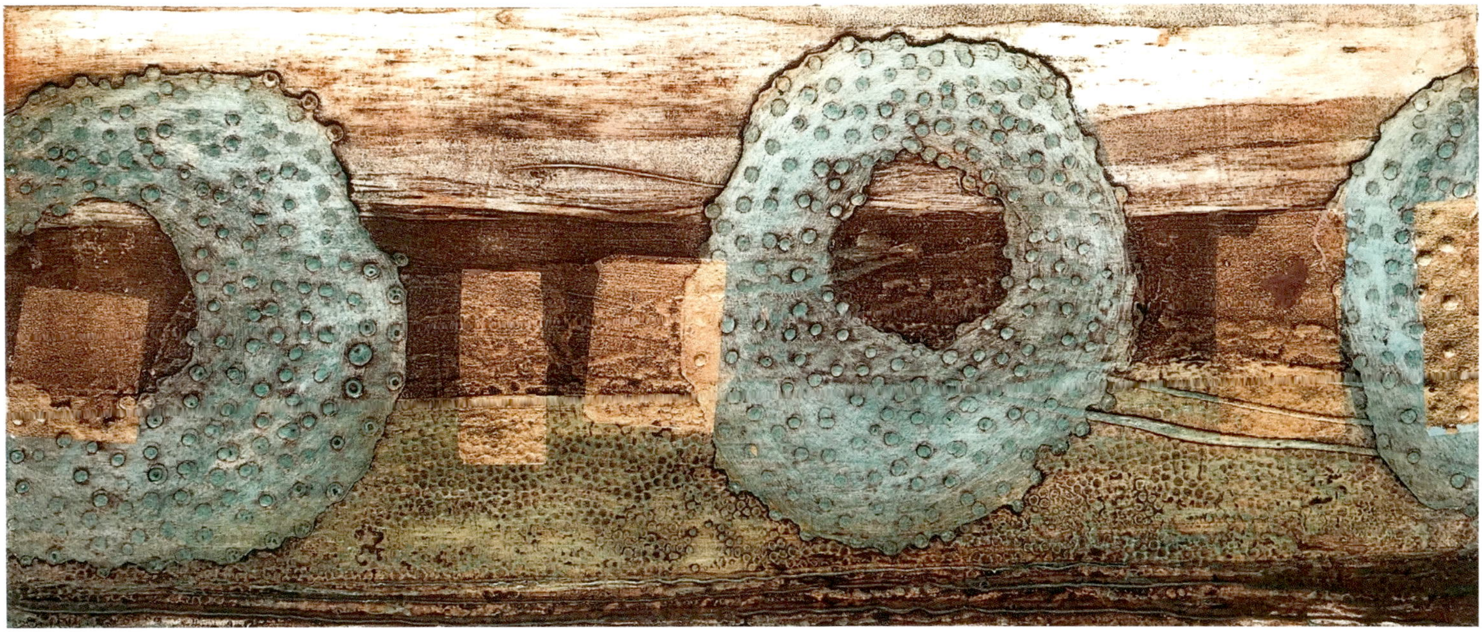

From top: 'Urchins' (collagraph with copper leaf), 21cm x 52cm, variable edition of 50; 'Fossil Flower' (collagraph with gold and copper leaf), 38cm x 55cm, variable edition of 50 – all Clare Maria Wood

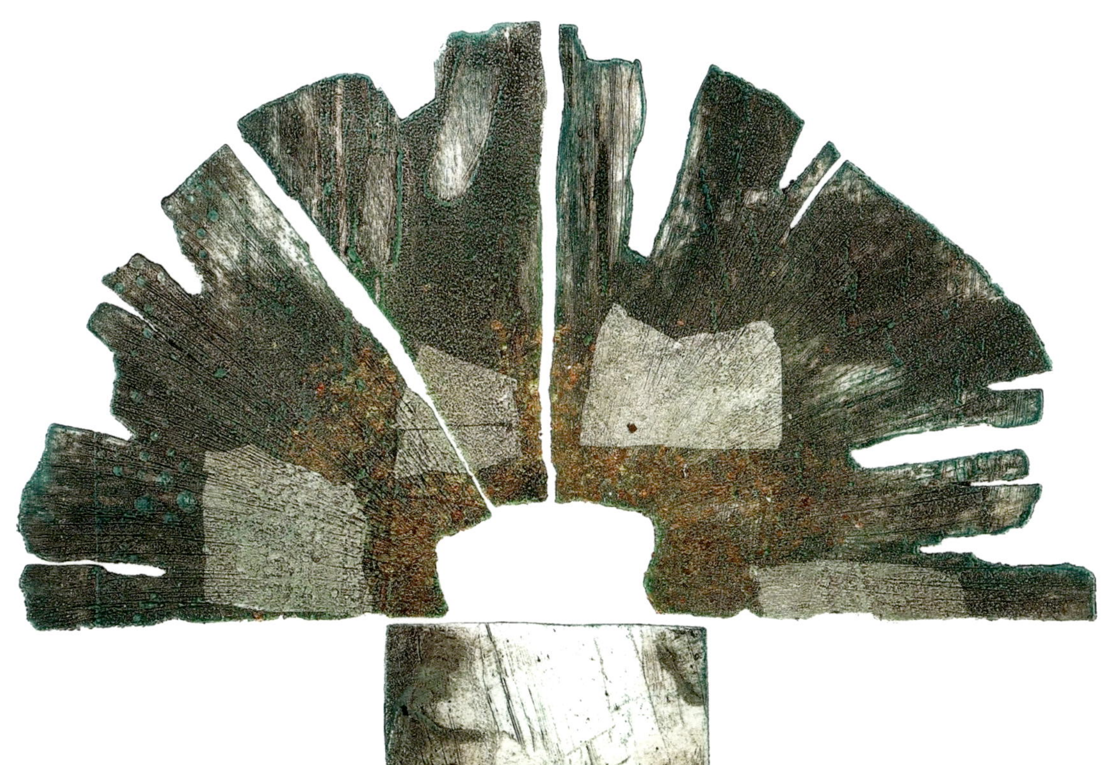

LEADERS IN PRINTMAKING

GAINSBOROUGH'S HOUSE PRINT WORKSHOP

Gainsborough's House Print Workshop is a well-equipped, professional and friendly printmaking resource. Located at the childhood home of the celebrated painter Thomas Gainsborough, the workshop adjoins a thriving museum and gallery, the jewel in the crown of the attractive Suffolk market town of Sudbury, set in the landscape that inspired him.

The Print Workshop welcomes artists, students and print enthusiasts of all abilities. Techniques taught include relief printing, etching, screenprinting, monoprinting and lithography. Courses are led by well-known, talented and experienced tutors, with Dale Devereux Barker, Carl Borges, Peter Brown, Emma Buckmaster, Michael Carlo, Anne Desmet RA, Megan Fishpool, Colin Gale, Jason Hicklin, Susan Jones, Jude Lockie, Sue Molineux and Annabel Ridley all exhibiting at the 2018 Cambridge Original Printmakers Biennale – along with Workshop Committee members.

Also included in the Biennale is a print by Thomas Gainsborough. Many etching techniques currently in use in the Workshop would be familiar to this innovative printmaker. *www.gainsborough.org*

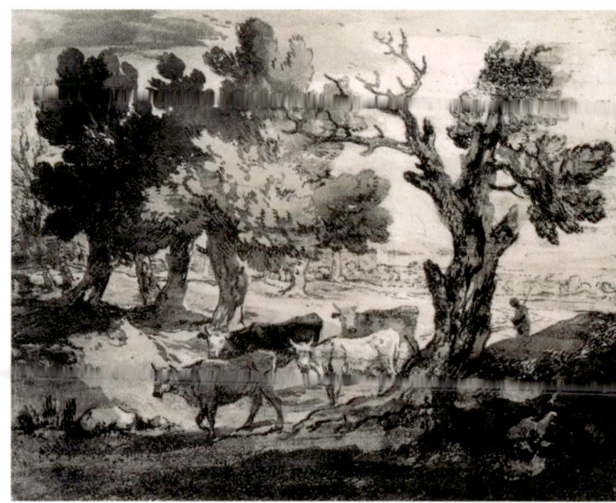

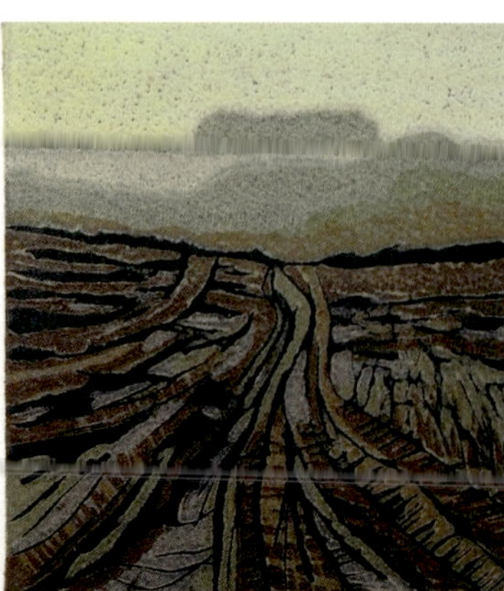

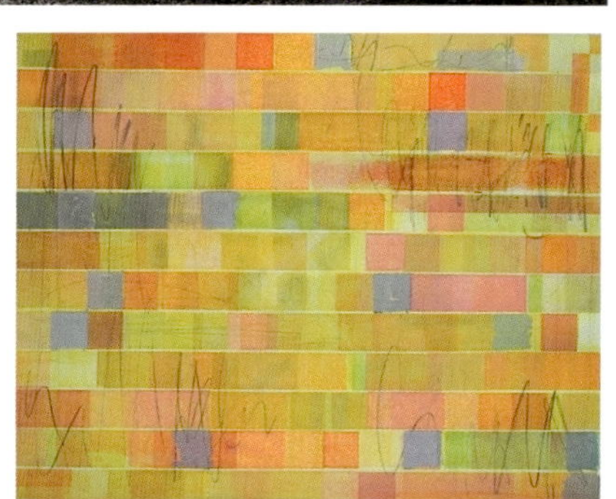

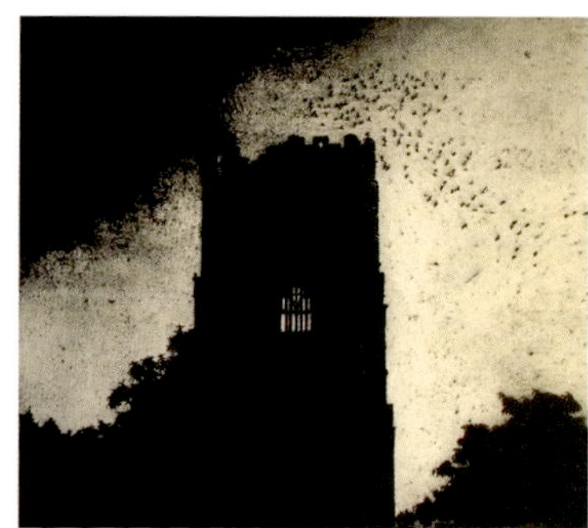

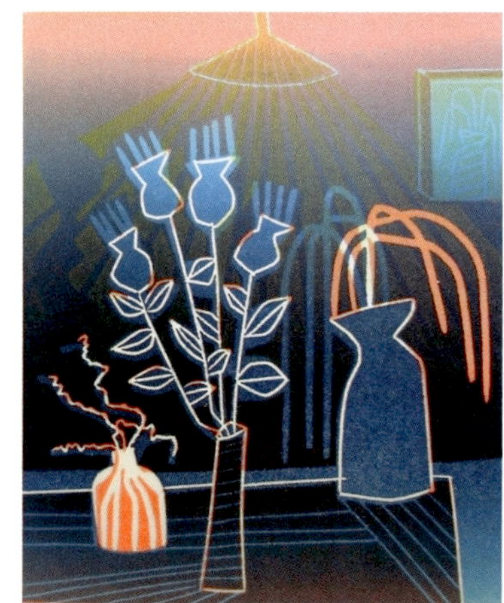

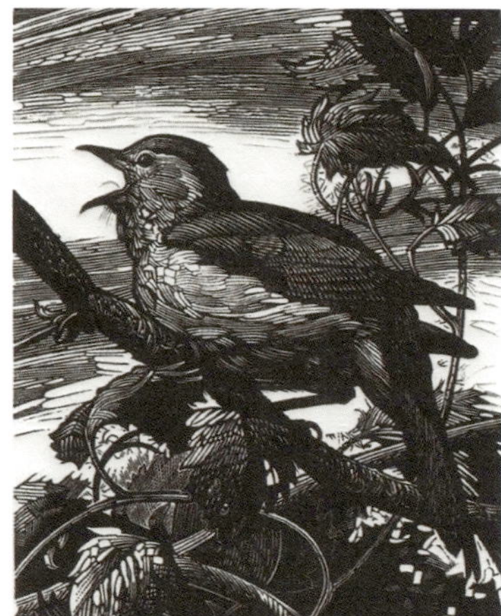

From top left, clockwise: *Thomas Gainsborough (1727-1788): 'Wooded Landscape with Herdsman and Four Cows 1785-1788' (aquatint and soft-ground etching); Michael Carlo: 'Earth 96' (reduction woodcut), 14cm x 14cm, edition of 15; Emma Buckmaster: 'Evening' (etching), 52cm x 54cm, edition of 20; Peter Brown: 'Nightingale' (wood engraving), 10cm x 7.4cm, edition of 70; Dale Devereux Barker: 'Interior III' (linoprint), 26.4cm x 28.6cm, unique; Colin Gale: 'Shutters' (relief print), 56cm x 76cm, edition of 8*

PARNDON MILL

Practising artists Liz Boast, Tania Scott Durrant and Kirsten Wilson run Parndon Mill Printmaking Studios at Parndon Mill, within a creative community of artists, craftspeople and designers. The collective is situated on the banks of the River Stort in Harlow, Essex. *www.parndonmill.co.uk*

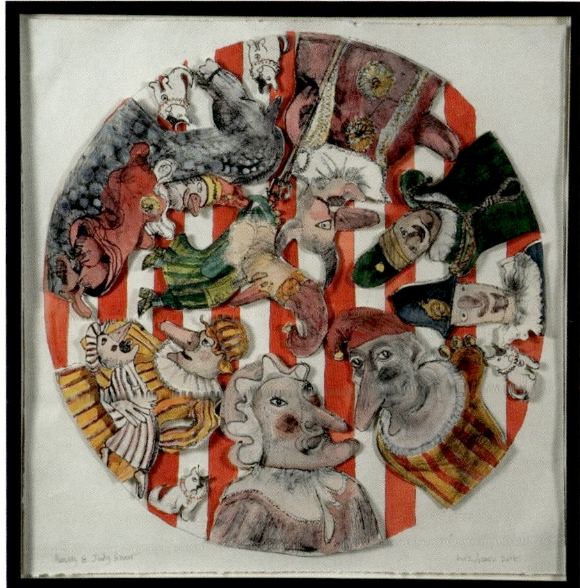

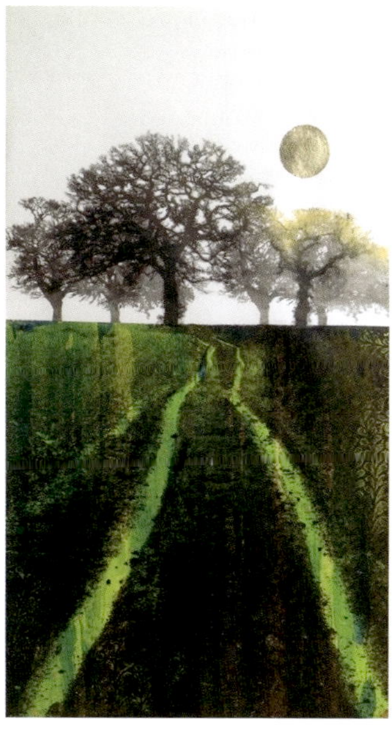

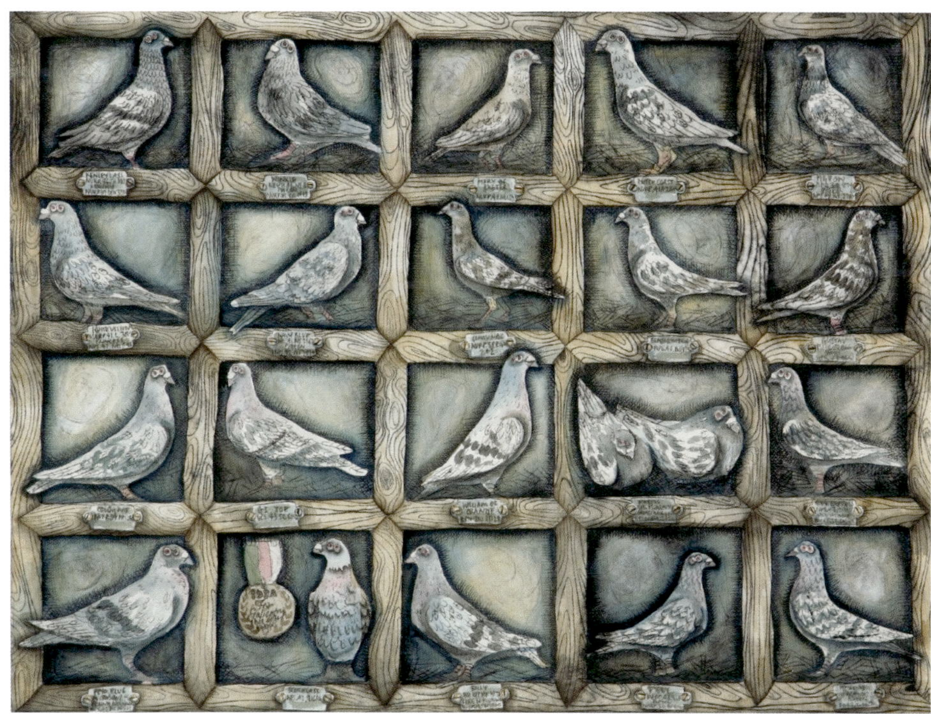

From top left, clockwise:

Liz Boast: 'Punch and Judy Show' (hand-coloured drypoint), 70cm x 70cm, edition of 10
Essex-based Liz uses drawings from her sketchbooks of her collection of old puppets, dolls and curiosities to make narrative prints using drypoint printing and watercolour.
www.lizboast.co.uk

Tania Scott Durrant: 'England's Green and Pleasant Land' (silkscreen monoprint), edition of 25
Tania, who lives in Hertfordshire, is inspired by walking and sketching in the beautiful rolling countryside around her home and by the dramatic landscape of the west coast of Scotland. She combines the subtle atmospheric marks created by spit bite etching with the flat block plates of linocut and screenprinting.
www.taniadurrant.com

Kirsten Wilson: 'MI14 (d)' (hand-coloured drypoint), 80cm x 100cm, edition of 10
Showing the decorated pigeons of the Second World War that were awarded the Dickin Medal for Bravery. They are all named and in their loft, some present and some missing in action. Hertfordshire-based Kirsten has always been drawn to detail and humour, often combining collage, her own marbled paper, drypoint, lino and screenprint.
www.kirstenw.co.uk

ANGLIA RUSKIN UNIVERSITY

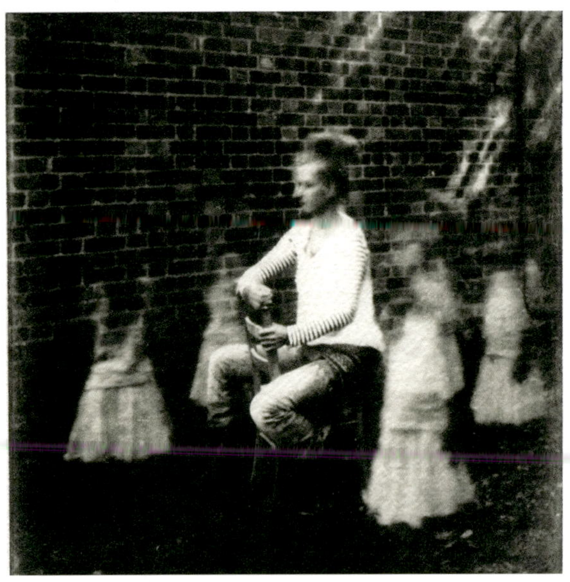

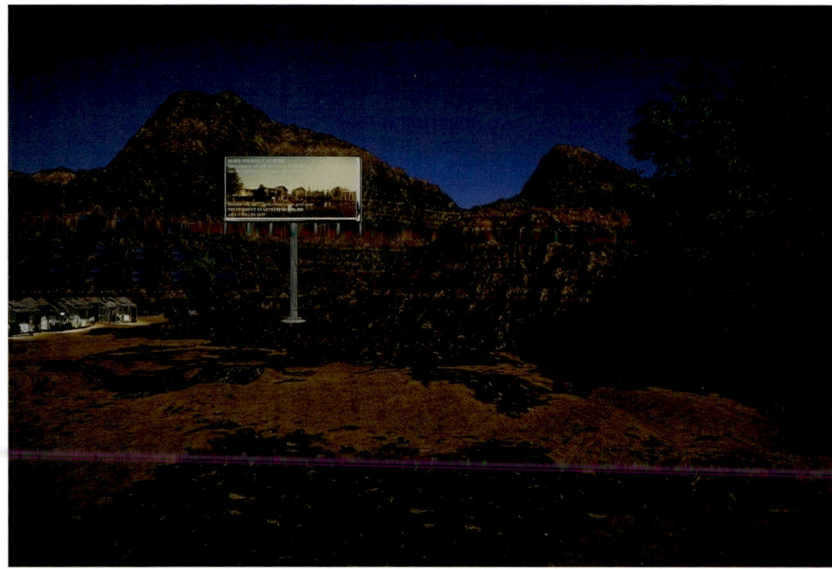

The work shown here is by a selection of MA Printmaking students and alumni.
www.anglia.ac.uk

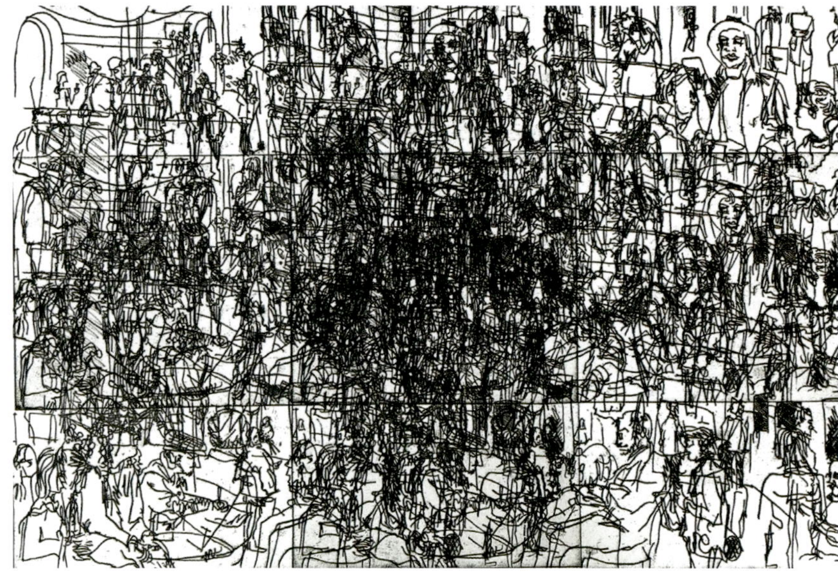

From top left, clockwise:
Julie Sleaford and Vic Dawson (ARU MA Photography and MA Printmaking Alumni): 'Uncertain Portrait #5' (Solarplate etching from a pinhole photograph made in the Mobile Laboratory for Extraordinary Research), 16cm x 16cm, artist's proof

Emily Godden: 'Reality Checkpoint' (POV screenshot from virtual reality experience)

Laura White: 'Saturation' (soft ground etching), 60cm x 40cm (approx). Laura describes 'Saturation' as "a response to the increase in the use of hand-held devices in our society".

Work from the following also features in the 2018 Biennale: students Jo Tunmer (see pages 120-122), Vicky Barker, Svetlana Atlavina, Sachiko Purser, Jim Brown, Paddy Ribeiro, Michelle Crowther, Mark Lonnie, Qianrong Wen and William Van-Boesschoten.

CAMBRIDGE REGIONAL COLLEGE

The following work is by some of the Printmaking specialists on the College's pre-degree UAL Diploma in Art and Design Foundation Studies course. "Each student has selected work from their final self-initiated major project, using research, exploration and evaluation to develop their experience of professional arts practice. Ideas are considered, questioned and experimented with to create an exploratory body of work on a topic or subject that has a resonance with each student; the outcome is the result of creative discovery, but the journey continues."
www.camre.ac.uk

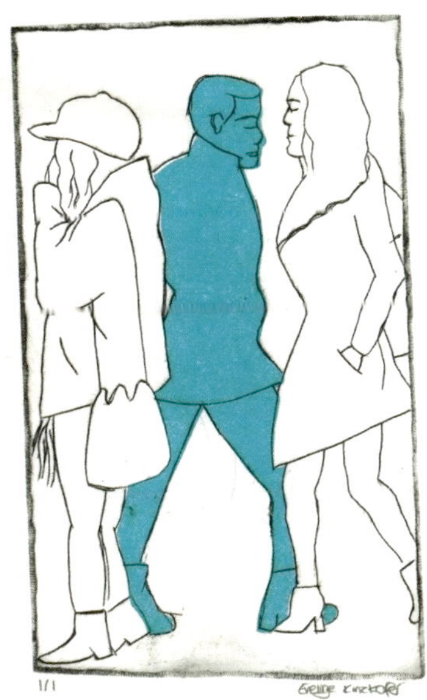

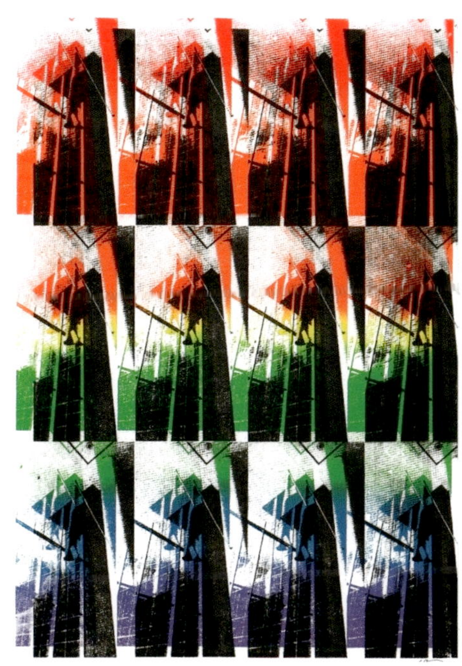

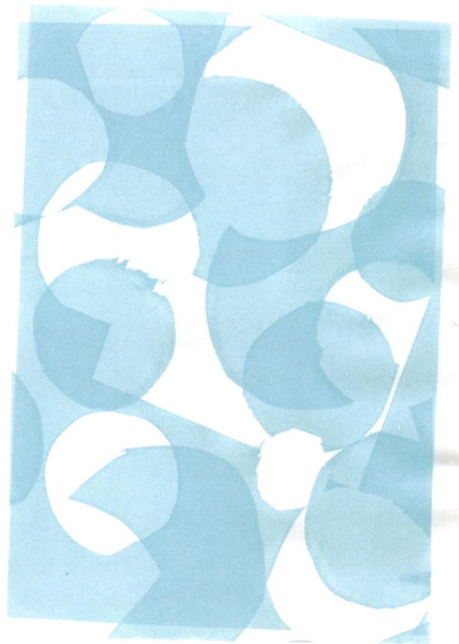

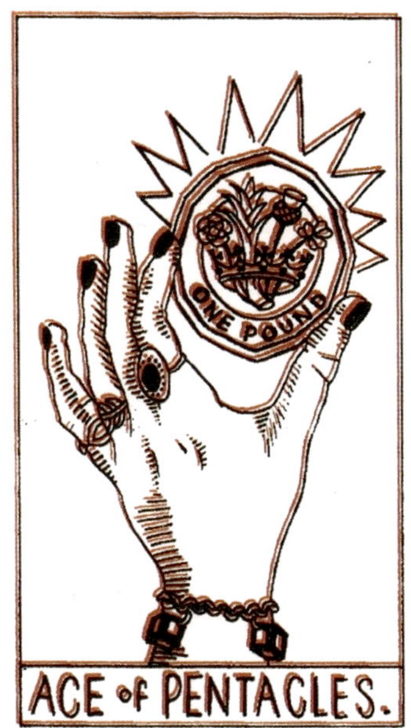

From top left, clockwise:
Eveline Kinzkofer: 'People' (drypoint on Perspex with chine-collé), 13cm x 22cm, unique. "Project based on 'daily travel' – what do you see on your commute?"

Georgia Stevens: 'Colour' (multi-colour layered photo screenprint), 20cm x 29cm, unique. "Project based on changing attitudes to homosexuality in art and culture."

Francesca Robb: 'Ace of Pentacles' (offset photo screenprint), edition of 6. "Project considering a contemporary interpretation of tarot card images." From original drawings.

Katie Sims: 'Patsample' (layered paper stencil screenprint, sample), 14.5cm x 22cm, unique. "Project based on personal exploration into pattern design and textile repeat."

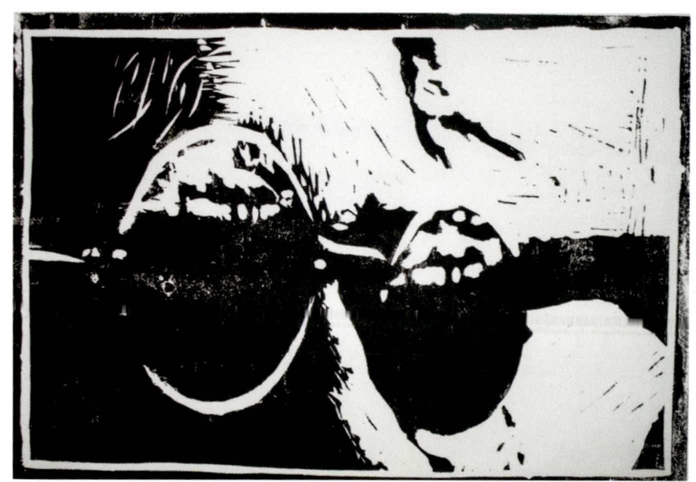

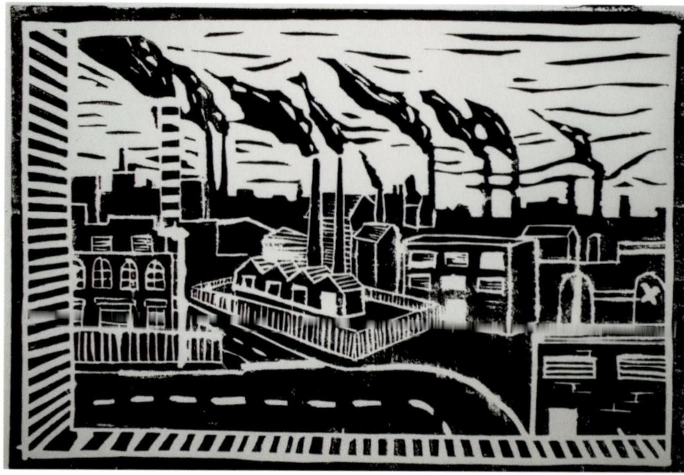

LONG ROAD SIXTH-FORM COLLEGE

Long Road is a specialist sixth-form college for 16- to 19-year-olds. The 2,200 students study for qualifications they need to progress into university or employment. The college offers a number of art and design courses, including: Art and Design Level 3 Diploma (Level 3 Applied Diploma); Art & Design (Level 2 Applied Diploma); Art, Craft and Design (A-level); and Foundation Diploma in Art and Design (Level 4 Foundation in Art & Design).

Former student Oscar Hart, 19, was at the time of writing about to start a Fine Art degree. "I am very open to new ideas, processes and media. That said, printmaking and painting are currently my main focus. In terms of printmaking – especially linoprints – one of my biggest influences is Fernando Feijoo. He was also my introduction to this medium. I also feel inspired by the Impressionists, as well as by early street photography.

"The purpose of my work is to capture candid and real moments of the everyday and of my life through the media of paint and print."

www.longroad.ac.uk

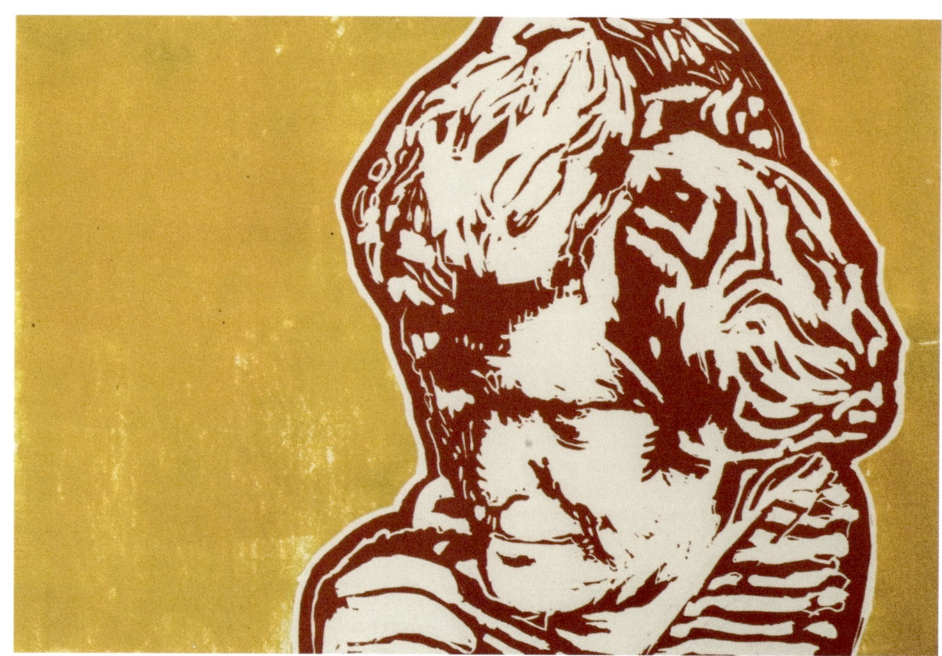

From top left, clockwise:
'Reflections'; 'Industrial Skyline'; 'Grandmother Portrait' (all linocuts), 20cm x 30.5cm, editions of 5

PRINTMAKING GLOSSARY

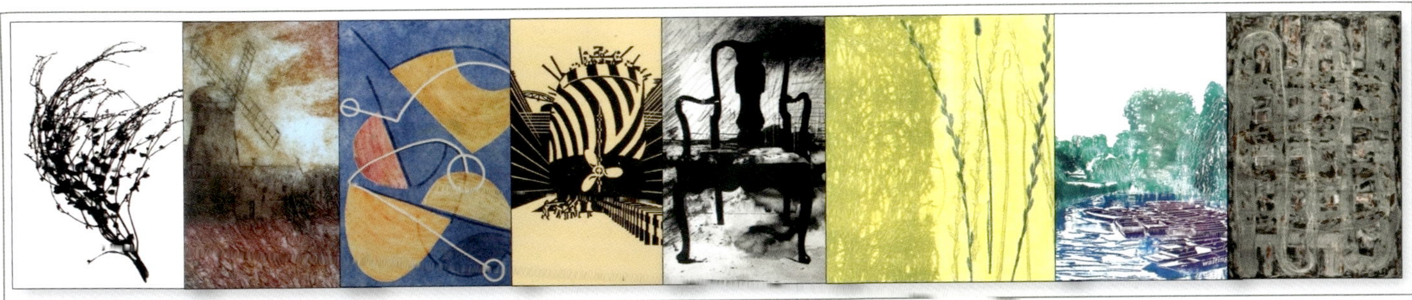

Original print: an image created from hand-cut or hand-drawn printing blocks, plates or stencils that are used to produce a limited number of prints, usually numbered and signed by the artist.
Relief print: made by cutting the image out of a flat surface, usually wood or lino. The remaining raised areas then form the relief block to which ink is applied by means of a roller.
Intaglio print: made by cutting into a flat surface by hand, as in engraving, or by using acid to burn into a metal plate, as in etching. The depth and density of the pits and hollows control the tone of the finished print.
Wood engraving: the image is cut with sharp tools into the end grain of a block of wood, usually box or lemonwood, in which very fine detailed work can be engraved.
Woodcut (also woodblock): the design is worked into the side grain or plank of the wood with the cutting generally following the direction of the grain. The grain itself can be incorporated into the design.
Linocut: the surface material is cut away from hessian-backed linoleum, a relatively soft material that can be mounted on to wood to give extra support. Multiple colours can be achieved by cutting multiple blocks of lino, or by inking, continuing to cut away and re-inking the same block (the reduction or reductive method). Vinyl can be used as an alternative to lino.
Etching: a flat metal plate (copper, zinc, steel) is first coated with an acid-resistant ground. The design is scratched through the hardened coating, exposing the metal below. The whole plate is then immersed in acid that burns or etches only the exposed areas of the metal plate where the design has been drawn.
Aquatint: a process used to etch large areas of even tone. A fine, even layer of acid-resistant powdered resin is dusted over the surface of the plate. When the plate is heated, the resin melts and fixes to the plate. The design is painted out with acid-resistant varnish. The acid bites into the metal plate between the individual grains of resin.
Drypoint: a sharp-pointed steel tool is used to inscribe directly into the surface of a metal or perspex plate. Not only is a line inscribed into the surface but a burr is pushed up that holds the ink and prints as a thick, velvety line.
Mezzotint: using a rocker – a flat steel blade with a fine serrated edge – thousands of tiny indented holes are made evenly over the entire surface of a copper plate. This will print as an even, rich, velvety black.
Screenprint (also serigraph and silkscreen): a fine woven mesh (originally silk, but today synthetic) is stretched tightly over a frame. Stencils are used to mask out the areas of the screen that are not to be printed. A sheet of paper is laid under the screen, then a flat rubber blade is drawn over it, forcing ink through the open areas not masked by the stencils.
Collagraph: a print made from a collaged or textured board. One method is to work in relief, applying a variety of materials on to the surface of a cardboard plate. Another approach is an intaglio method achieved by scoring lines into the surface and cutting away layers of card with a scalpel, thereby creating recesses that will hold ink.
Lithograph: a design is drawn or painted directly on to a prepared surface, originally limestone and today more usually zinc or aluminium. Once the image is drawn, the surface undergoes a chemical process, making the undrawn areas sensitive to water. The drawn areas remain sensitive to oil-based ink. During the printing process, the 'stone' is constantly dampened and the surface is inked up with a roller. The ink adheres to the greased areas and is repelled by the areas that are wet.
Monoprint/monotype: both are one-off print techniques in which an image, produced on a metal plate, sheet of glass or any other flat surface, is transferred to paper. There are two basic methods of working. In the subtractive approach, a metal plate or sheet of glass is inked up by means of a roller, and the image is produced by selectively wiping away the ink. In the additive approach, ink, paint or water-based media can be painted directly on to the plate. These methods can be used in combination with other print techniques.
Mixed media: a work produced using two or more printing processes.
Solarplate™ etching (also photopolymer plate): a light-sensitive metal plate is etched through the action of ultraviolet light. An opaque image on transparent film is placed on the prepared plate, then exposed to light before plain water is used to 'fix' the image before inking and printing.

ACKNOWLEDGEMENTS

Cambridge Original Printmakers (COP) would like to thank the following people and organisations for their help and support, without which the Biennale would be impossible to hold:

The external selectors: Elizabeth Armstrong, Kip Gresham and Morag Barnes

The prize-givers: John Purcell Paper, Hawthorn Printmaker Supplies, Awagami Factory, Intaglio Printmaker, Cambridge Contemporary Art and Church Street Gallery

The guest speakers: Paul Catherall, Jane Human, Louise Stebbing, Wuon-Gean Ho, Serena Smith and Andrew McDowall

The publisher, **Mascot Media**, would like to thank COP for the opportunity to work with them on this project, and acknowledges the cooperation of the committee and of the individual artists in the supply and use of their images.

This book is printed in the UK using paper certified by the **Forest Stewardship Council (FSC)**. Thanks to **Swallowtail Print** for helping us keep our carbon footprint as small as possible...

BACK COVER: the 3D Print Project

Old meets new! The 3D print project incorporates both traditional and contemporary printmaking technology – highlighting and harnessing the evolution in new technologies while still working with a hand-pulled original print.

An Albion relief printing press (circa 1850) was photographed using a DSLR camera and the images analysed using photogrammetry to plot its 3D form. The resulting edited digital file, sent to a 3D printer, produced a 2.5mm deep matrix (plate) of the compacted image of the Albion press.

Using a roller, the matrix was subsequently inked up – the details of the compression being picked out by the inking process. Printing the matrix by hand using the Albion press on to Fabriano Rosaspina paper took the project full circle; a traditional press providing the imagery for and from 3D imaging, thereby creating an informed dialogue between old and new.

A tracker (akin to a barcode) has been incorporated into the image of the Albion press printed on the back cover of this book, giving anyone scanning the image with the 'Augment' App on a phone or tablet the ability to view the Albion press in wonderful 3D.

A 3D printer, printing matrices, operated during Biennale 2018 along with the hand-pulled prints taken from them.

Cambridge Original Printmakers would like to thank Andy McDowall for his generous support – and also Camscan, Middlesex University and Polaroid 3D for their help in realising this project.

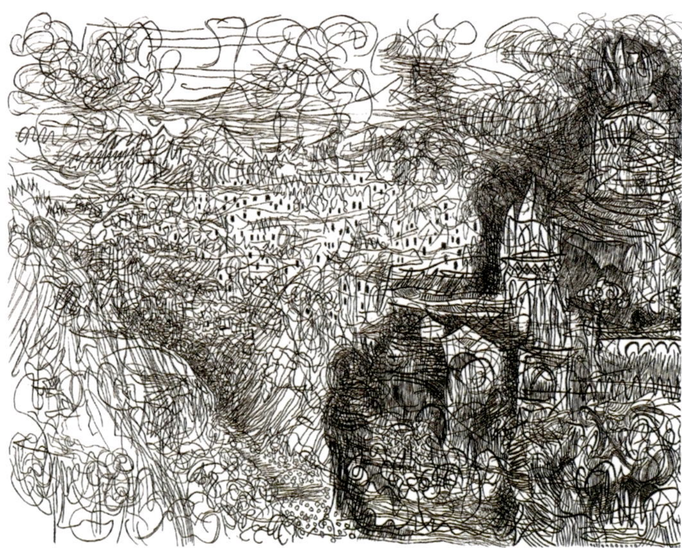

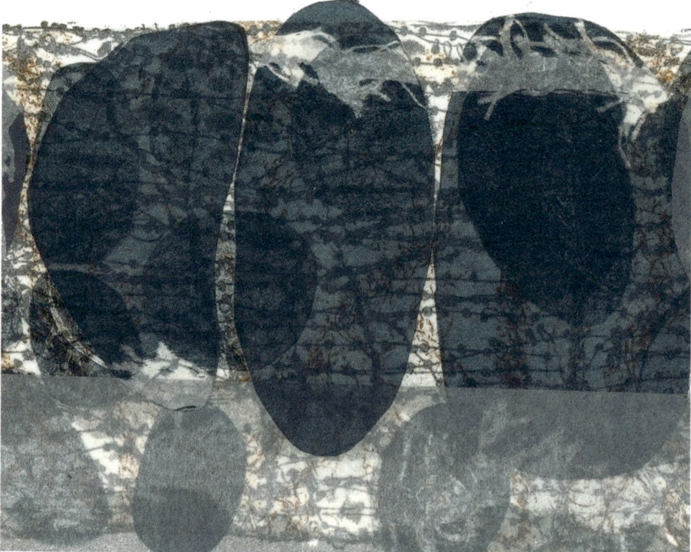

Left: Paul Hawdon – 'A View of Matera' (etching); Right: Tracey Ashman – 'Evocation XV (Series 1)' (monoprint and chine-collé)

Published in Great Britain in 2018 by
Mascot Media, Norfolk, UK.
Email: mascot_media@btinternet.com
www.mascotmedia.co.uk

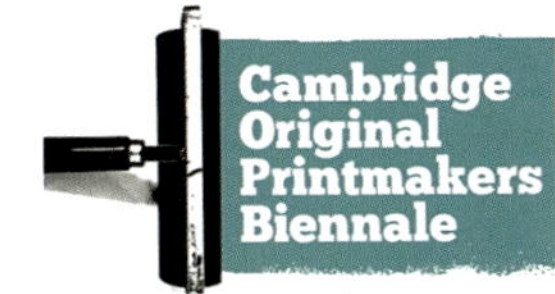

In partnership with Cambridge Original Printmakers

http://cambridgeoriginalprintmakers.com

A CIP catalogue record for this book is available from the British Library.

ISBN: 978 1 9998457 7 3

Designed by Marion Scott Marshall and Alan Marshall.
Edited by Marion Scott Marshall.

Printed by Swallowtail Print, Drayton Industrial Park, Taverham Road, Drayton, Norwich, Norfolk NR8 6RL.
Email: contact@swallowtailprint.co.uk
www.swallowtailprint.co.uk

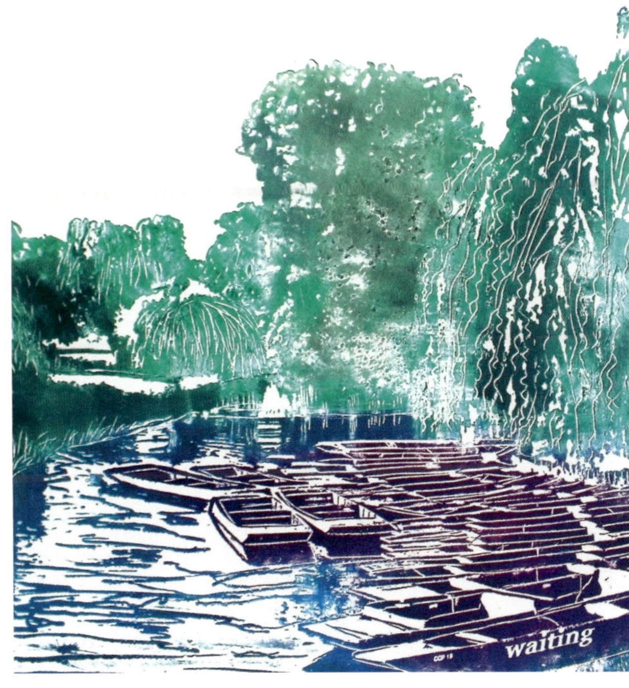

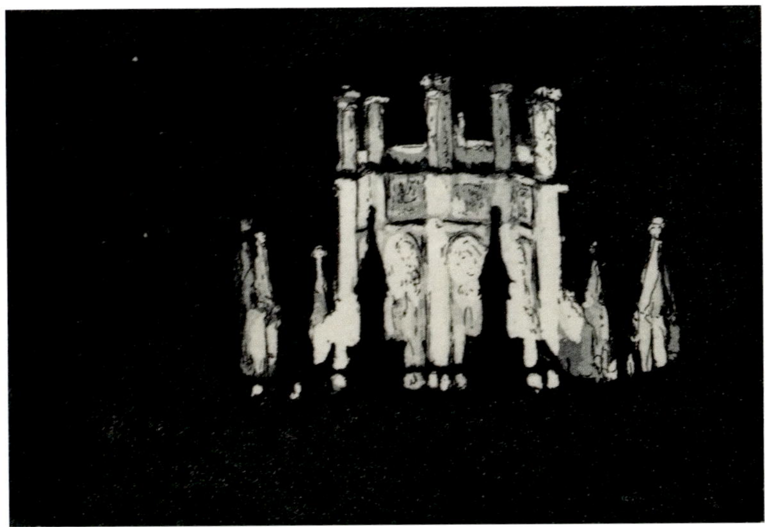

Title page: Iona Howard – 'Sedge Fen III' (carborundum, monoprint and drypoint). Above: Jo Tunmer – 'Seize the Day' (relief Solarplate etching). Left: John Preston – 'Floodlit Lantern, Ely Cathedral' (aquatint). Facing page, clockwise from top left: Kim Major-George – 'Hope Within, green' (collagraph); Jill Ogilvy – 'Blue Teacups' (monotype and drypoint); Geri Waddington – 'Wall Lizards' (resingrave engraving); Celia Hart – 'The Three Hares in Winter' (linocut).

Front cover artists

Top row from left: Edwin Wilson; Liz Hales; Jo Tunmer; Sue Jones. Second row, from left: Jackie Duckworth; Katharine Green. Third row from left: Gordon Chesterman; Bren Unwin; Ricardo Pimentel; Nina Sage; Ross Loveday. Bottom row from left: Roz Howling; Geri Waddington; Louise Stebbing; Constance Johnson.

LIMITED EDITION

CAMBRIDGE ORIGINAL PRINTMAKERS

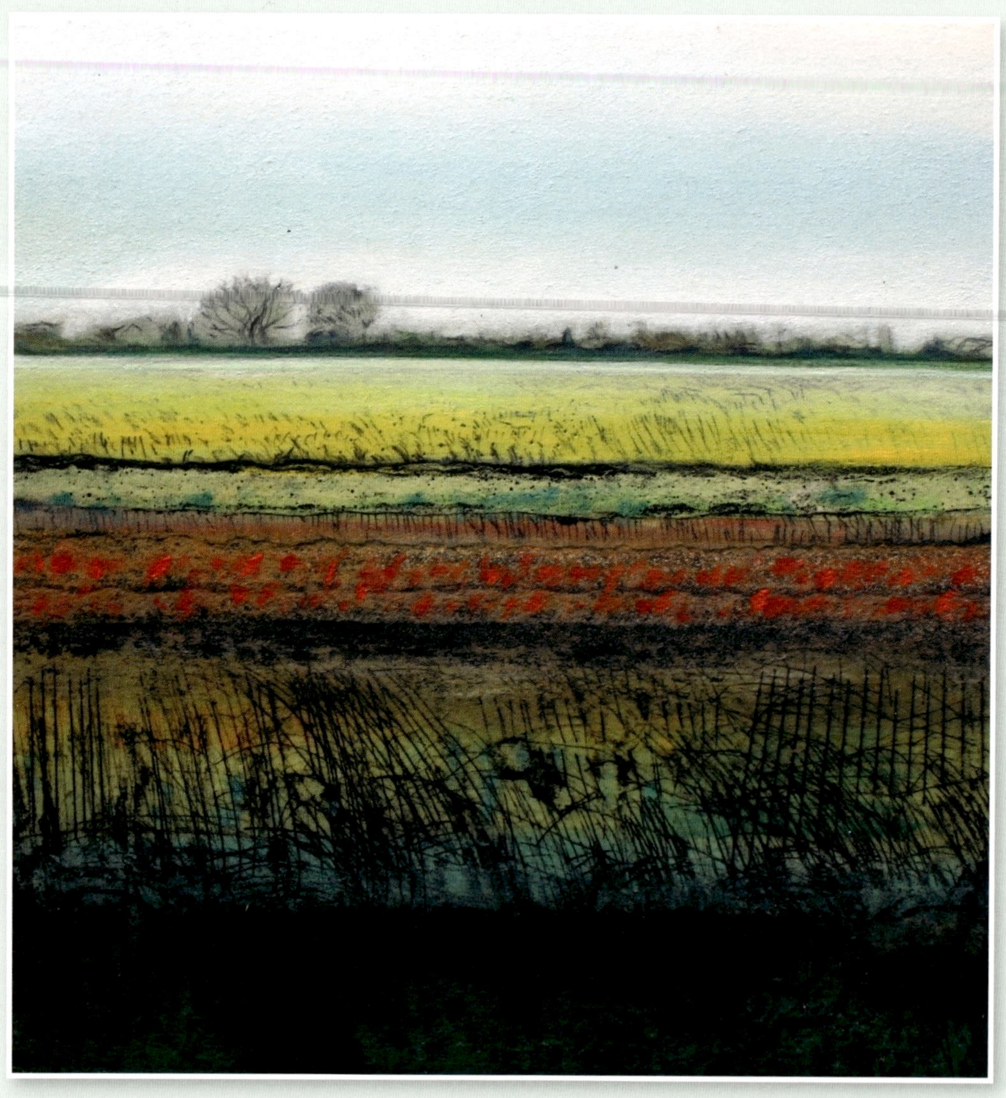

MADE IN NORFOLK BY MASCOT MEDIA